"Games and play are diverse, and one approach does not suit all of them. Here one can find tools that are appropriate for analysing games from simple to highly complex, while also taking into account their associated forms of play and game cultures."

—**Frans Mäyrä**, Professor of Information Studies and Interactive Media, Tampere University, Finland

"The book arms anyone interested in videogames with a rich vocabulary and an analytical toolset that is both deep and accessible. My students love how it guides them through the process and helps them uncover meaning by themselves. A must read!"

—**Víctor Navarro-Remesal**, Professor and Game Scholar, Tecnocampus, Universistat Pompeu-Fabra, Spain

Introduction to Game Analysis

This accessible, third edition textbook gives students the tools they need to analyze games, using strategies borrowed from textual analysis.

As game studies has become an established academic field, writing about games needs the language and methods that allow authors to reflect the complexity of a game and how it is played in a cultural context. This volume provides readers with an overview of the basic building blocks of game analysis—examination of context, content and distinctive features, and formal qualities—as well as the vocabulary necessary to talk about the distinguishing characteristics of a game. Examples are drawn from a range of games, non-digital and digital, and across history—from *Pong* to *Fortnite*—and the book includes a variety of examples and sample analysis, as well as a wealth of additional sources to continue exploring the field of game studies. This third edition revision brings the book firmly up to date, pulling in new examples and sources, and incorporating current key topics in this dynamic field, such as artificial intelligence and game streaming.

Introduction to Game Analysis remains an essential practical tool for students who want to become fluent writers and informed critics of games, as well as digital media in general.

Clara Fernández-Vara is Associate Arts Professor at the NYU Game Center, New York University. She teaches courses on game studies and narrative design, while also working as a game designer and writer. As a researcher, her main interest is in exploring the integration of stories and gameplay, the relationship between games and other media, and videogame history.

Introduction to Game Analysis

Third Edition

Clara Fernández-Vara

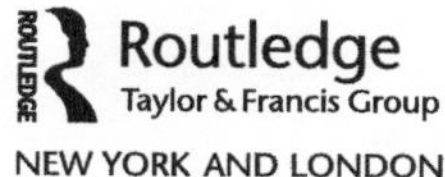

NEW YORK AND LONDON

Designed cover image: Cover illustration by Michael Rapa

Third edition published 2024
by Routledge
605 Third Avenue, New York, NY 10158

and by Routledge
4 Park Square, Milton Park, Abingdon, Oxon, OX14 4RN

Routledge is an imprint of the Taylor & Francis Group, an informa business

First edition published by Routledge 2014
Second edition published by Routledge 2019

Library of Congress Cataloging-in-Publication Data
Names: Fernández-Vara, Clara, author.
Title: Introduction to game analysis / Clara Fernández-Vara.
Description: Third edition. | New York, NY : Routledge, 2024. | Includes bibliographical references and index.
Identifiers: LCCN 2023055747 (print) | LCCN 2023055748 (ebook) | ISBN 9781032318349 (paperback) | ISBN 9781032410074 (hardback) | ISBN 9781003355779 (ebook)
Subjects: LCSH: Video games--Design. | Video games--Psychological aspects. | Video games--Social aspects.
Classification: LCC GV1469.15 .F46 2024 (print) | LCC GV1469.15 (ebook) | DDC 794.8--dc23/eng/20231204
LC record available at https://lccn.loc.gov/2023055747
LC ebook record available at https://lccn.loc.gov/2023055748

ISBN: 978-1-032-41007-4 (hbk)
ISBN: 978-1-032-31834-9 (pbk)
ISBN: 978-1-003-35577-9 (ebk)

DOI: 10.4324/9781003355779

Typeset in Warnock
by SPi Technologies India Pvt Ltd (Straive)

Contents

Figures

Preface to the Third Edition

This book is but a modest piece of evidence of the socio-cultural relevance and importance of games—ten years after its initial release, it is still in print in a new edition. Recent history has been louder and more eloquent in proving their importance—while the COVID-19 pandemic had millions and millions of people around the world hunkering down at home, isolated from friends and family, games became a channel to stay in touch. The timely release of *Animal Crossing: New Horizons* (2020) during lockdown, allowed players to fly off to different digital islands, visit friends, or swim out in the sea. Similarly, the runaway success of *Among Us* (2018) two years after its release was due to its online multiplayer features, which allowed people to connect with others, even if it was to try to get each other ejected into outer space. Online party games thrived as ways to goof off and tease friends in the evenings when people could not go out. Games have helped many people get through times of stress and trauma—part of their purpose was escapism, but another very important part was allowing people to get together in a virtual space and to share experiences.

At the same time, the current revisions to *Introduction to Game Analysis* have been written in a time of turmoil around the world, a world that is forgetting the importance of play as a community space of growth. Political polarization divides countries around the world into groups of "them vs. us," while issues like what bathroom one needs to use, fuel sources, or being able to have control over one's own body have become battlegrounds that should not have been ones in the first place. We need games more than ever—to explore, to experiment, to see the world through the eyes of someone we are not, to deal with conflict without hurting others. It is essential to understand how games are not only a cultural form, but serve a social function and create spaces for encounters, transformations, and imagining potential futures.

Acknowledgements for the Third Edition

The revisions of this book have been possible thanks to the input of my students at the NYU Game Center in recent years, as well as those who have been using the book as part of their courses in institutions all over the world. For this edition, I owe special thanks to Jay Guisao and Elizabeth Ballou for their comments and input on the manuscript, as well as my editor Sheni Kruger, and assistant editors Emma Sherriff and Grace Kennedy, for their assistance and support during these revisions.

Most of all, my perennial thanks go to Mateo and Matt, for showing me that, even in adverse circumstances, in the end we always have each other.

Preface to the Second Edition

Those of us who study games are in for a ride every day. Game studies involves many disciplines that must be in constant conversation, even though at times each field may use what sounds like a different language. Games—digital and non-digital—transform through the participation of players; in the case of videogames, they use technology that is constantly evolving and creating new opportunities to play. The economic models of games change constantly and strive to find new ways to both finance their creators as well as reach new audiences.

Because of the ever-changing nature of our object of study, a book on game analysis is but a snapshot of the state of the field at the moment of writing. Even though there is a core of works and concepts that are well known, the field does not remain the same for long. In the interval between the initial release of this book and this second edition, the world of games has transformed in ways that impact their study and analysis. The revisions in this volume are a response to these transformations, including expanded sections, new game examples, and updated references and ludography.

The growth of certain trends and the appearance of new phenomena needed to be reflected in this textbook. Some of these changes and evolutions are: the widespread use of video streaming as a way to understand and critique games, which has also become a mode of surrogate play; the increased ease of access to virtual reality and augmented reality technologies; and how diversity in game makers and players has become a mainstream discussion that both the games industry and academia are addressing. New games also have given me the chance to illustrate some of the building blocks that make up the analysis in certain ways as well. Last, but not least, the appearance of new types of resources, such as the repositories of magazines and computer games at The Internet Archive, has also changed the way that we access games, particularly older titles, that had been hardly accessible before.

In the time since this book was first published, I have also been a full-time professor at the NYU Game Center, where I have been teaching game studies and design classes. Many of the tweaks and additions to this book are responses to feedback from my students in these years, as well as tricks I have developed to help them learn to think about games critically and improve their academic writing.

In the writing of this second edition, I would like to thank the reviewers of the first edition, who sent me feedback that I have tried to address as well as possible. I also owe many thanks to Janet Murray, Todd Harper, T.L. Taylor, and Austin Walker, who provided essential feedback in key updates of the text. I am also very grateful to my editor, Erica Wetter, for her enthusiasm and support, without which this revised version would not have been possible. My students in the last five years, with their effort, struggles, and brilliance, have also contributed to the expansions in this book—my thanks to all of them for helping me become a better teacher every day.

The biggest and warmest thanks must go to my son Mateo and my husband Matt, who tolerate me absconding to write in coffee shops, and always welcome me back home with cuddles. I would not have been able to do this without you.

Acknowledgements for the First Edition

This book started as a class handout for undergraduate students, whose goal was to provide some guidelines for analyzing games as part of their assignment. I kept expanding the handout until it was actually longer than the assignment students had to write, until I realized that I had a lot to say about the topic.

First of all, thanks to my students over the years who have written game analyses, from whom I have learned the most in order to write this book.

Thanks to Mia Consalvo, who was the first to suggest that I should turn the handout into a book, and has provided a lot of support and feedback throughout the whole process of production.

The concept of this book and a good deal of its writing took place while I was a researcher at the Singapore-MIT GAMBIT Game Lab. My colleagues there, as well as collaborators and visiting scholars, provided much of the support and feedback that kept this book going: Doris Rusch, Geoffrey Long, Jason Begy, Konstantin Mitgutsch, Todd Harper, Abraham Stein, Pilar Lacasa, Jaroslav Svelch, David Finkel, William Uricchio, Philip Tan, Chor Guan Teo, and the rest of the GAMBIT staff and participants in our weekly research meeting.

Many thanks, as well, to Nick Montfort, who lent me a space to continue researching at The Trope Tank in MIT, and provided constant inspiration and challenges that have found their way into the book.

Thanks to all who provided resources and feedback as the manuscript was taking final shape: Jesper Juul, Mikael Jakobsson, Brendan Keogh, Chris Dahlen, Mattie Brice, Joel Goodwin, Nina Huntenman, T.L. Taylor, and the anonymous reviewers of the proposal.

My editor Erica Wetter and Simon Jacobs, editorial assistant, have been supportive and patient, and always had ideas and solutions whenever I was stuck. To both, many thanks.

The inspiration from this book comes from many years of writing literary analyses, which helped me come up with my own model to analyze media as texts. Thanks to my literature professors through the years, especially: mi padre, Jesús Fernández Montes y el otro Jesús en el Instituto Parla III, Robert Shepherd, Manuel Aguirre, and Philip Sutton, whose handouts on how to analyze a theatrical performance were the model I used for the original guide.

And, of course, this book would not be here without the unfailing support of my husband Matt, who is my living encyclopedia of games and gives me cuddles so I can keep going.

To all of them goes my gratitude. The faults in this work are my own.

1 The Whys and Wherefores of Game Analysis

▶ INTRODUCTION

Waiting in line on the first day of PAX East 2009, I overheard two videogame fans talking about *Dragon Age*. They were sharing their opinions about the game, which they had enjoyed. They talked about how the writing was great, as one could expect of Bioware, but the graphics still needed another pass; the smooth gameplay made up for some of the graphical glitches. The game was the right length; this mission was fun. Then they moved on to talk about a series of fantasy novels, whose title I did not pick up. According to these fans, the novels had very engaging characters, whose story across the novels was consistent but also surprising; they particularly loved how believable the dialogue was, which managed to blend contemporary language with a fantasy setting. The writing style was not pretentious and it built a world they wanted to be part of. They recapitulated their favorite chapters, and why they liked them.

What shocked me about this overheard conversation was the difference between how they discussed videogames and novels. While their opinion of *Dragon Age: Origins* (2009) rated a laundry list of high-level concepts of game reviews, they discussed fantasy novels from their experience as readers, using a much more specific vocabulary, and providing arguments based

DOI: 10.4324/9781003355779-1

on particular aspects of the novel. Their opinion of videogames was based on a series of sliding scales (gameplay, graphics, story), whereas their discussion of the novels centered on a more nuanced discussion on why they liked them.

The difference in discourse made me realize one of the main problems of videogame analysis and criticism. Videogame fans talk about games by borrowing terms from game reviews, which at the same time cover the talking points provided by marketing: Fantastic graphics! Immersive gameplay! Hollywood-like stories! It is not a problem of literacy—these two fans were able to provide thoughtful criticism, and they knew the game well. However, their vocabulary to talk about games was not on a par with how they discussed novels. In my own experience as a teacher, I have seen the same shift in students who can produce a thoughtful and solid film analysis, but then shift to a casual, shallow register when they write about a game. The guidelines presented in this book are based on my own experience as a media and game studies teacher, as a researcher and as a developer. Conversations like the one I overheard at PAX are part of my inspiration for this book—I want students who are passionate about games to snap out of their shallow discourse and use their knowledge to discuss games with the depth and nuance the games deserve, since students often demonstrate the knowledge and capacity they need. Although this anecdote took place more than a decade ago, the issues that I detected back then are still true. My goals also include reaching out to those who may not consider themselves *gamers* or *board game geeks*, but who would like to learn more about games by playing them. A third group this book is intended for are scholars with a background in the humanities and social sciences, who want to extend their appreciation of media to games, both digital and non-digital. Although they may feel comfortable applying the theories and methods of literature, film, or communication studies to games, the aim here is to highlight what the aspects of games are that not only define them, but also distinguish them from other media.

For those readers who may already come from established humanities or social sciences fields, the main hurdle to entering game studies is perhaps a pervading skepticism about whether games, digital or not, can become a medium worthy of study, as literature, theater, or film already are. To this day, games discourse is not usually associated with academic conferences or specialized journalism, but rather online streamers talking over the games they are playing for their audience, or newscasters talking about the latest game phenomenon as veiled advertising of the latest blockbusters. The academic study of games, however, is much older than people may think—Johan Huizinga's *Homo Ludens*, one of the foundational texts of game studies, discusses play as an essential aspect of cultural practice, and was first published in 1938[1], while psychologist Jean Piaget discussed the role of play in child development in his book, *La Formation du Symbole chez l'Enfant: Imitation, Jeu et Rêve, Image et Représentation* in 1945.[2] Although the field of game studies is relatively young in comparison with other disciplines, it is also becoming an established academic field rather fast. At the end of the 1990s, scholars like Espen Aarseth or Janet Murray started calling attention to games as their focus of study[3], the first issue of the academic journal *Game Studies* was published in July 2001,[4] while the Digital Games Research Association (DiGRA) conference started back in 2003.

As we will see in the following chapters, a sophisticated discourse on games does indeed exist and has been developed over several decades. A relatively limited group of scholars and a small number of practitioners and critics are familiar with this discourse, although those numbers are growing thanks to an increasing number of analytical works—articles, talks—that are more widely accessible. At present, mainstream videogame journalism and industry dominate the creation of analytical models in relation to popular culture—it is more likely that videogame fans will watch someone playing the game on Twitch while chatting to other users, listen to a podcast, or read a game development blog rather than peruse any of the papers given at the DiGRA conference, even though they are all equally available online. This is why these pages introduce readers to exemplary texts from a variety of sources, focusing on academic analyses of games.

The influence of marketing on the discourse, particularly in the area of digital games, is not negligible. Game reviews are one of the first (and often only) types of game writing that mainstream audiences are exposed to. This type of writing can be subject to a series of economic pressures that may condition its content. For example, publishers may provide journalists and videogame reviewers early access to the games provided they do not publish anything before a specific deadline, and the publishers may even dictate how much of the story of the mechanics the article can reveal.[5] Reputable game sites have a page with their editorial standards, which explain how the publication tries to avoid conflicts of interest, how their advertising is handled, and how they deal with review embargoes—these are declarations of intent that are part of an ethical journalistic practice in any publication.[6]

If a site posts any news that breaks the embargo, its staff may not get advance copies of games and publishers will withdraw their advertisements from the site, preventing the site both from having advance content and taking away revenue from advertising. In the streaming space, content creators hardly ever subscribe to ethical guidelines of this kind. Some of the most influential streamers can access preview versions of the game and access privileged information just as journalists do, which allows them to attract their audience, thus creating a relationship of convenience and interdependence with publishers. However, if the streamer breaches the trust of the publisher, particularly in the case of some of the largest companies, they can also be denied access in the future, or completely banned, therefore, being cut off from a key resource for their work.[7] An extreme case of conflict of interest is when some unscrupulous streamers also solicit codes to get free games from developers, at times arguing explicitly that their review will give "exposure" to their work, rather than working as detached critics. Subjectivity is inevitable (and even necessary) in reviews; the issue is that, in some specialized sources, the revenue model has the potential to influence the content to the point that some reviews are overtly biased toward the positive.[8] Disclosure of conflicts of interest is often part of the editorial policy of certain publication venues, for example—journalists may add a note if they got a review copy from the publisher or the developer.

There is a space for videogame reviews as consumer reports. Additionally, there are other types of journalistic writing, alongside the growing influence of streaming and podcasts, which are accessible to the general public and reflect on the cultural role of games and players. The state of videogame reviews is steadily changing—while there are new journalistic models and approaches, there are also challenges derived from new economic models, the misguided belief that artificial intelligence can replace human writers, and the subsequent depreciation of writing as a skilled trade. These are not problems that will be tackled directly here, but they are ongoing factors that influence current journalistic writing about videogames.

My concern is that there is no reason for writers outside certain specialized sites to replicate that kind of commercial discourse, particularly in academia. Scholars and journalists should be able to talk about what we consider relevant and meaningful with a certain level of nuance. That type of discourse can range from understanding our role as players and how our experience may differ from other people's, or being able to explain what it means to have a user interface that does not follow conventional configurations, or discuss the differences between player characters of different genders in terms of mechanics. There is so much more that game analysis can talk about beyond the quality of the graphics or the difficulty curve.

A more sophisticated way to talk about games is useful to scholars, creators and players. The aim of this book is to make the tools of academic analysis accessible to everyone. The number of schools which have incorporated the study of games in their curricula continues to grow, particularly in departments of social sciences and the humanities, and it is often difficult to know where to start or how the new subject fits with the rest of the materials covered. Game analysis is also relevant to practice-driven schools or computer science departments. This is because they need to be familiar with pre-existing works and what they have done in order to understand them, as well as create innovative games.

My aim is also to encourage everyone with an interest in games to learn more about them and produce thoughtful reflections. If you consider yourself a gamer who breathes and lives in game worlds, my aim is to take advantage of your expertise and apply it to examining games systematically, within a specific academic domain and approach. Having an extensive knowledge of games is obviously helpful to analyze games; in my classes, I try to take advantage of the personal investment my students already have as a motivation. My teaching focuses on the aspects of games that can provide material for analysis, their interrelationships, and how those aspects can be tackled from different perspectives. Analysis is also a tool for budding game designers, who can learn about diverse design aesthetics and develop a vocabulary to understand games better, as well as to communicate their designs to the people they work with. Being aware of the different processes that generate meaning in games is essential to understanding their role as a cultural and artistic expression.

The guidelines in this book should also be helpful to those who do not consider themselves game experts. The strategies here are not strict guidelines; they provide some considerations to be made when tackling games, a map of the different building blocks of the analysis, and a series of comparative examples. The idea is to help writers find their own way into games and how to talk about them, making use of what they already know, even if it is not in the field of games but of other media. We must also remember we do not have to limit ourselves to videogames, and that there are many types of games—playground games, card games, board games, arcade games, casual games, shooter games, escape the room activities, to name but a few—which can all be dissected and discussed.

By providing tools to analyze games in a cultivated way and promoting the generalization of academic discourse, my hope is that the readers of this book may realize that there are many ways to talk about games. Improving the discourse will allow players to engage with games in novel ways and become more critical of what they play. In filmic terms, it is similar to the difference between a "moviegoer," who is someone who goes to the movies regularly to be entertained, and a "cinephile," who is a more demanding audience member, has an extensive knowledge of film history, and can articulate the relevance of a movie and relate it to other works. In a similar way, we need more diverse ways to engage with games, ranging from the casual player to the "ludophile" who knows about the history and form of the medium in depth.

The foundation to a more sophisticated discourse on games is to understand them as *texts*. The methods I propose here are strategies for textual analysis applied to games, both digital and non-digital, derived from a humanistic background. This raises a set of questions, which I will address in the following sections: How are games texts? What is textual analysis? What can we learn through the analysis of games?

▶ HOW ARE GAMES TEXTS?

The term "text" is usually associated with the written word, which is also part of the dictionary definition. Because the practice of textual analysis has a strong tradition in the humanities, particularly in literature, the phrase has persisted in relation to reading and writing. As someone with a strong background in literature, I studied poems and novels, for example. When studying theater, however, it became evident that the text alone was not enough because the meaning of the text would also depend on the way the actor would deliver a certain line, and the context of the performance. In this case, the term "text" also applies to the performance of the play or an excerpt from it. "To be or not to be" means something different depending on the actor delivering it and the overall concept of the production, even if the words do not change. I realized that what *text* means extends to other artifacts that can also be objects of study: from literal text, such as a novel, philosophical essays, or historical documents, to non-written or even non-verbal text, such as movies or paintings, to sports events or broadcasts. This is not my discovery—French theorist Roland Barthes, in his book *Mythologies*, provides a classic example of how the concept of text can be applied to activities and artifacts that may also be a form of human expression.[9] The articles included in Barthes' book examine the cultural status of items such as red wine and detergents, to activities such as professional wrestling or striptease.

Textual commentary can also take many shapes and forms, such as a very systematic analysis that helps develop specific theoretical concepts. For example, Gérard Genette's *Narrative Discourse: An Essay in Method* is a book-long analytical take on Proust's multivolume novel *À la Recherche du Temps Perdu* [*Remembrance of Things Past*], which at the same time is developing a conceptual framework to understand general structures of narrative discourse.[10] A very different form of textual analysis can take advantage of the properties of digital media, creating a free-form multimedia essay, such as Peter Donaldson's article on Shakespeare's *The Tempest*, which invites the reader to explore the essay to convey the multilayered, complex nature of the play and one of its film adaptations, *Prospero's Books* (1991).[11]

This broad understanding of the term allows us to approach games as texts, whether they use cardboard, computers, or spoken words and gestures. We can study games as a cultural production that can be interpreted because they have meaning. Their cultural significance can derive from the context of play: who plays games, why and how, how the practice of playing relates to other socio-cultural activities and practices. Meaningful play also results from the player interacting with the systems and representations of the game. Thus, when we analyze games, we study meaning within the game (meaningful play) and around it (cultural significance). The text is not limited to the work itself, but also to where the text is interpreted and by whom.

If we consider games to be texts, we can also understand them better by analyzing what Gérard Genette calls "paratexts"—texts that surround the main text being analyzed, which transform and condition how the audience interprets that main text.[12] Texts such as the author's name or the title, reviews, or discussions about the work can predispose the audience to read the text a certain way. For example, some readers may be more willing to engage with a novel if the writer is a renowned author; if the work comes from a new novelist, readers may be more critical. Again, these texts do not necessarily have to be written, since we are using the term in a broad sense.

In videogame terms, paratexts would include the game cover, the instruction manual (in older games), the game's commercial website, reviews, and interviews with the developers, as well as other media, from other games to commercials or films that may have been inspired by the game or spawned by it. The way that a game is branded also becomes part of the paratexts of the game and how we understand it—branding creates expectations because it may belong to a pre-existing game series, or feature the name of a famous developer on the box. Extending Genette's concept to videogames allows us to understand how they become complex media artifacts in the light of these paratexts, since they provide further layers of interpretation. The building blocks described in the context area of Chapter 3 deal with the variety of paratexts that we can use to analyze the game.

One of the challenging issues when writing about games, particularly when bringing methods and approaches from literature, film, or communication studies, is whether games can actually be understood as a new way of communication. Mark P. Wolf entitled one of the earliest books in the game studies field, *The Medium of the Video Game*[13]; the word *medium* seems to imply that there is a message in them. Games as an expressive medium, however, are hardly a one-way method of communication where the designer "tells" a message to the player. The player is a necessary part of the text; it is difficult to find games where there is no player input,[14] as the game is not really a complete text without a player who interprets its rules and interacts with it. When we study games, we investigate how players engage with the text at different levels: how players understand the rules, and follow or break them; how players create goals for themselves; and how they communicate with each other, to name but a few. The materials can be very rich—Mia Consalvo's book, *Cheating*, deals with the different ways in which players define cheating in games, how they cheat, and how it changes the game.[15]

Players can also communicate and relate to each other through the game—after all, most games without computers are social activities. Therefore, some of the processes that can be studied if we consider games to be a medium are how players connect to each other through the game. Some games do incorporate responses to the designer, such as a table-top role-playing game where the players talk directly to the game master, or playground games where players are constantly inventing, negotiating, and arguing about the rules. In others, the cycle of feedback may take longer, with players posting on online forums what they like or dislike about a game, or streamers providing moment-to-moment commentary as they play. Even though games are not usually a two-way medium where the player can respond to the designer of the game, the necessary participation of the player and their interpretation constitute a cycle that can be understood as a medium. It may be the case that there is no designer to talk back to because it is a folk game (like Poker or Go Fish), which may prove that the communication is not between the player and the designer, but rather between the player(s) and the game. If players do not like Old Maid, they will not complain to the designer, even if there was one. If they do not like the rules, they will simply change them and adapt them to how they want to play.[16] Some games have made talking to the player about the game directly into an expressive device, such as *The Beginner's Guide* (2015) where the designer analyzes a series of incomplete game levels by a fictional game designer, or *Getting Over It with Bennett Foddy* (2017), a game of heightened difficulty where Foddy himself encourages the player to persevere and reflects on the nature of failure as the player struggles to advance in the game.

So, games are a strange medium, where the communication takes place as a constant cycle of players making sense of the game, figuring out what they want to do, and seeing what happens. It is a medium that, by necessity, establishes a dialogue between the game and the players, and among players.

Some aspects of games can be analyzed from the standpoint of other media, such as examining cinematics from a film studies point of view, or from visual design. The purpose of this book, however, is to call attention to how games are different from other media. Rather than limiting ourselves to thinking about games as a medium to convey messages, we can think of them as artifacts that encode certain values and ideas, which players decode and engage with as they play. Mary Flanagan argues that game developers should be more aware of the values that their games incorporate, and use them as an expressive device.[17] An example of the type of issue Flanagan talks about is the arcade game, *Death Race* (1976), whose creators thought it would be funny to have a game where the goal is to run pedestrians over, then marking a tombstone on the spot where the person was killed. Even with blocky graphics in black and white, the game caused one of the earliest controversies about videogame violence in the US.[18] *Death Race* was interpreted as a message inciting players to violence by people who did not play it; however, the creators and many players thought it was a fun game and did not think about the implications of their design decisions. Similar controversies repeat periodically, only the games get better graphics and sound and more complex design. What we can learn from this story is that games can be read differently depending on the audience, and that the system of the game embodies certain values which can also be the subject of interpretation. Once we accept that games are a type of text, we can analyze them as such.

▶ WHAT IS TEXTUAL ANALYSIS?

There are multiple methods to help us understand our reality, which change depending on the field we come from and what we want to learn. The practice of textual analysis cuts across different disciplines, both in the humanities and the social sciences: literature, philosophy, history, anthropology, communication and media studies.

Textual analysis is the in-depth study of a text in the sense discussed above, using the text as a sample or case study to understand a specific issue or topic. By using inductive reasoning and analyzing specific texts, we can develop general theories that can be applied to other works. The strategies of textual analysis go beyond interpreting the piece or event itself: part of it is trying to make sense of the text, while it may also address the varied ways in which different people can interpret it, as was the case in the *Death Race* controversy.

We have a general disposition to make sense of texts, often without formal training, in practices that can be observed in everyday life—conversations between friends after going to the cinema, reviews on consumer websites, book clubs, and discussions of last night's sporting match. We constantly try to unravel the texts that we engage with on a daily basis it is natural curiosity. The game fans whose conversation I overhead at PAX East were precisely doing informal text analysis, as a way to share and enjoy their media experiences and making sense of them together. It was precisely that impulse which probably took them to the convention in the first place, in order to find like-minded people with whom to talk about their favorite games and to partake of the culture surrounding games. Thus, analysis is not only a form of deeper engagement, but also of creating communities that play them critically and create a discourse based on those texts. Those communities may be academics, journalists, or fans; they may also be the practitioners who produce those texts and need a discourse to communicate with each other.

▶ GAME ANALYSIS FOR ALL

So, if we practice textual analysis naturally and we do it so often, what is the point of getting formal training? What are the benefits of learning academic methods for text analysis? Isn't that a bit of cultural snobbism? In everyday life, people may associate the academic approach to media analysis with highbrow film critics haunting arthouse cinemas, for example, who seem to speak another language and to whom general audiences find it difficult to relate. Academic critics may pan a film that may later become a cultural reference, encouraging the divide between everyday audiences and the academic realm. It has happened before—Alfred Hitchcock's *Psycho* (1960) was received with mixed reviews when it was released,[19] and yet today it remains a point of reference for filmmakers and critics alike.

Is this book encouraging an elitist approach to analyzing and discussing games? Well, yes and no. First of all, nothing will prevent the informal analysis of games, which is second nature to so many people. What is at stake here is fostering structured, systematic, and methodical ways to discuss games, similar to the ones that already exist for literature, film, theater, nonfiction, documentaries, and philosophy, for example. We need to construct an academic discourse that allows us to relate games to other media as well as other academic fields, to help expand and improve our knowledge. There is a need to include games in the map of academic study because the study of games is eminently interdisciplinary, as we will see. In the end, more sophistication is a means to broaden the types of discourse in relation to games, expanding the spectrum of ways of understanding them depending on one's background, the context of play, and so on. It is not that the preexisting discourse should disappear; rather, what we need is a wider variety of ways to talk about games.

Encouraging more sophisticated ways of discussing games is a way to include game knowledge as a form of cultural capital. Pierre Bourdieu defines *cultural capital* as the kinds of knowledge that allow one to acquire power and status, such as formal education and specific skills.[20] At the moment, the contribution of games and game studies to cultural capital is somewhat limited, mostly because the general knowledge of games is usually derived from the marketing of games and the generation of hype about certain titles, which trickles down to journalistic articles, blog posts, and online streaming shows. This type of knowledge is usually not as useful to acquire "power and status"; rather, it is often considered a waste of time. This is slowly changing in specific instances where expertise translates into specific status. For example, top e-sports players enjoy a reputation within their field and among their fans, and are able to make a living out of their gameplay—but they do not yet make as much money as what elite sports players may earn.[21] By improving the discourse on games, we can make it so that being well-versed in games can be admirable and knowing about games an intellectual currency.

Being able to discuss games in a cultured manner is not the exclusive realm of hardcore players—the key is not playing a lot, but playing well. What "playing well" means depends on the context. According to Drew Davidson, "playing well" in this context means enjoying the experience, understanding the game, and, more importantly, being able to explain what one likes or not and why, without using terms that marketing dictates.[22] One plays well by being able to understand the social set-up of a game, by interpreting games as a performative activity, by breaking down how participation in a fictional world is structured, by being able to appreciate the beauty of a system, by spotting the references to other games or other media, and tracing the variations or innovations with respect to other games. Understanding the complexity of games as activities, as well as their expressive means and features as aesthetic objects, implies expanding the ways in which we can enjoy games, digital or not.

The aim of textual analysis in general, and this approach to game analysis in particular, focuses less on making value judgments on the game and more on appreciating how we make sense of them. Creating a game canon, which includes games that are "good" or "the best" and which serve as a referent to all in the field, is not necessarily a way to improve game knowledge as cultural capital. A game canon lays a common ground, a series of compass points for those who enter the discourse, allowing us to chart the corpus of the texts that we study. A canon, however, can also limit the field of study, again by using elitism as a criterion. Moreover, often the prime candidates that would be popularly included in a game canon are bestsellers. If we think of digital games, the list could include works such as *Super Mario Bros.* (1985), *Halo* (2001), or *FIFA 23* (2022), once more displaying the power and influence of marketing. Determining which are the best games to label them as the games worth playing or analyzing is reducing our field of study. What we want is to expand the field—the method here provided is all-inclusive, where all games are worth studying, thus, opening up the possibility of discovering smaller, forgotten games, encouraging the practice of game archeology in order to highlight works that may have been overlooked, and finding new meanings in games that at first may have seemed trite. If our goal is to learn, there is so much that we can gather from playing flawed games, as well as the top of the crop.

BOX 1.1 THE PROBLEM WITH CANONS

One of the clearest markers of how a writer is thinking about their audience is how examples help illustrate the discussion. Many fields assume that the reader will be familiar with the texts referred to because they may be considered canonical and covered in foundational courses of the field. For example, scholars of English Studies are expected to know Shakespeare's key tragedies (*Romeo and Juliet* (1595), *Hamlet* (1602), *Macbeth* (1606), *King Lear* (1607), *Othello* (1604)), whereas film scholars should know *Citizen Kane* (1941) or *Goodfellas* (1990). In a similar way, in game studies, the assumption is that scholars will be familiar with *Pac-Man* (1980) or *Super Mario Bros.* (1985). On the one hand, canonical works provide us with a list of texts that serve as common referent to the participants in a discipline, so we do not have to explain every example from scratch. If you read an analysis from a field that is not yours, you will realize how difficult it can be to follow the argument if you are not familiar with the texts they are discussing. On the other, canonical lists across fields perpetuate works that are supposed to be "good," usually sidelining works that may be worth revisiting, as well as often marginalizing the work of diverse creators, especially women and people of color. In the case of game studies, the tendency is to focus on mainstream commercial games because they are more accessible, and more people may be familiar with them. This is one of the reasons why I encourage my students to find games that may have been overlooked, or may be unusual—lesser-known examples may be an undiscovered trove of knowledge, and may help highlight different creators whose work had not been noted before.

Games as texts can be tackled from two angles: as works connected to other works, or as works that can be read in different ways. In the first instance, we can look for what different games have in common, finding recurring patterns in their design, topics, aesthetics, and so on. Alan McKee calls this a structuralist approach,[23] which points to the work of theorists like Barthes, mentioned above, or Claude Lévi-Strauss, an anthropologist who discussed the commonalities between different cultures and societies. On the other hand, we can focus on the processes of sense-making while playing a game, the context in which it is played, and how it may be understood by different audiences. McKee calls these post-structuralist strategies, relating this approach to the work of scholars like Michel Foucault, Jacques Derrida, or Julia Kristeva. Going back to the *Death Race* example, a structuralist analysis would focus on how it continued the tradition of two-player arcade games, such as *Computer Space* (1971) or *Pong* (1972), or how driving in the game maps the two steering-wheel controllers to a top-down view of a field, or what the game may have to do with the movie that supposedly inspired it. Reading the game from a poststructuralist view, we could explore the question of why people who had not even played the game were so upset, and their understanding of what an interactive medium is, and compare it to the approach of the designers, documented in various interviews. Discussing how the game may seem very tame (or not) by today's standards and why may be another productive avenue of discussion.

This book provides an overview of a series of building blocks that can help writers following either approach, structuralist or poststructuralist. We can follow one or the other depending on what we want to learn from the game. My goal with this book is to provide a rich framework that allows us to understand the complexity of our subject matter and the multiplicity of ways in which audiences can engage with the texts.[24]

Game analysis is also a necessary tool to develop the concepts and vocabulary of game studies, which is still a relatively young field of study. Using an inductive method (that is, extracting general principles from specific examples), we can find overarching concepts that allow us to understand a wider range of games. These concepts allow us to relate games and their development, as part of the structuralist approach just described. Doug Church complains about the limited vocabulary to talk about games, particularly within the practice of game design, and calls for the development of what he calls "formal abstract design tools," derived from the analysis of specific games.[25] By examining closely the design of exemplary games, he comes up with concepts that allow not only to explain how the game works, but also to identify elements that can be used to understand other games and make design connections between them. One such example is "Perceivable Consequence: A clear reaction from the game world to the action of the player," which is identified both as a good element that helps the player know that their actions are meaningful in the game world, and as a design strategy to help the player understand the consequences of their actions in the game. There has been a growing number of academic works to develop those formal abstract design tools, in the form of reference libraries or dictionaries, such as the Game Design Patterns project, the Game Ontology, or the

Operational Logics approach.[26] The discourse of practitioners in the games industry has also expanded this vocabulary over the years—conference talks and online articles have helped generate new concepts, although these talks often do not use the rigor and systematic approaches that characterize academic discourse. The conceptual framework to understand how games tick and how we relate to games is, therefore, still a work in progress. Church's proposal to derive tools from the close reading of actual games and comparisons between them helps in developing those concepts in context. The strategy is not new—in the fourth century BCE, Aristotle generated the terms for his *Poetics* from the close reading of theater plays and epic poetry, creating a series of concepts that helped describe and compare the texts.[27] Following in Aristotle's steps, we can generate terms that allow us to describe games with nuance and depth.

▶ THE BUILDING BLOCKS AND AREAS OF STUDY OF GAME ANALYSIS

Starting an analysis can be daunting because there are so many things one can talk about. In order to ease our way into analysis, its building blocks can be divided into three interrelated areas: the *context*, the *game overview*, and the *formal aspects*. Each area comprises a series of building blocks, which writers can select to analyze a game. Think of these building blocks as plastic bricks that one assembles to construct the analysis: depending on the purpose of the analysis, the writer will use some pieces instead of others. These building blocks can be interrelated, so that in the same way that a door piece may need a hinge piece to build a doorway, there are analysis building blocks that usually go together. For example, when Camper discusses the graphic style of *La-Mulana* (2005), he uses two different building blocks: technology and the representation.[28] With respect to the technology, the game runs in current computers but it is developed to evoke the look of games developed for an older computer standard, the MSX2, whose processing capabilities were much more limited. Alongside the discussion of technology, Camper also discusses the aesthetics of the visual representation of the game, and how the careful choices to evoke a specific technology become an artistic statement.

There are many building blocks that we can use to construct the analysis of a game. This book presents three general areas in order to make them more accessible. Each different area may provide a different focus to our analysis:

the social sciences may focus on the context of the game or its reception, specifically in relation to players and communities, whereas game designers may want to discuss the formal aspects.

Interrelated building blocks can be the connection between the different areas, meaning that while we analyze a game, we are not limited to one specific set. In the example of *La-Mulana* above, the two building blocks fall into two different areas: while the technology used for the game and the technology it pays homage to are part of the context, the representation that recreates that technology is discussed as part of its formal qualities.

The following is a brief overview of the different areas of analysis of games. The introductions in Chapters 3, 4, and 5 will provide a more extensive description of these areas, as well as the building blocks comprising them.

Context The context of the game comprises the circumstances in which the game is produced and played, as well as other texts and communities that may relate to it. Although some literary scholars advocate that textual commentary should be limited to the text itself, as we will see later in the book, ignoring the context in which it is produced overlooks aspects that may be essential to understanding the text. The importance of context may be obvious in historical analyses, which must by necessity refer to the sociopolitical circumstances that produced texts like a newspaper article or a political discourse. There are other cases where the context is essential to disambiguate specific components of the text. For example, the Bible uses "thou" as the second person singular pronoun because that was the linguistic norm of the time; if a contemporary text uses it, it can be a sign of wanting to evoke a specific time period, or a reference to the Bible. In many fantasy videogames, such as *Ultima VII: The Black Gate* (1992), characters speak using "thou" as part of the language of the fantasy world in which they take place, marking that the action takes place far from everyday life. The same word can thus have different connotations depending on the context and who is reading it: what applies to a word can also be extended to a larger text. Thus, when we are analyzing a game, we have to take into account these other circumstances that may affect the way we understand it as a text. Even if one is not analyzing a game from a historical point of view, understanding its context is part and parcel of how we understand it, at times, even before starting to play.

An illustration of how context can affect the way we understand a game is *Resistance: Fall of Man* (2006). Its release met with the disapproval of the

Church of England because one of the levels takes place within Manchester Cathedral. The Church of England considered that having a battle within a digital version of the cathedral was a desecration, as well as copyright infringement.[29] The legal claims here were dismissed, although Sony, the publisher of the game, released a public apology about the level. This controversy is part of the context, and helps us understand the game, which seems to pride itself upon the realism of the locations to the point of copying real places.[30] The game takes place in an alternate history, so the similarities with the real world are an important part.

Game Overview This area focuses on the content, the basic features that distinguish the game from others, and how it has been read, appropriated, and modified by different audiences. These building blocks provide us with a summary that gives us an idea of what the game is about and who plays it, as a way to identify it.

The game overview covers the information that players need in order to get started. Players do not play games for their digital properties and structures, but because they mean something to them. Even as a pastime, games provide a means to relax and meditate, to become someone one is not, to explore, to learn about fantasy worlds as well as the real world, to make friends, or to blow off steam. Games can also be provocative texts that prompt players to create their own interpretations and parallel texts, such as creating their own levels, drawing their favorite characters, or writing stories based on the games they play. Although the analysis of fan-made texts is beyond the scope of this book, these paratexts (remember: texts outside of the work being analyzed but directly related to it)[31] can also help gain a deeper and complex understanding of a game.

When analyzing a videogame, one has to consider the player's position in the game. As a performance activity, the game is not complete until the player participates in it, and, therefore, the player is also part of the content of the game.[32] It is certainly an ambiguous position since the player is also part of the context of the game. It is very difficult to account for the role of the player in the game because different players will participate differently, and will, therefore, transform the text being analyzed. This also means that the person analyzing the game is part of it, too, and their approach to the game as players will also color how they understand it.

The design of a game usually encourages certain types of interactions, which is one of the aspects that we can explore. Games provide affordances, which define what the player can do, and curtail other actions, thus, defining the space of possibility of the game. For example, in *Super Mario Bros.* (1985), the player controls Mario, who can run, jump, and pick up objects, get rid of enemies by avoiding them or jumping on them, and grow larger by picking up a magic mushroom. This limited repertoire of actions allows Mario not only to traverse the world, but also to increase the final score. The game, however, does not let Mario talk to the enemies and ask them politely to pass by, or use the coins to buy a vehicle that would make him run faster. The intersection between what the player can do in the game and what is not afforded is the possibility space of the game.[33]

Formal Aspects The area dealing with the formal aspects studies how the text is constructed, the pieces that make it up. Verbal texts are made up of interrelated components: words, sentences, and paragraphs, at their most basic level. Word choices, patterns, and figures of speech are other components that literary analyses are concerned with. In cinema studies, being familiar with the vocabulary to refer to different types of shots, camera movements, and editing conventions is basic to writing a textual analysis of a film. In games, the formal aspects refer to the system of the game and its components (the rules, the control schemes), as well as how the system is presented to the player (interface design, visual style).

There are two humanistic approaches that base their methods on the formal analysis of their object of study: formalism and structuralism.[34] While formalism seeks to find the inherent components of a literary text at an abstract level, structuralism is the result of applying grammar-like structures to works beyond the verbal level, in order to understand where the meaning lies and how we make sense of that text. For instance, Vladimir Propp came up with what seems like a mathematical formula to describe a wide collection of Russian fairy tales, which is a typical example of the formalist approach to study literature.[35] He lists the typical lists of characters (the villain, the dispatcher, the helper, the princess, the donor, the hero, the false hero). Each of these characters has a specific function; for example, the donor provides an item that helps the hero during the adventure. Later on, Joseph Campbell's work on the Hero's Journey, also called the monomyth, can be conceived as a structuralist approach, since he parsed thematic commonalities in how the adventures of a hero cross cultures and ages.[36] This (often misunderstood) journey follows a very specific pattern:

> A hero ventures forth from the world of common day into a region of supernatural wonder: fabulous forces are there encountered, and a decisive victory is won: the hero comes back from his mysterious adventure with the power to bestow boons on his fellow man.[37]

Both formalist and structuralist methods have often been accused of overlooking the context by focusing exclusively on formal components over the content—the poststructuralist methods mentioned above are a response to the limitations of structuralism.[38] Although these reservations are not unfounded, it is also true that we can gain relevant insights by studying the structures of the text, how they relate to the content, and how these structures connect it to other works.

The method here proposed to study the formal aspects of games has a structuralist foundation as a conceptual tool to discuss games. Games are often structured systems, in the form of rule sets of computer programs, which are models that lend themselves to study of their form. According to Caillois, this type of organized play is termed "ludus," as it has specific regulations that constrain the activity.[39] Structuralism, however, can also be applied to study informal and unstable systems, such as make-believe play, which does not have hard rules and is made up as the players advance; Caillois calls this type of play "paidia": improvisational play, spontaneous, an opportunity for players to express themselves.[40]

The area of formal analysis may be familiar to writers coming from literature and film, where these approaches have long been applied. It may also be the most relevant to those interested in game design, as a way to understand how games work, as well as being able to communicate ideas to their development teams.

The building blocks of game analysis will be categorized under one of these three areas (context, game overview, formal aspects), giving us a glimpse of the richness and complexity of games, and the range of materials that we can comment on. The three areas are so interwoven it is difficult to talk about certain aspects of games without making references to others, so we spread them in three areas to facilitate mapping them.

The richness of games as a subject of study is such that not only can we write our class homework on games, but also theses and dissertations. One could spend a whole semester dissecting a single game from different points of view, as LeMieux and Boluk have done in their classes at University of California Davis—they have studied games such as *Super Mario Bros.*, *Doom* (1993), *Final Fantasy VII* (1997), and *Kentucky Route Zero* (2020).[41] There have been whole books written on games or game series, such as Dan Pinchbeck's *Doom: Scarydarkfast*, a monograph on *Doom*, its process of creation and design, as well as its cultural influence, or *World of Warcraft and Philosophy*.[42] There is so much we can explore and write about!

BOX 1.2 USING AI GENERATION TO WRITE YOUR ESSAYS

The popularization and easy access of tools that will generate texts based on a prompt has created a rush of students who use them to help ("help") them with their homework. Although there is a space for artificial intelligence tools and they can be very useful in specific contexts, when it comes to writing texts that need to show new insight and originality, they are simply not the right thing to use. There are many reasons why you should not be using tools that will generate your essays. Here are a few.

- If you are a student, you can run afoul of the policies of academic integrity and anti-plagiarism of your institution. Presenting work that you have not done yourself without proper attributions can be interpreted as dishonest and unethical. Plus, you are in school to learn, therefore, letting a computer cobble together an essay does not allow you to practice your new knowledge through writing.
- Essays generated with artificial intelligence are the result of a remix and regurgitation of texts that are already online and cannot generate original thoughts. AI cannot lead to new insights or ideas, nor is it able to string together an argument. Even if the essay sounds human, it tends to come across as a stream-of-consciousness rant, at times disorganized and repetitive, which makes for a poor essay. In the case of an analysis, the AI may resort to a variety of sources and formats that may not correspond to the type of essay the assignment may require. For example, if you are writing an academic essay, it may be taking the information from a journalistic website or a fan blog. Texts generated with AI are also very prone to rehashing biased or even bigoted information—they do not differentiate ideologies, but tend to make controversial or misinformed content appear as more important, just because they receive clicks both from people who either agree with the ideology or vehemently disagree with it.

(Continued)

(Continued)

- Continuing with the issues of sources, AIs can also "hallucinate"—they do invent sources, and citations, which may come across believable, but are completely fictional and we cannot find the source. For instance, if I ask ChatGPT to write my bio for a conference, it will invent a lot of information about me, including changing the institutions where I studied, and inventing publications and games I worked on. So, if you are thinking of asking an AI about a topic to find sources, you may waste quite a bit of time trying to find imaginary articles, books, or games instead of doing actual research. Web search engines (which have used AI for a long time, by the way) may take you to basic sources faster than an AI-powered writer.
- Artificial intelligence writers cannot quite do the job of a human writer—they lack the experience, the motivation, and the insight. One of the reasons why you may be in games is because you have a personal investment in them, and writing and analyzing them is part of that personal relevance. So, why outsource your passion to a computer?

▶ DEFINING THE AREA OF STUDY AND OUR AUDIENCE

In my classes, I often see students who want to say everything about their favorite game because the texts can be very rich indeed. They know the game backwards and forwards, and they talk about it with their peers all the time. This often results in students freezing when it comes to writing because they are overwhelmed by the sheer amount of information. Another common occurrence is that they try to cram everything they know into a single 1800-word paper, going from idea to idea but without really having a core argument. My method to assist students is usually asking them to stop and think about what they want to say, and focus on what makes the game noteworthy. The goal is to learn something new about the game, hopefully something that might have been overlooked or not noticed before. Part of my job also includes reminding students that they are not writing a blog post that their fellow gamers will read, but an academic paper where the teacher has certain expectations and standards, and which should be readable by people outside the class.

My trick to avoid being overwhelmed by the amount of material to discuss, or to fall into trite and not very productive discourse, is to be specific about what I am studying and who I am talking to, even before starting to write. By knowing who my audience is and what methods to use, I can be more effective in reaching my audience, as well as reduce the scope of what to say.

The approach of this book caters to scholars coming from a variety of disciplines within the humanities and the social sciences. This is still a broad audience, and different scholars may feel more at home with one approach instead of the other. Although game analysis is inherently interdisciplinary, we cannot use every method and discuss every single aspect of a game. In order to remain practical, we must identify the areas that we want to study, and which discipline we are addressing. Some of the questions we can ask ourselves to define the scope of our paper can be:

- What do I want to learn from the game?
- What is the field of study that I'm approaching it from?
- Who am I talking to? What do they know about games?
- What are the aspects of the game that are going to be relevant to the analysis?

The previous section briefly examined how different fields of study may tackle the games—we are not done with the multiplicity of fields yet. The discussion of the different building blocks in Chapters 3, 4, and 5 will include a connection to the specific discipline and methods they relate to.

Being aware of where we come from as authors, what we know best, and who we are writing for is a necessary exercise of introspection. It may be the case that the author is a teacher of literature who has decided to include videogames in their syllabus, as a way to appeal to their students. The methods and approach of literary analysis are relevant and useful to understand videogames. The literary scholar, however, should be careful not to lose sight of what makes games different from other media, by forgetting about their participatory nature or the social aspects of playing. In another case, the author may be a hardcore gamer who may have a lot of confidence in their knowledge of games. This is a great asset to have, but it may also get in the way of communicating one's findings to a readership who may not be as familiar with the games being discussed, and may get lost within the myriad specific names, jargon, and even in-jokes. The opposite can also be true—as a scholar, I often find myself trying to communicate my research work to game developers or fans who are not familiar with academic discourse. My strategy to talk about my work to commercial game developers or general audiences is to focus on basic theoretical concepts and ground them on examples. I cannot count on my audience knowing about literary theory or semiotics, but I can count on them knowing their games well.

▶ ARE WE READY?

There is still so much to be done in the field of game analysis. Rather than being afraid of it, we should be very excited about the possibilities. We can be pioneers in highlighting and arguing for the intellectual value of works that already have a cultural impact. Better still, we can become digital archeologists and discover an obscure game that turns out to be a wonderful work of art, and put it in the spotlight.

Not everybody who writes game analyses may be an avid gamer, but through analysis one can learn to appreciate games as cultural artifacts. The following pages do not intend to transform readers into videogame fans. After reading this book and applying it to your own work, some will still remain critical and skeptical about the status of games as art. That is okay because the goal of this book is not to evangelize, but to expand the variety of discourse as well as its quality. By enriching the discourse of games, we can also reach out to audiences in order to make it more widespread. The study of games must not be exclusive to a set of self-appointed experts. Everybody plays games—in playgrounds, on tables, with friends, with computers, with mobiles. Now, let us start thinking about what games can mean and how.

▶ NOTES

1 Huizinga, Johan. *Homo Ludens: A Study of the Play-Element in Culture* (Boston: Beacon Press, 1955).

2 Piaget, Jean. *La Formation du Symbole chez L'enfant: Imitation, Jeu et Rêve, Image et Représentation* (Neuchâtel: Delachaux Niestlé, 1945).

3 Both authors published key works in 1997: Aarseth, Espen J. *Cybertext* (Baltimore, MD: Johns Hopkins University Press, 1997); Murray, Janet. *Hamlet on the Holodeck: The Future of Narrative in Cyberspace* (New York: Simon & Schuster, 1997).

4 The issues of *Game Studies: The International Journal of Games Research* are all available online at: https://gamestudies.org/ (accessed November 4, 2023).

5 See, for example, how Bethesda set the terms of the release of reviews for *Fallout 4* (2015) in Schreier, Jason. "Fallout 4 Review Embargo Gets Embargo." *Kotaku*, November 5, 2015. Available at: https://kotaku.com/fallout-4-review-embargogets-embargo-1740855250 (accessed November 4, 2023).

6 You can read and compare the editorial policies of a variety of game review sites, or search for the editorial policies of your favorite publication online. See "Editorial Policy." *Kotaku Australia* (blog), May 3, 2021. https://www.kotaku.com.au/editorial-policy/ (accessed November 5, 2023); "Editorial Policy." *Rock Paper Shotgun*, n.d. https://www.rockpapershotgun.com/editorial-policy (accessed August 15, 2023); "Editorial Standards." *IGN Entertainment*, n.d. https://corp.ign.com/standards-and-practices (accessed August 15, 2023); Staff, Polygon. 2012. "Editorial Ethics and Guidelines." *Polygon*, October 19, 2012. https://www.polygon.com/pages/ethics-statement (accessed November 4, 2023).

7 This was the case with the leak of confidential images from one of Bungie's events online, which were traced back to a specific streamer. The streamer was subsequently banned from *Destiny 2* (2017–), an online game where he excelled and was the main subject of his channel, as reported in Chalk, Andy. "Bungie Says It Has 'Irrefutable Evidence' against Destiny 2 Streamer Accused of Leaking Confidential Content." *PC Gamer*, April 18, 2023. https://www.pcgamer.com/bungie-says-it-has-irrefutable-evidence-against-destiny-2-streamer-accused-of-leaking-confidential-content/ (accessed August 15, 2023).

8 A good discussion of the problematic economic model of certain game review websites is Walker, John. "A Response to PAR's Adblocker's/Games Press Article." *John Walker's Electronic House*, April 18, 2013. Available at: http://botherer.org/2013/04/17/a-response-to-pars-adblockersgames-press-article/ (accessed November 4, 2023).

9 Barthes, Roland. *Mythologies*. Trans. Annette Lavers (New York: Hill & Wang, 1972).

10 Genette, Gérard. *Narrative Discourse: An Essay in Method* (Ithaca, NY: Cornell University Press, 1980).

11 The essay is available online, Donaldson, Peter. "Digital Archives and Sibylline Fragments: *The Tempest* and the End of Books." Available at: http://shea.mit.edu/eob/ (accessed November 4, 2023).

12 Genette, Gérard. *Paratexts: Thresholds of Interpretation* (Cambridge: Cambridge University Press, 1997), pp. 1–15.

13 Wolf, Mark J. P. *The Medium of the Video Game* (Austin, TX: University of Texas Press, 2002).

14 For a detailed discussion of zero-player games, see Bjork, Staffan, and Jesper Juul. "Zero-Player Games. Or: What We Talk about When We Talk about Players."

In *Proceedings of the Philosophy of Computer Games Conference*, Madrid, 2012. Available at: www.jesperjuul.net/text/zeroplayergames/ (accessed November 4, 2023).

15 Consalvo, Mia. *Cheating: Gaining Advantage in Videogames* (Cambridge, MA: MIT Press, 2007).

16 For a rich and insightful discussion of how players adapt their game to their needs to play better, see DeKoven, Bernie. *The Well-Played Game: A Playful Path to Wholeness* (Lincoln, NE: iUniverse, 2002).

17 Flanagan, Mary, Daniel C. Howe, and Helen Nissenbaum. "Values at Play: Design Tradeoffs in Socially-Oriented Game Design." In *Proceedings of the SIGCHI Conference on Human Factors in Computing Systems*, CHI '05 (New York: ACM, 2005), pp. 751–760.

18 For a detailed history of *Death Race*, see Donovan, Tristan. *Replay: The History of Video Games* (Lewes, East Sussex: Yellow Ant Media Ltd, 2010), pp. 42–43 and Kocurek, Carly A. "The Agony and the Exidy: A History of Video Game Violence and the Legacy of *Death Race*." *Game Studies: The International Journal of Computer Game Research* 12, no. 1 (September 2012). Available at: https://gamestudies.org/1201/articles/carly_kocurek (accessed November 4, 2023).

19 See Smith, Joseph W. *The Psycho File: A Comprehensive Guide to Hitchcock's Classic Shocker* (Jefferson, NC: McFarland & Co., 2009) and also Crowther, Bosley. "Screen: Sudden Shocks." *New York Times*, June 17, 1960.

20 For the definition and discussion of cultural capital, see Bourdieu, Pierre. *Distinction: A Social Critique of the Judgement of Taste* (Cambridge, MA: Harvard University Press, 1984), pp. xvi–xvii, 73–75.

21 Nguyen, Mai-Hanh. "See How Much the Top eSports Teams, Athletes, and Their Organizations Make." *Business Insider*, January 11, 2018. Available at: www.businessinsider.com/top-esports-teams-players-salaries-2018-1 (accessed November 4, 2023).

22 Davidson, Drew. *Well Played 1.0: Video Games, Value and Meaning* (Pittsburgh, PA: ETC Press, 2009).

23 McKee, Alan. *Textual Analysis: A Beginner's Guide* (London: Sage Publications, 2003), pp. 9–11.

24 Another overview of methods and approaches to analyzing games from a different perspective can be found in Consalvo, Mia, and Nathan Dutton. "Game Studies—Game Analysis: Developing a Methodological Toolkit for the Qualitative Study of Games." *Game Studies: The International Journal of Computer Game Research* 6, no. 1 (December 2006). Available at: www.gamestudies.org/0601/articles/consalvo_dutton (accessed November 4, 2023). For a more detailed

discussion of methods for content analysis, see Consalvo, Mia. "Videogame Content Game, Text, or Something Else?" In *The International Encyclopedia of Media Studies: Media Effects/Media Psychology*, edited by N. Valdivia Angharad and Erica Scharrer (Oxford: Blackwell Publishing, 2013).

25 Church, Doug. "Formal Abstract Design Tools." In *The Game Design Reader: A Rules of Play Anthology*, edited by Katie Salen and Eric Zimmerman (Cambridge, MA: MIT Press, 2006).

26 The rationale and methods of these academic projects can be found in Bjork, Staffan. *Patterns in Game Design* (Hingham, MA: Charles River Media, n.d.), and Zagal, Jose P., Michael Mateas, Clara Fernández-Vara, Brian Hochhalter, and Nolan Lichti. "Towards an Ontological Language for Game Analysis." In *Changing Views: Worlds in Play* (Vancouver: University of Vancouver Press, 2005); Osborn, Joseph C., Noah Wardrip-Fruin, and Michael Mateas. "Refining Operational Logics." In *Proceedings of the 12th International Conference on the Foundations of Digital Games*, 27 (New York: ACM, 2017).

27 Aristotle. *Poetics*. Trans. Malcolm Heath (London: Penguin Books, 1996).

28 Camper, Brett. "Retro Reflexivity: La-Mulana, an 8-Bit Period Piece." In *The Video Game Theory Reader 2*, edited by Bernard Perron and Mark J. P. Wolf (New York: Routledge, 2009), pp. 169–195.

29 "Cathedral Row over Video War Game." *BBC*, June 9, 2007, sec. Manchester. Available at: http://news.bbc.co.uk/2/hi/uk_news/england/manchester/6736809.stm (accessed November 8, 2023).

30 "Resistance: Fall of Man—Game vs Real Life." *The Average Gamer*. Available at: http://www.theaveragegamer.com/2007/06/24/resistance-fall-of-man-game-vs-real-life/ (Accessed November 8, 2023).

31 Again, the definition of paratext comes from Genette, *Paratexts: Thresholds of Interpretation*.

32 The study of videogames as a performance activity is central to my work. You can read a summary of the main concepts in Fernández-Vara, Clara. "Play's the Thing: A Framework to Study Videogames as Performance." In *Breaking New Ground: Innovation in Games, Play, Practice and Theory: International Digital Games Research Association (DiGRA) Conference*, Brunel University, UK, 2009. Available at: www.digra.org/digital-library/publications/plays-the-thing-a-framework-to-study-videogames-as-performance/ (accessed November 4, 2023).

33 For a brief study of how game design defines the space of possibility, see Salen and Zimmerman. *Rules of Play*, pp. 66–67.

34 For an extensive account of the formalist and structuralist approaches and main proponents, see Eagleton, Terry. *Literary Theory: An Introduction* (Minneapolis, MN: University of Minnesota Press, 1996), pp. 2–6, 79–109. Structuralism here does relate to Alan McKee's definition above (see note 23).

35 Propp, Vladimir. *Morphology of the Folktale*. 2nd edn. (Austin, TX: University of Texas Press, 1968).

36 Campbell, Joseph. *The Hero with a Thousand Faces* (Princeton, NJ: Princeton University Press, 1972).

37 Ibid., p. 30.

38 Eagleton, Terry. *Literary Theory: An Introduction*, pp. 96–97.

39 Caillois, Roger. *Man, Play and Games* (Urbana, IL: University of Illinois Press, 1961), pp. 29–31.

40 Ibid., pp. 27–29.

41 LeMieux, Patrick, and Stephanie Boluk. "One Quarter, One Game: Approaches to Teaching a Single Game Seminar." In *Game Developers Conference: Educators Summit*, San Francisco, March 21, 2023.

42 Pinchbeck, Dan. *Doom: Scarydarkfast*. Landmark Videogames (Ann Arbor, MI: University of Michigan, 2013); Cuddy, Luke, and John Nordlinger. *World of Warcraft and Philosophy* (Chicago: Open Court, 2009).

2

Preparing for the Analysis

▶ INTRODUCTION

Before writing a single word, we need to do some groundwork. Playing the game is an obvious start, while gathering any information about the game that may be relevant to our analysis is also an important part of our work. How we play and why are going to influence our understanding of the game, so we must be aware of how our preparation affects what we are going to write later. This chapter discusses the implications of playing a game to analyze it, and gives an overview of the different sources that can provide us with the information that will help us make better sense of the game.

The first step is to budget your time. You may be a busy student with a crammed schedule. How much time can you realistically spend on this paper? This is important because you will do your best work when you are not writing against the clock, which is what most people do (including some of your teachers). You should estimate how much time you will spend:

- Playing.
- Reading.

DOI: DOI: 10.4324/9781003355779-2

- Writing.
- Rewriting.

It is easy to spend too much time in the first two phases, because they are the most fun—we play, we learn, we feel like we make progress. But we need to write too, and better sooner than later. Taking the first step to write can be intimidating—the essay in our head sounds great in concept, but once we start putting words down on paper—or with a word processor, most likely—then the limitations and issues of our writing become actual. Writer's block usually comes about when we get the feeling that we cannot live up to our original idea. One key to avoid spending too much time preparing, as a way to put off having to write, is to know that it is okay for the first draft to be bad, because we will revise it later. The best first draft is the one that is done and ready for rewrites. If there are other people available to read our work, take advantage of it. As a teacher, I find myself grading down papers just because the students wrote them in one sitting, and they made silly mistakes or explained things in a hurry. So, try to avoid writing your assignment at the last minute and make time for rewrites. I know well how hard it can be to find the time, but it is worth it in the long run—your work will be better, you will enjoy the process more, and you will feel a bit less stressed.

Our goal should be becoming an expert on the game. What *expert* means, however, is determined by what we want to achieve with our analysis. This means that expertise can be negotiable. Mastering the game can be a great way to learn a lot from it, since the best players also know their games very well. On the other hand, becoming an expert player requires dedication, and not everybody has the time, the inclination, or the talent to become a top-notch player. This is when other sources of information are critical to help us become experts. Even if we are professional players, paratexts will bolster our knowledge and we will do a better job. Becoming part of a game community will also help accessing the kind of knowledge and materials produced by that group of players. We may not need to be very good at the game either, particularly if we are analyzing how other people play or if we are interested in a concrete aspect of the game. As a rule of thumb, becoming an expert on a specific game involves learning everything we need to know to achieve the main goals of our analysis.

▶ YOUR ANALYSIS IS AS GOOD AS YOUR SOURCES

The Internet has changed the way in which we access information—it seems that all that we need to know is just a few mouse clicks away. Online journals and databases, as well as applications to manage scholarly references and documents, help us organize inordinate amounts of information. Moreover, when it comes to the study and writing of digital games, there are already several open-access, peer-reviewed journals that are available online, such as *Game Studies*;[1] many of the sources listed throughout the book are only available in digital form.

Easy access, however, also means that there are many sources that are not as reliable or sound as academic and journalistic writing may require. Anyone can publish content online—which means there is also a lot of poorly documented and argued junk. (There is also bad writing in print, but it usually has to go through an editing process.) Learning to identify which are the most reliable sources for your writing is a basic skill that one develops over time. This skill is particularly useful beyond scholarly work, since we live in an age when disinformation, bad faith discussions, and half-baked arguments pervade our day-to-day lives, taking advantage of the overwhelming amount of accessible information online. Here is a set of starting points to find reliable resources:

- *Print books are your friends*. There is plenty of relevant work that has been published in paper format that is not accessible otherwise, whether it is on games or something else. As we will see in later sections, not all your sources have to be directly related to games—bringing in approaches and sources from other fields can be a way of enriching the study of games and finding new perspectives. If you are a university student, odds are that there is probably a team of librarians willing to guide you through the resources of your library. So, go to the library and show your librarians some appreciation.

- *Editors and reviewers usually act as gatekeepers*. One of the issues with online resources is that there is hardly ever an editor or someone in a similar role who performs a quality check, if not of the specific piece of writing, at least in selecting the writer for their good quality. Look for sites that are selective with their publications by having an editorial board, or a curator.

- *Just because a blogger, website, or podcast is popular and has a lot of followers, it does not mean that they are an authority*. Granted, there are plenty of intelligent and insightful writers whose arguments you can cite, counterargue, or refine. Their writing can be a useful document of popular opinion, for example, if you want to discuss how the game was received. But if they refer to data or are giving a factual account, try to find a primary source instead. For example, if you are talking about the popularity of a game, look for sales figures or diverse reviews, do not take some over-general statement from a blog. If you want to refer to a theory from film or literature, resort to an authoritative source, such as a scholarly work, rather than somebody's general musings.

- *Look for the discourse generated by a scholarly work*. Many online journal databases and resources[2] allow us to know who has cited a particular work, particularly because the number of citations has become an index of quality for institutional purposes. The number of citations, however, may refer to other scholars who have refined the arguments, elaborated counterarguments, or outright refuted the work you have read. Some articles may be outdated, even if they are insightful, and there may be other scholars who have updated or extended those arguments more recently. Use the databases to find who has cited the work more recently and in what context—what you think is a new idea may have already been written.

Your sources can also serve as a source of inspiration to find a writing voice. Being critical of your sources can help you find what kind of writing you enjoy the most, so this attitude informs your own work and who you want to be as a writer. Is your aim to be a journalist who writes reviews that are on a par with some of the best film writing? Do you want to be a game scholar who writes close-readings of games like one would write of literary works? Are you a social scientist who wants to disseminate your findings to a large audience? The better your sources are, the better writer you can potentially become.

▶ PLAYING THE GAME CRITICALLY

The first step in writing a videogame analysis is not to write, but to play the game extensively. It may be tempting to start writing right away, particularly if you have played it before. Even if you have completed the game in the past, you should still revisit it, because playing a game for fun is different from playing it critically. Playing critically requires making a series of choices about how to play—since our choices may yield different information, we have to be methodical and aware of what we do while we play.

Before continuing, I must make a note. This chapter, and the book overall, focuses on the analysis of *digital* games. Non-digital games (card games, board games, playground games, etc.) pose a whole different set of problems. As we have discussed, games are a participatory medium and a performance activity, therefore, players are going to transform the text. A mother playing chess with her child will play a different game from that of two chess masters—the game may be the same but the context changes how it is played, including tweaks in the rules.[3]

Digital games also change depending on who is playing, but their digital components, where the computer provides a dynamic system whose behavior is predictable, make it relatively easy to reproduce some of the play situations. It is quite hard to reproduce a session of board or card games, where each social situation is unique and gives way to different negotiations, while we may be able to replicate a play situation in some types of videogames, particularly in the case of single-player games. The methods to obtain information for the analysis, which is what this chapter discusses, are closer to anthropological research, specifically what we call "participant observation," where the researcher is also part of the social group they are studying—this will be discussed in more detail below.

The special status of non-digital games does not mean that we cannot study board games, card games, playground games, "escape the room" events, or live-action, role-playing games (LARPs).[4] Many of the building blocks of the analysis described in the next chapters can be applied to understand non-digital games, too. It is the set-up and the methods that are going to be different and more complex, so they will not be discussed here in as much depth.

What Does "Finished" Mean? Establishing how much one needs to play the game in order to obtain relevant information is one of the first early decisions to make. Writing deadlines loom quickly and our articles/homework/reviews need to be sent out and read by others.

It may be easy to determine when a game is finished for certain types of games, particularly in the case of narrative games, for example, when there is a set number of missions, or when the player gets to the end of the story. However, tackling our texts this way is similar to how one would tackle reading a novel or watching a film, forgetting the interactive and systemic aspects of our games. Games are usually meant to be replayed and revisited—one does not only play *Settlers of Catan* (1995) or *Bejeweled 2* (2004) once, because they are dynamic systems that we engage with and try to get better at, either alone or with other people. Even in the case of narrative games, the contents are in constant expansion: for example, massively multiplayer online games (MMOGs) have an inordinate number of missions and periodical updates, as well as mini-games that we keep replaying, while other games extend their stories and challenges through new episodes of downloadable content. The interactions with other players, even if they are not designed, are also part of the game, and their participation can change how we play, from competing against other players to forgetting about the game and just hanging out, making friends in the virtual space.

Even in the case of games where the narrative marks that the game is at the end of a play-through, there may be different modes in which the game can be completed. We can choose different levels of difficulty (*Bioshock* (2007)) or different characters to control in the game (*Dragon Age: Origins* (2009)). Some games are so expansive that it may require hundreds of hours to find all the missions and explore all the nooks and crannies, as is the case of *The Elder Scrolls* series (1994–2013). In *The Elder Scrolls V: Skyrim* (2013), the expansiveness of the world is also increased by using procedural content generation, where the missions are generated and will be different when you play again using the Radiant A.I. system.[5] As games grow in complication and content, it will become evident that we cannot play the game in all modes, and it is going to be impossible within the time allotted to write the analysis. Therefore, deciding what "finished" means is the first step to define your analytical methods. Is it finished when you get to the end of the game? After you play for a number of hours? After you have completed a set of missions?

Interactivity and Critical Distance In academic writing, we appeal to critical distance as a necessary method to engage in critical analysis. The concept is relatively vague and not well defined, and usually refers to how scholars set aside their feelings about their object of study to analyze it critically, looking for the core of the text in a methodical and well-argued way. On the other hand, it is practically impossible to leave out subjectivity from writing since everyone has a point of view about their subject of the study. In the case of game analysis, achieving critical distance is problematic since the writer/player is also participating in the game.

Becoming a writer/player affects critical distance, which is unavoidable. The player is an essential component of the game, although there are certain types of analyses that may eschew the player's experience completely. This would be the case when analyzing the visual design of a game exclusively, for example. It is also true that this type of analysis will probably fall outside of game studies, following the methods of another discipline, such as graphic design, in the case just mentioned.

It is also easy to use oneself as reference for an "ideal player," even though we may not be. *Ideal* does not mean *optimal* player; rather, we look for an everyman of sorts, an abstract figure outside of cultural context and without preconceived ideas. This abstraction, although commonly used in literary studies or film criticism, is difficult to achieve. The sheer fact that we are tackling games systematically and critically sets us aside from most other players, so it is hard to consider ourselves average. Additionally, the better we get at playing a game, the rarer a player we become, since expert players are a minority. By being good at a game, we tackle it from a privileged point of view.

The field of phenomenology, which studies human experience, has a method that can help us in this case, called "bracketing."[6] According to this method, when we analyze the world based on our own experience, we reduce it to its essential elements, trying to eschew our subjective preferences and tastes. This requires conscious self-examination and consideration of who one is as a player, and requires a lot of literacy. As basic practice, we have to consider what type of player we are, and acknowledge that our experience playing may be different from other people's.

One way to solve this issue of critical distance may be having someone else play the game for us, or watching videos or streams of play-throughs and becoming observers of the game. This may work for certain types of analyses, especially if we focus on the player's behavior. But that is no excuse for not playing the game—we have to understand how the game works, how it positions the player, what types of thinking are involved in the game. Grabbing the controller or the mouse is still essential to gain insight on how the game works. Watching a video of an expert player does not make you into an expert yourself.

There is no solution to the problem of critical distance since literature and film analyses also have similar issues. In videogames, the critic also becomes a participant in the object of study; it cannot be helped. In preparing for an analysis, we have to be aware of what type of player we are, how we are tackling the game, and how that may affect our perception of the game.

BOX 2.1 EXERCISE: WHAT TYPE OF PLAYER ARE YOU?

Since we must be aware of what type of player we are, here are some questions that you can ask yourself to figure out your player profile. This exercise will also help you realize that you may be a different type of player depending on the game or the context.

What game genres do you like playing? (Feel free to add your own)

- Non-digital games
    - Card games
    - Board games
    - Sports
    - Playground games
    - Table-top role-playing games
    - Live action role-playing games (LARP)
- Digital games
    - Puzzle games
    - Adventure games
    - Visual novels
    - Computer role-playing games
    - Action-adventure games
    - Turn-based strategy games
    - Real-time strategy games
    - Racing games
    - Sports games
    - Multiplayer online battle arena (MOBA)
    - Battle Royale
    - Casual games
    - Free-to-play games
    - Experimental games
    - Massively multiplayer online games
    - Massively multiplayer role-playing online games
    - First-person shooters
    - Sandbox games/open world

(Continued)

(Continued)

- What do you play for?
  - Problem-solving
  - Achievements
  - Socializing
  - Exploration
  - Learning
  - Finding the optimal strategy
  - Relaxation/stress management
  - Self-improvement
  - Curiosity
  - Thrill
  - Becoming someone else
  - Expressing yourself
- What platform(s) do you use to play games?
  - Non-digital games
  - PC
  - Console
  - Mobile
  - Virtual Reality Headset
- How many hours do you play?
  - Not at all, this is homework.
  - 1–5 hours a week
  - 5–10 hours a week
  - 10–15 hours a week
  - 20+ hours

Based on your responses, write your own profile as a player. What types of games do you know best? Which ones are you good at? Which games do you not really play? Why do you like the games you like? There will be games you do not care about; why is that? You may realize that you play different genres for different reasons, so your profile may need different sections depending on the genre. This exercise will help you make explicit your own biases, not only about games, but also about how others may play games if they are different from you.

▶ WALKTHROUGHS AND CHEATS

Playing skills are a further issue in becoming experts in our game. For certain kinds of analyses, we need to become skillful at the game, but we may not have the time or the prowess to do so. Skill may not be the hurdle on every occasion—puzzles, quests, and missions may require players to solve problems in a specific way that may not always be obvious. It is often the case that we may have a deadline looming, meaning that we do not have enough time to figure things out on our own.

What cheating means depends on who is playing. Mia Consalvo, in her study of cheating in videogames,[7] found out that different players have different definitions of the term. For some players, cheating is identified as getting any outside information to play the game (including advice from friends); for others, friendly advice, walkthroughs, and guides are okay, but cheat codes and changing the code are out of the question; for another set of players, cheating only takes place when playing against other players because it means breaching a social contract, as in the case of online games. Therefore, before starting to write, we must be aware of our own definition of cheating as we are playing the game. The key questions to ask ourselves are: Are we okay with cheating? If so, why?

There are ways in which we can get better at our games, which may be necessary to our analysis, but may also affect how we play. Most games for all platforms may allow different types of cheats, which alter the standard rules. These cheats can be devices to obtain infinite lives or health, jump to any-level, unlock extra items, exploits that allow infinite resources, to name but a few. They are usually part of the game, either because they are tools that the game developers used to fine-tune it, or errors in the programming that allow behaviors that were not designed by the developers. There may also be external devices to cheat, such as programs that are loaded along with the game. All these can change what would be the critical path, and may skew the results of what we want to obtain in the analysis. For example, it would not be very accurate to talk about the difficulty curve of a game if we have been using cheat codes all along.

Walkthroughs and strategy guides are another resource that can affect the experience of the player, since rather than figuring things out on our own, we get help from other players who have already mastered the game. This is particularly true in narrative games, where figuring out who to talk to or how to solve a puzzle is not a matter of skill, but problem-solving and thinking. Even after having played through on our own, these guides can help us learn about parts of the game we may have missed, for example, particularly if there are hidden quests or areas. Therefore, the status of these resources is somewhat ambiguous in game analysis. On the one hand, they provide us with an advantage that the everyman player may not be expected to have. On the other, they give us additional information that will help us know more about the game, and they are sources that provide us with valuable information, from expert players as well as from the developers themselves, at times, as is the case of some game guides.

Outside information, in the form of guides, walkthroughs, or tips from other players, and devices to assist one's play, such as cheat codes, hacks, or game loaders, are all ways to expand what Consalvo calls "gaming capital"[8] The term refers to the practices of players and how different preferences define different types of players. Gaming capital includes the types and amount of knowledge of players, therefore, by resorting to extra information and resources, we extend our gaming capital. Our gaming capital defines us as players, so we have to consider how our gaming capital is set up and what kind of analysis it will help us produce.

In the specific context of analyzing a game, the implications of using cheat codes and walkthroughs are less ethical (playing fair) and more methodological (how do these guides affect the way that we understand the game?). After all, different kinds of cheats can all be tools to help us play the game, but then we steer away from being a standard player or following the critical path. Since these are resources, they should be included as part of your methods in case you decide to use them. More will be said about using one's own experience as a reference in Chapter 4. For now, it should be noted that the circumstances of play, including cheats and walkthroughs, are part of the analytical methods used here.

▶ GATHERING INFORMATION ABOUT THE GAME

Traditionally, textual analysis in the humanities tends to limit itself to the information within the text—what is not included in the text is not part of the analysis, because the text should speak for itself.[9] This way of analyzing text may not be the most productive, since it overlooks the fact that we never approach a text in a void—we have previous knowledge and a sociocultural background that frame how we understand the text. We cannot categorically affirm that all that there is to analyze is encapsulated in the text—if you try to read a text in a language you do not speak, you will not understand it, since we all need to bring our own linguistic knowledge to understand a message.

We can compare reading in a language we do not understand to the appreciation of abstract paintings, such as the color studies of Mark Rothko or Jackson Pollock's action painting, for example: if we are not familiar with the theories and practices of contemporary art, the concepts that inspired those paintings will be lost to us. We need to know more about the sociocultural circumstances in which a work was produced, such as the techniques used, other works of art by the same artist, or contemporary works that the paintings may have been inspired by or were responding to, for example, how these paintings were received and how they figure in the history of art are also part of how we can appreciate them.

The same goes for games: every game alludes to a family or genre, and is developed within a media landscape; the games that we have played before inform how we play new ones.[10] In the same way that the techniques of painters may be important in certain types of art critique, knowing the technology that a game has been developed for is also important, because that gives us information about what the platform can afford to do. How a game has been received in news pieces, reviews, academic criticism, tells us about its influence and how others have made sense of the game before us. Knowing about the context of a game is a way to become experts on it. In certain types of analysis, such as historical analysis, it may be the one key knowledge you need, independently of your skills.

Thus, the method of textual analysis I propose here includes the discussion of the context in which the game is created and played, incorporating methods from media and cultural studies into the analysis of games. According to this method, the writer should be familiar with the context of the game as well, because no cultural artifact is created in a void. As discussed in Chapter 1, every text is surrounded by other texts, starting with the box and manual of the game or the website we download the game from. Games also make references to other games, thrive on conventions inherited from a specific genre, or break off those conventions. For example, the game *The Secret of Monkey Island* (1990) featured a combat system that was quite novel at the time. The key to sword fighting is not being a skilled swordsman, but rather knowing the wittiest insults to fend off your opponents and make them lose their concentration. Thus, fighting becomes a dialogue game, where the player has to choose which insult to use. These mechanics were reused in later games of the series (*The Curse of Monkey Island* (1997) and *Escape from Monkey Island* (2000)), but have also been appropriated by later games, both as homage and as a way to revamp them. For example, the game *The Shivah* (2006) uses dialogue for two rabbis to fight against each other. Fighting is then a dialogic battle, where the trick is responding with questions, as a rabbi would do, to thwart the opponent.

The context is also necessary to understand how players may tackle the game, depending on where they come from: What does the game assume the player already knows? How does the context create specific expectations?

How does the game tap into cultural assumptions or social conventions? For example, the game *Nintendo Land* (2012) for the WiiU includes short tutorials for every single game. These tutorials were meant to teach players how to use the controls since it was a novel technology that used a tablet as a controller, along with the remote-like controllers already featured on the Wii. In the USA and Europe, this was the game the console came bundled with during its launch, because it was meant to introduce players to the new technology and its possibilities. Therefore, when analyzing *Nintendo Land*, it is important to take into account its status as a launch title, as well as being developed by the manufacturers of the console itself. The examples above have demonstrated how the context is also part of the game itself and should not be overlooked. In Chapter 3, we will see how a third of the building blocks of the analysis consists of elements related to the context.

When we look for the context of our game, one of the first things we want to find is what has been written about it, whether it is academic or journalistic. An Internet search will probably be helpful in finding some information right away, but the top hits on the list may not be the most useful or insightful. Remember: you have to be selective about which sources you will use in your analysis. Reviews of mainstream games are abundant, Internet forums are full of opinionated posters, but how are they helping us understand the game better? Both of these resources give us a sense of how well or badly received the text may be, but the goal of our analysis is not regurgitating a general opinion as if popular perception is the only authoritative voice. Writing a game analysis where you are just repeating popular takes on a game will hardly provide any insight. You do not necessarily want to contradict everybody else; the goal is to articulate something that is new and helps us understand the game in a new light. The same caution in selecting our resources must go into who we choose to argue against: a clumsily written review or a misinformed writer who has only played the first 30 minutes of a 30-hour game are easy to counter, but you will prove yourself to be a better critic if you find better works to discuss. Therefore, make sure that your sources are at least as insightful as you may hope to be. Again, your analysis will be as good as your sources. (And remember to check your library too.)

If we find very few or no references about the game after an intensive search, we already have the basis for a preliminary argument: the game has been overlooked, so our thesis statement must articulate why the game is important and deserves our attention. In the case of games about which a lot has already been written, your goal should be finding out what aspects of the game have been discussed before. Your analysis should find novel ways to tackle those aspects or, better still, find what has been overlooked and expand on it. Repeating what others have said will help you provide context, but your goal should be providing new insight on the game you are discussing.

A few keystrokes may call up an avalanche of links and references, so before becoming overwhelmed by the sheer amount of information at hand, remember that your goal is to be selective. For example, if you want to focus on the role of sound to create a narrative in a first-person shooter, walkthroughs or reviews may not be the most useful resource. Sound design is unfortunately often overlooked, so you probably want to look for specialized sources, such as academic papers on sound and narrative in other media, articles in trade magazines, or, if you are lucky, interviews with the sound designer, for example. A dearth of discussion on a specific aspect gives you a clear prompt to look for writings on the general topic, or articles that may discuss a similar aspect in another game or medium for the sake of comparison.

One healthy habit when preparing research work is to keep track of your sources—it can be as basic as having a document where you list the books, articles, and links that are useful. There are also tools that are designed precisely to maintain a database of bibliographic references—these are particularly useful if you write papers often; if you are studying for a Masters or PhD, they are an essential tool. Having a database is useful because you do not have to find the sources every single time, and you keep all your references in the same place. There are many free tools to do reference management—the one I used for this book is Zotero,[11] but there are other options, both free and commercial, to help you keep track of your references, including URLs of resources or copies of the articles themselves as a .pdf file. Keeping good track of all your references is key when it comes to finishing off the analysis, as we will see in Chapter 7.

▶ OVERVIEW OF POSSIBLE RESOURCES

There are many sources that can help us know about our games and their context, as well as gaining insight on their contents. The following sections cover some of the possible resources you may want to examine to learn more about your game.

Game Box and Manual The most immediate resource that can provide us with important information about the game is the box and the manual, if you have a physical copy of the game. This is true of digital and non-digital games. A physical copy gives us the release date and the publisher and in the case of commercial board and card games, it will display the number of players and the publisher. For videogames, we will see who the developer is. Boxes also include the instructions for the game and the cover of the game lets us know how it was presented commercially. As we will see in Chapter 3, it can also provide us with information about ratings or recommended player ages, giving us a clue to what the potential audience of the game is. The images on a box also indicate the type of game the marketing department wants players to believe it is: if the *Call of Duty* series was marketed with cartoony characters and colorful landscapes, it would be trying to appeal to the wrong audience, since their core players seem to identify the games they look for with greyish blues and browns and pseudo-realistic computer graphics. Game covers and boxes can also change from country to country, so we can get some insight by comparing how the game was marketed in different countries, particularly if the cultural context of the game is relevant to our analysis. For example, Figure 2.1 compares the

FIGURE 2.1 Comparison between the covers for the game *Ico* (2001)

covers of *Ico* in the USA (left) and in Japan (right). The US cover shows the protagonists explicitly, imitating a film poster, while the Japanese cover (used in the rest of the world) imitates Giorgio de Chirico's surrealist painting style and makes the landscape the protagonist. While the US box tries (poorly) to invoke its storytelling, the other cover invokes the wistful romantic tone that the derelict environments of the game create.

In the specific case of modern videogames, however, these are mostly accessible online, and new releases will hardly ever have a boxed copy. Digital downloads have become the main channel to access games; in the case of mobile games, it is the only way to access any title. The download page of a game is, at times, all the information that we can have access to as part of its context, and that information may be very scant—most of the time, we will get the name of the developer and publisher. If we're lucky, there may be a link to their webpage for further context—see Figure 2.2 as an example from the Apple store. The page information features standardized fields, however, it may not give us access to the credits of the game or its country of origin.

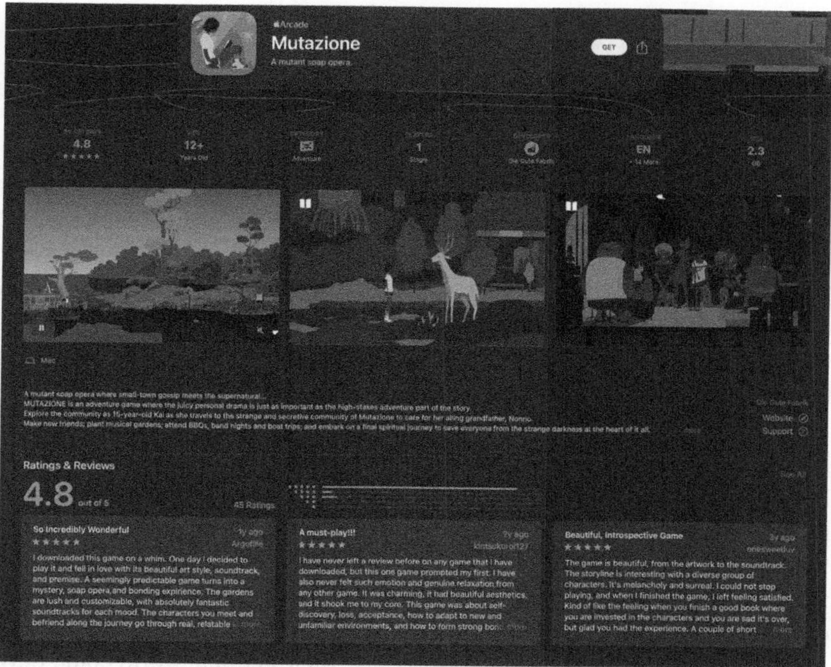

FIGURE 2.2 Apple Arcade store page for the game *Mutazione* (2019)

On the other hand, an online portal can provide us with additional contextual information that we cannot obtain from physical box. For example, the Steam portal page often includes links to recent news about the game, trailers and demo videos, and user reviews (though user comments and reviews should always be taken with a pinch of salt, as we will see below). In mobile app stores, we can also see the version of the game and a list of the changes over time. This additional information is just one click away, and something that physical releases cannot quite offer us as a source.

It is important to remember that these pages are also very volatile and may become inaccessible for a variety of reasons. For example, if we try to access a link to a download portal from a different zone from where it was released, say, we have a link of a game released in the United States but our device zone is set to the European Union, we may get an error. The portal may decide to close access to the app, or the developer may withdraw it from the store, which will also make it unavailable. Therefore, digital downloads are a double-edged sword, making some contextual information easily available, while other information becomes scarce and also unstable.

Manuals are also important—for commercial board games, they are essential for players to know how to play. In the case of modern videogames, they often include the instructions of how to play as a tutorial in the game itself, so it is always worth having a look at the manual of the game if there is one. The manual will often include the list of people who made the game, which in certain cases may only be accessible until you complete the game. Digital delivery of games is becoming more and more popular, so this information may not be physically available—in this case, finding the official website can provide us with the information about how the game was presented and delivered. Even in the case of web games which do not have any manuals, it is always worth looking for the original website where they were hosted, since that will likely provide basic contextual information.

Manuals are essential when studying early games, particularly in the case of home consoles and home computers, where some computer platforms used unusual keyboard mappings for the controls. For instance, the Sinclair Spectrum computers often mapped the direction controls for left and right to O and P and up and down to Q and A, a configuration that is not used in computer games nowadays. In the case of early arcade games, the cabinet was key to understanding the game, because their fictional world could only be represented in rough strokes, given the limited memory of their platform and low resolution of the visuals. With just a few kilobytes of RAM, there was not much room for elaborate cinematic cut-scenes either. The game manual, the box, or the cabinet allowed developers to include the narrative premise, along with the descriptions of the controls of the game. For example, in the book *Rules of Play,* the discussion about game narratives starts with a quote from the manual of *Super Breakout* (1981), which talks about spaceships and force fields, whereas the visuals of the game portray a strange tennis match against a wall.[12] Using paratexts to expand the fictional worlds of the game was very common in many of the arcade, console, and home computer games of the 1980s, where cabinets, manuals, and boxes were both a marketing device and a place to provide more information about the game.

Game Reviews Reviews help us understand how a game was received at the time of release. After some time, it is also worth considering how game reviews may differ from the reception to the game, or from how the game is regarded a few years later. Some publications, such as the British magazine *Retro Gamer,* used to include a section of "retro reviews" where they compare the reviews of a specific game at the time of release with how it would be reviewed at present. Although there are many reviews online, you should also look at print magazines, particularly for older games. *The Internet Archive* is an invaluable resource to find many of these magazines, coming from a variety of countries (see Box 2.2).[13] For more recent games, there are aggregate websites that include the ratings of critics and compare them with the ratings of users. These ratings, however, should be tackled with much skepticism, since these aggregate punctuations can be swayed by a variety of factors. For example, groups of users may decide to review-bomb a specific title because they disagree with a certain portrayal in their content, or there may be coordinated groups of fans who raise the rating of a game. Marketing companies can also write fake reviews of their games, or have their employees artificially raise their user reviews[14]—although users often have a keen eye to spot these over-flattering comments. These phenomena may not reflect the opinion of a significant number of players, or even of people who have actually played the game, but may be the result of users who may know how to manipulate these systems and twist them to represent a certain reflection of a game. We live in times where bots and troll farms are used to flood and undermine online discussions, often to incense the public and create a discourse of extreme opinions. Aggregate ratings websites are an easy target for these groups to distort the reception of a specific work, whether it is games, films, books, or television shows.[15]

BOX 2.2 THE INTERNET ARCHIVE

Although I warned you about using Internet sources above, it is also true that one of the most useful resources in my work every day is The Internet Archive (www.archive.org). Founded in 1996, it is a non-profit digital library of internet sites as well as other cultural artifacts, which are digitized and made available online.[43] Its Open Library is a formidable collection, that includes films and books in the public domain, old-time radio programs, NASA images, and concerts of The Grateful Dead, amongst a myriad other documents and media artifacts.

The Internet Archive is an invaluable resource for game studies in many ways, particularly if you study digital games. Here are some of the sections that can be the most useful when analyzing games:

- *The Wayback Machine* (https://archive.org/web/, accessed November 5, 2023) allows access to pages that may not be available anymore, such as fan pages, old versions of official websites, or older news sites, thus, we can find primary sources and cite them as a webpage. Some resources in this book are linked through this tool.
- *The Software Library* (https://archive.org/details/softwarelibrary, accessed November 5, 2023) allows access to tens of thousands of software titles, including an impressive number of old digital games which are otherwise very difficult to play, let alone run, unless you can access the hardware that runs them. This is also where the Flash games and animations mentioned below are preserved and made available, and their numbers grow every day. What is more, the games are playable on your browser, so you can check them out immediately. Many of them also have the file ready so you can run it in an emulator yourself.
- *Computer Game Manuals* (https://archive.org/details/gamemanuals, accessed November 5, 2023), as its name indicates, collects game manuals from many games from the 1980s until the end of the 1990s. Manuals are part of the context of the game, as we saw above, and they are also very easy to misplace. Even if you get hold of an original copy of a game, the manual may not always be there. Manuals are also essential to play older games, such as the ones found at the Internet Archive's own Software Library, because the controls may be very different from the ones you may be used to.
- *The Computer Magazine Archives* (https://archive.org/details/computermagazines, accessed November 5, 2023) includes general computing magazines, as well as game magazines in English as well as Spanish, Italian, German, Polish, Portuguese, Russian, Arabic, and Japanese among others. These magazines help us understand how a game was received at the time of release; we can even find walkthroughs and cheats that may not be available otherwise. The magazines are also fully searchable, so you can find mentions of a game or specific article quite fast.

(Continued)

(Continued)

- *Speed Runs* (https://archive.org/details/speed_runs, accessed November 5, 2023) is a video collection of playthroughs of games the fastest way possible. They do not constitute a standard way of completing a game, but can give us insights on glitches and exploits, as well as how expert players may tackle the game.
- *The Machinima Archive* (https://archive.org/details/machinima, accessed November 5, 2023) is an academic resource produced in collaboration with Stanford University to preserve the art form of machinima, which uses 3D game engines to produce films.

As with all your sources, you should always check the origins of the materials you find in the Internet Archive and pay attention to the metadata of each entry—the dates of the magazine, the version of the game, the edition of the game, or who uploaded the materials, amongst other things. Going through this archive with a critical eye can yield great results.

So when reading reviews, take into account the context in which they appear, what the goal of the reviewer may be, and what may be the factors that could condition the opinions of the writer.

Academic Articles If your analysis is academic, it should be situated within the pre-existing literature and make references to relevant works that may have already dealt with the game at hand. Although the practice of game analysis is not as widespread as in other humanities fields, there probably are academic articles and theses that deal with the game that we are focusing on. There are articles and dissertations dealing with specific game genres, which may include references to your game, or games that are similar. Many of these works will be discussed throughout the book, so their discussion will keep appearing in different sections.

Press Releases and Advertisements In the same way that game boxes provide us with information about how the game is presented to players, press releases and advertisements can tell us a lot about the perceived audience of the game (at least in terms of marketing). Different television advertisements from different countries can tell us a lot about the context in which the game is released, and how it may vary from country to country. If the analysis focuses on the cultural context of the game, comparing different ads is not only fun, but can also be very productive. Print magazines can be a good source, since who the magazine is aimed at already gives us an idea of who marketers think the audience is. We can also find many television advertisements online as well, which can be informative even if they are out of the context of the channel and the programs that the ad may have been shown in. Internet ads, on the other hand, are going to be difficult to track unless you are analyzing a contemporary game.

In the current digital landscape, the main way to advertise games is not on television, but rather online game trailers, which are distributed through social media and online publications. The release of these trailers becomes an event in itself, especially if they are announcing an anticipated title. They are so important, that in the last few years trade fairs like E3 have been substituted by online events, where publishers announce their new catalogues in hour-long presentations or supercuts of trailers. These online events have become more widespread during the pandemic, where it was not possible to hold in-person events; they have also proved that developers can reach audiences directly without the need of trade shows. Trailer releases also generate their own discourse and speculations, which become part of the context in which the game is released, to the point that, at times, the reactions of fans to a trailer may influence the game development, and games may change based on the reception of a specific preview of a game.

Newspaper Articles Apart from game magazines, there can be mentions in the general press that may provide relevant information about the game we are analyzing. The sole mention of a videogame outside of the specialized press should immediately prompt the question of why it is being mentioned. Established newspapers in the English-speaking press, such as *The Guardian* or *The New York Times*, now have their own sections of games in their online version. The magazine *Los Angeles Review of Books* also includes reviews of videogames, although they are published months and even years after their release.[16] The fact that there is a section of these outlets devoted to games demonstrates their cultural impact and relevance. Bear in mind that at times the marketing departments of big publishers arrange for interviews and feature articles about their games in the general press, as part of their publicity campaign to reach a wide audience—something that is also frequent in the marketing campaigns for other media. In the past, a game could acquire certain relevance outside of gaming circles, which may not have been intended by marketing (at least openly). The recurring controversies whenever a game of the *Grand Theft Auto* series (1997–2013) was released, for example, tended to focus on their violence and notorious portrayals of the crime world. However, the more widespread accessibility of games and the growing number of videogame players of all ages, as well as the increasing popularity of board games as a social activity, has helped redirect the discourse about games and normalizing their analysis as activities that shape our everyday life. In the past, articles in the non-specialized press would perpetuate misunderstandings about what videogames are, including accusations of videogames making players violent or antisocial.[17] Therefore, when looking at a newspaper article on a game, especially a videogame, make sure to check its date as well as the author. More recent articles tend to have authors who are knowledgeable about games and therefore write columns or articles from the point of view of a specialist, as opposed to general journalists who may not be as familiar with the topic, or who write about games just because of the shock value of the story.

Developer Diaries and Talks One of the objections usually raised against traditional literary criticism is that it gives too much weight to the presupposed intentions of the author. In literary theory, New Criticism called this *intentional fallacy*, arguing that the intention cannot be proved by the text nor is it relevant.[18] (This concept will be referred to again in Chapter 3, which starts discussing context as an area of analysis.) All we should care about is what is in the text, which is all the evidence we need. However, this position also assumes that works are produced in a void, which is another fallacy. Games are cultural artifacts, and as such, they are the product of their time and socio-cultural context.

We are lucky enough to have a variety of resources to learn more about what the game developers were thinking as they made the game. Some games actually document their creation process publicly, in the shape of blogs or developer videos, some even stream their development process as they are working on the game, showing their process and also conversing with fans as they work. In a rare example of games with a wealth of information available, Jordan Mechner kept a diary while he was developing his two first games, *Karateka* and *Prince of Persia*, which he released first in fragments in his own blog and then published in their entirety as books.[19]

There is also a growing number of special collections in specific libraries, where developers have donated their documents for others to study. For example, The Strong Museum in Rochester, NY, counts with the International Center for the History of Electronic Games, including Mechner's document collection, or the papers of Dani Bunten (designer of *M.U.L.E.* (1983)).[20] The University of Texas in Austin hosts collections of documents from some of the notable game developers who have worked in the city, such as Richard Garriott, creator of the *Ultima* series (1979–1999) or Warren Spector, producer of *Deus Ex* (2000) amongst many other titles.[21]

Developer interviews may also include some of the questions that we are seeking answers for. These resources also have to be taken with a pinch of salt—normally they are part of the marketing campaign, and usually cover some of the same points advertisements do.

The actual design documents or development files can provide us with invaluable insight about the process of production, although getting hold of them can be difficult. Not many of these documents are freely available, either online or in special collections in libraries. In the case of older games, at times the original code has been lost—often because the storage technology has become obsolete or has degraded over time. For recent games, most commercial developers (particularly of AAA games) are overprotective of their development process, because they do not want to reveal too much information.

Developer Retrospectives "Insight is 20/20 hindsight," or so the saying goes. Thus, some of the resources that can allow us to learn more about the development process of a specific game are released after the game is finished, what used to be called "postmortems," which are relatively popular in industry publications and conferences. The term "postmortem" has become less popular, mostly because the connotations of the word may mean that a game is "dead" after release, while the point is precisely that they come to life into the world to be played; we will therefore use the term "developer retrospective," although looking for "postmortem" will certainly yield substantial results when looking for these documents and presentations. These retrospectives are written after the game has been released, or are presented in conferences, often some time after the release has passed. Some of the conclusions reached in these reflections are the result of achieving some distance from one's own work over time, and although they retell how the developers recall the process, they are also less tainted with publicity in sight. *Game Developer Magazine*, now out of circulation, has many issues available online. One of their recurring feature articles was game postmortems, which is the type of resource we are looking for.[22] The Game Developer's Conference hosts the so-called Classic Game Postmortems, where developers talk about the development process of games that are now held in high regard, such as *Alone in the Dark* (1992),[23] *Fallout* (1997),[24] or

Rez (2001).[25] Most of them are available to watch online. Some of these self-reflections, as well as interviews where developers reminisce about their work, are good sources, although the accounts should be taken with a pinch of salt—these stories may be biased by romantic or disenchanted notions too, and they may or may not have marketing purposes behind them.

This list of possible resources can help you become an expert on your game, but you may not need to consult all of them for your analysis. The more you know about your game, the better prepared you will be to write. It is also too easy to spend a lot of time playing the game and checking resources, so select what kind of information will be the most useful for your game. The goal is to get around to writing, which is when the process becomes more challenging but also more rewarding.

Resorting to Pre-Existing Theories to Understand Games Certain types of game analysis will resort to theories and frameworks, either to explain the game, or as examples that help us understand those frameworks, as we will see in Chapter 6. The field of game studies is growing, but part of what we are doing right now is borrowing theories from other media to understand games better. Throughout the book, we will see how the key is using those theories as a tool to study games and generate new insights, maybe leading to new theories as a result.

You should not feel limited by having to find works that are directly related to games. Although there is a significant body of work written about games, it is not very large if we compare it to other fields. So, if you just look for game-related sources, you will bump up against a wall very soon. The key is that the study of games is eminently interdisciplinary, because it can be approached from a wonderful variety of points of view—this is the precisely the multiplicity and variety that this book is addressing. So, learn from other disciplines and see how they help you understand games in a novel way. Bernard Perron, for example, examines the different levels of signification in videogames based on his knowledge and previous work on horror film,[26] as Krzywinska does in her work on *Resident Evil* and *Undying*.[27] James Paul Gee applied his understanding of literacy and sense-making to write a book on how videogames can teach things,[28] while T.L. Taylor approached the study of virtual worlds using methods borrowed from ethnography.[29] In my own case, my literary training and drama studies have helped me understand games as an activity related to other types of performance, such as theatre, rituals, or sports.[30] In all these cases, the key is realizing that the application of the theory to games, and more specifically to digital games, is going to challenge the theories we use. It is very likely that there is not a complete correlation between the environment the theories were developed for and the study of games. And that is okay—the clash and the challenge are precisely where we can produce new knowledge.

▶ ACCESS TO THE GAME AND ACCOUNTING FOR YOUR SOURCES

When we write about a game, we need to provide precise information about the games that we have been playing, in the same way that we cite the people whose work and concepts we are using to support our argument. Remember—your paper is as good as your sources, so be sure to include detailed information about the game(s) that you are talking about. This information should go beyond the title and year—for example, there are myriad versions of *Pac-Man* (1980) for almost any digital platform you can think of. The platform and the developer are also essential in order to identify the specific version of the game that you are talking about, even when it is very likely that your reader may be familiar how *Pac-Man* works.

It is most likely that you will be analyzing a game that you already have access to, because of your own choosing, or because, hopefully, your teacher has made sure the game is available. However, if you are the adventurous type, or want to do some game archaeology and find games that are off the beaten path, you may come across some obstacles. In the case of older games, you may not have the original platform that it was developed for. It could also be the case that the platform was never released in your part of the world: for example, the Amstrad personal computers were only distributed in Europe; the MSX computer standard was only used in computers in Japan, western Europe, and Brazil; while the TRS-80 was only available in the USA. This means that, even if you get hold of the original platform, you may not be able to plug it in, because of different television standards and/or electrical voltage.

In the same way that books have different editions that may include revisions, new introductions, critical essays, and comments, games can have different versions depending on the platform, where the affordances of the technology may actually bring about fundamental changes to the game. The original version of the game is called in the industry the "reference build," which is the one that is worked on first and then translated ("ported," in industry jargon) to other platforms. Often the reference build is the version of the game that was released first; if a game is released for several platforms simultaneously, one would need a bit more research to know which one is the reference build—often developers will keep mum about that information, though.[31]

Digital games at times depend very heavily on their hardware, making it difficult to play even when we can technically run the code in the computer. For example, the Mattel Intellivision home console has a small keyboard controller whose configuration is essential to play certain games, which only computer keyboards with a numeric pad may be close to. In a more dramatic example, the Nintendo Zapper is a peripheral designed for the Nintendo Entertainment System, and some games are specially developed for it, *Duck Hunt* being the most famous example. This piece of hardware will only work on a cathode ray tube (CRT) television, and not with current high-definition televisions. So even though it technically runs on an emulator, *Duck Hunt* (1984) is only really playable as designed if you have the complete hardware set-up. As specialized hardware encouraging gestures and special set-ups keeps appearing over the years, as is the case of the Playstation Move, the Microsoft Kinect, the Nintendo WiiU, or virtual reality (VR) headsets and wands, the challenges of running their games as years go by increases, unless any of these hardware designs become a standard or a model that is handed down from platform to platform. So far, most of these specialized peripherals usually only work with one specific console model, and become outdated in the next generation.

You may have to run the game in an emulator, that is, a program that behaves like a computer inside another computer. Emulators work as separate programs in a computer, or as an application on a mobile device; The Internet Archive also has a growing collection of older games that run in the computer browser (see Box 2.2). Continuing the comparison with book editions, using an emulator is like using a facsimile of a work—a photographic copy of a book, manuscript, or print that replicates the visuals of the material source. In literature and history scholarship, at times we need original texts, such as a manuscript with the author's notes, or the original edition of a book where we can see how a specific word was printed, because that may provide different interpretations of the text—there are pieces of Shakespearean scholarship that discuss how a single word is printed in different editions, for example. Those original documents may be difficult to access, and may only be available in a specific library where one needs special permission to read and manipulate those documents. In a similar way, we use emulators when we cannot access the original game, but that also means that the game will be somewhat changed.

If we play an emulated version of *Kaboom* (1981), for instance, we will probably not be using the controllers that the game was designed for, the game paddles for the Atari VCS. As we have seen already, and will continue to discuss in the following chapters, the material circumstances in which we play the game are part of the experience; so an emulator counts as a different edition of the game. Figure 2.3 shows *Knight Lore* (1984), developed for the MSX, running on an emulator for OSX.

The controllers may not be the only problem. Continuing with the Atari VCS, one part of the hardware that is difficult to emulate is the Television Interface Adapter (TIA), the main computer chip that generated the image, sound, and read the input from the joysticks, which handled and generated data for CRT televisions.[32] The CRT television generated images line by line

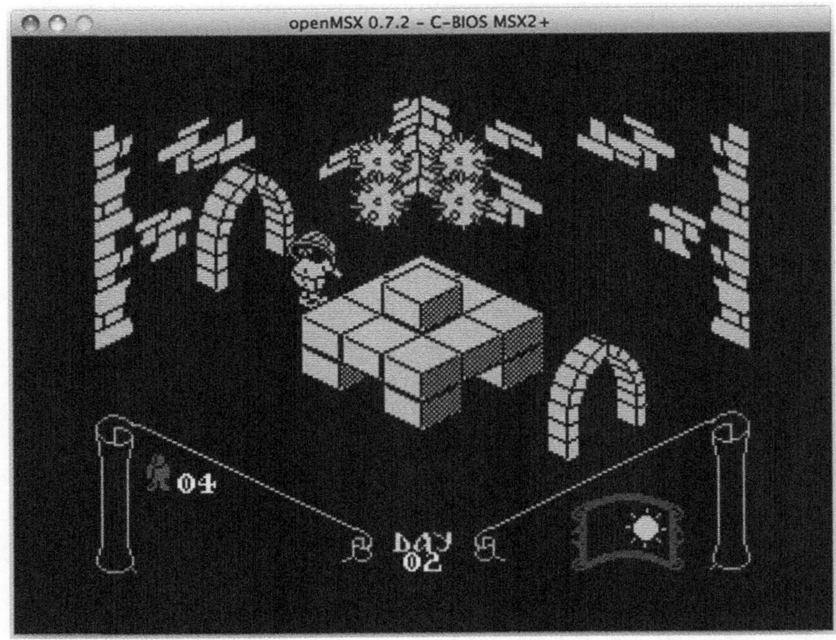

FIGURE 2.3 ***Knight Lore*** **(1984), developed for the MSX, running on an emulator for OSX**

at a specific rate, which is different from that of current computer monitors, so when we run those same games on an emulator, the images are going to flicker to the point that some games may be unplayable, such as *Pac-Man* (1980) or *Frostbite* (1983).

Ports are another way to play games when there is no other access to them. At times it cannot be helped: *Spacewar!* (1961), one of the earliest videogames in history, ran in PDP-1 computers that were not very common in their time; now they are even rarer, because there is only one in working condition running at the Computer History Museum in California.[33] The original code has been preserved, fortunately, and then retranslated to newer computers across the generations. It is unlikely that anybody writing about the game will play it in its original form, with its oscillator monitor transformed into a star field, or using the repurposed controllers, but at least we can get a sense of the gameplay. The material aspects of gameplay that we miss, we can reconstruct by looking at documentation.

In a way, a port is a translation of the game from one platform to another, extending the parallels between book editions and games. Unlike emulation, ports usually mean recoding the game, which usually changes some of its features, from screen resolution and colors to playing the music differently. For example, *Asteroids* (1979) in its original arcade version used a vector graphics monitor, which means the graphics were displayed with beautiful straight lines and glowing vertices, rather than the pixilated CRT image. In the Atari VCS port (1981), the ship and the asteroids became colorful splotches on the screen, which flickered a lot because the console could not support more than a few moving sprites on the screen. Figure 2.4

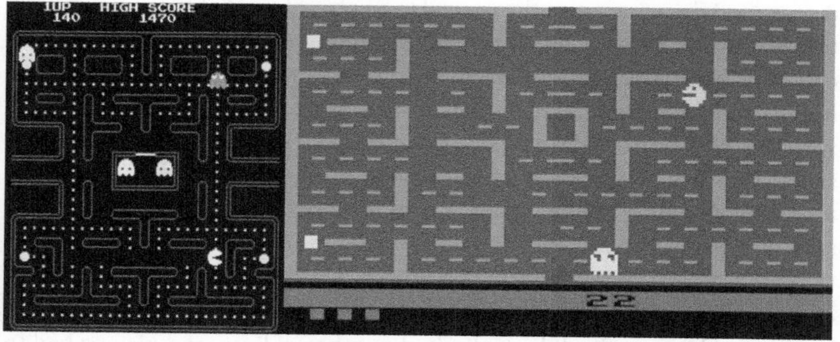

FIGURE 2.4 Comparison between the original version of *Pac-Man* (1981) and its Atari VCS port (1981)

shows a comparison between the original version of *Pac-Man* (1981) and its Atari VCS port (1981).

Non-digital games can also have different versions, just like books do—games may tweak rules, or include different tokens. The database *Board Game Geek* is an invaluable resource to keep track of these different editions, because it lists different editions of games, not only through time but also in different countries.[34] The database depends on user content, so the way the information is gathered is not necessarily systematic and its curation may not be rigorous, but the sheer number of contributions from users, including photographs of different versions of a game, makes it into a key resource to understand the history and background of board and card games. (Archivists of board and card games should also start thinking about facsimiles, incidentally.)

Do not forget to account for the version of the game that you are analyzing, and do not take for granted having access to games—it may be more challenging than it seems. On the other hand, you should not give up on discussing a game just because it is technically difficult to run. As we have seen, there are different ways to get around that.

▶ SECONDARY SOURCES

Continuing with the issue of access, technical issues can be only part of the problem. We may want to analyze a game that is an event, a be-there-or-be-square type of thing, a performance. Other times, it may be hard to get the game running, or get hold of the material. These games are important to discuss and document and they can also be part of our field of study. I mentioned Roland Barthes' essay on professional wrestling in Chapter 1[35]; we can find the equivalent of fleeting events in games, too. Event games are important, since they relate to performance art. Alternate reality games, such as *The Beast* (2001), a tie-in of the movie *Artificial Intelligence* in the same year, or *I Love Bees* (2004), a game to promote another game, *Halo 2*, took place within a specific amount of time. Even though some of the websites or information are still available online at the time of writing, in order to play the actual game, you had to be there. Another example of this type of event game is *GlitchHiker* (2012), a Global Game Jam game that became "extinct"—the game itself had a limited number of lives, and players had to keep playing to keep it alive. The moment the game had no more lives, the game was deleted from the server and could not be played any more.[36] If we have not been part of these event games, and yet we want to analyze them, the context becomes essential: videos, manuals, websites, descriptions. Theatre scholars do this all the time—they may have seen a play a long time ago, so if they want to discuss it in a paper later on, they look for production photos, interview the people who took part in it, read reviews, watch video recordings. The goal is to reconstruct the event as much as possible, both to keep a record and to give a sense to the reader of what the game was like, on top of the given goals of generating insight on the object of study.

Even modern games are liable to becoming inaccessible overnight. *P.T.* (2014) is a short, first-person horror game released as a free download in the Playstation Network. Those who completed the game realized it was a trailer for what would have been a new instalment of the *Silent Hill* series—the title stands for "playable teaser." When the game that *P.T.* was an introduction to was canceled,[37] Konami—publisher of both—decided to also pull the teaser from the Playstation Network store, rendering it unavailable unless one had the data already downloaded in their console.[38] *P.T.* is a fascinating game at many levels. The player must traverse a corridor over and over again, looking at things and opening doors to invoke a terrifying ghost. Some messages are written in different languages, which was intended as a device to have players all over the world collaborating and solving the riddles in the game. But, unless one has played it or has access to a Playstation 4 with a copy of the game in its hard drive, any analysis of the game needs to use secondary sources to learn about it. Fortunately, *P.T.* was extremely popular, so there are many let's play videos, reviews, as well as a myriad webpages with interpretations and careful breakdowns of the game.[39] None of them are quite the same as playing the game first-hand, especially because it is a horror game, but it is possible to reconstruct the game in quite a bit of detail.

More recently, the End-Of-Life of the software platform Adobe Flash meant that thousands of web games have become inaccessible to play online, after Adobe decided to stop updating and supporting the platform at the end of 2020.[40] The plug-in necessary to play Flash games does not run in most modern browsers anymore, so in order to be able to play many of the games that thrived from the mid-2000s to the mid-2010s, one has to resort to alternatives, from in-browser emulators, to initiatives to port flash games into open standards such as HTML5. Adobe's corporate decision meant the disappearance of important web games such as *Crimson Room* (2004) one of the first escape the room web games, or the original version of

Cannabalt (2009), which helped popularize the endless runner genre. Different initiatives, such as the collaboration between The Strong Museum of Play and the website Kongregate,[41] or The Internet Archive's work of preservation of Flash games and animations,[42] have helped salvage an important part of digital creations.

Although not having access to the original game is not ideal, and you should always play the game you are analyzing, reconstructing a game through its paratexts can be a legitimate method. If this is the case, where you do not get to play the game, you should still make a note of it in your analysis. This is valid academic practice, where we can mention that a quote is from another text instead of the original, if we cannot gain access to the source.

A voice of warning: do not use paratexts as a way to avoid playing the game, in the same way that some lousy literary students use *Cliff's Notes* or your country's equivalent of summaries and comments that supplement a novel, so they do not have to read it. If the game is available in some manner, play it. Reading Wikipedia does not turn you into an expert on any games either—it is the start, but not the end of your research.

▶ PLAYER DATA

Certain types of analyses, geared toward the social sciences, study player behavior. Here, the focus of the analysis shifts to the activity of play itself, rather than the game. The researcher can record play sessions or interview the players about their experiences, and then use that data, rather than the game, as the focus of the analysis. For larger-scale works, gathering and analyzing player data can be a way to complement the formal analysis of a game or types of games—for example, Jesper Juul, in his study of casual games, used interviews with players to complement his own insights on the genre.[44]

This book does not focus on player data gathering and analysis, but on the study of the game itself, taking the problematic stance of "ideal player" as its main guideline (similar to film or literary analyses).[45] However, the next section provides a short introduction to how to obtain player data from the ethnographic study of virtual worlds.

Preparing to Analyze Virtual Worlds The analysis of online virtual worlds is a case apart, but relevant enough to the study of games that it deserves a section here. The study of virtual worlds is so specialized that there is at least a separate handbook providing guidelines for it already.[46] According to Boellstorff et al., a virtual world is a multiuser virtual space, where players can navigate and explore and interact with the objects in it.[47] These worlds are online and therefore provide a shared social space where users can interact and communicate, using an avatar as their representation in it. For our purposes, the main difference with other types of digital games is that these are *persistent* worlds, that is, the user does not have to be there for the world to change and evolve. The study of virtual worlds is usually related to the social sciences because the focus is more on studying the players and their social environment than on the formal qualities of the game.

Virtual worlds may not necessarily be games—for example, *Second Life* (2003–) is a virtual environment where there may be games, but that's not the point. *There* (2001–2010; 2012–) is also a virtual world where people meet and maybe create content. Another relevant example here is *Habbo*, formerly known as *Habbo Hotel* (2000–), an online community for teens and young adults. Its model has been imitated by other communities, and also saw a boost of users during the COVID-19 pandemic, since it was an easily available social space where one could meet friends online. These virtual worlds are usually thrown in with digital games because so many of them are games and the controls are based on their conventions. The first online world, *MUD1* (1978), was conceived as a game.[48] There are many massively multiplayer online role-playing games (MMORPGs) (*World of Warcraft* (2004–), *EVE Online* (2003–), *Final Fantasy XIV* (2010–2012; 2013–), or puzzle games (*Puzzle Pirates* (2003–)) that gather thousands of players day to day; virtual reality (VR) is also facilitating a growing number of online communities, such as *VRChat* (2014–).

The preparations to study a virtual world are somewhat more extensive and even more self-conscious than the ones this chapter has covered so far. If in any game analysis we have to be aware of what type of player we are, how we present and conduct ourselves in a virtual world has the potential to affect our research, since it will make users/players respond to us socially. Amongst the factors that we have to take into account, Boellstorff et al. list the following factors as essential for consideration before we start studying a virtual world:[49]

- *Equipment used*: virtual worlds tend to be computer-based, although virtual worlds can also be accessed on consoles or and mobile devices, such as *Genshin Impact* (2020–). The equipment we enter the virtual world with is going to condition how we experience it and, more importantly, how we communicate with others. For example, a slow computer or connection, or an old mobile device may be the cause of lag in our communications in the world, and therefore not allow us to keep up with other players.

- *Learning how to play the game*: the process of becoming an expert in the game should start with reading the instructions in order to be able to get around and interact with people, as before. There will be specialized commands and strategies that we can learn by interacting with the members of the virtual world, and that may be part of what we want to study.
- *Selecting a subcommunity*: virtual worlds can be expansive and large, therefore, we have to select which aspects of it we are going to study. It can start with being aware of different servers and subcommunities, as well as playing modes (e.g., player vs. player or player vs. environment).
- *Committing to a schedule*: because virtual worlds are persistent, when we analyze a virtual world we have to keep up with key events of the community that we are studying. That means that there may be scheduling issues that may affect our real life; this involves a level of commitment that is not as common in other types of game analysis.

I will talk more about this in Chapter 6, which will discuss more specifically how these data become the basis to analyze game communities.

The version of the text we access is something that we must note in the humanities, but in the case of games, it becomes even more important, given that the material circumstances in which we play the game may change not only the experience, but also affect the audiovisual representation as well as the design. Chapter 7 gives a brief account of how to account for your sources in your final work.

THE PROBLEM WITH SPOILERS

Culturally, we have become accustomed to privilege the personal experience of media. Alfred Hitchcock managed to create a buzz around his movie

Psycho in 1960 because he wanted to create expectation, as well as surprising the audience when the protagonist gets killed midway through the movie. Did I spoil that for you? Probably not, since the scene where she dies is one of the most iconic moments in film history. At the time, it was pretty shocking because it went against the audience's expectations. Nowadays, many films and TV shows rely on surprising the audience with twists and reveals, so much so that there many people who want to experience the surprise themselves and try to avoid getting the story spoiled at all costs.

The experiential aspects of a game are essential in order to understand it, so at times there is a reluctance to spoil the experience for others. At times, a twist or surprise is the only thing that will keep the game going. For example, Brenda Romero's board game Train (2009) is presented as a minimalist train game where players compete to bring passengers from one station to another—the meaning of the game changes completely when the destination of the train is revealed to be one of the Nazi concentration camps during World War II. The game counts on people not knowing the twist before starting to play, so having spoiled the game for you now, you will play it differently, if you ever have the chance to. The thing is, in order to communicate what is remarkable about the game, I needed to explain how the information that is revealed changes how the game is played—usually players stop the game once they realize the role that the game is putting them into.

In its worse incarnation, the resistance to spoil a game may derive from an extreme personal attachment to games, where some people find it impossible to put any distance between the game as the text being analyzed and themselves. Whether to spoil the game or not is a fine line to tread—the rule of thumb is to think of what the goals of your analysis are. If you are trying to get other people to play the game, as would be the case of a review, you probably do not want to give away its secrets. Other times, it is precisely by revealing the twist of a game that we can make clear why it is important. That is the goal of Brendan Keogh's *Killing Is Harmless*, for example, when talking about *Spec Ops: The Line* (2012), where he writes a book-long close reading of the game to provide an in-depth interpretation of its themes.[50] Game critic Joel Goodwin sets out to spoil *Cart Life* (2012) for his readers because that's when he can make clear what makes it truly remarkable;[51] in contrast, Chris Dahlen, talking about the same game, tries to not spoil it to pique the interest of the readers and to get them to play this independent game that deals with the struggles of the American working class.[52] We will discuss both articles in Chapter 6.

In the case of humanistic writing, it seems that the no-spoilers policy goes against the writing tradition of the field, because the assumption is that the reader is familiar with the text/game, and if not, the writing has to provide enough information to understand it. Spoiling the game is part of being able to discuss it in depth, so it is important to be able to talk about it without constraints, and not spoiling your readers' experience should not be one of them. It is fine to warn the reader early on that you are not going to withhold information—it seems to have become part of the etiquette of writing about games. But if you find yourself resistant to revealing the secrets of your game, you may be letting your emotional attachment to playing games get in the way of your understanding them. Incidentally, I get games spoiled by reading my students' analyses every semester, so spoilers are part of the job of being a game scholar.

▶ THE READINESS IS ALL

Getting ready to write the analysis is the fun part. You are learning, exploring, and playing games! It is fun even if you do not really like the game you have to play. (It can happen, believe me.) The good news is that you will learn from games you hate as well—some of the games that I had to play for my research made me really frustrated, and yet they have turned out to be really useful for examples throughout my career, including this book.

Learn how to budget your time, though. It is easy to get lost in the exploration and information gathering, because it feels rewarding, while actually starting to write can give you a bit of vertigo. Chapter 3 provides a breakdown of some of the building blocks of the analysis, so you can identify which ones are the most relevant or interesting to what you want to write.

BOX 2.3 WALKTHROUGH ON HOW TO PREPARE TO ANALYZE A GAME

This is a step-by-step description of how to set up and gather information about your game. Throughout the process, be sure to take notes, either summarizing key ideas, or jotting down your own impressions. It will make it easier to start writing and prevent writer's block later on.

(Continued)

(Continued)

Step 1: Gathering Basic Contextual Info

- Get a copy of the game, preferably original, since it will provide you with contextual information through the box or manual, or the portal to download the game.
- If the copy of the game does not have a manual/box, find them online, if they exist.
- Find advertisements for the game (commercial, print ads, official website, trailers) as well as reviews (both at the time of release and contemporary if it is an older game).

Step 2: Learn How to Play the Game

- Read the game manual/go through the tutorial.
- Get familiar with the controls.
- Find the difficulty level that you are comfortable with or that you may be interested in playing.
- Explore the different game modes. Decide which one you will focus on.
- Decide what it means to finish the game, and what it means to cheat.
- Why is the game interesting? What parts of the game should you be focusing on?

Step 3: Play the Game

- Play however much you need to finish the game, or, if you are studying players, watch somebody playing it.
- Always take notes of your gameplay.
- You are not writing a walkthrough (those are readily available, both commercially and by volunteers/fans).
- Take notes of whatever is relevant to your analysis (read the following chapters to decide the building blocks):
    - Surprising aspects of the interaction.
    - Assumptions made by the game (e.g., in the representation, in the design).
    - Frustrations/things that are broken.
    - Recurring patterns (in the design, themes, etc.).
    - Relationships with the context.
    - Elements of the design that may appeal to the audience.
    - What the game is about based on the mechanics (vs. what it says on the box).
- If you are doing a historical analysis, find elements that may point to its socio-historical context, such as references to the real world made through characters, writing, or audio-visual representation.

After playing the game, you should have a sizeable amount of information to start writing. Chapter 3 provides a breakdown of how that information can be classified and identified as different building blocks—it may also provide you with pointers to types of information that you may need to write your analysis and that you may not usually pay attention to.

NOTES

1 There are several open access journals available online that are fine resources for academic work on games. Game Studies: The International Journal of Computer Game Research was the first available at: www.gamestudies.org (accessed November 4, 2023).

2 Some popular databases that are easily accessible are Google Scholar (https://scholar.google.com, accessed November 4, 2023) and Semantic Scholar (https://www.semanticscholar.org/, accessed November 4, 2023). Be mindful that these are search engines that use algorithms and artificial intelligence to select the works—Semantic Scholar focus precisely on "popularity" as a metric—and algorithms also have biases. In practice, do not just stick to the top results.

3 As an example of one method to study non-digital games, see Mackay, Daniel. *The Fantasy Role-Playing Game* (Jefferson, NC: McFarland & Company, 2001). The author uses his own group of role-players to inform his theoretical approach.

4 An example of collected works on live-action, role-playing games is Stenros, Jaako, and Markus Montala, eds. *Nordic Larp*. 1st edn. (Stockholm: Fëa Livia, 2010). There is also the *International Journal of Role-Playing*, whose articles deal with both table-top and digital role-playing. Available at: http://ijrp.subcultures.nl/ (accessed November 4, 2023).

5 "Radiant A.I." *Elder Scrolls*. Available at: http://elderscrolls.fandom.com/wiki/Radiant_A.I. (accessed November 4, 2023).

6 Van Manen, Max. *Researching Lived Experience: Human Science for an Action Sensitive Pedagogy* (Albany, NY: State University of New York Press, 1990), p. 187.

7 See Consalvo, Mia. *Cheating: Gaining Advantage in Videogames* (Cambridge, MA: MIT Press, 2007), pp. 83–105.

8 Ibid., pp. 3–5.

9 This approach has been inherited from the New Criticism movement in the mid-twentieth century, where the main method was close reading, and the analysis focused on self-referentiality within the text. See Eagleton, Terry. *Literary Theory: An Introduction* (Minneapolis, MN: University of Minnesota Press, 1996), pp. 38–46, for an overview of this literary theory movement. Chapter 6 discusses close reading as a method to analyze games, but always within context.

10 For a detailed discussion of this last point, see Juul, Jesper. *A Casual Revolution: Reinventing Video Games and Their Players* (Cambridge, MA: The MIT Press, 2009), pp. 66–78.

11 More information on the tool is available at: www.zotero.org/ (accessed November 4, 2023).

12 Salen, Katie, and Eric Zimmerman. *Rules of Play: Game Design Fundamentals* (Cambridge, MA: The MIT Press, 2004), p. 377.

13 *The Internet Archive: The Computer Magazine Archives.* Available at: https://archive.org/details/computermagazines (accessed November 4, 2023).

14 This was the case of several employees from Telltale, who gave perfect scores on Metacritic to *Jurassic Park: The Game* (2011) on the day of release. This called the attention of other users, who quickly realized that the people writing the reviews worked for the company that made it. The practice was publicly denounced as being an example of conflict of interest. More details in Sinclair, Brendan. "Jurassic Park User Reviews Abused." Gamespot, November 18, 2011. https://www.gamespot.com/articles/jurassic-park-user-reviews-abused/1100-6346288/ (accessed November 11, 2023).

15 See the case, for example, of how the reception of the film *Star Wars: Episode VIII—The Last Jedi* (2017) on social media was so polarized, not so much by users, but bots, trolls, or sock puppets, who used their reaction to the movie as a way to put out their political messages, aligned with right-wing causes. See Bay, Morten. "Weaponizing the Haters: 'The Last Jedi' and the Strategic Politicization of Pop Culture through Social Media Manipulation." *First Monday*, November 1, 2018. https://doi.org/10.5210/fm.v23i11.9388.

16 See, for example, this review of Bloodborne (2015), published in 2023: "Game Wonder: On FromSoftware's 'Bloodborne' and H. P. Lovecraft's 'The Haunter of the Dark.'" Accessed November 12, 2023. https://lareviewofbooks.org/article/game-wonder-on-fromsoftwares-bloodborne-and-h-p-lovecrafts-the-haunter-of-the-dark/

17 As an example of how mainstream journalism has treated videogames in a misinformed way in the past, see Dutton, Nathan, Mia Consalvo, and Todd Harper. "Digital Pitchforks and Virtual Torches: Fan Responses to the Mass Effect News Debacle." *Convergence: The International Journal of Research into New Media Technologies* 17, no. 3 (August 1, 2011): pp. 287–305.

18 The intentional fallacy was one of the arguments in favor of reading the text separately from its context, so rather than trying to guess what the author meant, critics looked for meaning in the text itself. The problem with New Criticism, however, is that they also tended to read the text as having a single reading that spoke for itself, without contemplating that different readers may have different interpretations. For a more detailed discussion on intentional fallacy, the issues that New Criticism had with authorial intention, and a critique on that stance, see Eagleton, Terry. *Literary Theory: An Introduction* (Minneapolis, MN: University of Minnesota Press, 1996), pp. 38–46.

19 Mechner, Jordan. *The Making of Prince of Persia: Journals, 1985-1993* (Charleston, NC: ICG Testing, 2012); Mechner, Jordan. *The Making of Karateka: Journals 1982-1985* (CreateSpace Independent Publishing Platform, 2012).

20 "International Center for the History of Electronic Games," January 27, 2014. Available at: www.museumofplay.org/about/icheg (accessed November 4, 2023).

21 Dolph Briscoe Center for American History. "Videogame Archive." https://briscoecenter.org/projects/videogame-archive/ (accessed November 12, 2023).

22 The complete collection of *Game Developer Magazine* is available at the Game Developers' Conference Vault: www.gdcvault.com/gdmag (accessed November 4, 2023).

23 "Classic Game Postmortem: Alone in the Dark." Available at: www.gdcvault.com/play/1015840/Classic-Game-Postmortem-Alone-in (accessed November 4, 2023).

24 "Classic Game Postmortem: Fallout." Available at: www.gdcvault.com/play/1015843/Classic-Game-Postmortem (accessed November 4, 2023).

25 "Classic Game Postmortem: Rez." Available at: www.gdcvault.com/play/1023187/Classic-Game-Postmortem (accessed November 4, 2023).

26 Perron, Bernard. "The Survival Horror: The Extended Body Genre." In *Horror Video Games: Essays on the Fusion of Fear and Play,* edited by Bernard Perron (Jefferson, NC: McFarland, 2009), pp. 121–167.

27 Krzywinska, Tanya. "Hands-On Horror." In *Screenplay: Cinema/Videogames/Interfaces,* edited by Geoff King and Tanya Krzywinska (New York: Wallflower Press, 2002), pp. 206–223.

28 Gee, James Paul. *What Video Games Have to Teach Us about Learning and Literacy*. Second Edition: Revised and Updated Edition (New York: Macmillan, 2007).

29 Taylor, T.L. *Play between Worlds: Exploring Online Game Culture* (Cambridge, Mass.: The MIT Press, 2006).

30 Fernández-Vara, Clara. "Play's the Thing: A Framework to Study Videogames as Performance." In Breaking New Ground: Innovation in Games, Play, Practice and Theory: International Digital Games Research Association (DiGRA) Conference, Brunel University, West London, 2009. Available at: www.digra.org/digital-library/publications/plays-the-thing-a-framework-to-study-videogames-as-performance (accessed November 4, 2023).

31 For a fuller discussion on how different versions of a game can compare to a book edition, see Fernández-Vara, Clara, and Nick Montfort. "Videogame Editions for

Play and Study." Technical Report. *The Trope Tank*, June 5, 2014. Available at: http://dspace.mit.edu/handle/1721.1/87668 (accessed November 4, 2023).

32 Montfort, Nick, and Ian Bogost. *Racing the Beam: The Atari Video Computer System* (Cambridge, MA: The MIT Press, 2009), pp. 45–55.

33 "Restoration | PDP-1 Restoration Project | Computer History Museum." https://www.computerhistory.org/pdp-1/restoration/ (accessed November 12, 2023).

34 "BoardGameGeek." https://boardgamegeek.com/ (accessed November 12, 2023).

35 Barthes, Roland. "The World of Wrestling." In *Mythologies* (New York: Hill & Wang, 1972), pp. 15–25.

36 Johnson, Jason. "Dead Pixels." *Unwinnable*, August 2, 2012. Accessed November 12, 2023. https://unwinnable.com/2012/08/02/dead-pixels/

37 Crecente, Brian. "Silent Hills Canceled, Konami Confirms." *Polygon*, April 27, 2015. Available at: www.polygon.com/2015/4/27/8503201/silent-hills-canceled-konami-confirms (accessed November 4, 2023).

38 McWerthor, Michael. "Konami Pulling Silent Hills Teaser P.T. from PlayStation Store - Polygon." *Polygon*, April 25, 2015. Available at: www.polygon.com/2015/4/25/8498359/silent-hills-teaser-p-t-playstation-store-konami (accessed November 4, 2023).

39 Hernandez, Patricia. "The Next Silent Hill Already Has Bonkers Fan Theories." *Kotaku*, August 14, 2014. Available at: https://kotaku.com/the-next-silent-hill-already-has-bonkers-fan-theories-1621737836 (accessed November 4, 2023).

40 "Adobe Flash Player End of Life." https://www.adobe.com/products/flashplayer/end-of-life.html (accessed November 12, 2023).

41 The Strong National Museum of Play. "The Strong Partners with Kongregate to Preserve Flash Games." https://www.museumofplay.org/press-release/the-strong-partners-with-kongregate-to-preserve-flash-games/ (accessed November 12, 2023).

42 Campbell, Ian Carlos. "The Internet Archive Is Now Preserving Flash Games and Animations." *The Verge*, November 20, 2020. https://www.theverge.com/2020/11/19/21578616/internet-archive-preservation-flash-animations-games-adobe

43 "Internet Archive: About IA." Available at: https://archive.org/about/ (accessed November 4, 2023).

44 Juul. *A Casual Revolution*, pp. 175–218.

45 A good reference for gathering and analyzing subject data is Seidman, Irving. *Interviewing as Qualitative Research: A Guide for Researchers in Education and*

the Social Sciences (New York: Teachers College Press, 2006) or Creswell, John W. *Research Design: Qualitative, Quantitative, and Mixed Method Approaches* (Thousand Oaks, CA: Sage Publications, 2003).

46 Boellstorff, Tom, Bonnie Nardi, Celia Pearce, and T.L. Taylor. *Ethnography and Virtual Worlds: A Handbook of Method* (Princeton, NJ: Princeton University Press, 2012).

47 Ibid., p. 7.

48 Bartle, Richard. "Hearts, Clubs, Diamonds, Spades: Players Who Suit MUDs." In *The Game Design Reader: A Rules of Play Anthology*, edited by Katie Salen and Eric Zimmerman (Cambridge, MA: MIT Press, 2006), p. 769.

49 Boellstorff et al. *Ethnography and Virtual Worlds*, pp. 72–75.

50 Keogh, Brendan, Daniel Purvis, Rob Zacny, and Benjamin Abraham. *Killing Is Harmless: A Critical Reading of Spec Ops: The Line*. 1st edn (Stolen Projects, 2013).

51 Goodwin, Joel. "Ahead… The Stars." *Electron Dance: Words on PC Gaming*, January 17, 2012. Available at: www.electrondance.com/ahead-the-stars/ (accessed November 4, 2023).

52 Dahlen, Chris. "Chasing the Dollar," *Unwinnable: Life with Culture*, February 28, 2013. Available at: www.unwinnable.com/2013/02/28/chasing-the-dollar/ (accessed November 4, 2023).

3 Areas of Analysis 1: Context

▶ INTRODUCTION

After preparing for our analysis, we are ready for the next stage: identify what we are going to write about. As Chapter 2 described, we, as writers/players, need to play in an analytical way, as well as learn as much about the game as possible. At this point, it should be obvious that there are many aspects that we can analyze. Even a game that may appear simple can be the subject of in-depth analysis—see, for example, Richard Rouse's careful and exhaustive breakdown of *Centipede* (1980b).[1] One could write a whole book on a single game too; an early example of this is *Pilgrim in the Microworld*, where the author describes how he tried to master *Breakout* (1978) for Atari VCS.[2] In our case, it is more likely that we have to write a paper or short article instead of a book, which means we have to be very selective on which parts of the game we are going to tackle.

The next step is, therefore, to determine which components are relevant to the analysis. The following chapters describe and justify its possible building blocks, and they can be used to identify topics of discussion in relation to our game. Rather than providing a uniform model, these guidelines acknowledge a variety of contexts and purposes for analysis, which may have a series of common interconnected components. These building blocks can,

DOI: 10.4324/9781003355779-3

therefore, be configured in diverse ways, adapting them to the multiple frames of analysis that this book is catering to. Each building block can also constitute a topic on its own, which can be expanded to be the core of a full analysis. Each description of the building blocks provides some examples to help you understand how the block can get different discussions started.

Some building blocks will be more familiar than others, depending on your academic background, because they relate to content and themes from different disciplines. Formal elements may resonate if you are a literature or film student, whereas if you are in a media or cultural studies department, you may feel at home discussing the cultural context. Budding sociologists and psychologists may be more comfortable with the study of players and player communities.

The different sections of the analysis are not an organized checklist of what should be included, nor should they follow a strict order. This list provides a map of the different aspects that can potentially be included. Chapter 6 explains how different configurations of these components can generate different types of analysis depending on your goal, whether you are writing a journalistic review, a formal analysis, or an historical overview, amongst other models.

There are three main areas in each analysis, which were already introduced in Chapter 1: (1) the *context* of the game; (2) an *overview* of what distinguishes it; and (3) its *formal qualities.*

1. Providing the *context* helps us situate the game historically, culturally, socially, and economically. Videogames are the product of their time, therefore, learning about the socio-cultural and industrial environment in which they were produced is crucial to understanding them,

2. An overview of the game's *main defining elements* helps readers situate themselves by explaining briefly what the game is about. This section is common to all types of analysis, as we will see in Chapter 6, although focusing exclusively on the content may be the subject of some specific models of journalistic game reviews, which are closer to consumer reports. By taking into account how the game was played, appropriated, and transformed by the community, the analysis also acknowledges that games are a human activity, not merely a set of rules or code in a computer.

3. The *formal qualities* of the game are not limited to technical specifications, or a breakdown of specific design features that may be typical of some game reviews. An analysis of the formal aspects must inquire how they work, hypothesize why they are there, and, most importantly, how they relate to the player's experience.

The following pages describe the different building blocks included within each area. It will soon become obvious that many of those blocks are connected; in more than one case some may seem to discuss similar aspects of the game. This is why this model is flexible—depending on the goal of the analysis, some discussions will be better addressed by resorting to different building blocks.

▶ CONTEXT HELPS UNDERSTAND THE GAME

Taking the context into consideration allows us to frame the discussion. In Chapter 2, we examined how learning about the context is part of the process of becoming an expert on the game in question. Whatever the goal of the analysis, the context and factors of production are also part of the game. For starters, context can provide information about the purpose and reason for the game and its content. Nevertheless, one should be careful when attributing certain aspects of the game to the context, falling into the so-called *intentional fallacy*.[3] Intentional fallacy is first assuming that one can figure out what the author was thinking when creating a work, then believing that this presupposed intention is the key to deciding the value and meaning of the work.[4] In the study of videogames, one may establish causal connections between context and content that are easy to dispute and disprove. For example, they are often a team effort, meaning that it is as problematic to establish a single authorship, as in film studies; technology and marketing may strongly shape the final result, or at least its perception by audiences.

It may be tempting to skip on contextualizing the game, particularly when one is short on space. However, in the same way understanding the game in its context helps one understand it in a more nuanced manner, it also helps our readers situate the framing of our discussion and what aspects of the game we are going to focus on. With every analysis, we should contribute to creating a sense of history, and show how texts are interconnected, just as in any other academic discipline.

During the process of situating the game, a preliminary decision we need to make is how much the context will discuss the audience in relation to the game. As discussed in Chapter 1, it is difficult to exclude player experience; when our experience is included, we need to qualify and define it. If the purpose of the piece is to discuss the economic circumstances of the release of a game, for example, accounting for the control scheme may not be relevant, particularly if it follows pre-existing conventions, such as those of first-person shooters. If the game requires special controllers, as is the case of music games like *Rock Band* (2008), then the control scheme becomes relevant to the distribution of the game, since it requires more retailer space, and also becomes more expensive than other games. It is also true that, in these cases, the analysis may fall into the conventions of some other discipline (business, in this case), since player participation is what makes games different from other media.

The socio-cultural context is essential to understanding games produced in cultures different from the one in which the analysis is written. The protagonists of *Osu! Tatakae! Ouendan* (2005) are the members of a cheering squad or *ouendan*; although they are often considered Japanese male cheerleaders, their movements and music are iconic in Japan, but unfamiliar in most other countries. The role of the *ouendan* is to encourage and cheer for sports teams, often directing the chants of the fans. In the game, the goal is to get the *ouendan* to complete their dancing and cheers to give strength to people in distress, changing the context of the cheering from sports to everyday situations. The equivalence may be obvious to Japanese players, while these black-clad shouting men may seem exotic or baffling to players from the rest of the world.

Understanding the differences between where a game is developed and where it may be played is also very relevant to game designers. The global distribution of games makes the process of localization not only necessary but also part and parcel of the development process. Continuing with *Osu! Tatakae! Ouendan*, the game was remade for its Western version, *Elite Beat Agents* (2006), so that the *ouendan* became a squad that brought together the image of the US government's men in black with *The Blues Brothers*, creating new characters because there is not a direct cultural equivalent.[5] Translation can also affect game development—for example, in *The Secret of Monkey Island* (1990), the player must find "something that will attract attention, but have no real importance." The item in question is a red herring, which turns out to be a pun in English but does not make any sense in other languages, so the puzzle is lost in translation. Localization may change a game from version to version, often undermining their initial purpose.

▶ WHAT COUNTS AS CONTEXT?

The context of the game refers to the circumstances in which it was produced, which may have a bearing on the final result and condition its reception. Some contextual factors may have a direct relationship with the artifact, such as the people who participated in the production, the material circumstances of production (hardware, software), and the history of the production, to name but a few. On a larger scale, the context can extend to socio-historical events that took place while the game was made, or when and where the game was released. For example, *Propeller Arena: Aviation Battle Championship* for the Sega Dreamcast was cancelled in 2001 after the September 11th attacks. It was a battle flight simulator where planes had to zip through city buildings during dogfights; it so happened that one of the levels looked startlingly similar to New York. The similarity between the images in the news and the declining market of the Dreamcast console led to the game not being released, in spite of its being practically complete. However, the final version of *Propeller Arena* was leaked online, and there is a fan site of a game that was never released.[6]

The context can also be made up of other media, what I called in Chapter 1 *paratexts* based on Genette's definition.[7] These media texts (reviews, TV advertisements, game boxes, manuals, machinima) around the game we are analyzing are part of how the audience makes sense of it. Chapter 2 provided an overview of what these paratexts may be—they can (and should) be part of your sources as you prepare for the analysis.

▶ CONTEXT: THE BUILDING BLOCKS

The following section is a breakdown of the different elements that may define the context of the game. They are listed from aspects and factors directly linked to the production, to elements that may be circumstantial to the game. These elements are:

1. Context Inside the Game
2. Production Team

3. Game Genre
4. Technological Context
5. Socio-Historical Context
6. Economic Context
7. Audience
8. Relations to Other Media

Context Inside the Game One of the first things that we must define is what parts of the game we will be talking about. Many current mainstream games are very long and include multiple levels, different modes, a set of characters to choose from, and even expansion packs and downloadable content. Given their depth and breadth, it may be impossible to cover one single game in a paper, an article, or even a book. Even if our object of study is a smaller-scale game, it is always good practice to determine which features will be analyzed as a way to focus the discussion.

In order to identify which aspects of the game will help us situate our discussion, we have to figure out how the game is structured and divided. Play modes or levels of difficulty are ways of dividing gameplay in general. If we are talking about a specific segment during gameplay, there are other markers that we can use, such as different levels, stages, or locations. In the case of story-driven games, the narrative can also be structured in such a way that it provides different chapters, episodes, or quests that we can identify as units.

Stating which aspects are central in the analysis itself is also basic good practice. Including this information early on, such as which mode the game was played in, the character(s) that were used, or levels that were played, situates the work within the game itself, as well as making explicit what has been omitted. Justifying the choice of playing a game in a certain mode also helps explain the position of the writer with respect to the game in question.

A good example of how different points of entry may evolve into different analyses is *Super Smash Bros. Melee* (2001). In its single-player mode, it is a side-scrolling fighting game where the player must tackle obstacles and enemies in sequence. The player can also choose from various game types, each presenting different types of challenges, from fighting enemies one after another, to racing, to target practice. *Super Smash Bros. Melee* is more popular for its multiplayer mode, in which up to four players can fight against each other. Players may fight individually or in teams; there are five different game types, and each one of them determines the winner through different rules. In the standard mode, the last player standing is the winner, whereas in coin mode, the player who collects the most coins that pop up after hitting an enemy wins. The multiplayer mode also lets players set their own rules to play, such as establishing a time limit or number of rounds; thus, there are multiple combinations that players can determine. Letting players configure the rules means the game can be adapted to a variety of contexts for the multiplayer mode, from organized competitions[8] to informal settings like a college dorm.[9]

When the analysis deals with a concrete section, it is also useful to connect it to the rest of the game, and discuss why that section is important. It helps the reader locate the part of the game that is being discussed, in case they choose to play it themselves. Providing as much information as possible allows readers to then go and play the game themselves later if they so wish—one possible way to make up for the impossibility of "quoting" from a game.

Questions to identify the context within the game:

- What level/chapter/mode of the game is being analyzed?
- Why is this part of the game relevant to the analysis?
- How does this segment relate to the rest of the game?
- When does it take place in the course of the game?
- How does one get to that point in the game?
- What happens in this section?
- Is the gameplay in this section different from the rest of the game?
- Does the game require a strategy different from the rest of the game?

Further Reading

Zagal, Jose P., Clara Fernández-Vara, and Michael Mateas. "Rounds, Levels and Waves: The Early Evolution of Gameplay Segmentation." *Games and Culture* 3, no. 2 (2008): 175–198.

BOX 3.1 EXERCISE: MAPPING GAMEPLAY

As a way to understand the game that you are analyzing and its complexity, take some time to map how the gameplay is structured. This is not a physical map of the game, but rather a tree or chart that provides the layout of the different ways of segmenting the game. How can you structure and segment gameplay in your game? Which segments of your game are you going to tackle?

You can map the game in two basic ways:

A) **Gameplay Modes**: This map may be the easiest, since it can be traced by following the menu options in the game that relate to gameplay. For example, this is how we would map *Super Smash Bros. Melee*:

- single-player mode
  - regular match
    - classic mode
    - adventure mode
    - all-star mode
  - event match
  - stadium
    - home-run contest
    - target test
  - multi-man melee
  - training mode
- versus mode
  - melee
  - special melee
  - tournament mode
  - custom rules

This tree was basically extracted from the menus of the game. I left out the menu options that referred to save games, trophies/achievements, or sound settings, for example, and just focused on the options that affect gameplay. Making an initial map like this helps you visualize the content of your game, so you can pinpoint which aspects you are tackling. For example, if you are analyzing how a community plays *Super Smash Bros. Melee*, you will have to specify that they are playing the Versus Mode, and within that, which submode they are playing, and which rules they chose.

(Continued)

(Continued)

B) **Story Structure**: Mapping the game like this is a bit more complex, since it requires having played through the game already; if you have not completed the game, you will probably have to look for a walkthrough or guide. The narrative breakdown can take a long time to map in this case. If we are talking about a mission or quest-based game, there will be core segments and side segments of the story, so the map will not necessarily be a list of chapters. We have two basic ways to map story-driven games, depending on whether we focus on the events or the areas. A map of the events would be like the index of a book—see how we would map *What Remains of Edith Finch* (2017), where the player has to revive the memories of the members of the Finch family, going back five generations.

- Molly (11 December 1937–13 December 1947)
- Barbara (31 October 1944–31 October 1960)
- Walter (26 August 1952–21 March 2005)
- Calvin (25 April 1950–23 September 1961)
- Sam (25 April 1950–16 June 1983)
- Gus (20 June 1969–8 November 1982)
- Gregory (12 January 1976–19 December 1977)
- Lewis (27 December 1988–21 November 2010)
- Milton (19 May 1992)
- Edith "Edie" Finch (8 April 1917–5 December 2010)
- Edith Jr. (14 February 1999–18 January 2017)

Each of these chapters has its breakdown into different events, also segmented in the form of interrelated narrative puzzles; a list of those puzzles would help us make a more detailed map of the game.

In contrast, a role-playing game or MMORPG may be easier to account for by focusing on the locations of the game. For example, this is how we would tackle *Fallout* (1997):

1. Vault 13
2. Shady Sands
3. Vault 15
4. Raiders
5. Junktown
6. The Hub
7. Necropolis
8. The Glow
9. Brotherhood
10. Boneyard
11. Military Base
12. Cathedral

(Continued)

(Continued)

It is possible to provide a breakdown of each area by listing the quests associated with it. For example, let's look at how we would map the first area, Vault 13, based on the quests:

1. Calm the rebel faction.
2. Destroy the Mutant leader.
3. Destroy the source of the Mutants.
4. Find the water chip.
5. Find the water thief.

This exercise should help you get a sense of the scope of the game, and select which aspects of it you will analyze, as well as a first reminder that you need to communicate to your reader which aspects of the game you will be discussing.

Production Team In Chapter 1, we mentioned how paratexts influence how we interpret a text; the name of the author is one of these paratexts. For example, certain game developers, such as Roberta Williams (*King's Quest* series, 1984–1998), Hideo Kojima (*Metal Gear* series, 1987–2015) or Sid Meier (*Civilization* series, 1991–2016), have a status that creates certain expectations about their work. The same goes for certain companies, such as Blizzard or Bethesda, which are associated with specific game worlds or game genres. For some fans, their favorite developers can do no wrong. Identifying who has participated in the development of a game can provide us with important information about the influences and the history of the production. It is not a matter of highlighting the personalities behind the game as much as it is pointing out and revealing more about the process of how the game was made, and especially of the human factors that are part of the creative process.

Acknowledging the human factors in the production is a first step in relinquishing the concept of games as a factory product and towards their status as an art form, opening up new types of discourse, and keeping technological or economic arguments in check. The games industry worldwide is notorious for being particularly grueling—there is a higher percentage of employees who leave the industry every year than in other tech industries (10% as opposed to 6%), and the average age of people in key roles is also lower than in other technologies, meaning that there are not enough people who stay long enough to garner sufficient experience to lead teams, for example.[10] The industry has traditionally relied on the "passion" of employees for what they do, which eventually chases away people who may want job security and keeping a work-life balance—and passion can wane after months of working very long hours with no rest. In order to understand a game as a commercial product, it is important to be aware of the capitalistic practices that lead to their release, and that they are artistic works created by teams of people with rare talent, but developed as if they were a factory product. The video series *People Make Games* has provided a series of videos exposing some particularly egregious industry practices; their investigative journalism pieces are a great way to understand the circumstances in which many of the games we play are produced.[11]

In terms of defining the context, the production team will immediately serve to make connections with other games that may have been made by the same people. It can also relate the game to other media, if the personalities involved are not necessarily part of the videogames industry. Many developers work within a specific genre or provide their own style, which connects the game being analyzed to the rest of their work. Looking at their previous games can shed some light on certain aspects of the game, such as the recurring concerns of the team, how they innovate from one game to another, or whether they are breaking off from the genres that they usually work on. For example, the Japanese company Square (1983–2003) is usually identified with role-playing games, thanks to the fame of the *Final Fantasy* series (1983–2023). In its early days, the same team also produced shooter games such as *3D World Runner* (1987), or racing games such as *Rad Racer* (1987). Calling attention to the variety of designs Square produced can be the starting point, for example, to examine later works, such as *Final Fantasy VII* (1997), which includes racing and fighting in the form of mini-games.

The collaborative nature of the production of many videogames makes it problematic to determine their authorship. Game studies has yet to see a debate like the one that took place in film studies in the 1960s between Andrew Sarris and Pauline Kael. Sarris followed the school of French criticism and advocated that the director was the author of a film, while Kael reclaimed the title for the screenwriter.[12] Videogames have set up a more pressing dilemma, even when marketing departments and the industry itself often encourage the cult of personality to sell more games. Who is the "author"? The game designer? The creative director? The lead programmer? The lead artist? The producer? The marketing department? The voice actors? Can players be considered authors of the game, too, since the game cannot start without them? How is the player an author of user-generated content? Who we consider an author of the game is both a construction *of* discourse and constructed *by* discourse.[13] Therefore, being aware of what the figure of the author means with respect to the game, and who is identified as such, is a necessary exercise even before starting to write.

Identifying the author of a videogame may not be easy, so whenever an individual is singled out, it should be because it helps generate the context of the game, and establishes clear relationships with certain creative approaches, in videogames or other media. Making an argument to disprove the sole authorship of an individual may be a productive exercise to counter the marketing strategies of singling out personalities as authors, similar to how Pauline Kael did when she claimed that the screenwriter Herman J. Mankiewicz was the real author of *Citizen Kane*, and not Orson Welles, the director.[14]

A further issue in trying to determine the authorship of the game is that its makers may not have been credited. In the 1980s, Atari did not list the names of the engineers who worked on their cartridges, which caused many of their best programmers to leave and create their own company, Activision.[15] Many home computer games were circulated with no names attached to them, particularly if they were distributed in magazines as code to be typed into the computer. The absence of this information makes it difficult to establish the context of the game, since identifying the developers may provide further historical information about the game.

Some games are made by a sole developer, who is credited in the game, which makes it easier to identify the author of the game. This was true of many games developed for home computers in Europe during the 1980s, where developers were often computer hobbyists. For instance, Matthew Smith created *Manic Miner* (1983) and *Jet Set Willy* (1984), two of the most popular games for the ZX Spectrum, and a cornerstone in the design of European platform games. Paco Menéndez, along with graphic designer Juan Delcán, created *La Abadía del Crimen* (1987), an unofficial adaptation of Umberto Eco's *The Name of the Rose* (1983).[16] The game remains one of the most influential games in Spanish game development to this day, its narrative complexity inspiring other Spanish developers to make other games freely inspired by Eco's novel, such as *Murder in the Abbey* (2008), as well as multiple remakes and updates for new platforms. The latest update of the game includes an English version, and it is available on the online platform Steam.[17]

Many of the factotum game makers these days are independent developers, often working on experimental games. They are either single developers or work with very small teams, such as Christine Love (*Analogue: A Hate Story*, 2012), Dietrich Squinkifer (*Dominique Pamplemousse*, 2014), or Cosmo D (*Betrayal at Club Low*, 2022). The works of these developers are often presented as "art games" which may or may not have something to do with how they are presented as the work of individuals rather than as commercial products.

Singling out specific personalities from a team can also provide further connections to other games, helping to establish a larger context, or relating the game to other media. The forays of artists from other media at times bring the prestige of the artists to the game, as is the case of the manga artist Akira Toriyama, of *Dragon Ball* fame, who designed the characters for the *Dragon Quest* videogame series since 1986, as well as *Chrono Trigger* (1995). The first game (to my knowledge) to include a soundtrack by a famous musician was *Captain Blood* (1988), which featured songs by electronic music composer Jean-Michel Jarre. From the realm of writing, Douglas Adams famously collaborated with game designer Steve Meretzky both in the videogame adaptation of *The Hitchhiker's Guide to the Galaxy* (1984) and *Bureaucracy* (1987). More recently, George R.R. Martin provided the world building of *Elden Ring* (2022), developed by FromSoftware, famous for their story-rich action role-playing games such as *Demon's Souls* (2009).

Videogames have been a medium for artistic experimentation for different artists across media for decades. Poet Robert Pinsky wrote the interactive fiction piece *Mindwheel* (1984), while Brian Eno worked on the score of *Spore* (2008), which generates different music depending on the choices of the player and the context of the actions. More recently, *NBA 2K17* (2016) included a career mode whose story was written and directed by Aaron Covington, one of the co-writers of the film *Creed* (2015). Artists who work in other media can also help us draw comparisons across media, or focus on a specific aspect of the game related to other media (e.g., visual art, music, cut-scenes, writing).

Questions to discuss the relevance of the production team;

- Who made the game, a team or an individual?
- What other games have been made by this production team?
- How does the game relate to the previous and/or later work of that team?

- Are there any team members whose contribution can be considered to be distinctive? How?
- Are there any collaborators who are artists in other media? What is their contribution to the game?

Further Reading

Grossman, Austin, ed. *Postmortems from Game Developers: Insights from the Developers of Unreal Tournament, Black and White, Age of Empires, and Other Top Selling Games*. 1st edn. San Francisco: CMP Books, 2003.

Jorgensen, Kristine, Ulf Sandqvist, and Olli Sotamaa. "From Hobbyists to Entrepreneurs: On the Formation of the Nordic Game Industry." *Convergence 23*, no. 5 (2017): 457–476.

Juul, Jesper. *Handmade Pixels: Independent Video Games and the Quest for Authenticity*. Illustrated edition. Cambridge, MA: The MIT Press, 2019.

O'Donnell, Casey. *Developer's Dilemma: The Secret World of Videogame Creators*. Cambridge, MA: The MIT Press, 2014.

BOX 3.2 THE ISSUE WITH CREDITS

One of the recurring challenges of studying games is to know who has *actually* worked on them. When we refer to a novel we refer to the author; in film and television, there are opening and closing credits. Audiences have a sense that these texts have been created by people. Game credits, however, are often more complicated to determine than those for other media. We have already pointed out the difficulty of discussing authorship in games, particularly when it is made by teams. But apart from the issues of collective authorship, an additional problem is determining who has made the game, which can allow us to draw connections with other games and other contexts.

In the case of older games, it can be hit and miss—programmers for early computers may not have had enough computer memory to include their own name in the code or the game, since every letter counted. In commercial games of the 1980s, for example, the names of the engineers who programmed the games were left out from the box—we have already mentioned the origins of Activision above. Famously, Warren Robinett wrote his name in a secret room in *Adventure* (1980) for Atari 2600; it was both an easter egg and also a way to claim his work.[18]

(Continued)

(Continued)

Even with recent and up-and-coming releases, it is not always obvious who worked on a game. I find myself scrambling to figure out who has worked on a game right after it has been announced, because there are no listings of the credits on the game's website or press kit. This omission may be for a variety of reasons. Giving public credit to creators means acknowledging that there are creative individuals who can claim their contribution to a project. In the game industry, what is most common is to be paid for the work one does for a game, what is legally called "work for hire." In some exceptional cases, some teams receive a bonus if the game does well. Successful games are re-released into different platforms, often taking advantage of the work of the original team, but they do not get to see any money. Their names may not appear in the credits of the re-release, while the owners of the intellectual property reap the benefits because the game is an asset to exploit economically. Not crediting the original creators closes the door for them to claim part of those benefits.

In other cases, we have game makers who choose to use a pseudonym, as artists often do, or not reveal their name because they may want to protect their privacy. This is particularly poignant since a variety of creators have been harassed online, or their personal information revealed online, by certain loud, opinionated, and reprobate fans. Game makers at times forfeit publicizing their authorship in order to have some peace of mind.

Even when a game is released with credits, these may not be completely reliable, because of the internal politics of a company. The marketing department may dictate who is credited in the game, often to highlight the figure of a sole person as the main creative driving force, because also acknowledging other contributors may undermine the myth of the "creative genius" that the advertising wants to generate. In other cases, the credits may leave out people who left the project before it was released for whatever reason, even when they have done the bulk of the work; in some egregious cases, their names have ended up in the "special thanks" section of the credits. There is no regulation on how people should have their work acknowledged in the credits, and at times people cannot even say publicly that they worked on something, even after the project has been announced. The situation has been so ugly that the International Game Developers Association (IGDA) started a Special Interest Group on Game Credits, which released its first set of guidelines to prevent many of these issues with a guide for developers.[19] Some of the recommendations include not removing the names of staff members who have left before a game has launched, and that the credits should appear in the game and not be something the player has to unlock, which is likely evidence that these rules are addressing problems that have occurred often enough that they need to be highlighted. The IGDA, however, does not have any way to enforce these guidelines—they are just recommendations.

(Continued)

(Continued)

For those of us writing an analysis, it is important to know who worked on the games—it is part of the context, allows us to connect a game with others through the people who worked on it, or with other works. But finding out who made a contribution to a game at times may require some additional research. Discovering this information can be rewarding—for example, Aaron Reed has done some remarkable "archeological" work to figure out who were the authors of different text games in the 1970s, by digging up magazines, books, and documentation, allowing us to follow the genealogy of games that are cornerstones of game history.[20] In any case, be aware of the difficulties of determining who has worked on a game, and the factors that may influence who appears on the credits of a game.

Game Genre Defining a genre is not easy in any medium, since there are many ways to define the term depending on the domain discussing it. In general, the genre of a media artifact—such as literary works or film—is associated with certain formal features and cultural assumptions; that is why understanding the context of the game is vital to establish the genre of a game. Game genre can be defined by commercial interests, industrial practices, academic definitions, or journalistic articles, although often those definitions are more buzzwords than actual thought-out definitions. After all these years, defining genre is still a challenge in literature and film, as well as a favorite topic of discussion.

Game genres help in grouping and classifying games, thus also helping to form relationships and distinctions between different works; it is a way to organize the enormous corpus of the object of study. In all media, genres are usually associated with a series of conventions, which are in constant transformation and create new genres.

How do we define a game genre? We can start with their formal characteristics. Most games base their rules and mechanics on pre-existing ones, which allows us, for example, to classify board and card games in families.[21] Some board game families can be race games with similar layouts and rules to Ludo/Parcheesi, or different variations of chess, such as Xiang-Qi in China, or Shogi in Japan.

Definitions of genre can be multiple and can contradict or undermine each other. We could argue that there are formal features that define a videogame genre, particularly those related to how the player interacts with the game. For instance, a first-person shooter can be distinguished by the combination of a first-person point of view and the player being able to shoot within a navigable three-dimensional environment. Games such as *Wolfenstein 3D* (1992), *Unreal Tournament* (1999), or *Half-Life* (1998) are classical examples of the genre. The definition, however, can be put to the test with some borderline cases. Is *Operation Wolf* (1987) a first-person shooter? It does have a first-person point of view, and the player controls a set of cross-hairs while they navigate the space, although only moving side to side, while first-person shooters typically allow the player to move in the four compass directions.

Conventions are a nebulous category that can help us define a genre. A set of features becomes conventional once it is used from game to game. Some examples of game conventions are control schemes: the point-and-click menu interfaces of early graphic adventure games require the player to compose a sentence by clicking on words from a menu and objects on the screen. Fighting games such as *Soulcalibur II* (2002), or *Super Street Fighter IV* (2010) combine the directional input with button presses, so that the right movement and button press, when properly timed, can result in a complex fighting move.

Genre conventions also help situate a game within certain traditions of design and development, although often the history of influences and derivations may be difficult to track down. Juul discusses how the history of tile-matching games can be traced differently, depending on which arguments are provided, or rather, *who* is providing the arguments.[22] In spite of the difficulty, and that there is not a unique way to establish the influences of a genre, it is a useful exercise, since situating the game within a tradition helps us understand how a game may be innovative or ground-breaking. For example, *Half-Life* (1998) has been recognized for integrating a story in a first-person shooter, which, before that, had not been a genre particularly prone to narratives. Being one of the first to include a specific feature is what may make the game worth studying.

Conventions can also become transparent to seasoned players, so it is easy to forget about them if you are analyzing a genre you know well. On the other hand, conventions may be insurmountable barriers to those new to a genre. For example, non-experienced players will find it difficult to navigate the space of a first-person shooter, where looking and walking have separate controls. In identifying the genre, we have to step back and realize which conventions the game may follow.

Apart from formal features or conventions, the context in which the game is played can also construct the genre. For example, the rubric *casual games* seems to be a wide-reaching label that may be considered a genre, but in fact it encompasses many different types of games that may be considered genres in themselves. Puzzle games, hidden-object games, or tower defense games can all be labeled *casual* and yet they all have different mechanics. *Casual* can also be a brand imposed by marketing departments, in order to make the game appealing to audiences who may not consider themselves gamers, but still like playing videogames.

The fictional world of the game may also define the genre, as is the case with survival horror games. In these games, the player is trapped in an environment infested with monsters (from zombies to ghosts to mutants), which chase the player. Often the player has to destroy them, as in *Resident Evil* (1996), where the player explores a house overrun with zombies; it is also possible that the player must run away without getting hurt, as in *Amnesia: The Dark Descent* (2010), where the player controls someone who does not remember who he is, but knows that he needs to avoid darkness; he cannot fight the monsters that chase him, only run away. In both cases, the key is usually to escape an extremely hostile environment, hence the *survival* label.

In an even more confusing situation, the same label may define different types of games. For example, the term *arcade* is quite problematic—while some people use it specifically for games released in arcade cabinets, others invoke the term to designate fast-action games in general, whose controls are relatively simple (direction pad plus two to four buttons). Labels may also come and go—while in the late 2000s *advergames* was a common buzzword at games conferences, by 2012, *gamification* had taken over as the new fashionable label for games designed to attract customers. Now, downloadable games that are initially free but then have customers pay for further content introduced the term *free-to-play* (shortened as F2P, and also referred to as *freemium*); now it is generally accepted that many games will have in-app purchases after being downloaded for free, or will need a subscription. As you read this, there is probably yet another fashionable term to refer to this type of game in the works.

Given the complexity of determining genre, the best way to tackle it is to be aware of what your own definition is and where it comes from. In defining the game genre, one should think about what it means, who defines it, and, if using one's own definition, explain it for the sake of clarity. One can also base the definition on somebody else's work: you can start looking it up on Wikipedia, which has good overviews on certain topics, but be sure to check scholarly sources such as *The Routledge Companion to Video Game Studies*, which can provide pre-existing definitions as well as citations to other works dealing with the genre.[23]

Questions to identify the context within the game:

- What genre does the game belong to? According to whose definition?
- Which features of the game identify it as an example of that genre? Are these features inherent to the game, or are they paratexts?
- How does the game break off or subvert the genre it is labelled with?

Further Reading

Arsenault, Dominic. "Video Game Genre, Evolution and Innovation." *Eludamos. Journal for Computer Game Culture 3*, no. 2 (2009): 149–176.

Egenfeldt-Nielsen, Simon, Jonas Heide Smith, and Susana Pajares Tosca. *Understanding Video Games: The Essential Introduction*. 4th edn. London: Routledge, 2020, 52–57.

Juul, Jesper. *A Casual Revolution: Reinventing Video Games and Their Players*. Cambridge, MA: The MIT Press, 2009, Chapter 4: "Innovation and Clones: The Gradual Evolution of Downloadable Casual Games," 79–102.

Kagen, Melissa. *Wandering Games*. The MIT Press, 2022.

Wolf, Mark J.P. *The Medium of the Video Game*. 1st edn. Austin, TX: University of Texas Press, 2002, Chapter 6, "Genre and the Video Game," 113–134.

Wolf, Mark J.P., and Bernard Perron. *The Routledge Companion to Video Game Studies*. 2nd Edition. London: Routledge, 2023.

Bloomsbury books: Approaches to Digital Game Studies. https://www.bloomsbury.com/us/series/approaches-to-digital-game-studies/. Accessed November 4, 2023.

BOX 3.3 EXERCISE: GENRE HISTORY

Trace the genre and influences of the game you are analyzing, based on Juul's map of tile-matching games.[24] Start by defining the genre with a list of features that characterize it. Based on that genre, what games does it relate to? What are the features that connect it directly to other games? Which ones are common? Which ones are different? Are all the games listed part of the same genre, or does it bring different game types together?

If you are in a classroom, trace the history of the same game and then compare notes with your classmates. What are the assumptions that each genre history is based on? What knowledge of the game did each person use to trace the history?

Technological Context The technical platform can influence what type of game you are dealing with. The term *platform* refers here specifically to the technology that the game is built for—not only the hardware (consoles vs. PC; portable gaming consoles vs. smartphones), but also game engines to create games within a specific genre or format (Adventure Game Studio, RPG Maker, Ren'Py), or even general development platforms (Unity, Unreal Engine, Godot). The study of games based on their platform belongs to the larger area of *platform studies*, which is a specific approach within the study of digital media and creative computing, as proposed by Montfort and Bogost,[25] who advocate the humanistic study of applications at the platform level, in order to understand the processes that constitute their foundation. Their book, *Racing the Beam: The Atari Video Computer System*, offers an in-depth example of how platform-based analysis sheds light on the relationship between the technology and the game design, and how game developers can overcome the limitations of the platforms creatively. Other books in the series have done the same with other platforms, from the Nintendo Entertainment System,[26] the Gameboy Advance,[27] or the home computer BBC Micro.[28]

Mentioning the platform of a game is a basic requirement in any game analysis because it helps us identify a specific version of the game, but this building block may also overlap with the contents of the game overview. Again, it is not only an issue of providing clear references; at times, games may change substantially from platform to platform. For example, the original MSX version of *Metal Gear* (1987) differs substantially from the NES version released later that year—not only are the graphics different because of the varying graphic capabilities of each platform, but each version also has different level design, because it was developed by a different team. Listing the platform is similar to including the edition of a book, as already discussed, because it helps readers locate the original text one is writing about. Most times, the platform is something that may only need to be mentioned in the references; other times, discussing the platform can become the core of your analysis.

Determining the original version of the game being played, whether it is modified and how, can become an essential part of the technological context of the game, particularly if the analysis encourages the reader to play the game. Establishing which version of the game you are discussing, however, could be a bit complex at times, which may complicate the access to the game for your readers. This is the case of games that get regular updates and expansions online, which may fix technical issues or add new features. For example, it was not possible to play the original version of the massively multiplayer online role-playing game *World of Warcraft* (2004–), because the periodic updates and expansions changed the game from its original state. Fans who wanted to play the version of the game as it was in 2004 had to find a pirated copy of the game and run their own servers, until 2017 when its developer, Blizzard, decided to release *World of Warcraft Classic*, the original version of the game.[29] That "classic" version has also been updated and received expansions, including new ones different from those of the original game.[30] Other ways to change the game that may affect the platform include workarounds to gain advantage, such as entering cheat codes and using preloaded programs to change the original settings of the game. The role of cheating was already discussed in Chapter 2: if the changes to the game make it easier or more accessible, this should be reflected in the writing, since these modifications are part of the methodology of the analysis.

Technology can also be an essential factor in the development and distribution of the game, with certain types of designs only being possible once a certain technology is available. The history of virtual worlds illustrates this very clearly:[31] the first virtual world was *MUD1*, a text game developed by Roy Trubshaw and Richard Bartle in 1978. Like many of the early virtual worlds, *MUD1* was created in a university, which made its availability very limited. As dial-up connections became more widespread and affordable, online virtual worlds not only became possible but also more populated. Early virtual worlds were one of the features offered by services providers such as CompuNet in the UK or Compuserve in the USA in the mid 1980s.

The advent and spread of the World Wide Web in the mid-1990s meant another expansion for virtual worlds, which made it easier to develop graphical virtual worlds, and have a larger group of players. The growth of the Internet facilitated the appearance of massively multiplayer online virtual worlds. The technological context, in this case, overlaps with the economic context, because what is important is not only that the technology existed, but also that it was readily available. Even having online virtual worlds had been the initial idea of some of the first developers in the early 1980s; the development of better online technologies and their steady spread are what facilitated larger, more complex virtual worlds.

One last aspect to be taken into account is the use of emulation, and ports, which was discussed in Chapter 2. The limitation or extended affordances of the platform can remove or add features, at times even more noticeably than in an emulator. For instance, the iOS version of the game *Karateka* (2012) includes a set of keys overlaid on the screen to control the player character; the game also allows player to unlock a "rewind" feature that allows players to try the last challenge again rather than starting the game over if they lose. Different versions can also substantially change things like the processing performance, the image display, or the sound quality, which may be issues we can discuss in our analysis.

A platform provides a set of limitations, mainly technological, that developers can embrace or work around. Discussing how the platform may encourage certain types of interactions can help us understand the relationship between the game and the materials it is built upon. As a current example, games for smartphones may not have graphics as lavish as those of current home consoles; their controls are also simplified, since the touchscreen may only allow tapping, holding, and dragging, without complex button combinations. Thus, the types of interface in mobile games are usually not particularly complex, from drawing cards in solitaire games, to moving puzzle pieces, to dragging and releasing to fire objects, as in *Angry Birds* (2009). When shooting games are ported to smartphones, their controls have to be simplified—the complex button combinations of a console controller cannot be reproduced in phones with small buttons or touchscreens. For example, *Fortnite: Battle Royale* (2017–), players in mobile platforms have to navigate menus to change weapons or abilities, whereas on PC players can change weapons just by pressing the key associated with that specific weapon.

Understanding the platform also helps determine whether a specific aesthetic of the game is a result of the technology or a choice of the developers. For example, the black-and-white graphics of *Uninvited* (1986) originated in the monochrome monitor of the Apple I1GS; a current game using similar graphics, such as *Return of the Obra Dinn* (2018), makes it a style choice to create the looks of a Macintosh Plus, also monochrome, but with 3D navigable environments.[32] At times a game may be developed precisely to evoke a past platform—the game *La-Mulana* (2005) has already been mentioned in Chapter 1. The game was developed using the color palette and graphics resolution, as well as chiptune music, similar to those of the MSX computer standard. Camper argues that the game creates a retro-style that vindicates a long-outdated technology that is also relatively obscure.[33] Thus, the platform it is developed for and the one that it is imitating present an aesthetic choice, which also provides us with opportunities to discuss the formal aspects of the game.

Questions that help define the technological context of the game:

- Which platform(s) was the game developed for? Which version played is the object of analysis?
- How do the technological affordances and constraints of the platform define the game?
- How does the game overcome the technical limitations of the platform?
- Does the game evoke some other technology, different from the one used to play? If so, how and why?
- Which version of the game is being played?
- Are there any technical additions or modifications to the game? If so, how do they change it?

Further Reading

Camper, Brett. "Retro Reflexivity: La-Mulana, an 8-Bit Period Piece." In *The Video Game Theory Reader 2*, edited by Bernard Perron and Mark J.P. Wolf. London: Routledge, 2009, pp. 169–195.

Custodio, Alex. *Who Are You?: Nintendo's Game Boy Advance Platform*. Cambridge, MA: The MIT Press, 2020.

Gazzard, Alison. *Now the Chips Are Down: The BBC Micro*. Cambridge, MA: The MIT Press, 2016.

Jones, Steven E., and George K. Thiruvathukal. *Codename Revolution: The Nintendo Wii Platform*. Cambridge, MA: The MIT Press, 2012.

Maher, Jimmy. *The Future Was Here: The Commodore Amiga*. Cambridge, MA: The MIT Press, 2012.

Montfort, Nick, and Ian Bogost. *Racing the Beam: The Atari Video Computer System*. Cambridge, MA: The MIT Press, 2009.

BOX 3.4 EXERCISE: PLATFORM COMPARISON

Compare two versions of the same title for different technological platforms, especially a game and its port to another platform. In the case of contemporary games, compare the home console or PC version with the same title for portable consoles, smartphones or tablets, such as *Fortnite: Battle Royale* (2017–), *Among Us* (2018) or *Genshin Impact* (2020–)—all of these are easily available. For older games, compare an arcade game, such as *Pac-Man* (Namco, 1980) or *Burger Time* (1982), with a version for home consoles, such as the Atari VCS, the Commodore 64, or the Nintendo Entertainment System (NES). Do the features of the game change? If so, which of those changes have to do with the technology? How do they change the game experience?

Socio-Historical Context Situating the game within the social and historical circumstances in which it was produced is a basic strategy of some kinds of textual analysis. The dates when a game was made, released, and played provide information related to some of the building blocks already discussed, such as the expectations of developers and audiences, in terms of what the technology can do or the design conventions of that moment, for example.

Games can also be reactions to current events, or reflections on past historical events. Tristan Donovan identifies many of the games developed in the mid-1980s in the UK as *British Surrealism,* because of their bizarre visuals, inspired by the likes of *Monty Python*.[34] In one of these games, *Wanted: Monty Mole* (1984), a mole breaks into a mine populated by strange enemies, such as hairspray cans or sharks. Donovan considers it a take on the miners' strike, a violent struggle between the National Union of Mineworkers and the British government, which ended up with the defeat of the miners. The mine that Monty breaks into is owned by a character called Scargill, named after the president of the miners' union at the time.

The intersection of cultures, as well as the take of one culture on another, can also be the source of commentary. The study of the process of localization is probably one of the most productive cultural aspects of videogames, since it not only involves linguistic translation but also cultural adaptation, as noted in the case of *Osu! Tatakae! Ouendan* in Chapter 2. The cultural intersection can involve multiple areas—*Ganbare Gorby!* (1991) features former Soviet leader Mikhail Gorbachev as its hero. The player must help Gorby, the cartoon version of Gorbachev, fight soldiers and keep a factory working, to provide people with food, medicine, and videogames. Significantly, the main character became a young boy for the Western version of the game, and the title was changed to *Factory Panic*.

Questions to identify and discuss the socio-historical context:

- When and where was the game made?
- How is the historical period reflected in the game?
- Which aspects of the game reflect the culture that produces it?
- If the game has been localized, how has it changed from its original version?

Further Reading

Donovan, Tristan. *Replay: The History of Video Games*. Lewes, East Sussex: Yellow Ant Media Ltd, 2010: Chapter 9, "Uncle Clive," and Chapter 10, "The French Touch."

Hanli, Geyser, and Pippa Tshabalala. "*Return to Darkness: Representations of Africa in Resident Evil 5*." 2011. Available at: www.digra.org/wp-content/uploads/digital-library/11312.58174.pdf. Accessed November 4, 2023.

Pruett, Chris. "The Anthropology of Fear: Learning About Japan through Horror Games" *Loading ... 4*, no. 6 (2010). Available at: http://journals.sfu.ca/loading/index.php/loading/article/view/90. Accessed November 4, 2023.

Economic Context How a game is distributed, marketed, and monetized is part of its economic context, and affects how it reaches its audience. The means of distribution do not only pertain to publishers, who may find deals to sell the game in brick-and-mortar shops as well as online outlets, where a slot on the main page of a game portal or app store can make or break a game. There have been multiple channels of distribution of videogames over the years, from printed copies of the code to BBS servers, to music tapes or floppy disks in plastic zip bags that developers personally mailed to their customers. The economic models vary greatly from game to game—from a subscription-based massively multiplayer online game (MMOG) to a one-time purchase for a console game. A web game will be monetized differently from a downloadable PC game or a game for mobile. Some games are free because players have to watch advertisements in order to play or unlock items, while other games may have been paid for by an institution to educate or make players aware of a specific issue, or make money by gathering and selling your data. A publisher may also determine the content of a game by commissioning it to a studio, or may specialize in specific genres or types of games. Another model of distribution is now imitating television and movie streaming, where one can get a subscription to game packages every month, such as the Xbox Game Pass, PlayStation Plus, Humble Choice or Apple Arcade. This gives access to a selection of games, which may change every month, so players can try new games. In this last case, the focus is on the service, and at times in the exclusive titles for it, rather than the individual games themselves.

The number of economic resources available to a developer also conditions the presentation and polish of the game. While large developers, such as Square Enix, can afford to hire hundreds of people and spend several years on their next big title, small development teams may have to release games more often, or of much smaller size, in order to keep in business.

The economic context may be defined by the location in which a game is produced, as well as when it was made. During the 1980s in Europe (and to some extent in the USA), the videogames industry was started by computer hobbyists in the UK, Spain, or France. Lone developers or small teams sold their games to publishers or retailers willing to sell them. At the same time, in the countries under Soviet influence there were no commercial ways to distribute software as well as hardware, which prompted players to come up with their own ways of distributing and creating games, from piracy to creating clones similar to other Western games.[35] In contrast, Japanese video games were a product derived from toy companies like Nintendo, while software development companies and engineers were the main drivers of the North American games industry.

More recently, we have seen how smaller developers often resort to crowdfunding in order to finance the development of their games, which in some cases allows players to participate in the process of development, but which also creates expectations about what the game is going to be like in ways that had not been possible before,[36] Conversely, the ease of downloading content to mobile platforms has made the so-called free-to-play model grow very fast, so that players download the game initially for free, and then gain access to additional content through microtransactions, including purchasing levels, special items or in-game currency that allows players to unlock special abilities. The content can be cosmetic, including characters or costumes, but in other cases it can also include game levels, power-ups, or weapons, to name a few examples. Some players and designers look down on this model, because these games first entice the player to play, and once they get into it, they become really difficult in order to get players to pay so they can keep playing—what it is often derisively referred to as "pay to win." Each economic set-up implies different policies of production and marketing, as well as different audiences, and not all of these configurations refer to what is legal or ethical. A recent example of how the economic set up can affect a game is the legal dispute between Epic Games vs. Apple in 2020. Epic Games challenged the revenue cut that Apple took from each purchase made through the App store, and tried to circumvent Apple's payment system. Apple then accused Epic of breaching their contract and blocked the game *Fortnite* from their app store. As a result of this legal strife, *Fortnite* is unavailable in iOS, Apple's mobile operating system; even though the game can be installed in Mac OSX, it does not support cross-play, meaning players can only play with others who are also playing on Mac OSX. Epic seems not very interested in doing business with Apple, and as a consequence, Apple users are cut off from one of the most popular games worldwide.[37]

Questions to identify and discuss the economic context:

- Is the game a commercial product or not?
- Who was the publisher of the game?

- How was the game distributed?
- What is its business model (if any)?

Further Reading

Consalvo, Mia, and Christopher A. Paul. "If You Are Feeling Bold, Ask for $3': Value Crafting and Indie Game Developers." In *DiGRA '17 — Proceedings of the 2017 DiGRA International Conference*. Melbourne, Australia: Digital Games Research Association, 2017. Available at: www.digra.org/wp-content/uploads/digital-library/124_DIGRA2017_FP_Consalvo_Indie_Game_Developers.pdf. Accessed November 4, 2023.

Egenfeldt-Nielsen, Simon, Jonas Heide Smith, and Susana Pajares Tosca. *Understanding Video Games: The Essential Introduction*. 4th edn. London: Routledge, 2020, Chapter 2.

Keogh, Brendan. *The Videogame Industry Does Not Exist: Why We Should Think Beyond Commercial Game Production*. Cambridge, Mass.: The MIT Press, 2023.

Kerr, Aphra. *The Business and Culture of Digital Games: Gamework and Gameplay*. Thousand Oaks, CA: SAGE, 2006.

Sheff, David. *Game Over: Press Start to Continue*. Wilton, CT: Cyberactive Media Group Inc/Game Pr, 1999.

Svelch, Jaroslav. "Selling Games by the Kilo: Using Oral History to Reconstruct Informal Economies of Computer Game Distribution in the Post-Communist Environment." In *Game\Play\Society: Contributions to Contemporary Computer Game Studies*. Munich: Kopaed, 2010, pp. 265–277.

Audience The discussion of the audience relates to the economic context of the game. Games are often developed with an audience in mind, the type of players who are mostly going to play it, which, for commercial games is understood as the market. Figuring out who the audience is and, more importantly, how the game is trying to appeal to them expands the socio-economic background of the game.

Determining the intended audience is not always obvious, although there are some easily accessible sources that can provide us with that information. The different rating systems in different countries are a good starting point—the ESRB in the USA, PEGI rating in Europe, and CERO in Japan provide basic information on the age range the game may be intended for. The discrepancies between rating systems, or a critique of the content of the game in comparison with how it has been rated, can give way to good discussions on how game audiences are construed by rating systems, for example.

The advertising of a game, as well as the media in which that advertising appears, can provide more information on who is expected to play it. The gender, age, and looks of the people appearing in the advertisement can give us a hint of who they want their audience to identify with. For example, the US TV advertisement for *Pole Position* (1982) for Atari VCS shows a whole family who participates in the game—a traditional American white, middle-class family who are going on a leisure ride in the suburbs and get sidetracked into frantic car racing. A few years later, the commercial for *The Legend of Zelda* (1986) shows two boys playing together, in an attempt to appeal to a different demographic (male players between 11 and 14 years old). The advertisements themselves can be fascinating texts to discuss, but if you end up doing so, you will probably not be analyzing the game itself. The channels of distribution, tackled in the previous building block, can also be a strong indicator of who may be playing the game—casual game portals, for example, have an audience of their own, made up of their regular visitors.

Who the game is intended for affects the design and types of representation of the game, which may be another section of the analysis. Juul observes how the general category of casual games presents some common traits, such as easy controls (e.g., mouse clicks or gestural interfaces) or *juiciness* (excessive audio-visual feedback for every action and event in the game).[38] On the other hand, games intended for niche audiences, such as flight simulators, may expect players to make an investment, either in the form of time commitment or money. *Microsoft Flight Simulator* (2020) is played better with dedicated controllers and by having good knowledge of how to pilot a plane, given how complex and detailed the simulation is.

Early games from the 1970s and 1980s, as well as experimental games, are more difficult to understand as appealing to a specific audience. Many early games were closer to technology demonstrations rather than being considered commercial ventures, such as *Spacewar!* (1961) or *Pong* (1972). Some experimental games, on the other hand, could be considered "games for games' sake" works that defy the technology and the conventions of game design, and might even seek to make an expressive point. These games might require players to adapt to them, rather than being made for a specific audience, such as *Line Wobbler* (2015), a dungeon crawler that runs on a single physical line of lights, which the player has to move within or dodge in order to win.[39] There is an implied audience for experimental games—members of experimental game communities, the public attending a game exhibit or the venue where it will be presented, game connoisseurs, or players who in general look for non-commercial, unconventional games. Where the game is presented and discussed provides information about who the implied audience is, and how it may be received differently. For example, Anna Anthropy's *Dis4ia* (2012) is a game she made about her experiences of gender dysphoria and hormone replacement therapy. It is a biographical game for its creator, as well as an important example of the use of metaphors as part of game design. Its initial release took place alongside hundreds of other games in Newgrounds, a space for hobbyist games. On the one hand, the game is a collection of mini-games that was right at home with other experimental, eclectic work, The game is also a deeply personal work, which has been discussed in the context of art games as well as queer works, and exemplifies how gameplay can use metaphors expressively. What the game means depends on the context in which it is discussed.

Realizing how a specific game design may try to appeal to a range of audiences requires relating this building block to the formal analysis. Issues such as control schemes, levels of difficulty, or play modes are all design features that can accommodate players with different levels of proficiency and experience. For example, *Rock Band 2* (2008) allows players of different skills to play together by letting each player select their own difficulty level. While it includes online scoreboards for players who want to prove their prowess to the world, it also features a no-fail mode, in which the whole band can continue playing even if they are all making mistakes, because the point is to play together and get through the song rather than getting a high score.

In short, in order to identify the audience, we must look both at some of the paratexts of the game (game ratings, advertisements, distribution channels), as well as examine the game through other building blocks, such as game difficulty or interfaces.

Questions to identify the audience of a game:

- What is the rating of the game?
- Who was the game marketed to and how?
- Which elements of the game may appeal to specific audiences?
- If the game has different modes, what kinds of players may those modes be intended for?

Further Reading

Chess, Shira, Nathaniel J. Evans, and Joyya JaDawn Baines. "What Does a Gamer Look Like? Video Games, Advertising, and Diversity." *Television & New Media 18*, no. *1* (2017): 37–57.

Egenfeldt-Nielsen, Simon, Jonas Heide Smith, and Susana Pajares Tosca. *Understanding Video Games: The Essential Introduction*. 4th edn. London: Routledge, 2020, Chapter 2, pp. 168–183.

Shaw, Adrienne. *Gaming at the Edge: Sexuality and Gender at the Margins of Gamer Culture*. Minneapolis, US: University of Minnesota Press, 2015.

Young, Bryan-Mitchell. "*The Disappearance and Reappearance and Disappearance of the Player in Videogame Advertising*." Paper presented at DiGRA Conference, Tokyo, Japan, 2007.

BOX 3.5 EXERCISE: WHAT MAKES A GAME HARDCORE?

This exercise is meant to help you learn how a game appeals to its audience, and how it tries to tailor itself to players. First of all, choose a "hardcore" game, such as a first-person shooter, real-time strategy game, or role-playing game. There are two ways to go about this exercise.

A) If you consider yourself a gamer, find a friend or relative who does not play games or does not think of themselves as a gamer. Teach this new player how to play the game. They do not have to master it; the focus is studying the process of first learning the game in two or three hours.

The report of your experience should address these issues:

- What were the most difficult parts of the game to learn? Why?
- What was the easiest thing to pick up? Why?
- What did your subject do that was surprising?

B) If you do not play videogames regularly or at all, find a friend or relative who does consider themselves a gamer, and ask them to teach you how to play the game. You do not have to master the game, just see how much you can learn in two or three hours.

- What were the most difficult parts of the game to learn? Why?
- What was the easiest thing to pick up? Why?
- What did the person teaching you take for granted that you did not know how to do?

Relations to Other Media Revisiting a series of events or a set of characters through different media has happened for many, many centuries. The stories of Greek mythology were told in poetry and plays, depicted in paintings, statues, and bas-relief. Videogames have become the latest medium that these stories can be extended to, as a participatory space to explore worlds, events, and characters. The studies of adaptation, which have focused on the translations between novels, theater, and film/television, for example,[40] are now being challenged not only by the multiplicity of media, but also by having stories that expand across several media. The study and practice of different incarnations of a fictional world through different media have been dubbed *transmedia storytelling*, a practice different from adaptation. Transmedia storytelling focuses on the presentation of different aspects of a fictional world across different media, rather than on how story events may be retold in a different medium. *The Matrix* franchise (1999–2003) is a canonical example of a transmedia property, since the main narrative became fragmented across different media, inviting audiences to go from one medium to another to explore the whole story.[41]

Discussing the relation between a game and other media is a practice that directly relates games to other disciplines, such as literature, film, or media studies in general. In analyzing the game, however, one should be careful with reading the game the same way one would carry out a critical analysis of a film or a short story. The purpose of this book is to present a framework that highlights the nature of videogames and what distinguishes them from other media forms; although one of the strategies is establishing similarities with other types of media analysis, it is also true that the participatory nature of videogames should not be discounted. Therefore, in discussing a videogame in relation to other media, the role of the player and the rules of the game should not be forgotten—after all, the experience of the player is one of the common aspects between building blocks of the analysis. For example, Matthew Weise resorts to the term *procedural adaptation* to explain how survival horror games adapt horror movie conventions into a participatory media artifact.[42] The worlds of zombie movies, particularly the films directed by George A. Romero, also have rules, which are translated into rules of the fictional world of the game. Weise notes how the infectious nature of the zombie disease, for instance, is notably absent from videogames directly inspired by the Romero films, such as the *Resident Evil* series (1996–). Although translating this rule might make the games a more faithful adaptation of the films, it would also make the game more difficult, so game conventions prevail to make the game more playable.

The sources of inspiration of a game can be multiple—a game could be part of a franchise or a tie-in for a movie. Often, some games are released along with a Hollywood film as a way to take advantage of the publicity of a movie. As part of the creation of expanded fictional universes, now we see games that expand and are in dialogue on the worlds of franchises such as the Marvel Cinematic Universe, Star Wars, or The Witcher. Some games that try to make the best of the licensed properties they are based on, beyond using the license as part of the brand recognition for a game, such as *Battlestar Galactica: The Board Game* (2008), which uses the stories of the TV show to shape its systems of resource management as well as hidden identities, or Telltale Games' *The Walking Dead: Season One* (2012), which makes its gameplay focus on choices to tackle the life-or-death situations as its core challenge.

Some videogames may be inspired by other works, but not necessarily be an adaptation. *Eternal Darkness: Sanity's Requiem* (2002) is clearly inspired by H.P. Lovecraft's Cthulhu mythos, and although it includes references to the stories, the game creates its own world and stories. The games in the *Grand Theft Auto* series (1997–2013) seem similarly inspired by the worlds of movies and television, with the experience of driving in *Grand Theft Auto: Vice City* (2002) strongly echoing the television show *Miami Vice* (1984–1990), for example. Another Rockstar game, *L.A. Noire* (2011), takes the film *L.A. Confidential* (1997), alongside other films within the noir detective genre and the novels of James Ellroy, as sources of inspiration for its missions, tone, and presentation.

At times, not being able to secure the rights for an adaptation may force the game to create a distinctive identity— *Dead Rising* (2006) includes a disclaimer on its cover explicitly stating that it is *not* an adaptation of George Romero's film *Dawn of the Dead* (1978). However, many of the scenarios of the game are clearly inspired by situations in the movie. Mapping these similarities, in the case of unofficial adaptations, can reveal relationships between games and other media that may not be evident at first.

Other games are also an important source for videogames. Non-digital games, such as sports games, card games, board games, or even playground games, can be implemented in digital form, as was the case of the game of *Solitaire* (1989) that came packaged with the Windows operating system. Discussing how digital media transform the game is an obvious but productive avenue. Continuing with the case of *Solitaire*, what the digital version adds is the ability to go back to a specific combination of cards, and to restart if the player gets to a dead-end state. In the case of sports games, some productive questions can be how a team sport becomes a single-player game, or how the effort required in a specific sport is translated as an effort while playing the videogame. In all these cases, the section on formal analysis provides the building blocks to develop this discussion.

Another non-digital game source may be a specific rule set from tabletop role-playing games, such as *Dungeons and Dragons* (1974) or *GURPS* (1986).[43] Although the digital implementation of the system may seem, straightforward, the player's experience may be different—combat that may take several minutes in a live environment may be finished in seconds in its computer version, depending on whether the combat is turn-based or not. Games have also developed their own role-playing system, even if it was inspired by a table-top rule set. *Fallout* (1997) developed its SPECIAL system after a deal to use GURPS fell through.[44] The violence and gore depicted were too much for Steve Jackson's games, so they did not grant the developer Black Isle the license to their system, even though it had already been implemented in the game.

Games can share the same character, even if they are completely different genres. For example, Mario is the star of his own series of platform games, as well as being a playable character in the *Mario Kart* series (1992–2014), *Super Smash Bros*, series (1999–2017), and *Super Mario Strikers* (2005–2007), to name but a few. Whether this character-sharing is a matter of marketing, or a case study of transmedia storytelling can be a good subject of discussion.

Questions to plot the relation of a game with other media:

- Is the game part of a media franchise?
- Is the game adapting a pre-existing work (another game, a film, a book, a play)? What does it take from the work? What is left out?
- Is the game inspired by a pre-existing work? How so?
- How do the rules of the game relate to the other media artifacts?
- How much does the player need to know about the other media in order to play?

- What is the role of the player in the game compared to the role of the audience in other media incarnations?

Further Reading

Fernandez-Vara, Clara. "The Game's Afoot: Designing Sherlock Holmes." In *Proceedings of DiGRA 2013: Defragging Game Studies*. Atlanta, GA, 2013. Available at: www.digra.org/digital-library/publications/the-games-afoot-designing-sherlock-holmes/. Accessed November 4, 2023.

Jenkins, Henry. *Convergence Culture: Where Old and New Media Collide*. New York: New York University Press, 2006.

Ryan, Marie-Laure. "Transmedia Storytelling: Industry Buzzword or New Narrative Experience?" *Storyworlds: A Journal of Narrative Studies 7*, no. 2 (2015): 1–19.

Weise, Matthew. "The Rules of Horror: Procedural Adaptation in Clock Tower, Resident Evil and Dead Rising." In *Horror Video Games: Essays on the Fusion of Fear and Play*, edited by Bernard Perron. Jefferson, NC: MacFarland, 2009, pp. 238–266.

▶ TO SUM UP

Discussing the context surrounding the game—paratexts, factors of production, and socio-economic and historical setting—situates the discussion and creates a series of connections with other building blocks. These blocks can also be the main discussion point of the analysis, as Chapter 4 describes, such as an historical analysis, the study of a specific game community, or focusing on the materiality of the platform of a specific game. While the context establishes what the game may have in common with other games, the overview and the formal analysis establish what sets the game apart.

▶ NOTES

1 Rouse, Richard. *Game Design: Theory and Practice*. 2nd edn. (Plano, TX: Wordware Publishing, 2001), pp. 5–68.

2 Sudnow, David. *Pilgrim in the Microworld* (New York: Warner Books, 1983).

3 See Chapter 2, note 14.

4 Baldick, Chris. *Concise Dictionary of Literary Terms* (Oxford: Oxford University Press, 1996), pp. 110–111.

5 Engadget. "Creating Osu! Tatakae! Ouendan and Its Recreation as Elite Beat Agents," March 8, 2007. https://www.engadget.com/2007-03-08-creating-osu-tatakae-ouendan-and-its-recreation-as-elite-beat.html (accessed November 14, 2023).

6 *The Propeller Arena Fan Site.* Available at: https://propellerarena.neocities.org/ (accessed November 4, 2023).

7 Genette, Gérard. *Paratexts: Thresholds of Interpretation* (Cambridge: Cambridge University Press, 1997), pp. 1–15.

8 Jakobsson, Mikael. "Playing with the Rules: Social and Cultural Aspects of Game Rules in a Console Game Club." In *Situated Play, Proceedings of the Digital Games Research Association (DiGRA) Conference*, 2007. Available at: www.digra.org/digital-library/publications/playing-with-the-rules-social-and-cultural-aspects-of-game-rules-in-a-console-game-club/ (accessed November 4, 2023).

9 Kolos, Hillary. "Not Just in It to Win It: Inclusive Game Play in an MIT Dorm." Thesis, Massachusetts Institute of Technology, 2010. Available at: http://dspace.mit.edu/handle/1721.1/59731 (accessed November 4, 2023).

10 Bain & Company. "Beyond the Love of the Game: Talent in the Video Game Industry," October 4, 2023. https://www.bain.com/insights/beyond-the-love-of-the-game-talent-in-the-video-game-industry/ (accessed November 14, 2023).

11 "People Make Games—YouTube." https://www.youtube.com/@PeopleMakeGames (accessed November 15, 2023).

12 See Sarris, Andrew. "Films in Focus." *The Village Voice*. April 15, 1971.

13 See a discussion of issues of authorship in general in Foucault, Michel. "What Is an Author?" In *The Foucault Reader*, translated by Paul Rabinow. New York: Pantheon Books, 1984, pp. 101–120.

14 Kael, Pauline. "Raising Kane." *The New Yorker*, February 12, 1971.

15 Donovan, Tristan. *Replay: The History of Video Games* (Lewes, East Sussex: Yellow Ant Media Ltd, 2010), pp. 90–93.

16 For a history of *La Abadía del Crimen*, from its inception to the technological achievements and current status as a cult title, see Esteve Gutiérrez, Jaume. "La Abadía Del Crimen." *Well Played* 6, no. 2 (June 29, 2017). http://press.etc.cmu.edu/index.php/product/well-played-vol-6-no-2/ (accessed November 14, 2023).

17 "The Abbey of Crime Extensum on Steam." Available at: http://store.steampowered.com/app/474030/The_Abbey_of_Crinie_Extensum/ (accessed November 4, 2023).

18 Robinett, Warren. 2006. "Adventure as a Video Game: Adventure for the Atari 2600." In *The Game Design Reader: A Rules of Play Anthology*. Cambridge, Mass.: MIT Press.

19 The website of the Special Interest Group, alongside the latest version of the guide, are available online at "Game Credits – IGDA." n.d. https://igda.org/sigs/credits/ (accessed September 17, 2023).

20 Reed, Aaron. *50 Years of Text Games: From Oregon Trail to AI Dungeon*. First. Oakland, California: Changeful Tales Press, 2023.

21 Partlett, David. *The Oxford History of Board Games* (Oxford: Oxford University Press, 1999).

22 Juul, Jesper, "Swap Adjacent Gems to Make Sets of Three: A History of Matching Tile Games." *Artifact* 1, no. 4 (2007): 205–216.

23 Wolf, Mark J.P., and Bernard Perron. *The Routledge Companion to Video Game Studies*. 2nd edn. Taylor & Francis, 2023.

24 Juul, Jesper. "Swap Adjacent Gems to Make Sets of Three: A History of Matching Tile Games." *Artifact* 1, no. 4 (2007): 205–216.

25 Montfort, Nick, and Ian Bogost. *Racing the Beam: The Atari Video Computer System* (Cambridge, MA: The MIT Press, 2009), pp. 145–150.

26 Altice, Nathan. *I Am Error: The Nintendo Family Computer/Entertainment System Platform* (Cambridge, MA: The MIT Press, 2015).

27 Custodio, Alex. *Who Are You?: Nintendo's Game Boy Advance Platform*. MIT Press, 2020.

28 Gazzard, Alison. *Now the Chips Are Down: The BBC Micro* (Cambridge, MA: Tie MIT Press, 2016).

29 Frank, Allegra. "World of Warcraft Classic Is an Official Vanilla Server." *Polygon*. November 3, 2017. Available at: www.polygon.com/2017/11/3/16603922/world-of-warcraft-classic-announced-trailer-wow-blizzcon-2017 (accessed November 4, 2023).

30 Welsh, Oli. "World of Warcraft Classic Is Becoming Its Own Game—Is Fortnite OG Next?" *Polygon* (blog), November 10, 2023. https://www.polygon.com/23954103/world-of-warcraft-classic-fortnite-og-nostalgia

31 See Bartle, Richard. “Making Places.” In *Space Time Play—Computer Games, Architecture and Urbanism: The Next Level*, edited by Friedrich von Borries, Steffen P. Walz, and Matthias Bottger (Basel: Birkhäuser Verlag, 2007), and Hunsinger, Jeremy, Lisbeth Klastrup, Matthew Allen, and Richard Bartle, eds. “From MUDs to MMORPGs: The History of Virtual Worlds.” In *International Handbook of Internet Research* (Dordrecht: Springer Netherlands, 2010), pp. 23–39.

32 PlayStation.Blog. “How Lucas Pope Created the Unique 1-Bit Art Style of Return of the Obra Dinn, out this Week on PS4,” October 17, 2019. https://blog.playstation.com/archive/2019/10/17/lucas-pope-on-return-of-the-obra-dinns-art-style (accessed November 16, 2023).

33 Camper, Brett. “Retro Reflexivity: La-Mulana, an 8-Bit Period Piece.” In *The Video Game Theory Reader 2*, edited by Bernard Perron and Mark J. P. Wolf (London: Routledge, 2009), pp. 169–195.

34 Donovan. *Replay*, pp. 117–118.

35 Svelch, Jaroslav. “Selling Games by the Kilo: Using Oral History to Reconstruct Informal Economies of Computer Game Distribution in the Post-Communist Environment.” In *Game\Play\Society: Contributions to Contemporary Computer Game Studies*. Munich: Kopaed, 2010, pp. 265–277.

36 Planells, Antonio José. “Video Games and the Crowdfunding Ideology: From the Gamer-Buyer to the Prosumer-Investor.” *Journal of Consumer Culture* 17, no. 3 (2017): 620–638.

37 For a detailed but accessible summary of the lawsuit and its ruling, see Robertson, Adi. “A Comprehensive Breakdown of the Epic vs. Apple Ruling.” *The Verge*, September 12, 2021. https://www.theverge.com/2021/9/12/22667694/epic-v-apple-trial-fortnite-judge-yvonne-gonzalez-rogers-final-ruling-injunction-breakdown (accessed November 16, 2023).

38 Juul, Jesper. *A Casual Revolution: Reinventing Video Games and Their Players* (Cambridge, MA: The MIT Press, 2009), pp. 45–50.

39 More information and photos of the game available at “Line Wobbler.” Robin Baumgarten’s game experiments, November 4, 2014. Available at: http://wobblylabs.com/line-wobbler (accessed March 11, 2024).

40 Chatman, Seymour. *Story and Discourse: Narrative Structure in Fiction and Film* (Ithaca, NY: Cornell University Press, 1980).

41 Jenkins, Henry. *Convergence Culture: Where Old and New Media Collide* (New York: New York University Press, 2006).

42 Weise, Matthew. “The Rules of Horror: Procedural Adaptation in Clock Tower, Resident Evil and Dead Rising.” In *Horror Video Games: Essays on the Fusion of Fear and Play*, edited by Bernard Perron (Jefferson, NC: MacFarland, 2009), pp. 238–266.

43 Gygax, Gary, and Dave Arneson. *Dungeons and Dragons* (Tactical Studies Rules (TSR), 1974); Jackson, Steve. *GURPSBasic Set*. 1st edn. (Steve Jackson Games, 1986).

44 “SPECIAL,” *Fallout Wiki*, last modified December 17, 2013. Available at: http://fallout.fandom.com/wiki/SPECIAL (accessed November 4, 2023).

4

Areas of Analysis 2: Game Overview

▶ INTRODUCTION

When we start writing an analysis, we must always be clear about what we are actually analyzing. It is always useful to include a summary of what the game is about, both to provide an overview for readers who may not be familiar with the game itself, and to make explicit how we understand the game. For example, one writer may focus on the complexity and richness of the systems in *Tactics Ogre* (1995), a tactical role-playing game, whereas another writer may care more about the rich branching storyline and how the narrative relates to the game mechanics.

In fields like literature, writers often assume that the reader is familiar with the work at hand, in particular, if the text is part of a specific canon. Assuming that all readers have the same knowledge of games is taking too much for granted, particularly because of the heterogeneity of contexts of production and play already discussed in the previous chapters. Again, textual analysis can be used as a tool to discover obscure games or introduce readers to games they are not familiar with, thus contributing to the creation of a varied videogame corpus one game at a time.

DOI: 10.4324/9781003355779-4

This area covers the building blocks that comprise the game overview, which is a descriptive section that allows the reader to identify the game, and whose goal is to distinguish it from other games. More importantly, through these building blocks, we can introduce what makes the game deserve our analysis. Every analysis will require some of these blocks to identify the game in discussion; some of them can be explained briefly while others will be superfluous. Some of these building blocks overlap with others in different areas. Discussing some of them in depth may provide insight, but that is most likely to happen in the counterpart blocks that belong to the other two areas: the context and formal elements.

The purpose of the overview is to complement and extend the information that would be provided in a citation. Chapter 7 will discuss how citations may be too limited to provide enough context about the game; this area of analysis provides the space to elaborate on what distinguishes the game from others.

Some writers mistakenly understand a game overview as a summary of the story of the game, similar to how literary or film analyses provide a synopsis of a novel or a movie. Story-driven genres, such as role-playing games or adventure games, may lend themselves to a summary of the events of the story, but even doing that may not really allow us to understand why the game is special. Plus, reducing a game to a story misses the participation of the player as well as the rules and limitations that are part of games. While some games may have a series of events to mark the progress of the game, in other cases, the story events are irrelevant to the gameplay. This does not mean that the story premise or the events of the story do not have room in the analysis, since they can be central to the experience. However, you should keep in mind that discussing exclusively the story of the game may situate the analysis in the realm of literature or film, for example, instead of dealing with the game itself. So remember—the story summary is only one of several blocks that you need to discuss the game; retelling the narrative events is not analyzing the game.

This area refers to the most common blocks providing the information that helps to identify the game, as well as providing the preliminary grounds to explain what sets it apart. Chapter 6 will show in more detail how this overview becomes part of practically every analysis.

▶ GAME OVERVIEW: BUILDING BLOCKS

Although some of these building blocks may also be considered formal elements of the game, they belong in this area because they are also general features that can be found in most games. The building blocks that make up the game overview are:

- Number of Players
- Rules and Goals of the Game/Game Modes
- Game Mechanics
- Spaces of the Game
- Fictional World of the Game
- Story
- Gameplay Experience
- Game Communities.

Number of Players Listing a basic piece of information like the number of players allows us to learn more about how players take part in the game. It is a formal feature that is always included in the boxes of commercial games, both digital and non-digital. Videogames are often designed for a single player, whereas non-digital games commonly require several people in order to be able to play and involve social interaction. The number of players and how they relate to each other are particularly relevant to analyses focusing on the social context of the game and how it is played, because it sets up not only how the player relates to the game itself, but also how they relate to each other.

There can be many configurations in which the number of players can combine. This section will follow the player interaction patterns proposed by Fullerton (see Figure 4.1),[1] which helps explain how players can tackle the game.

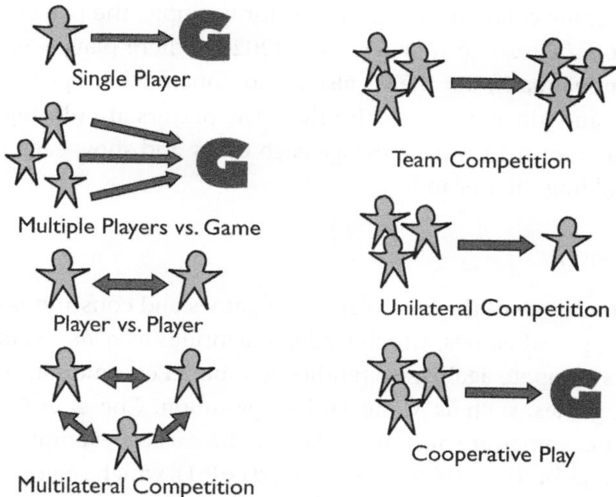

Figure 4.1 Different multiplayer configurations
Source: adapted from Fullerton (2019)

Single Player vs. Game

This is one of the most common configurations in videogames, where the player plays against the computer. On the other hand, non-digital single-player games are rare, because playing games is traditionally a social activity. Peg solitaire and different types of card solitaires refer to the "single player" in the title, although some consider them puzzles rather than games. These supposed borderline cases may be the source for an interesting discussion—a jigsaw puzzle does not require multiple players, but it can be put together communally and there are game books such as *Fabled Lands* or *Destiny Quest* that combine a "Choose Your Own Adventure" structure with characters stats and dice rolls, as if they were a single-player role-playing game of sorts.[2]

Multiple Players vs. Game

This is an uncommon configuration of players, where players are individually competing simultaneously but not against each other. What sets aside this type is that there is no interaction between players (as opposed to the cooperative play below), so this configuration appears in games of pure chance, such as Bingo or Roulette. However, there are more recent games that challenge this definition because they consist of several players trying to beat the game collaboratively. This is, for example, the player configuration of *Animal Crossing: New Horizons* (2020), where players engage with the game individually, but there's also a component where players can visit each other, and gift items to each other. The players are playing the same game, while they are able to message each other and show each other how they are building their islands.

Player vs. Player

Competition is one of the basic drivers of games and constitutes one of the four basic types of games, which Caillois identifies as *agon*.[3] Games where two players compete against each other is a model common in some of the oldest folk games, such as Mancala, Backgammon, Chess, or Go. The origins of digital games are also multiplayer—the earliest examples are games such as *Tennis for Two* (1958) or *Spacewar!* (1961), which required two people playing together. Digital single-player games became more common in home computers, whereas early game consoles would usually provide options for both single and multiple players.

Multilateral Competition

Games can also have more than two players pitching against each other. Card games, such as Poker, or board games such as *Settlers of Catan* (1995) or *Risk* (1957), push players to compete against each other to become the single winner. Multilateral competition has also become tremendously popular among online games, with the abundance of "Battle Royale" games available, such as *Fortnite: Battle Royale* (2017–), where players have to survive in a hostile environment and be the last player standing, all while gathering resources and means to attack other players. Although the battle royale genre is very popular with shooter games, the model has also extended to other game genres, as is the case of *Tetris 99* (2019), where 99 players play *Tetris* online, and try to be the last player without an overflowed screen, all while sending additional blocks to other players by clearing large swathes of blocks in their own screen.

Team Competition

Players can unite against other players, so players collaborate against another team. This configuration is common in competitive sports, such as Basketball or Hockey. Digital games have also incorporated team competition thanks to online play, as is the case of *Counter Strike* (2000).

Local multiplayer games are also more frequently incorporating teams that compete against each other—*Rocket League* (2015) brings together model car driving and football, whereas the arcade game *Killer Queen* (2013) pits two teams of five players against each other in paired game cabinets.

Unilateral Competition

There are games where one player competes against the rest, and the other players collaborate to defeat the player who is "it." This configuration is common in playground games like Tag or Blind Man's Bluff; it also makes for very interesting gameplay in board games and digital games. It would appear that the player that is singled out is at a disadvantage, so, in order to balance the game out, the one player against everyone else is given complete information.[4] This configuration is typical of games where there is a "traitor" that is trying to sabotage the common goal that the rest of the players are trying to achieve, as is the case of *Among Us* (2018), where players are running a spaceship and they are trying to figure out who is on their side and who is trying to kill the rest of the crew. That changes the goals of that player to trying to sabotage and defeat the other players. Another example of this configuration is the Nintendo GameCube's *Pac-Man Vs.* (2003), where three players play the ghosts of Pac-Man on the big screen, and one player plays Pac-Man in the small screen of a GameBoy Advance. The players who play the ghost can only see their most immediate surroundings on the screen, while the person who controls Pac-Man can see the whole labyrinth, just as in a regular *Pac-Man* game. A similar configuration can be found in the game *Luigi's Ghost Mansion*, which is part of the collection of games in *Nintendo Land* (2012). One player controls the ghost that haunts the mansion in the Wii U controller, which has its own screen, while up to four other players try to hunt the ghost down on the television. As in *Pacman Vs.*, the information on each screen is different, since the ghost remains invisible on the television screen—players will know when the ghost is near when their controllers start to vibrate.

Cooperative Play

Collaboration is the counterpart to competition—in the same way that a single player can be pitched against a game, there can be a group of players who collaborate to achieve a single objective. An interesting example of this can be found in some of the games of the New Games Movement of the 1970s, which promoted large-scale collaborative games. One of the games is the Lap Game, where players sit on each other's laps to create a circle; the challenge is to get as many people as possible sitting together in a circle.[5] In a more recent example, "escape the room" events require teams of people to solve interlinked puzzles within an allotted amount of time—an individual player could solve all the puzzles on their own, but not before the time is up. Another example would be the board game *Pandemic* (2008), which requires players to fight against different diseases spreading in different regions. Each player is a specialist with different strategic abilities to fight the disease, so players need to collaborate in order to win the game. This board game encapsulated the importance of collaboration against a common problem in its gameplay, anticipating the challenges that the world faced during the actual COVID-19 pandemic of 2020.

In digital games, cooperation as a core mechanic has become more common as a player configuration. For example, the game *Tick Tock: A Tale For Two* (2019) is an adventure game were players have to run different versions of their game in separate platforms. Each player will get different information and will see different parts of the world. By sharing information, players will help each other solve the puzzles in their version of the game and solve the mystery together. Players can play in the same room (but without looking at each other's screens), or be apart and talking to each other on the phone or voice chat. In other digital games, cooperative play may be an additional mode, rather than the main player configuration. For example, there are certain quests in *World of Warcraft* (2004–) that a single player cannot complete on their own, such as defeating a particularly powerful enemy; players then need to organize a raid in order to complete the challenge.

Fullerton's classification provides a handy breakdown of different player configurations. However, there are still a few factors that we need to take into account when we discuss the number of players of a game, such as whether players play simultaneously or in turns, and how the players connect to each other.

When multiple players take turns, they can be either playing the same game against each other, as is the case of Chess, or they may be taking turns in playing different games at the same machine. This latter case is called *hot-seat multiplayer*, a common feature of early arcade videogames,[6] in which a player would play until they lost one life in the game, then leave the seat to the other player, alternating until both players exhausted all their lives.

Games such as *Galaga* (1981) or *Defender* (1980) featured hot-seat multiplayer, thus promoting people to play together in the arcade and compete against each other to reach the highest score.

If simultaneous play is possible, particularly in the case of digital games, then we have to think about how the game supports all players. We need to identify whether the game can be played by all in the same machine or in different interconnected machines. An example of a simultaneous multiplayer game is *Goldeneye* (1997), a first-person shooter where the screen is split to show each player their separate view. If each player plays on a different machine, we also need to figure out how the games are linked. Some games use a local area network (LAN) to connect either computers or consoles, where people can be playing in the same room. Players can also connect remotely to a server, where game sessions may be ad hoc and ephemeral, where a player initiates the game, and others may join or drop (e.g., *Counter Strike*, 2000). Some games may choose their online players randomly (*Mario Kart DS's* online mode, 2005), while others may allow private servers to be set up (*Minecraft*, 2011).

The scale of the game is also another factor that we may have to discuss. Massively multiplayer online games (MMOGs) are their own world quite literally. Unlike the online multiplayer games just described, games such as *Everquest* (1999–) or *EVE Online* (2003–), as discussed in Chapter 2, take place in a persistent virtual world, that is, a computer space that continues existing after players have logged off.[7] MMOGs are also social spaces, where players can establish a wide variety of relationships about them, from the lone wolf who just wants to complete quests alone or explore the world, to people who want to make friends, or to compete with others or even just be a nuisance and spoil other players' games.[8] Part of defining an MMOG, therefore, includes making at least a basic reference to how players interact with each other and with the world—the virtual world *Second Life* (2003–) may not be considered a game by some because there is no competition or quests, but it shares many of the conventions of MMOGs, such as the control scheme; it also allows its inhabitants to create games for others. In contrast, *Minecraft* (2011) does have persistent online worlds that can be accessed by players, although their numbers are not considered "massive" because the original expectation was that servers will be set up by users, not the developer. Some servers can host several thousand players,[9] however, which may not be considered "massive", but it is still quite substantial. In the case of analyzing an MMOG, this building block is going to connect to blocks such as game communities, where we can discuss players' relationships in more depth.

Collaboration and competition may also change through the game, or there may be different modes that the game supports, so that the relationship between multiple players may also shift during gameplay. In the multiplayer mode of *LittleBigPlanet* (2008), there are certain areas and items that can only be reached by collaborating with other players; on the other hand, at the end of the game, each player has a score depending on the number of items they have picked up throughout the level.

Another example of this is how games may have different multiplayer configurations. *Rock Band* (2007), for example, features a variety of multiplayer modes, from one to four people playing together a song, to two different sets of players playing against each other to see who achieves the highest score in a song. Competitive multiplayer gameplay can take place in two modes: Tug of War, in which two bands take turns playing different sections of the same song, or Score Duel, in which two bands play the same song to see who achieves the highest score. The different features associated with multiplayer configuration show how the approach to using distinctive features can work to define and distinguish a game.

Questions to explain the different configurations related to the number of players:

- How many players can play this game together?
- Do players compete against each other?
- Can players collaborate?
- Do players team up?
- Are the players together in the same physical location or remotely?
- If they play remotely, how do they connect with each other?
- How do players communicate with each other (if at all)?

Further Reading

Björk, Staffan, and Jesper Juul. "Zero-Player Games. Or: What We Talk about When We Talk about Players." Paper presented at The Philosophy of Computer Games Conference, Madrid, 2012. Available at: www.jesperjuul.net/text/zeroplayergames/. Accessed November 4, 2023.

Egenfeldt-Nielsen, Simon, Jonas Heide Smith, and Susana Pajares Tosca. *Understanding Video Games: The Essential Introduction*. 4th edn. London: Routledge, 2020, pp. 150–152.

Jakobsson, Michael. "Playing with the Rules: Social and Cultural Aspects of Game Rules in a Console Game Club." In *Situated Play: DiGRA 2007 Conference Proceedings*, Tokyo: Akira Baba, 2007, pp. 386–392.

BOX 4.1 EXERCISE: HOW MANY PLAYERS CAN PLAY THIS GAME?

The number of players is often featured on the box of a game, both in the case of board games as well as digital games. The number of players is a formal feature that may be more flexible than it says on the box. This exercise invites you to explore how many people may be able to play the game and how.

Think about how the number of players, as well as their roles, may change depending on how players decide to play. How can a single-player game be played by multiple people? A good example are adventure games, where several people can play together at the same time: everyone looks at the screen to see what happens, and then they discuss what to do, while one person carries out the commands. Players may also take turns in playing a game that requires skill, such as a platform game or a fighting game, if they want to complete a mode, thus using collaboration as a way to tackle the competitive aspects of the game. Conversely, one player can try to control all the characters in one game, for example, and see if it is even possible. This experiment involves choosing a game and finding the boundaries of how many people may be able to play together (or not). By exploring potential reconfigurations of the number of players and how they play, we can learn how players appropriate and transform a game, as well as hypothesize which features of the game afford these transformations. For example, adventure games can be played by many people collaboratively because most of their challenges do not depend on skill but on puzzle-solving, so players can think aloud with others to figure out the different puzzles. Turn-based collaborative games, in contrast, may be playable by one player, whereas real-time competition may not allow for a single person to control all the players. Although this exercise can be examined in an essay discussing the hypothetical number of players, it is probably best carried out by actually trying to play the game with others.

Rules and Goals of the Game/Game Modes The challenge of every game analysis is to get across what the game is like, even if the reader has not played it. Thus, one of the first things we have to do is explain the basic rules.

When new players are introduced to a non-digital game, they usually get a brief introduction of the basic rules and the win condition, which may be followed by a test play-through where more nuanced restrictions are explained. A game analysis does not have to reproduce a complete version of the game manual; summarizing the main rules and constraints usually suffices to convey an idea of what the game is about.

For example, a summary of the rules of Monopoly (1935) would read something like this:

> Monopoly is a board game in which players become real estate magnates, buying properties in a city and building them. The board is a single-track circuit (what Parlett would call a *race game*),[10] which makes players go around. Each turn, a player throws two dice to determine where their token lands. Each square may be a property for sale, which the player can buy, or which may already be owned by someone else. Players can build inside their property—the more buildings in the square, the more other players have to pay whenever they land on that property after a dice roll. The goal is to trade properties and buildings, so they yield high profits at the expense of the other players. The winner of the game is the last player who is still in good standing after all the other players have declared bankruptcy.

At times, mentioning the genre or family the game belongs to becomes shorthand for explaining the core mechanics. In table-top games, we have trading-card games, trick-taking card games, or live-action role-playing games, to name but a few; in digital games, we have first-person shooters, point-and-click adventure games, or racing games as a few examples. The genres evoke a set of conventions that can help us avoid giving a long description of complex rules, which in certain cases may be the only thing we need in our analysis (although, as discussed in Chapter 3, defining genre and conventions is a whole problem of its own).

In the case of digital games, however, we do not always know all the rules. The system is usually a black box and the player needs to figure out how it works—in fact, this can be one of the pleasures of playing a videogame. So, it is not easy to write the rules of a videogame; what we write in this case is the goals of the game, and a summary of the game mechanics, which indicate what the player can do (see next building block). The rules of the game can be explained in depth as a strategy guide, such as a list of the different weapons and their stats for a first-person shooter game. For instance, the strategy guides for *Animal Crossing: New Horizons* (2020) list when and where each type of bug and fish are going to appear, so players know which ones they may be missing, and when to get them.[11] These guides show how the game works in certain depth; for the purposes of the overview, this type of guide helps us understand how a specific area or feature works. There are also online tools that allow players to predict the price of turnips, which in the world of the game are a type of investment with fluctuating price, or what the weather is going to be like. These tools reveal the algorithms that determine when events take place, but which may appear as random to players. (See also "Rules of the World" building block, discussed in Chapter 5.)

The goals of a game at times can be tricky to identify. Some games may not have an end state, and yet they will still have a goal. This is very common in early arcade games such as *Galaxian* (1979), a 2D shooter game where the player controls a spaceship and must destroy incoming waves of enemy ships. The player must brave the attacks for as long as possible to achieve a high score. *Pac-Man* (1980) and *Donkey Kong* (1981) famously feature *kill screens*—they only have a limited set of levels, because designers thought that no player would get that far in the game. In this block, we focus on the goals set by the game design, not necessarily the ones players can come up with (which can be their own relevant topic).

Looking at the instructions of the game is a good place to start the summary, because they give us a gist of the game mechanics. The *Pong* arcade cabinet (1972) famously features two sentences as instructions: "Insert Coin. Avoid missing ball for high score." It is wonderfully concise, but it needs to be expanded a bit in order to get across how the game works: there are two paddles on each side of the screen, which each player slides up and down in order to hit the ball and send it to the other side.

Other times, the rules and goals of the game may not be your run-of-the mill mechanics, or are tied with specific meaningful interactions, so explaining the rules may be the core of our analysis. For example, it is notable how when talking about the game *Cart Life* (2011), it ends up being necessary to explain the rules in certain detail. Chris Dahlen summarizes the game thus:

> *Cart Life* is a game about running a street cart. It's a retail simulator, like any number of "tycoon" games on the market, where you have to start a business and balance several concerns: stocking supplies, watching costs, dealing with random setbacks and weighing a risky growth plan against the safety of the low-grossing products you're accustomed to.
>
> But *Cart Life* is not only a retail sim. It also tells a gut-wrenching story about people who are down on their luck and almost broke, and who start a small street business as a way to get back on their feet.[12]

The rest of the game review explains the rules in relative detail. Joel Goodwin, in another review of the game, combines the explanation of the different rules and goals with his experience of playing the game.[13] This is because *Cart Life* is a very peculiar artifact—a simulation of running a street cart that turns some of the conventions of strategy games against the player, by not providing the player with help or power-ups, or even an agenda to remember what to do. Time passes and it is very challenging to achieve all the goals set for the day. *Cart Life* is an example of *procedural rhetoric*, where the procedures of the game imply and convey a certain meaning as the player plays the game[14]; it is therefore necessary to explain not only the novel mechanics but also what they mean.

Games may also have different play modes, something already noted in Chapter 3. In relation to this building block, different modes usually imply different rules, or at least variations on a common set of rules. For example, *Combat* (1977) uses different modes to introduce variations on the basic rules of the game. It is a two-player game where each player controls an army vehicle of the same type (tanks, biplanes, or jets) to fight each other. In each mode, players choose which type of weaponry they will use in the match, from straight or guided missiles to bouncy bullets that will ricochet on the borders of the screen. The combinations of ships and weapons create 27 different game modes.

In contrast, modern games may feature diverse modes with different goals. The different modes of *Super Smash Bros. Melee* (2001) have already been discussed in Chapter 3; each mode might be considered a different game and analyzed independently from each other.

When a game has different modes, be explicit about the variety in the rules, mostly because it means that the rules of the game may be different. Even when we focus on a single mode, it should be clear to the reader that there are different ways to play the game. An overview of the rules is also the setup of a formal analysis, which explains them and breaks them down.

Questions that help describe the rules and goals of the game:

- What are the rules of the game? What are the constraints and affordances provided to the player?
- Is there a goal in the game? Does achieving the goal end the game?
- What are the different modes of the game? How does each mode change the core rule set of the game?

Further Reading

Egenfeldt-Nielsen, Simon, Jonas Heide Smith, and Susana Pajares Tosca. *Understanding Video Games: The Essential Introduction*. 4th edn. London: Routledge, 2020, pp. 122–126.

Fullerton, Tracy. *Game Design Workshop: A Playcentric Approach to Creating Innovative Games*. 4th edn. Boca Raton, FL: CMP Books, 2019, Chapter 2 "The Structure of Games" and Chapter 3 "Working with Formal Elements."

Salen, Katie, and Eric Zimmerman. *Rules of Play: Game Design Fundamentals*. Cambridge, MA: The MIT Press, 2004, pp. 116–266.

BOX 4.2 EXERCISE: GETTING TO THE CORE OF HOW TO PLAY A GAME

Explain how to play the game you are analyzing to someone who does not know much about games, especially if it is digital, without showing them the game. If possible, explain it in person rather than in written form, so that they can ask you questions about what they do not understand. The aim of the exercise is to practice summarizing how a game works, as well as to recognize which aspects of the game rules one may be taking for granted. What are the basic rules to get someone started on the game? Which aspects of the game are easier to understand? Which ones are more difficult to pick up? How can showing the game itself facilitate the explanation?

Game Mechanics Related to the rules of the game, this building block accounts for the regulations applied to player behavior. While the rules of the game above describe the game in formal terms, and will probably be easier to explain for non-digital games or games with a few rules, games with complex rules and rich game worlds may be better served by explaining what the player can actually do. We already saw some of the issues derived from generalizing player experience in Chapter 2. Our own experience is always difficult to generalize because there can be myriad ways to play a game, and players can bend the rules and come up with their own goals, so one should be aware of those differences and qualify them.

A helpful concept to understand the difference between the rules of the game and gameplay is the distinction between the *rules* and the *mechanics* of the game.[15] While the rules can dictate how the game works, the mechanics refer to the rules that establish how the player participates in the game. Some game designers, like Chris Crawford, identify the mechanics as the *verbs* of the game: the palette of actions available to the player.[16] For example, in *Super Mario Bros.* (1985), the verbs include *run, jump, pick up*; the rules of the game, on the other hand, dictate how the enemies move, or how the score increases. In *Super Street Fighter IV* (2010), the mechanics define the varieties of punching and kicking, which combined yield a wide range of verbs. Each character may have moves that are unique to the character, from the famous *hadouken*, which allows hitting the opponent from a distance, to a stranglehold.

A clear example of the difference between rules and mechanics is Will Wright's first game, *Raid on Bungeling Bay* (1984). The player controls a helicopter and needs to bomb six different factories while dodging the attacks from below. The rules of the game establish how the world works. The factories keep building technologies that the enemy will use against the player and there are also boats that bring supplies from one factory to another. There is a complex system by which, the more they remain intact, the stronger the attacks will be over time. The mechanics refer only to what the player can do, which is to pilot the helicopter and bomb the factories.

For the sake of brevity, and if it is relevant, the analysis may focus on the core mechanics of the game. Salen and Zimmerman provide a clear definition of what a core mechanic is:

> A core mechanic is the essential play activity players perform again and again in a game. Sometimes, the core mechanic of a game is a single action. In a footrace, for example, the core mechanic is running … However,

> in many games the core mechanic is a compound activity composed of a suite of actions. In a first-person shooter game such as *Quake*, the core mechanic is the set of interrelated actions of moving, aiming, firing, and managing resources such as health, ammo and armor.[17]

Thus, we have a set of verbs that make up the vocabulary of possible actions in the game. By identifying the core mechanics, we can figure out what the game is actually about. The consonance or dissonance between the set of verbs and the supposed theme of the game can be a source of discussion, as we will see in Chapter 5.

Questions whose responses allow describing the gameplay of a game:

- What does the player do in the game?
- What are the verbs that describe the basic actions?
- What are the core mechanics of the game? How are they meaningful?
- Which actions are less frequent?
- How does the player perform the actions in the game?

Further Reading

Crawford, Chris. *Chris Crawford on Interactive Storytelling*. 1st edn. New Riders Games. Berkeley, CA: New Riders, 2005.

Sicart, Miguel. "Defining Game Mechanics." *Game Studies: The International Journal of Computer Game Research 8*, no. 2 (2008). Available at: http://gamestudies.org/0802/articles/sicart. Accessed November 4, 2023.

BOX 4.3 EXERCISE: COUNTING THE VERBS

Take the game that you are analyzing and list its core mechanics in the form of verbs. How many verbs are there? Are there combinations of verbs that allow for new actions?

Use that list to compare the game to another, finding their commonalities and differences. For example, compare *Deus Ex* (2000), an action role-playing game, with a first-person shooter, such as *Bioshock* (2007). They are both first-person narrative games, but based on their verbs, what are the commonalities? What sets them apart?

Spaces of the Game The term *space* can have a multiplicity of meanings in relation to games. It can be the space in which the game takes place, how it is divided, and how it is arranged (a *level*, which we will discuss in Chapter 5); it can also refer to the space of possibility, that is, the range of potential actions and events. Since this area is concerned with discussing what sets the game apart from others, the first thing to look at in terms of space is whether its configuration stands out from others or relates to the other aspects of the game in a productive way. Let us see what this means in more detail.

A first step to identify the space of the game is to determine the relationship between the game actions and the activities of everyday life. The recovered concept of Huizinga's *magic circle* has become a common defining concept of games, mainly because games take place in a ritual space, that is, a space where the rules of everyday life do not quite apply.[18] In a game of Chess, for example, the King is the most valuable piece on the board, but only if a game is being played—otherwise it may only be a piece of plastic. In a sport like basketball, for example, if players touch the ball with their feet while in the court they are breaking the rules. Many sports usually define the field in which the rules are in effect—when the players or the ball go out of bounds, the game stops. Card games define a space by sitting around a table or a circle of players, so that it becomes a space of agreement.

Defining the boundaries of the circle or whether the circle actually exists is one of the challenges when analyzing certain games.[19] Alternate reality games, for example, thrive on the ambiguity of using real-world spaces, and not acknowledging that they are games in the first place. In a different example, the augmented reality game[20] *Pokémon Go* (2016–) made players go out into the streets to hunt Pokémon, and train them in virtual gyms, which were located in real-world locations, encouraging new types of social interactions as well as ways to shield oneself from everyday life.[21] The ambiguity of space can be a great topic to tease out from the standpoint of many fields—from its ontology (that is, how it exists and constructs a reality), to the social implications of creating a space of play, to the design challenges of effacing the magic circle.

In the specific case of videogames, the space is defined by the relationship between five different planes, as Michael Nitsche argues:[22]

1. Rule-based space: "defined by the mathematical rules that set, for example, physics, sounds, AI, and game level architecture."

2. Mediated space: "defined by the presentation, which is the space of the image plane and the use of this image including the cinematic form of presentation."

3. Fictional space: "that lives in the imagination, in other words, the space 'imagined' by players from their comprehension of the available images."

4. Play space: "meaning space of the play, which includes the player and the videogame hardware."

5. Social space: "defined by interaction with others, meaning the game space of other players affected (e.g., in a multiplayer title)."

Every videogame will establish different relationships between each plane. Some of these spaces (e.g., the play space, the social space) may be considered part of the context of the game, which was discussed in Chapter 3, as the physical and social context of the game. The relationship between these planes is what defines the primary space of the game.

The videogame itself also creates a virtual space, which is mediated, rule-based, and fictional, as Nitsche describes. The discussion of the spaces of the game can focus on how it is constructed in relation to these three planes. Jenkins argues that the practice of game design is *narrative architecture*,[23] so that designers create spaces to explore and navigate at the same time the player becomes part of a fictional narrative world. Movement through the space, contests, and exploration, thus, become basic qualities of the space of the game.

The space is rule-based because the way in which the objects in the game move is also regulated. For example, in Monopoly (1935) the pieces can only move clockwise and from square to square; in Chess, every piece can only move on the board following a specific pattern. In digital games, these rules are part of the code—the designer has to determine the objects' movement in order to implement them in the game. There is also a distinction between the rules and the game mechanics that apply to movement. Arcade games are a clear example—in the game *Galaxian* (1979), the player can move the spaceship at the bottom side to side and shoot at any time (see Figure 4.2). The enemy spaceships also move side to side, but they can also leave the formation and twirl around, moving up or down; they can only shoot the

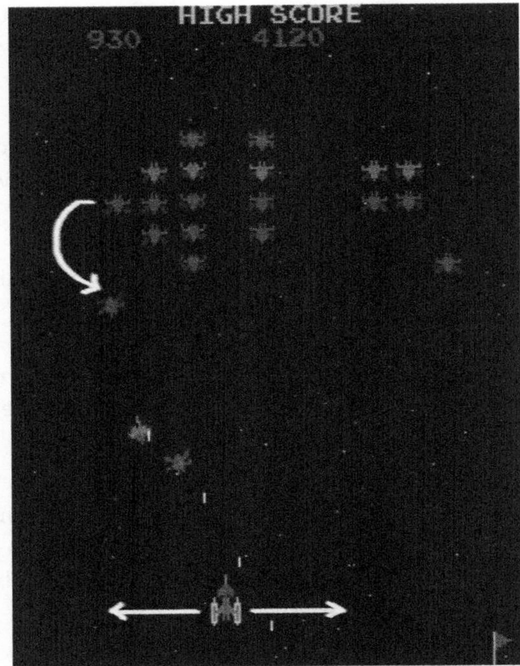

Figure 4.2 **In *Galaxian*, the player controls the ship at the bottom, while the ships move sideways and then flow down the screen**

player while they are moving, though. The difference between how the player ship and the enemy ships move creates an asymmetry between them—they cannot move and attack their opponent in the same way. The rules that define how objects move in the world indicate the *cardinality of the game world*, whereas the rules that refer to the movement player mechanics define the *cardinality of gameplay*.[24]

Derived from its rule-based nature, the space is also structured and segmented. In board games we have squares or tiles, for example, in digital games, the space is mediated, and we interact with it through the screen.

There can be different ways in which the space is structured. The space can be divided into screens, for example, the different levels in *Donkey Kong* (1981) or *Pitfall!* (1982) use separate screens; once one screen is traversed successfully, the player can move on to the next. The design can also structure how the player moves in the space—in *Bioshock* (2007), for example, each new level has certain areas that are locked, which open up after the player figures out how to open a door and fix the access to it, or kills an enemy. How the player sees the world of the game, and how the space shapes the way the player interacts with it, create a structure for the navigation and gameplay actions. The Levels and Level Design building block in Chapter 5 describes how to analyze these configurations in more detail.

The mediated space and how it is represented to the player may be familiar to those with a background in film and media studies. The space can be represented two-dimensionally, like a cartoon, or in three dimensions. It is relatively easy to apply concepts such as the *mise-en-scène* (how the spatial elements are composed), or how each shot constructs the space. Mark J.P. Wolf produced one of the earliest theoretical approaches to examining the space of videogames based on comparisons with film shots, a common analytical approach to games since the camera provides a point of view in the world for the player. (The definition of *point of view* will be unpacked in Chapter 5.)[25]

The difference with spaces represented in photography, film, painting, or even literature is that videogame spaces are *navigable*:[26] the player participates in the space and may change or manipulate the objects in it. Digital media also allow spaces to be non-topographical, so we cannot physically map them and they can also defy the laws of physics. The labyrinths of the Atari VCS version of *Adventure* (1979) are famous for warping the space, while the core mechanics of *Portal* (2007) involve opening space portals to reconfigure the space and the way that it is navigated, turning navigation and reconfiguration into the challenge of the game.

When defining the fictional space of the game, the first question to ask is whether it can be considered a world. While games like *Bioshock* introduce rich environments with a story, it is difficult to discuss the fictional world of *Tetris* (1987). Even fighting games, where there is an implied fictional world, are difficult to discuss in terms of that world, since the player cannot navigate or take action on it—the only thing the player can interact with is the other player. We will deal with the fictional world in the next building block. Examining the play space of the game helps us understand how it is played in its physical context, and what assumptions have been made about how players need to interact with the game. For example, games using gestural interfaces usually take a large space to move around—*Dance Central* (2010) requires the space of a living room so the Kinect device can capture your whole body, and may be hard to play in a smaller living room, let alone a bedroom. Some VR technology set-ups initially required setting up sensors (called *lighthouses*) to play a game where the player can walk around a virtual world, so a home VR set-up would need a large empty space in order to move without bumping into real furniture. The cumbersome set up of these VR technologies has now been replaced by more efficient devices—users just need a headset and controllers in order to navigate the virtual space, acknowledging that not all players may have a physical space to play because they live in small apartments or a dorm room.

The social space of the game is particularly relevant to multiplayer games because the relationships between players are also part of the game. This should be obvious in the case of board games, but it is not very different in the case of local multiplayer or party videogames, as well as online games. The opportunities provided to taunt each other, give instructions, or mislead your opponents can make or break a game. For example, the game *Overcooked* (2016) is a cooperative cooking game that requires players to talk to each other in order to prepare ingredients, cook, and serve them, as well as keep a good supply of clean dishes. If players do not tell each other what they are doing or what needs to be done or they do not listen, it is impossible to succeed—very much like in a real kitchen job.

But a game does not have to be multiplayer for the social space to be relevant to our analysis—in the Number of Players building block, I already mentioned how adventure games can be multiplayer because people can get together and discuss what to do. The core challenge of these games is often based on problem-solving, which can be done in groups. I have run events where a room full of people played text adventure games, by having one person typing the commands, while the room discussed and shouted out what they wanted to do.

There are hardware platforms whose design encourages games that take advantage of the possibilities of the play and social space of the game. For example, the last three generations of Nintendo consoles (Wii, WiiU, and Switch) all provide affordances to play games beyond a single player in front of the screen. The Wii was first to focus on gestural interfaces as a way to control the games—rather than as add-on hardware—as well as facilitating party games, which attracted a lot of people who did not consider videogames their kind of pastime. The WiiU has a controller with a screen, which could be used as a standalone console without a larger screen, or as a parallel screen to the main one. The screen in the controller can be used as a device to create asymmetrical information in a multiplayer game (see *Luigi's Mansion* mentioned in the Number of Players building block above), or as a way to divide the player's attention and create tension during gameplay. For instance, *ZombiU* (2012) is a survival horror game which used the game controller screen to display the inventory. Unlike other games, where you can pause while going through the items the player character carries, it meant that if the player wanted something from their backpack, they had to look for things while they could be attacked by a zombie any time. The design of the Nintendo Switch is a step further into considering the use of the play and social space—it is portable but can also be connected to a large screen; it is supposed to facilitate playing a multiplayer videogame any time by having its controllers detach from the main console. The console can thus be reconfigured depending on the play and social space in which its games are going to be played.

Questions to describe the space(s) of the game:

- How does the game create a space distinct (or not) from everyday life?
- What is the relationship between the game and the physical space it is played in?
- How is the space represented (2D/3D)?
- What is the point of view of the player?
- How can the player navigate the space?
- How do the objects in the space move?
- How is the space divided?
- How are the objects arranged in the space? Are they supposed to help or hinder the player?

Further Reading

Egenfeldt-Nielsen, Simon, Jonas Heide Smith, and Susana Pajares Tosca. *Understanding Video Games: The Essential Introduction*. 4th edn. London: Routledge, 2020, pp. 129–139.

Fernández-Vara, Clara, Jose P. Zagal, and Michael Mateas. "Evolution of Spatial Configurations in Video Games." *In Worlds in Play: International Perspectives on Digital Games Research*, edited by Suzanne De Castell and Jennifer Jenson. New York: Peter Lang, 2007, pp. 159–168.

Huizinga, Johan. *Homo Ludens: A Study of the Play-Element in Culture*. Humanitas, Beacon Reprints in Humanities. Boston: Beacon Press, 1955.

Nitsche, Michael. *Video Game Spaces: Image, Play, and Structure in 3D Worlds*. Cambridge, MA: The MIT Press, 2009.

Wolf, Mark J.P. *The Medium of the Video Game*. 1st edn. Austin, TX: University of Texas Press, 2002, Chapter 3.

Fictional World of the Game A fictional world is the imagined world in which the actions and events of a game take place. Identifying the game world helps to establish connections with other games and media as part of their context, as discussed in the previous area. Covering the fictional world in the overview allows us to identify the theme of the game, what happens in the world, and which conventions and stories the world may evoke in the player.

As discussed above, not all games have fictional worlds—it is difficult to think of *Tetris* or Poker requiring the creation of an imagined world. Many games present a fictional world within which the player interacts: *Grand Theft Auto IV* (2008) takes place in Liberty City; the *Monkey Island* series (1990–2022) takes place across different fictional islands of the Caribbean. Fictional worlds are not exclusive of digital games—games of make-believe create imagined worlds, such as cops and robbers, space opera, or a fairy kingdom. Table-top role-playing games also thrive in building fictional worlds—the *Planescape* campaign setting is a world that encompasses different planes of existence which link several worlds from *Dungeons and Dragons*, interconnected through dimensional portals.[27]

Explaining the basic functions of a fictional world sets up player expectations, since different worlds will have different agents, events, and actions associated with them. For example, the *King's Quest* adventure game series (1984–2016) is set in a fairy-tale world, so we can presuppose we will be the hero or heroine of the tale, there will be magic enchantments, witches and wizards, kings and queens, princes and princesses, peasants and innkeepers, gnomes, and other magical beings. Breaking spells and solving riddles are going to be some of our basic interactions derived from fairy tales.

On the other hand, the fictional world of *Mass Effect* (2007) evokes the space opera genre, with trans-galactic voyages, planets inhabited by a variety of alien races, and advanced technology as a way to tackle and solve problems. In contrast, the world of the *Assassin's Creed* series (2007–2023) uses different historical settings for each instalment, from the Middle East in the twelfth century, to the American Northeast during the American Revolution, to Egypt during the Ptolemaic period. These settings are brought together by the core premise of the game, which is the use of a technology in the fictional present, the Animus, that allows its users to experience the memories of their ancestors in the form of a virtual simulation—in a way, they are a game within a game. The world of *Assassin's Creed* is therefore both each individual historical world and how the Animus allows players to explore them. Thus, the fictional world and the rules are interdependent—the extent of this interdependence will be dealt with in Chapter 5, in the Relationship between Rules and the Fictional World building block.

The fictional world also sets up a theme, which can be in consonance (or not) with the actions that the player has to do. Soren Johnson discusses how theme is different from meaning, so what the box of the game may indicate may be different from what the players actually do in the game. For example, *Spore* (2008) is not about evolution, but rather about building and growing (creatures, vehicles, cities, civilizations) and sharing.[28]

Questions to identify and discuss the fictional world of the game:

- Where does the game take place?
- Is the fictional world associated with a specific genre (sci-fi, fantasy, mystery, etc.)?
- Is the fictional world based on an actual historical setting?
- What is the player's role in the fictional world?

Further Reading

Brand, Jeffrey E., Scott Knight, and Jakub Majewski. "The Diverse Worlds of Computer Games: A Content Analysis of Spaces, Populations, Styles and Narratives." In *DiGRA '03 - Proceedings of the 2003 DiGRA International Conference: Level Up*. Utrecht, 2003.

de la Maza, Antonio José Planells, Antonio José. *Possible Worlds in Video Games: From Classic Narrative to Meaningful Actions*. Pittsburgh, PA: ETC Press, 2017.

Wolf, Mark J.P. *Building Imaginary Worlds: The Theory and History of Subcreation*. 1st edn. London: Routledge, 2012.

Story The fictional world is the setting for the events of the story of the game. This is why games with less fleshed-out fictional worlds, such as fighting games or racing games, usually have less complex stories, which are also traditionally less related to what the player actually does in the game.

The application of the term *story* to games is problematic, first, because there are many games that are difficult to understand as stories, *Tetris* (1987) being a typical example. However, fictional worlds in games are so common we must wonder how games may aim at creating narrative experiences. AAA developers certainly seem to display narrative aspirations in works such as the *Uncharted* series (2007–2017) or the *Metal Gear* series (1987–2018). In some cases, presenting a summary of the story premise of the game—if there is one—helps in introducing the fictional world of the game and its starting point. For example, this can be one way to summarize the story premise of *Mask of the Rose* (2023):

> The game starts in an alternate version of London in 1862, in the aftermath of a cataclysm that has caused London to sink underground and become separated from the rest of England. While the government and Queen Victoria are nowhere to be seen, a new set of masters rule the sunken world. The player can explore the newly arranged streets of London, meet its inhabitants, take on jobs and try to figure out the mysteries behind the catastrophic relocation of the city—the story of who they are is all up to the player.

If determining the story of the game seems complicated at first, we have some tricks up our sleeve. The blurbs featured in boxes or download pages can provide a quick summary of the story of the game, which we can then quote. Independent games, for example, often have a section in their website with their press kit materials, which often include a summary of the story premise of the game. It is important to remember, however, that those blurbs are written by the marketing department, and might be misrepresentations of the game. (That also means that discussing how marketing presents the game and what the game is actually about can be a good starting point for an essay.) Bringing your own take on the story is part of the contribution and originality of your analysis.

The story premise is a high-level summary that introduces the reader to the world and the story of the game. The equivalent in film and television jargon is the term *log line*, a one-sentence summary of the plot and what makes the story distinctive. Since the term *story* has already been identified as complex, it is a good exercise to think about what the term means in relation to the game we are analyzing. The story of the game can be defined within two main domains: the story of the fictional world and the story of the player.

In relation to the fictional world of the game, there are two levels of the story:

- Story of the game world: the events that have happened in the world before the game starts. This story may or may not be part of what the player does in the game. Many games have this without being necessarily story-driven, such as *Mirror's Edge* (2008), a first-person *parkour* game, or the *Wipeout* racing games (1995–2012).
- Gameplay may be based on discovering this story, as is the case with detective games: *Gabriel Knight: Sins of the Fathers* (1993), *Myst* (1993), the *Blackwell* series (2006–2014), *Mask of the Rose* (2023).

In contrast, the story of the player comprises the events that happen as the game play unfolds. I am going to use Marc LeBlanc's terms, although I am tweaking the definition to make it encompass a more flexible explanation of story:[29]

- *Embedded storytelling*: the events have been pre-set by the developers as a series of milestones or specific set of actions that the player needs to perform to advance. One way to pre-determine the events is to represent them in the form of pre-set texts or cut-scenes, as in the *Metal Gear* series. Another way is to make a sequence of narrative events into something that the player has to do. Many point-and-click adventure games, such as *The Secret of Monkey Island* (1990), use puzzles as a way to set those events; role-playing games such as *Mass Effect* use quests as a way to pre-determine specific events, even if they change, depending on the choices of the player.
- *Emergent storytelling*: the story events that are generated as the player interacts with the fictional world. This is more common in the simulation genre, where there is a complex system with many variables that the player can tackle in many different ways. The key here is that the

> story events are propitiated by the system, but not necessarily anticipated by the developers. Simulation games such as *The Sims* series (2000–2023) or strategy games such as the *Civilization* (1991–2016) series are typical examples of these. There is also a whole genre of games using procedural content generation, where the world and events are different every time a game starts, which can also give way to emergent storytelling. Games such as *FTL: Faster Than Light* (2012) or *Darkest Dungeon* (2016) use generated spaces and challenges (the first one in outer space, the other in a deep dungeon) to create dramatic situations and make players face one dilemma after another.

The story of the game is often a combination of both embedded and emergent storytelling, for example, the *Grand Theft Auto* series (1997–2013) is recognized for having a rich world where the player can do a great variety of things (from car stunts to driving a cab or an ambulance, or playing videogames within the videogame), yet, at the same time, there is a specific story arch in each game that consists of a series of pre-determined missions. Even in the case of adventure games, where the events are often pre-established, there is often a good deal of exploration and experimentation in the world that can be considered a type of emergent storytelling. There is also a game design school that can be termed *simulationist*, which aspires to create story-driven game-rich worlds that will generate fulfilling dramatic stories, combining computer role-playing games that encourage the player to tackle the challenges with their own play style, finding solutions that may not have been predicted by the developers. Games such as *Deus Ex* (2000) attempt this approach; the *Dishonored* series (2012–2017) is derived from the same game design school. Emergent storytelling is one of the current challenges of story-driven game design, where the simulated world would encourage multiple replays that would allow the story to be completely different each time.

In summary, the story of the game does not consist merely of providing a synopsis, as one would do when analyzing a film or a novel. We also have to take into account the level at which the story takes place and how it relates to gameplay.

Questions to identify and discuss the story of the game:

- What is the story premise of the game?
- Who does the player control (if that is the case)?

- What has happened in the fictional world before the game starts? How does it relate to the gameplay of the game?
- How do the player's actions constitute events in the game?
- Which events of the story are told in non-interactive media? Which happen during gameplay?
- How does the system of the game bring about story events?

Further Reading

Egenfeldt-Nielsen, Simon, Jonas Heide Smith, and Susana Pajares Tosca. *Understanding Video Games: The Essential Introduction*. 4th edn. London: Routledge, 2020, Chapter 7.

Kirkland, Ewan. "Storytelling in Survival Horror Video Games." In *Horror Video Games: Essays on the Fusion of Fear and Play*, edited by Bernard Perron. Jefferson, NC: MacFarland, 2009, pp. 62–78.

Klevjer, Rune. "In Defence of Cutscenes." In *Computer Games and Digital Cultures Conference Proceedings*. Tampere: Tampere University Press, 2002.

BOX 4.4 EXERCISE: WHAT MAKES A GAME STORY-DRIVEN?

This exercise should help you identify if your game is story-driven or if it is a game with a story. The first step is summarizing what the player does. Can it be condensed in the form of a story? If it can, then make a short timeline of the game, or at least of a segment of the game, or in the case of branching storylines, just represent a walkthrough of the game. Draw a line and mark the most significant events in the story. What does the player do for that action to happen? Does the player actually carry out the actions in that event? Or is that event a cut-scene given as a reward to the player (e.g., the story mode of fighting games like *Street Fighter IV*)? Do the player's actions actually consist of revealing the story events that have happened in the past (e.g., *Myst*)?

The more you can map the events of the story to actions carried out by the player, the more confident we can be that a game is story-driven. If the events of the story are a reward for certain actions and the gameplay is not part of the events, you are playing a game with a story. You will be identifying where the game is on a spectrum, rather than whether it is one or another label.

Gameplay Experience By providing a brief account of what playing the game is like, the reader can get the gist of the gameplay even if they have not played themselves. However, we have already seen how summarizing the experience of playing the game is certainly tricky, since generalizing each player's personal experience is practically impossible. On the other hand, the experience of the player can also be crucial to understanding the game, so much so that the analysis can focus on experience itself. In general, the focus on this building block should not be on whether playing the game is "good" or "bad"—which is overtly subjective—but rather how the player is a participant in the game, and how players can understand the game as they play. So, a good prompt to develop this block is to ask oneself: "What does the player *do*?"

There are basic methods by which player experience can be accounted for in an analytical way. On the one hand, the gameplay and experience of players can be documented, usually through ethnographic work, or the analysis can focus on the author's own experience, recorded in notes, diaries, or audio/video recordings. (There was an overview of this in Chapter 2, and there will be more about it in Chapter 6, when the analysis of game communities is discussed in more detail.)

A brief account of the gameplay experience, in an abstract, less subjective mode, looks something like this:

> *Dance Dance Revolution* (1999) is not really about dancing, but rather hitting the giant buttons on the pad to the rhythm of the music. In higher difficulties, the player's feet stomp so rapidly that it looks more like running than dancing—the arcade cabinet includes a railing around them so players can support themselves while they race. Only the most skillful players can look like they are actually dancing, by moving their arms in unison with their feet and even twirling around; otherwise, most players look like runners in place, focusing on the game screen.

The abundance of players streaming their gameplay and *let's play* videos provides us with an additional resource to understand better how players may experience the game, given that we see them play, narrate what they are doing, and, often, react to the events in the game. One should be aware, however, that streamers are also performing for an audience, so their work may be stylized, dramatized, or otherwise optimized to attract viewers—the self-awareness of streamers does affect the style and presentation of their gameplay. However, streams can still be information that we can use in our analyses. Comparing how someone else plays the game with our own experience can help us bring a new perspective on what the "experience" is like, and realize the subjectivity of the term.

For the overview, the idea is to provide an account of what playing the game is like. One thing is explaining the rules and mechanics of the game or the story events; the other is explaining what the experience is like and the types of interactions the game encourages. This building block is subjective, which is okay, but be aware of it. When this building block becomes central to the analysis, we have a personal account, which, as we will see in Chapter 6, is a very specific type of analysis where subjectivity is both our best and worst asset.

Questions to discuss player experience:

- What is the attitude of the player toward the game? Is it amusing/threatening/scary, etc.?
- How does the player respond to the challenges in the game?
- If the game is multiplayer, what type of interactions take place between players?

Further Reading

Keogh, Brendan, Daniel Purvis, Rob Zacny, and Benjamin Abraham. *Killing Is Harmless: A Critical Reading of Spec Ops: The Line*. 1st edn. Stolen Projects, 2013.

Leino, Olli, Hanna Wirman, and Amyris Fernandez. *Extending Experiences*. Rovaniemi: Lapland University Press, 2008.

Sudnow, David. *Pilgrim in the Microworld*. New York: Warner Books, 1983.

Taylor, T. L. *Watch Me Play: Twitch and the Rise of Game Live Streaming*. Princeton Studies in Culture and Technology. Princeton, NJ: Princeton University Press, 2018.

BOX 4.5 EXERCISE: PLAYER-WATCHING

One of the easiest ways to realize how a game is an experience is just by looking at how people play the game. Watch somebody play a videogame—if you do not have a willing subject at hand, there are plenty of videos online of players who record themselves and their families playing together, as well as streamers who provide commentary on the games they play live, often also broadcasting their own faces alongside the game (though remember that they are also performing for an audience).

Rather than describing what is on the screen, note how they react to the game. Games that use motion-sensing devices, such as the Xbox Kinect, the Joy-Cons for Nintendo Switch, or the DualSense controller for Playstation, provide us with even more information about how players engage physically with the game.

How does their face express emotion? Are they smiling or serious? Does it look like they are making a mental or physical effort? What are they doing with the rest of the body? Are they leaning forward/backward? Are they shifting on their seat?

Players' facial gestures and body language provide a novel point of view to analyze games. Can we differentiate someone playing a horror game from someone playing a real-time strategy game? How do different people engage with the same game?

Game Communities Games can create a community of players in and around them. While the Audience building block described in Chapter 3 referred to players as an abstract concept, this building block analyzes the communities that are formed in or around a game. The way this building block contributes to the overview is to establish how relevant the community is to the game.

The community may be peripheral, which means they are not integrated as part of the game itself. There may be fan communities that are created around a game or game series, similar to how fan communities may be created around television shows, films, books, you name it. A marketing department or game distribution services may encourage the creation of these communities by hosting official forums, for example—they are interested in knowing how players receive the game, what the specifics are of the abstract concept of audience they had before the game was released. The role of community managers is increasingly relevant to game development, especially in online games that are living services; independent developers also use applications such as Discord or Twitch as a way to grow and cultivate the community around their games. Forums, Discord servers, fan wikis, as well as other types of player-created content, help us learn more about the game and how it is actually played.

There are communities of players that create content for the game, often using tools provided by the game itself. Games such as *LittleBigPlanet* (2008) incorporate tools to access content created by other players, whereas *Animal Crossing: Happy Home Designer* (2015) allows players to decorate homes, inside and out, share their designs, as well as importing other players' designs and modify them. These communities of developers can help us understand the formal aspects of a game, based on the expertise they need and how they may support and teach each other how to develop content, as well as the types of topics and designs that they create and how they may subvert the tools provided— this will be discussed at more length in Chapter 5.

Games can also create a community of players inside them, as is the case of massively multiplayer online games. The fictional world of the game is always online; it is persistent, a space where players can come in and interact with others as well as with the world of the game. These virtual worlds become social structures with economies and history. Players who participate in them also have to decide how they want to present themselves in the community. At times the identity is limited to a name or a handle, because there is not an avatar, as is the case of online board games, while pet breeding games, such as *NeoPets* (1999–) or the now defunct MMOG *Faunasphere* (2009–2011), have the player's animal collection as the signifier of their identity. In other cases, the identity of the player is defined by the look of their avatar and their behavior in the world. The looks can be as detailed as the 3D renderings of *World of Warcraft* (2004–) or *Genshin Impact* (2020–), or as cartoony as *Puzzle Pirates* (2003–) or *Ragnarok Online* (2002–). There will also be different types of players, with different goals and attitudes toward the game.[30] Studying online game communities is literally entering another world, which this book can only give you a peek into—the analysis of game communities will be discussed in Chapter 6.

The increasing ease with which one can stream one's gameplay online has also opened the floodgates to the creation of communities around a specific game, which watch other people play, and comment on each other.

Streaming also led to experiences such as Twitch Plays Pokémon, where a set-up connected *Pokémon Red* (1998) to the input of the chat that runs alongside video streams on Twitch, allowing players to control the game through their text input.[31] More than 60,000 players at a time were watching the stream, many of them inputting commands to play the game, until the game was completed. This social experiment was so successful that the channel has continued broadcasting this type of crowdfunded play at the time of writing,[32] and also spawned a whole category of channels that allowed the audience to control the game called "Twitch Plays."[33] Although these streams were a fad for a few years, the TwitchPlaysPokemon twitch channel is still active at the time of writing, and has continued streaming gameplay of different Pokémon titles with the input of their audience.[34]

In analyzing the specifics of players as a whole, we need to determine the relationship between the players and the game, how it is motivated, and how it relates to the content of the game.

Questions to define the game community of a game:

- Are there groups of players around the game? What tools do they use to get together?
- Does the game provide tools for the players to interact together (e.g., chat windows, exchange of content, meeting spaces)?
- Does the game create a community in its fictional world?
- What is the common interest that made the game community get together in the first place? How is it different from other game communities related to the same game?

Further Reading

Bartle, Richard. "Hearts, Clubs, Diamonds, Spades: Players Who Suit MUDs." In *The Game Design Reader: A Rules of Play Anthology*, edited by Katie Salen and Eric Zimmerman. Cambridge, MA: The MIT Press, 2006.

Pearce, Celia, and Artemesia. *Communities of Play: Emergent Cultures in Multiplayer Games and Virtual Worlds*. Cambridge, MA: The MIT Press, 2009.

Taylor, T.L. *Play Between Worlds: Exploring Online Game Culture*. Cambridge, MA: The MIT Press, 2006.

Yee, Nick. "Motivations for Play in Online Games." *CyberPsychology & Behavior* 9, no. 6 (2006): 772–775.

Zimmerman, Joshua J. "Computer Game Fan Communities, Community Management, and Structures of Membership." *Games and Culture*, December 13, 2017.

▶ TO SUM UP

The building blocks that comprise the overview give the reader a gist of what the game is about, to get across its main features and make it intelligible to readers who may not be familiar with it. It is always useful to provide a summary of these building blocks, even if the analysis focuses on some other topic entirely, as we will see in Chapter 6. This area is mainly descriptive, so analyses where these building blocks are predominant will usually be closer to reports, or personal accounts of gameplay.

Many of these building blocks relate to building blocks in other areas, so they can also be expanded as a combination of related building blocks (e.g., number of players as a formal element, the relationship between game spaces). The relationships between these building blocks can also become the foundation for including further building blocks, and the main topic of an analysis. In the following area, for example, the relationship between rules and the fictional world becomes an important topic of discussion, which explores the tension between the system and the representations in the game.

▶ NOTES

1 Fullerton, Tracy. *Game Design Workshop: A Playcentric Approach to Creating Innovative Games*. 4th edn (Boca Raton, FL: CRC Press / Taylor & Francis Group, 2019), pp. 59–64.

2 Morris, Dave, Kevin Jenkins, Jamie Thomson, and Russ Nicholson. *Fabled Lands: The War-Torn Kingdom* (Fabled Lands, 2010); Ward, Michael J. *Destiny Quest: The Legion of Shadow* (London: Gollancz, 2012).

3 Huizinga, Johan. *Homo Ludens: A Study of the Play-Element in Culture*. Humanitas, Beacon Reprints in Humanities (Boston: Beacon Press, 1955), pp. 30–31; Caillois, Roger. *Man, Play and Games* (Urbana, IL: University of Illinois Press, 1961), pp. 14–19.

4 Fullerton. *Game Design Workshop*, p. 63.

5 Fluegelman, Andrew. *The New Games Book* (Garden City, NY: Dolphin Books, 1976).

6 Zagal, Jose P., Clara Fernández-Vara, and Michael Mateas. "Rounds, Levels and Waves: The Early Evolution of Gameplay Segmentation." *Games and Culture* 3, no. 2 (2008): 175–198.

7 Boellstorff, Tom, Bonnie Nardi, Celia Pearce, and T.L. Taylor. *Ethnography and Virtual Worlds: A Handbook of Method* (Princeton, NJ: Princeton University Press, 2012).

8 Bartle, Richard. "Hearts, Clubs, Diamonds, Spades: Players Who Suit MUDs." In *The Game Design Reader: A Rules of Play Anthology*, edited by Katie Salen and Eric Zimmerman (Cambridge, MA: The MIT Press, 2006).

9 The list of most popular *Minecraft* servers shows how many of them can host around 1000–2000 players. Available at: https://minecraft-server-list.com/sort/Popular/ (accessed November 4, 2023). The most popular servers at the time of writing can host up to 9999 players. Available at: https://minecraft-server-list.com/server/292028/ (accessed November 4, 2023).

10 Partlett, David. *The Oxford History of Board Games* (Oxford: Oxford University Press, 1999).

11 See Animal Crossing Wiki. Available at: http://animalcrossing.fandom.com/wiki/Animal_Crossing:_New_Leaf (accessed November 4, 2023).

12 Dahlen, Chris. "Chasing the Dollar." *Unwinnable: Life with Culture*, February 28, 2013. Available at: www.unwinnable.com/2013/02/28/chasing-the-dollar/ (accessed November 4, 2023).

13 Goodwin, Joel. "Ahead… The Stars." *Electron Dance: Words on PC Gaming*, January 17, 2012. Available at: www.electrondance.com/ahead-the-stars/ (accessed November 4, 2023).

14 Bogost, Ian. *Persuasive Games: The Expressive Power of Videogames* (Cambridge, MA: The MIT Press, 2007), pp. 28–44. The concept will be discussed in more length in the Values and Procedural Rhetoric building block in Chapter 5.

15 Sicart, Miguel. "Defining Game Mechanics." *Game Studies: The International Journal of Computer Game Research* 8, no. 2 (2008). Available at: http://gamestudies.org/0802/articles/sicart (accessed November 4, 2023).

16 Crawford, Chris. *Chris Crawford on Interactive Storytelling*. 1st edn. New Riders Games (Berkeley, CA: New Riders, 2005), pp. 91–110.

17 Salen, Katie, and Eric Zimmerman. *Rules of Play: Game Design Fundamentals* (Cambridge, MA: The MIT Press, 2004), p. 316.

18 Huizinga. *Homo Ludens,* pp. 10–14; Salen and Zimmerman. *Rules of Play,* pp. 94–98.

19 Consalvo, Mia. "There Is No Magic Circle." *Games and Culture* 4, no. 4 (October 1, 2009): 408–417.

20 *Alternate* Reality Games and *Augmented* Reality Games share initials (ARG) and are both examples of how the space of the game can be layered and complex, but they are different types of games (see Glossary).

21 Humphreys, Lee. "Involvement Shield or Social Catalyst: Thoughts on Sociospatial Practice of Pokémon GO." *Mobile Media & Communication* 5, no. 1 (January 1, 2017): 15–19.

22 Nitsche, Michael. *Video Game Spaces: Image, Play, and Structure in 3D Worlds* (Cambridge, MA: The MIT Press, 2009), pp. 15–16.

23 Jenkins, Henry. "Game Design as Narrative Architecture." In *First Person: New Media as Story, Performance, and Game,* edited by Noah Wardrip-Fruin and Pat Harrigan (Cambridge, MA: MIT Press, 2004), pp. 118–130.

24 For further definitions and discussions of the different types of cardinality, see Fernández-Vara, Clara, Jose P. Zagal, and Michael Mateas. "Evolution of Spatial Configurations in Videogames." In *Worlds in Play: International Perspectives on Digital Games Research,* edited by Suzanne De Castell and Jennifer Jenson (New York: Peter Lang, 2007), pp. 159–168.

25 Wolf, Mark J.P. *The Medium of the Video Game.* 1st edn (Austin, TX: University of Texas Press, 2002), pp. 51–76. See also Nitsche, *Video Game Spaces,* pp. 69–79, and Perron, Bernard. "The Survival Horror: The Extended Body Genre." In *Horror Video Games: Essays on the Fusion of Fear and Play,* edited by Bernard Perron (Jefferson, NC: McFarland, 2009), pp. 121–167.

26 Murray, Janet. *Hamlet on the Holodeck: The Future of Narrative in Cyberspace* (Cambridge, MA: The MIT Press, 2001), pp. 129–137.

27 Cook, David, "Zeb" Robh Ruppel, Dana Knutson, Tony DiTerlizzi, and Rob Lazzaretti. *Planescape Campaign Setting (Advanced Dungeons and Dragons)* (Wizards of the Coast, 1994).

28 Johnson, Soren. "GD Column 11: Theme Is Not Meaning (Part I)." *DESIGNER NOTES.* Available at: https://www.designer-notes.com/game-developer-column-11-theme-is-not-meaning-part-i/ (accessed November 4, 2023); "GD Column 12: Theme Is Not Meaning (Part II)." *DESIGNER NOTES.* Available at: https://www.designer-notes.com/game-developer-column-12-theme-is-not-meaning-part-ii/ (accessed November 4, 2023).

29 LeBlanc, Marc. "Tools for Creating Dramatic Game Dynamics." In *The Game Design Reader: A Rules of Play Anthology*, edited by Katie Salen and Eric Zimmerman (Cambridge, MA: The MIT Press, 2006).

30 See Bartle. "Hearts, Clubs, Diamonds, Spades: Players Who Suit MUDs," and one of the main revisions/critiques of Bartle's types, Yee, Nick. "Motivations for Play in Online Games." *CyberPsychology & Behavior* 9, no. 6 (2006): 772–775.

31 Ramirez, Dennis, Jenny Saucerman, and Jeremy Dietmeier. "Twitch Plays Pokémon: A Case Study in Big G Games." In *Proceedings of the 2014 DiGRA International Conference*, 2014.

32 "Twitch Plays Pokémon." *Twitch*. Available at: www.twitch.tv/twitchplayspokemon (accessed November 4, 2023).

33 Twitch. "Announcing the 'Twitch Plays' Game Category." *Twitch Blog*, January 13, 2016. Available at: https://blog.twitch.tv/en/2016/01/13/announcing-the-twitch-plays-game-category-55149935ad79/ (accessed November 18th, 2023).

34 *TwitchPlaysPokemon - Twitch*. Accessed November 18, 2023. https://www.twitch.tv/twitchplayspokemon.

5

Areas of Analysis 3: Formal Elements

▶ INTRODUCTION

The final area of analysis deals with the formal elements of the game. This approach relates to literature and film studies, fields where the formal description usually lays the foundation for the analysis. A description of the formal elements alone, however, may not be too useful—we need to explain how the formal elements work, how the player relates to them, why it is important to pay attention to them. Chapter 4 has already provided the building blocks to identify and describe the game and differentiate it from others. So how do the formal elements contribute to the analysis?

The formal elements are concepts and terms that help us describe the game in detail, extending its general description to detailed components, and providing insight about how it works and how it is played. This is why these building blocks are likely to appear in any type of game analysis that requires describing very specific aspects of the game with a certain level of nuance; they allow zooming in on how the game is made.

A breakdown of the formal elements is not a mere description of the design components of the game; understanding how these pieces come together should be the basis to provide insight about it. Formal elements provide a

DOI: 10.4324/9781003355779-5

material and systematic description, but they do not mean much outside of the context of play and their relationship with player experience. In literary and film studies, the relationship between form and content is a basic strategy to understand literary and cinematic works; in games, knowing how the formal elements interrelate and how players make sense of and interact with them is what helps us understand why the game is remarkable (or contemptible). The goal is not only to admire how the game is done, but how the formal elements relate to player experience.

The practice of analyzing a game formally is also particularly relevant to game designers, who must understand and be able to describe formal aspects as part of their trade. Critical game analysis is a basic skill to make games and to create one's own design palette—Richard Rouse, in his book *Game Design: Theory and Practice,* includes formal analyses of games (namely, *Centipede,*1980; *Tetris* 1987; *Loom,* 1990; *Myth: The Fallen Lords,* 1997; *The Sims,* 2000) as a way to exemplify each design concept that he discusses in the book.[1] All these analyses are framed historically, so the reader understands how these games innovated with respect to other works and how they influenced later games. Rouse's close readings are great examples of the kind of game analysis that designers, both in training and accomplished, should read and produce in order to learn how to communicate and understand their own practice better.

The limitation of analyzing games formally, however, is that the existent vocabulary is in constant development, just as games as a medium keep evolving and changing, as discussed in Chapter 1. The terminology used to describe game elements comes from a variety of sources. Some of the most extended terms come from the industry itself, others are borrowed from fields like film or marketing, and a smaller portion is derived from the academic field. There is not a wide consensus about what the basic terms are—new technologies and game designs give way to novel ways of interacting that need names, and the community of practice of developers is constantly catching up to generate new vocabulary to refer to these elements and trends. Specialized websites and trade and academic conferences are all venues that can help creating consensus, since the terms become established the more we use them. Even then, the different ranges of interested parties in games result in a variety of jargon depending on the context in which the game is being discussed. Defining one's terms is important, or else these different discourses just generate buzzwords, words that sound good and everyone thinks they know what they mean but mean something different for everyone, from *immersion* to *artificial intelligence.*

BOX 5.1 BEWARE OF BUZZWORDS

One of the recurring issues that I have to constantly remind my students about is being careful with using buzzwords. In Chapter 3, I already mentioned that labels for games come and go. There are terms that become fashionable, and everyone uses them, and then they disappear a few years later. Buzzwords are often the result of overuse of a term, which is invoked constantly and without taking into account the nuance of its meaning. This has to do a psychological phenomenon called *semantic satiation*,[2] which accounts for how a word can lose its meaning by repeating it a lot, so the word becomes a set of separate sounds and letters, and the meaning is gone. You can try it yourself—choose a word, preferably a noun, and repeat it aloud over and over again. After a bit, it just becomes a sound, not what it means.

Defining your terms is essential to your writing—Chapter 6 explains the process and reasoning in more detail. In the area of formal analysis, it is relevant because every term requires precision and clarity, whereas buzzwords usually invoke vague ideas, and may not really make the point you are trying to make, plus you may be using a term that is more complex or has a longer tradition than you may have assumed.

One such term that almost every student of mine uses at some point is *immersion*. It is a term that plagues games journalism, marketing and industry, and has given way to many academic discussions and analysis. But it is also a complex term—every semester I spend at least a whole class session just to break it down to my students. One of the most popular definitions is Murray's, who defines it as one of the essential properties of digital environments.[3] She initially defines it as "the sensation of being surrounded by a completely other reality ... that takes over all of our attention, or whole perceptual apparatus."[4] The rest of the chapter where Murray discusses the term explains different ways in which the participation in this other reality is structured, how the boundaries are established, and how different components contribute to the active creation of belief, which is what gives the player the sense that they are part of the fictional world of the game. Immersion in games involves a complicated process—from how we negotiate the space of the game with everyday life, to how we become part of its world, to how we actually feel that we are part of that space—McMahan separates these three aspects with different terms (*immersion, engagement*, and *presence)*,[5] whereas Ryan discusses immersion both as a phenomenon that can be found in literature, and that digital media incarnates in a new way; her types of immersion are spatial, temporal, and emotional.[6] The literature on immersion is long and wide, so when stating that "the player is immersed in the world," you have to understand which aspects of the process the statement is referring to. This is important because there are authors (myself included) who question the concept of immersion that implies separateness

(Continued)

(Continued)

from the real world, the feeling of being cut off from reality—rather, feeling involved in an activity like games requires players to negotiate their understanding of everyday life with what they do in the game.[7] Alternate Reality games are prime examples of how one can be really into a game and have to be aware of the actual physical space.[8]

Another buzzword that my students (and some scholars who will remain unnamed) often use lightly are *procedural rhetoric*, which is how participating in a process can convey meaning;[9] while currently the phrase *artificial intelligence* seems to pervade the news and academic circles as a blanket term, whereas it may refer to a specific area of research, such as procedural content generation, machine learning, or large language models (LLMs). These are all legitimate terms which refer to complex ideas and fields; using them as a way to refer to an intuition about a game or computing concept does not make one sound knowledgeable about the topic—on the contrary, trusting big words to lend authority to our analysis may indicate one's ideas may be half-baked. So, remember: choose your terms carefully.

Chapter 1 mentioned how Church proposes generating a vocabulary based on analysis, so the terminology derives from aspects of actual games.[10] Analysis can thus become the tool to expand and generate our games lexicon, one game at a time. The panorama to generate that vocabulary is rather grim, however. Diverse projects have attempted to create a terminology in the past, almost single-handedly. Some have come both from practitioners (The 400 Project list by Hal Barwood and Noah Falstein, as well as books by Ernst Adams, Bob Bates, and Richard Rouse III)[11] and academia (Game Ontology, Game Design Patterns, Operational Logics).[12] The main problem is not the quality of the work—these are all worthy projects, which have made contributions of different importance to game terminology. Generating a game vocabulary is not a matter of writing a dictionary of terms, but rather compiling a set of interrelated concepts in the form of frameworks, which indicate how the ideas connect to each other and provide a context and application of those terms. That is, it is not enough to make up a word to call a specific element—it must have a context in which to apply it. You can get a dictionary for a language, but if you do not know the grammar or a bit of the culture that uses the language, you will not really be able to speak it. (Plus memorizing a list of words is quite boring unless you take memorizing data as a personal challenge.)

Concepts and terms also have to catch on within the community—the jargon of a specific discipline is also the result of social consensus and, therefore, the vocabulary derives from the community of practice of developers, academics, and critics. You may want to call an uneven level of difficulty *Fred,* but if nobody else uses the name, you are not really contributing to the vocabulary, even if the concept may help you explain levels of difficulty to others very precisely. Therefore, individual efforts to create a vocabulary, although a good analytical start, may not have as much impact as contributing to a communal framework, which is not quite established in game studies.

In order to build up your vocabulary to talk about games, some of the important factors include being familiar with the discourse of the communities of academics and practitioners, keeping up with publications, and constantly playing games, old and new. By being a part of the game community and continuing to explore, you will also find new areas that may need frameworks to understand them better.

An analysis of the formal aspects of a game involves identifying the elements that help us generate new knowledge about the game first; the next step is to establish relationships between elements, as well as other building blocks. For example, we have already mentioned how defining a genre through its formal traits is an interesting challenge in any medium, since what seems like the core of a genre naturally changes through time and adapts itself to reflect new cultural trends. Take first-person shooters, as mentioned in the discussion on Game Genre in Chapter 3: they involve a first-person point of view and shooting at anthropomorphic entities, that is, animals or things that look like people. That accounts for games such as *Operation Wolf* (1998), *Doom* (1993), and *Half-Life* (1998), for example. Each of these games has different control schemes: while *Operation Wolf* was originally an arcade game where the player only controls the crosshairs, in *Doom,* the point of view and movement go together, while *Half-Life* separates point of view and movement. Apart from slightly different control schemes, they also have different fictional worlds—*Operation Wolf* puts the player in the role of the rescuer in exotic lands, just like John Rambo in the eponymous film series, whereas the fictional world of *Doom* is a dungeon where the player kills monsters. In contrast, *Half-Life* has a complex fictional world (the Black Mesa Research Facility) and is usually recognized for being one of the first games where narrative was part and parcel of gameplay within the first-person shooter genre.[13] It is in the mapping of the commonalities and differences that we can identify both the innovations of a game as well as its belonging to a specific tradition.

Another productive aspect of analyzing the formal properties of a game is to explore the relationship between the rules and the fictional world of the game. Although fictional worlds are not exclusive of digital games (tabletop role-playing games thrive on creating them too), the formal properties of a game should provide us with insight on how they contribute to player experience. They are one entryway into what makes the game remarkable and different from others.

BOX 5.2 EXERCISE: LEARNING FROM "BAD" GAMES

What makes a game "good" or "bad" is very subjective—understanding games in binary terms is not necessarily helpful to understand games better or contribute to improving the games discourse. Part of generating a richer understanding of games includes using more nuanced terms, and avoiding absolute terms. One example of why this divide is not so useful is because, at times, games that may be considered "bad" can teach us a lot about games, because they make their formal traits evident by botching them. Select a game that may have been regarded as not very good quality—look for the lowest ratings in specialized games or a list of "worst games," for example. Get hold of a copy of the game and play it. Remember: playing games you do not like is an essential part of studying and making games.

The next step is to articulate why the game is "bad," and do not limit yourself to just finding different ways to say: "This game is terrible." Here are a few factors that you may want to take into account:

- Is the game boring or confusing? Why?
- Are the technical aspects of the game poorly implemented? Is the game buggy? How so?
- Does the game use stereotypical or biased representations?
- Is the game difficult in an uninteresting manner? How and why?
- Is the audio-visual quality what makes it poor (e.g., visual design, voice acting, sound design)?

Find specific examples to explain any of these aspects to reinforce your argument. Do not forget the redeeming qualities of the game:

(Continued)

(Continued)

- Does the game aim at innovating but does not succeed?
- Is it just one aspect of the game that spoils what might otherwise be an interesting game?
- What may be the redeeming qualities of the game?

In this case, the context is essential to fully understand the game. For example, saying that an early 3D game for PlayStation, such as *Metal Gear Solid*, or Nintendo 64, such as *Super Mario 64* (1996), has bad graphics in comparison with current platforms shows a lack of historical perspective—these graphics were state of the art when the game was released. Whether what is "bad" in the game is intentional or not may also be important—the game *Desert Bus* (1995) requires the player to drive a bus from Tucson, Arizona, to Las Vegas, Nevada, in real time, without being able to pause the game and with the bus veering slightly to one side to require the player's input constantly. *Desert Bus*, derived from a concept from the comedians Penn and Teller, presents an unfair challenge on purpose, thus turning gameplay into something closer to performance art—how long can you bear to play?

Although intentionality is always difficult to determine, as already discussed in Chapters 1 and 3, the context may help us understand the reasoning behind the game. You can always document yourself on the origins of the game and determine why specific elements may not be the best quality, from naïve developers to rushed production times to purposeful parody. You may realize that a "bad" game is merely flawed, or that it may actually have been developed as a joke, as an experiment, or as a special challenge for players.

▶ FORMALISM AND NARRATIVE

Certain parts of the discourse about games, in game studies as well as journalism, talk about formalism and narrative as opposite approaches to understanding games and game design. I find this division baffling, since at the beginning of my academic career I had to do a lot of formalist work in order to talk about narrative in games. This discourse seems to make certain assumptions about what formalism is without quite defining it, which is the main issue—this is a clear example of why it is important to define one's terms. Therefore, in order to understand formalism, let us define what it is first, and then we can understand where this apparent division may from.

In its origins, formalism was a school of thought in literary studies. Formalists tackle the components of a text and how they are organized, but do not concern themselves with what those components may mean in depth, or how they relate to their context. This approach describes what elements make up a text, while avoiding interpreting its context: for example, literary formalism focused on the form—structures, literary devices and techniques, imagery, rhyme. According to Eagleton,

> [f]ar from seeing form as the expression of content, [formalists] stood the relationship on its head: content was merely the 'motivation' of form, an occasion or convenience for a particular kind of formal exercise. *Don Quixote* is not 'about' the character of that name: the character is just a device for holding together different kinds of narrative technique.[14]

Similarly, formalist approaches to games have represented the fictional world of the game as a device at the service of the rules of the game, or as decoration that is slapped on the system of the game, considering any aspects that may have to do with narrative as secondary to the rules.

In any new field, formalism is often a necessary phase, since scholars need to take apart and identify the components of what they are studying—formalism is necessary so that we can actually tackle our object of study. At the beginning of the 2000s, many of the scholars writing about games worked on definitions, classifications, and ontologies, because we needed names for the things we were going to analyze and interpret later. The work of the so-called ludologists tended to be more formal, partly because it was paving the way for the study of (digital) games as a distinct new field, and in some cases as a way to extricate the games from studies of narrative which, again, was treated as secondary. Some of the discussions in the early years of game studies revolved around what was termed the ludology vs. narratology approaches.[15] Subsequent work has proved that this divide was not necessarily adversarial[16] and, now, it has become clear that it is difficult to talk about games without taking into consideration how they may be presented as a narrative form. The dichotomy, however, has somehow survived and still pops up in social media discourse, journalistic articles, and even in academic conferences.

Narrative aspects can be formalized; those formal approaches help us analyze games in terms of their storytelling. In game studies, Jenkins lists the types of storytelling in games in relation to how players can make sense of them or how the story changes depending on player's input.[17] The authors of *The Game Narrative Toolbox* list types of text that writers have to write for a game, showing how formal analysis can help creators understand their craft.[18] My own dissertation included a breakdown of the formal elements that allowed us to identify what adventure games are and what distinguishes them from other genres. These are examples of classifications, taxonomies, and definitions that break down the components of the narrative aspects of games—all formal approaches to narrative.

The opposition between form and narrative seems to stem from thinking that games are mainly systems, and that narrative is incompatible with them. The roots of formalist studies in the humanities, however, precisely come from systematic approaches to literature—we have already mentioned Propp's *Morphology of the Folktale* as a work whose purpose was to identify the formula of a collection of Russian fairytales.[19] Propp's "formula" was what, decades later, computer scientists have used to teach computers how to write fairytales, for instance.[20] Formalism has its roots in literary theory and is part of the field of narratology; in a way, they are inextricable.

In game design practice, narrative designers come up with systems that integrate the storytelling of the game—from quest systems that keep track of what the player has achieved and what they have left to do, to procedurally generated content that will make parts of the game be different whenever the player starts. The sticking point is that narrative systems are very difficult to extricate from meaning, from their interpretation—they go hand in hand, and they cannot just be flowcharts, diagrams, or numbers on a spreadsheet. These systems invoke worlds, relationships, and events, and they become more concrete and less abstract while players play. In short, these systems demonstrate that it is indeed very difficult to have games that are purely abstract and isolated from their context, and reveal one of the main limitations of formalism.

One aspect of formalism that is important to remember, however, is that it has been recurringly criticized because of the way it looks at its object of study out of context—originally, it was a more "scientific" way of approaching humanities work. One of the critiques raised about ludology was how these early works tend to leave out the study of players and the context of play, for example. While formal approaches help us identify the parts of a game, they do not tackle how the game is meaningful—what it means to players, how they are cultural artifacts, and yes, what stories they tell. Some of us, players and designers, can admire the beauty of a well-designed system and get lost in its dynamics. But systems can also tell stories, which at times can become deeply ingrained in culture. For example, in the book

Playing Oppression: The Legacy of Conquest and Empire in Colonialist Board Games, Mary Flanagan and Mikael Jakobsson provide a history of how colonialist ideology has become ingrained in game design practice. The genre of 4X games (named after its four key verbs: Explore, Expand, Exploit, Exterminate) uses mechanics that reproduce the strategies of colonial empires by appropriating resources, growing them, and benefitting from them, while disregarding the populations that produced them and the origins of the labor of that expansion—people were another resource that could also be discarded. Making yet another 4X game that focuses exclusively on its mechanics, without taking into account the history and ideological baggage they imply, unwittingly reinforces the ideological tropes that originated those mechanics in the first place.[21]

To sum up, formalism is an approach that is necessary to describe and break down what we study, but focusing on the formal aspects exclusively can lose sight of what the game means, how it can be interpreted, and the connotations of its mechanics. In any case, formalism is also applied to the narrative of games, and they are not necessarily separate.

FORMAL ELEMENTS: BUILDING BLOCKS

The building blocks referring to the formal elements of a game are the following:

- Rules of the World
- Diegetic vs. Extradiegetic Rules
- Save Games
- Relationship between Rules and the Fictional World
- Abstraction
- Values and Procedural Rhetoric
- Procedural Content vs. Hard-Coded Content
- Game Dynamics

- The Gap between the Player and the Game: Point of View
- The Gap between the Player and the Game: Entity and Object Manipulation
- Control Schemes
- Alternative Controllers
- Difficulty Levels/Game Balance
- Representation (Visual Design, Sound Design, and Music)
- Representation and Identity
- Rule-Driven vs. Goal-Driven Games
- Levels and Level Design
- Choice Design
- Cheats/Mods/Hacks/Bugs.

Rules of the World Not all games present fictional worlds, as argued in Chapter 4—it is hard to think about Sudoku as having a world that we interact with, since there are no characters, for example. When the game has a fictional world, it usually follows a set of rules—in the case of videogames, it is out of necessity, since the computer needs to follow instructions in the code to generate the representation of the world and how it will respond to players' input. The implementation of the fictional world constitutes the game world of the game.

The game world is a simulation that the player participates in—simulation in this case does not necessarily mean that there is a real-world counterpart, but rather that there is a world that the player inhabits and participates in.[22] How that world works and what are its implied values of the system are two of the main issues that this building block can deal with. For example, Liberty City in *Grand Theft Auto IV* (2008) is a city where pedestrians take a stroll on the sidewalk, cars run at normal speed on the road and follow traffic rules, and the day/night cycle changes every 20 minutes. This could be called a simulation of the real world within certain limits.

The difference between what is possible in the game world and what the player is allowed to do is another area that can yield productive discussion. For instance, in the main mode of *Halo: Combat Evolved* (2001) characters talk to each other in cut-scenes, but the player cannot choose when to talk or what to say. Which actions are available or not is the direct result of design decisions; these decisions are part of what we can discuss in this building block.

In the non-digital space, creating the world and its rules may be part of the game mechanics. In Live Action Role-Playing games (LARPs), a phase of the game may be devoted to creating the rules and limits of the world that players are going to play. Some of these games that are about creating worlds—*Dialect* is a game about a world, where the players tell the story of a community by creating its language, and how the language reflects its values.[23] So in certain cases, the goal of the game may be creating the rules of the fictional world itself.

Questions to identify the rules of the fictional world:

- How does the game world operate independently of player input?
- What does the game world allow the player to do?
- What does the game prevent the player from doing?
- What kinds of events and behavior does the game world reward or encourage? Which ones are discouraged?
- Are there any game world rules that the player can determine or modify?

Further Reading

Egenfeldt-Nielsen, Simon, Jonas Heide Smith, and Susana Pajares Tosca. *Understanding Video Games: The Essential Introduction*. 4th edn. Routledge, 2020, pp. 201–213.

Juul, Jesper. *Half-Real: Video Games between Real Rules and Fictional Worlds*. Cambridge, MA: The MIT Press, 2005, Chapter 4: "Fiction."

BOX 5.3 EXERCISE: MATCHING THE VERBS WITH THE FICTIONAL WORLD

The Fictional World building block in Chapter 4 has already discussed how Soren Johnson points out that the theme of the game and what we do in the world may be different things; in the same chapter, the Game Mechanics block included an exercise which listed the verbs of a specific game in order to identify the mechanics. Now let's take a further step, which will help us establish the Relationship between Rules and the Fictional World building block below.

This is a continuation from the game mechanics exercise in Chapter 4. Examine the fictional world of the game, and make a list of potential verbs in it—what would the inhabitants in the world do? What would the actions of the main character be? For example, there are many games that have Sherlock Holmes as their protagonist. Based on what we know about the character from the stories, some of the verbs listed would be: investigate, examine, interrogate, experiment, smoke, fight, put on disguises.

Now, look at the list of core mechanics of the game. Do they overlap with the verbs of the game? How do the actions of the player relate to the fictional world? How does it define the role of the player in the world? Continuing with the Sherlock Holmes example, if we are analyzing a game such as *The Mystery of the Mummy* (2002), the main verbs are examine, pick up, place, and open door. There is nobody to interrogate, and the events of the case are displayed just as the player figures out how to open yet another door. There is a disconnect between what the player does and what the fictional world adds to the game, much in the way that Soren Johnson discusses in his article "Theme Is Not Meaning."[24]

When the fictional world and the verbs are in agreement, the game seems to "click." For example, in *Grand Theft Auto IV*, many of the mechanics really have to do with thieving: the player cannot buy cars, but must hijack them; there is no button to talk to pedestrians, but there are several actions related to handling weapons, shooting, and punching. The verbs of the game dictate that we go around Liberty City behaving like a criminal.

Finding the connections between what the player does, how the world works, and what the fictional world is about helps us understand the (common) dissonance between the rules of the game and the rules of the world.

Diegetic vs. Extradiegetic Rules The terms diegetic and extradiegetic come from the field of film studies, where diegetic elements belong to the fictional world and can be experienced by the characters in it, and extradiegetic elements are for the players but do not belong in the world of the game.[25] For example, when you play *Grand Theft Auto: Vice City* (2002), you can listen to the radio in any of the cars, and the radio stations comment on what happens in the world, so the music is diegetic, whereas the music that plays in *Final Fantasy VII* (1997) during combat is not accounted for in the fictional world, and the characters fighting cannot hear it—the music is extradiegetic.

In a similar way, there are rules of the game that are part of the fictional world and others that are not. Some game elements may not be fictionalized, such as the game score, external achievements or badges, subtitles, and volume controls. In contrast, there are times where elements that would not seem to belong to the fictional world are fictionalized. For example, in *Animal Crossing: New Leaf* (2013), in order to access the Internet to visit the towns of other players, the player has to go to the station to take a train to go to cities far away, instead of bringing up a menu that says "connecting to the Internet."

Extradiegetic elements are often crucial to understand the game and motivate the player. Music soundtracks are prime examples of how extradiegetic elements are part of gameplay, mostly as feedback to the player on the actions of the game. The music in *Metal Gear Solid 2: Sons of Liberty* (2001), for instance, not only sets the mood, it also tells the player whether the soldiers are looking for the player character or not; if they are, it expresses how intensely they are searching.

Extradiegetic rules directly affect how we play because they are still the rules of the game. Selecting the level of difficulty or the goals of the game, to name a couple of common extradiegetic rules, directly affects what the player can do in the game and what is rewarded. Game achievements/trophies/badges are usually extradiegetic notices that mark the progress of the player, often giving hints about somewhat absurd goals that the game will acknowledge and reward, from placing novelty masks on zombies (*Dead Rising*, 2006) to killing an enemy with a toilet (*Half-Life 2*, 2004). The achievements in turn can point to extradiegetic elements too, such as completing the game in less than 24 hours (*The Beatles Rock Band*, 2009); or not playing the game in five years and in ten years (*The Stanley Parable*, 2013). In this last case, this achievement is very much part of the themes of the game, which address the player directly and challenge the player's expectations about what one can do in a videogame.

Exploring the boundaries between what is part of the world and what is not can give way to productive essay questions:

- Why does Mario have three lives?[26]
- Why is there an option to change the level of gore in *Diablo* (1996)? Who is it for?
- Who is the voice of *Adventure* (1977) that addresses the player throughout the game, starting with "Welcome to Adventure!"?

Questions to identify diegetic vs. extradiegetic rules:

- Which elements of the game do the inhabitants of the world sense and respond to?
- Which actions are explained as a narrative event? Which ones are not?
- Which rules are associated with an event in the world, and which are regulated in a menu?

Further Reading

Galloway, Alexander R. *Gaming: Essays on Algorithmic Culture.* 1st edn. Minneapolis, MN: University of Minnesota Press, 2006.

Jørgensen, Kristine. "Time for New Terminology?: Diegetic and Non-Diegetic Sounds in Computer Games Revisited." In *Game Sound Technology and Player Interaction: Concepts and Developments.* Hershey, PA: IGI Global, 2011, pp. 78–97.

Save Games Save games are a type of extradiegetic element that deserves its own building block. In digital games, the computer can store the state of the game, so one can go back to that state later on. Whether save games are possible, when, and how are all important to how the game will be played.

Arcade games do not have a save state, because the key is to keep players putting in coins whenever they die. Console games, particularly in cartridge-based systems, often have limited space to save the game, forcing the player to stick to a single playthrough where, once the game is saved, you cannot go back. Current home computer games, for example, often let players have multiple saved games, so that one can play the game to a certain point and then go back and try different choices, for example. Some games, such as *Sonic the Hedgehog* (1991), only let the player save at certain points of the game, for example, after finishing a level, so if the player fails before arriving to the save point, the progress until then is lost and the player needs to start over.

As technologies clear off the limitations of the number of save games, where and when to save becomes a stylistic choice, as well as shaping the difficulty. *Hydorah* (2010) is a PC game that evokes the limitations of arcade games by only allowing players to save their progress five times per playthrough, so players need to strategize their save spots. Its upgraded version, *Super Hydorah* (2017), lets players save as many times as they want, in consonance with the conventions of modern consoles. Another example of the stylistic use of save games can be found in the *Souls* series (2009–2022), where the player can use bonfires as a checkpoint. In that checkpoint, the player character replenishes their health points, but it also has the effect of respawning enemies, which means the player may have to fight them again or have learned how to avoid them or defeat them faster. The use of the bonfires in the *Souls* series is in tune with the themes of the games, which have to do with pervading death and learning from one's mistakes in the next life. Frequent saves can also be counterbalanced with making it difficult to undo player decisions. *Bioshock* (2007) saves the game automatically whenever the player is near one of the checkpoints (called *vita-chambers* in the game). That way, players will not lose their progress if they forget to save their game; they can take more risks and be bold when attacking enemies. On the other hand, it does not let players undo their previous actions and every decision will stay with them until the end of the game—something that is core to the game concept, since the accumulated choices of the game will result in one out of two different endings. How often we can the save the game, if at all, conditions how we play. The more often we can save, the more the game is letting us experiment and take risks; the less often we can save, the more demanding the game will be of the player.

The current generation of consoles, as well as game portals, requires that players create an account to play games, which also allows them to upload their save games to the cloud. Thus, players can play across consoles, and at times even across platforms, although this often involves a subscription fee to a specific service. The models of games as service has therefore turned save games into part of an online identity, which can be accessed independently from the type of hardware used.

Questions to identify the formal aspects of the save game feature:

- Can the player store the game state and stop playing and come back to that state?
- Can the player save at any time or only at specific points?
- Is there a limit on the number of saved games a player can have?

Further Reading

Juul, Jesper. "Introduction to Game Time." In *First Person: New Media as Story, Performance, and Game*, edited by Noah Wardrip-Fruin and Paul Harrigan. Cambridge, MA: MIT Press, 2004, pp. 131–141.

Rau, Anja. *Reload—Yes/No: Clashing Times in Graphic Adventure Games*. Copenhagen: IT University of Copenhagen, 2001.

Tobin, Samuel. "Time and Space in Play Saving and Pausing with the Nintendo DS." *Games and Culture 7*, no. *2* (March 1, 2012): 127–141.

Relationship between Rules and the Fictional World As a continuation of the previous building block, another important formal aspect to discuss is the relationship between the fictional world of the game and the rules. The exploration of these relationships is similar to how literary and film studies discuss the relationship between form and content, how the themes of a story are also expressed through the language, structures, and repetition, or film editing. In the case of games, the fictional world can bring a set of behaviors attached to it, which are often related to genre fiction. For instance, in *Red Dead Redemption* (2010), the player has to recreate scenes inspired by Western movies, from cow herding to gambling, to shoot-outs, to gunslinger duels. In contrast, *Outlaws* (1997) is a first-person shooter also set in the Wild West, which consists of a continuous series of shoot-outs, but nothing else. As a third example with a similar setting, *Westerado: Double Barreled* (2015) is also inspired by Western films, and follows a revenge plot structure. The player has to figure out who killed their family, and they can do that by either talking to people, and running errands, or shooting around. Every action has a consequence, so the rules of the game focus on making choices, similar to how films such as *A Fistful of Dollars* (1964) required the protagonist to carefully navigate the social space and get to know the factions before shooting anybody.

Thus, the fictional world can telegraph some of the behaviors that the player is expected to perform in the world, without telling the player explicitly what to do—Janet Murray calls this *scripting the interactor*.[27] Investigating which rules may be implied by the fictional world, whether they are implemented and how, is another topic that can lead to productive discussion. Matthew Weise has done this extensively with reference to horror films and how they have inspired different survival horror games, studying the process of what he calls *procedural adaptation*, which is examining how the rules of the fictional world in film or literature have translated into digital games.[28] One of the most striking examples is how horror games such as the *Resident Evil* series (1996–2017) featured zombies, but infection as a way to spread the zombie disease was not a rule of a game. This was true of many other zombie games until *ZombiU* (2012) was released—in this example, one zombie bite will infect the player character who will effectively die; the player will then control a new character, while they will have to find their previous zombified character, at times even having to fight them, in order to find the items they were carrying when they died.

These different aspects that define the rules and the fictional world are the focus of a specific discipline in game development, which we call *narrative design*. Although some developers believe that narrative design is only writing the story, in practice, we see how what the player does in some games may also be a narrative. Therefore, designing interactions that are also meaningful in a narrative context is an additional expressive avenue of game design. A clear example of the discord between gameplay and narrative is found in *Super Mario Bros.* (1985), and any of the titles of the series. Why does Mario pick up coins throughout the game? Narratively, they could be money for Mario to pay Princess Peach's ransom, but that's not the case—collecting them allows the player to gain an extra life, a non-diegetic element that is difficult to explain in narrative terms, as mentioned in the building block above. In contrast, an excellent example of narrative design can be found in *Battlestar Galactica: The Board Game* (2008), where the fictional world creates a dramatic premise that also generates drama during gameplay. Humanity has been wiped out from all the planets, except for those people who were out in space—this is what happens at the beginning of the TV show that the game is based on. In the game, players are aboard the *Battlestar Galactica*, and have to manage their resources at the same time that they are being chased by their enemy, the Cylons. One of the players is secretly a Cylon, and their goal is to sabotage the escape operation. Resource management as well as traitor mechanics,[29] which are common game design elements, are two of the ways in which the board game embodies the events of the TV show.

Clint Hocking coined the term *ludonarrative dissonance*[30] as a way to define the lack of coherence between the narrative of a game and what the player does in it. In the blog post where he defined the term, he critiques how *Bioshock* (2007) seems to promote one ideological approach through its game mechanics, which is directly contradicted by the narrative of the game. Hocking's term caught on in the game development and criticism communities, to the point that its overuse has made it lose the nuance and significance of its original definition and now it is close to having become a buzzword (see Box 5.1 Beware of Buzzwords). Part of the problem is also that some designers and critics invoke it as if it were a required feature of games, much as how the term *immersion* has worn out after repeatedly frivolous use. The term helps identify the disconnect between gameplay and the fictional world, but it does not mean it is compulsory—there is a lot of expressive potential in the mismatch between what the player does in the game and what the game is about, if this mismatch is done purposely. For example, in *Unmanned* (2012),[31] the player becomes a US soldier who bombs foreign soil remotely by using an unmanned attack aircraft, and then goes back home. The game deals with the everyday life of this soldier, from shaving and driving to work, to piloting drones and launching missiles, then taking a break for a smoke. It is a game about war, but it is precisely the separation from it that makes the game uncomfortable. The theme of detachment is reinforced formally by presenting the game in a split-screen that divides the player's attention while the player has to click to carry out different actions. The dissonance between what the player does in the game and the expectations created by war games makes of *Unmanned* an interactive critique of modern warfare (pun intended).

Questions to determine the relationship between the rules and the fictional world:

- How does the fictional premise of the world dictate the interactions in the game?

- Who is the player character and what are the kinds of actions that we associate with a character of its type?
- How are the interactions in the game in consonance (or not) with the narrative set up by the fictional world?

Further Reading

Fernandez-Vara, Clara, and Matthew Weise. 2020. "Making Worlds into Games—A Methodology." In *World-Builders on World-Building An Exploration of Subcreation*, edited by Mark J. P. Wolf, 1st edn. Routledge, pp. 73–92.

Johnson, Soren. "GD Column 11: Theme Is Not Meaning (Part I)." *DESIGNER NOTES*. Available at: https://www.designer-notes.com/game-developer-column-11-theme-is-not-meaning-part-i/. Accessed November 4, 2023.

Johnson, Soren. "GD Column 12: Theme Is Not Meaning (Part II)." *Designer Notes*. Available at: https://www.designer-notes.com/game-developer-column-11-theme-is-not-meaning-part-ii/. Accessed November 4, 2023.

Abstraction This building block derives from the relationship between the fictional world of the game and the rules discussed above. Specifically, it refers to the level of detail in which the fictional world has been implemented, and how much nuance of interaction is provided to the player. The concept of level of abstraction accounts for describing the degree of nuance; it refers to how a specific model is implemented as a game system. Juul refers to the level of abstraction of a videogame as the border between the fictional world and how it is implemented in the rules, within which the player can operate. "[T]he player can only act on a certain level, outside which the world is either crudely implemented ..., simply represented ..., or simply absent..." [32] Juul uses *Cooking Mama* (2006) as an example, where the fictional world is a kitchen, but the possible actions in it are more limited than in real life: for example, cucumbers can only be cut in a specific way, and one cannot order takeout instead of cooking. The parts of the game that are not relevant to gameplay have less functionality (e.g., the player sees a picture of the dish that they cooked, but there is no action to eat it), or are not implemented at all (e.g., the player cannot visit the rest of the house). Following this logic, the events in the fictional world that cannot take place as a result of the game system will either be represented or left out.

Whereas Juul understands the level of abstraction as a border between the simulation and the fictional world, it is more productive to interpret it as the area of intersection between rules and the fictional world. Thus, the level of abstraction is the amount of overlap between both. Figure 5.1 illustrates how the overlap may give way to different degrees of abstraction. A smaller overlap, where either the rules or the fictional world present a larger area in Figure 5.1, indicates a less fine-grained system. The larger the area of overlap between rules and the fictional world, the higher the fidelity in the simulation.

The level of abstraction can also be applied to the rules that establish how the player interacts with the simulation and how much nuance it provides. For example, in *Half-Life 2* (2004), the player character must gain momentum in order to make a longer jump because of the detailed physics system of the world, whereas, in *Yoshi's Island: Super Mario Advanced 3* (2002), the player character may jump in mid-air, but there is no inertia. It also indicates that there are aspects of the world that the player cannot interact with. For instance, in *Grand Theft Auto IV* (2008), the player can buy clothes, but cannot buy a car, only steal it; only certain buildings have doors that allow entering them, the rest are there as part of the décor.

The differences between *Red Dead Redemption, Outlaws*, and *Westerado: Double Barreled* in the previous building block show how a similar fictional world can be implemented with different levels of nuance: *Red Dead Redemption* allows the player to walk and ride around the world, with a wide

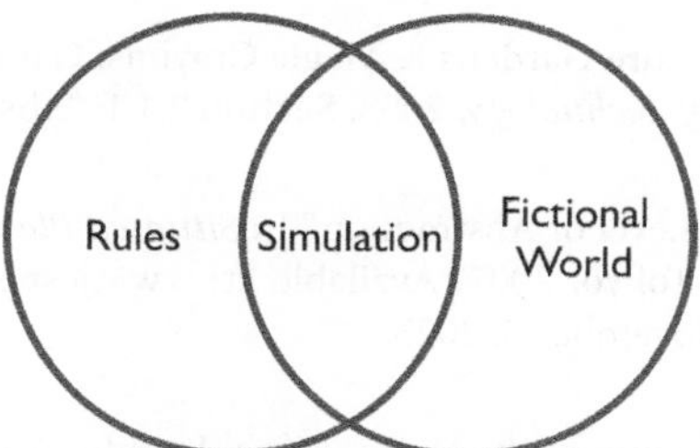

Figure 5.1 The overlap between the rules and the fictional world is the simulation; the more overlap there is between rules and world, the more nuanced the simulation will be

spectrum of actions, such as riding a horse or gambling; *Westerado* also has an open world to explore but at a much smaller scale, the player can either shoot other characters, or talk to them and choose what to say; finally, *Outlaws* has the most reduced interaction, since it only allows the player to navigate the space and shoot.

Talking about levels of abstraction helps in determining how complex a simulation is, and what aspects of the world have been implemented or are just represented.

Questions to determine the relationship between the level of abstraction in a game:

- Which aspects of the fictional world can the player interact with?
- Which aspects of the fictional world are represented (i.e., the player cannot interact with them)? Think of cut-scenes, background images, or anything that builds the fictional world but that the player cannot affect.
- Which aspects of the fictional world have been left out? Why?

Further Reading

Fernández-Vara, Clara. "From 'Open Mailbox' to Context Mechanics: Shifting Levels of Abstraction in Adventure Games." In *Proceedings of the 6th International Conference on Foundations of Digital Games: FDG'11*. New York: ACM, 2011, pp. 131–138.

Gingold, Chaim. "Miniature Gardens & Magic Crayons: Games, Spaces, & Worlds." *Georgia Institute of Technology*, 2003, Section 2.1.1: "Abstraction."

Juul, Jesper. "A Certain Level of Abstraction." In *Situated Play: DiGRA 2007 Conference Proceedings*. Tokyo, 2007. Available at: www.jesperjuul.net/text/acertainlevel/. Accessed November 5, 2023.

Wolf, Mark J.P. *The Medium of the Video Game*. 1st edn. Austin, TX: University of Texas Press, 2002, Chapter 2.

BOX 5.4 EXERCISE: SIMULATION VS. REPRESENTATION

Choose two games that present similar fictional worlds—we saw the comparison between *Outlaws*, *Westerado*, and *Red Dead Redemption* above, which all take place in a world inspired by Westerns. Examine what parts of the fictional world can be interacted with, and which ones are left out. List the verbs of each game—is there any overlap? Which verbs are the same? Which ones are different?

By looking at which parts of the world the player can interact with, we can establish the level of nuance and which aspects of the game have been selected, so two games may take place in the same world, but they may be designed to be different experiences. For instance, games such as *SimCity* (1989), *SimCopter* (1996), and *The Sims* (2000) arguably take place in the same world. However, each one chooses a different part of the world to interact with—in *SimCity*, the player is the mayor, who works more as a city planner; in *SimCopter*, the player is a helicopter pilot who has different missions, from redirecting traffic to transporting injured people to hospitals. Players could also create cities in *SimCity* and then import them into *SimCopter* to play in them, showing how even when the space may be the same, the verbs in them will be different (managing and planning vs. flying). *The Sims* uses a different level of abstraction—the role of the player is closer to that of a puppet master, rather than managing cities. The player guides a group of people in their everyday life, builds their house, but not the whole city. Even though *SimCity* and *The Sims* both feature complex simulations of the world, they use different levels of abstraction of the world itself. This is also shown visually: we do not quite see the citizens in the earlier instalments of the game, whereas in *The Sims* we see the map of our neighborhood but not the town.

Values and Procedural Rhetoric How the game world is regulated can also express a set of cultural and social values that we can identify and critique as part of our analysis as well as part of our design methods.[33] What is simulated or not, and what is considered positive or negative in the rule set, can also express an ideology. For instance, *The Sims* (2000) games allow same-sex couples; as Gonzalo Frasca discusses, a conservative version of the game may not have allowed same-sex relationships, or even have included sex as part of the game mechanics.[34]

The ideological stances at times can be oversimplified, or set up to generate or avoid controversy, so what the game sanctions and encourages is considered positive, what it punishes may be negative. For example, the racing game *Carmageddon* (1997) gives players extra points for running over pedestrians.[35] On the other hand, *Fallout 3* (2009) and *Fallout: New Vegas* (2010) do not let players kill children, in order to avoid controversy. In this case, the rules of the game world are designed to prevent a backlash in the real world.

Since the rule sets of games can reflect an ideology, we can also see how a game can make an ideological statement. The term that describes how this happens is *procedural rhetoric*, which is the use of system processes persuasively.[36] A clear example of this is *Papers, Please* (2013), where the player becomes an immigration officer in a fictional communist country, who has to examine the documents of every incoming traveler. It is up to the player to decide whether the traveler can enter the country or not because each traveler correctly processed—whether it is by letting them in or stopping them—helps the player earn money to sustain their family, whereas mistakes result in fines or not getting any money at all. The game presents the player with constant dilemmas, such as listening to the pleas of travelers who have fake documents but want to join their family in the country, or taking a bribe to let someone in, thus running the risk of losing everything just to get a bit more money to help the player character's family. By taking on the role of immigration officer, the player can see the unfairness of border control and political oppression, both in the faces of the people who go through the border and through the difficult choices that they have to make.

A more subtle example of how games can make ideological statements is *80 Days* (2014), which is loosely based on Jules Verne's novel *Le Tour du Monde en Quatre-vingt Jours* (1873), and is set in a decolonized, multicultural steampunk world. The player controls the valet Passepartout, at the service of Phileas Fogg, and has to make decisions as to where to go, how to manage their luggage, and who to talk to and what to say. By choosing a character who is not the original protagonist of the story, the game shifts the focus from the imperialism and privilege that define Fogg to the story of those who did not have a voice in Verne's novel. Additionally, many of the choices that the player has to make seem unfair because they do not seem to change the events of the story; Passepartout is not the hero, even though he does encounter revolutions and riots, which he may participate in but not lead. He is not there to change the world—the choices are limited to how the player wants to traverse it. The player cannot control how the characters they encounter behave, only how Passepartout will react to them. *80 Days* is a reaction against what the game narrative designer, Meghna Jayanth, calls "entitlement simulators," which are games that help the player get what they want.[37]

In analyzing how a game exemplifies procedural rhetoric, we have to beware of games that use *graphical skins*, as Bogost calls them,[38] where the ideology is tied to the representation rather than the system. For example, PETA released an online game called *New Super Chick Sisters* (2010) to denounce the cruelty that was used by the corporation to raise and slaughter chickens. The game is supposed to imitate *New Super Mario Bros.* (2006), where the player picks up chickens to save them and has to avoid burgers and fries. The information about the practices of the corporation is delivered through cartoony cut-scenes and pop-out text, but has nothing to do with why we are going around picking up chickens and jumping over burgers with evil red eyes.

Questions to identify the values of a game and if it uses procedural rhetoric:

- What does the game reward? What does it punish?
- What inclusions or omissions in the game can reflect an ideological stance?
- What are the elements of the game that express socio-cultural and ethical values?
- How does the game express its ideology? Is it integrated into the rules, or is it part of the cut-scenes and representation of the game?

Further Reading

Bogost, Ian. *Persuasive Games: The Expressive Power of Videogames*. Cambridge, MA: The MIT Press, 2007.

Flanagan, Mary, and Helen Nissenbaum. *Values at Play in Digital Games*. MIT Press, 2014.

Frasca, Gonzalo. "Simulation versus Narrative: Introduction to Ludology." *In The Video Game Theory Reader*, edited by Mark J.P. Wolf and Bernard Perron. 1st edn. London: Routledge, 2003.

Mitgutsch, Konstantin, and Narda Alvarado. "Purposeful by Design?: A Serious Game Design Assessment Framework." In *Proceedings of the International Conference on the Foundations of Digital Games: FDG'12*. New York: ACM, 2012, pp. 121–128.

Sicart, Miguel. *The Ethics of Computer Games*. Cambridge, MA: The MIT Press, 2009.

BOX 5.5 EXERCISE: SERIOUS GAMES

Select a so-called serious game, whose purpose is to educate about/raise awareness about/critique a specific issue. Some of the resources above will provide you with examples, you can also find a good selection at the Games for Change website www.gamesforchange.org/games/ (accessed November 5, 2023). Apart from this list, any game that is created for educational purposes, instructional purposes, or as part of an activist initiative will work (plus it is rather probable it is available online). After playing them, examine these specific aspects to evaluate the values that they are setting forth, and the effectiveness of their message. These are based on the use of the Design Assessment Framework proposed by Mitgutsch and Alvarado.[39]

- Purpose: What is the goal of the game? What is it trying to achieve? What values does it try to transmit?
- Content and information: What is the information that the game is trying to get across? What is the game trying to teach?
- Game mechanics: What are the rules of the game? What are the main verbs of the game? How hard/difficult is it?
- Fiction and narrative: What is the fictional world of the game? How does the context relate to the content it wants to get across?
- Aesthetics and graphics: How does the game set up a tone and environment to the player?
- Framing: Who is the game intended for? How much are they supposed to know about games before playing?
- Cohesiveness: Can we consider the game as using procedural rhetoric? Are the values that the game tries to convey integrated in the mechanics? Does the audience it is intended for actually play this type of game?

Note how some of these aspects relate to building blocks mentioned in this book already, such as the fictional world, the audio-visual presentation, or the audience. This is a somewhat advanced mode of game analysis.

(Continued)

(Continued)

By using these elements as a guide, you can evaluate how successful (or not) a serious game is. If you go back to the exercise that examined the relationship between rules and fiction, you will find that part of the problem is that what we do has little to do with the message that the game wants to get across.

Procedural Content vs. Hard-Coded Content How the content is generated can be a defining feature of the game that we are analyzing. This distinction is difficult to understand if you do not know some basic programming, but you can probably understand it once you see it.

The content of a game can be data that is *hard-coded* in the game: graphics, text, sound. Hard-coded data can be a music file, or a graphics file. When a game has a lot of files that are hard-coded, they take a lot of memory/storage space. This content is also presented always in the same manner, which means it does not usually change from game session to session. *Procedural content,* on the other hand, consists of giving the computer the instructions on how to create that content. Chris Crawford refers to this dichotomy as *process intensity vs. data intensity*: while the processes are abstract and an indirect way of creating content, data is concrete and direct.[40] To draw a comparison, instead of providing a file with a recording of a specific melody (which would be the data), procedural content tells the computer how to generate a type of melody, providing the score along with how to change it in specific circumstances. For example, the music should play faster if the player is at the end of a level, or change the key from major to minor if a scary enemy is waiting in the next room. In some cases, providing the instructions takes less space than the data itself, or rather than the amount of content that the instructions would generate. It is like do-it-yourself furniture: the package and the instructions take less space than the actual piece of furniture; only imagine that there are multiple ways to assemble pieces to make different types of furniture.

The difference between these two types of content gives way to rather different experiences. For example, *The Legend of Zelda* (1986) and *Rogue* (1980) are both top-down, tile-based games where the player goes around fighting monsters in dungeons and finding different objects that help improve (or at times, impair) the abilities of the player character. *The Legend of Zelda* is a game where the content is hard-coded—the game maps are always the same, items will always be in the same locations—and the behavior of the game entities is always the same to the extent that players can optimize a path to complete the game in a short time by playing repeatedly. In contrast, *Rogue* is famous for using procedural generation to create its maps, and to spawn different enemies and power-ups across the levels in the game, and where the player has to try to complete the game in one go—if the player character loses all the health points, the game ends; restarting the game means having a fresh new dungeon, different from the previous one.

When developing hard-coded content, the developer creates a series of data that will be shown always in the same manner. The content is controlled and optimized to be presented in a specific way. At the moment, we can assume that most of the content in games is hard-coded, for example, cut-scenes that always happen in the same way, character graphics, text. Procedural content generation, on the other hand, is a very promising area in games research and development, and it means that the system itself will generate part of the content for the player—for example, maps that are always different, quests for the player, the music score, non-player characters. Games such as *Rogue* are famous for generating most of their content procedurally—this also means that it may not be possible to complete the game, since the levels generated are not optimized or play-tested to be completed. Games that use this approach to design are called *roguelike*, and include the so-called dungeon crawlers such as *Diablo* (1996), where the story is hard-coded but the levels are different, or *Spelunky* (2009), which is a platform game where the levels are also generated. *FTL: Faster Than Light* (2012) is a real-time strategy game which generates the planetary systems and events that the player will face, so that the maps and challenges always result in a different story for the player. Even shooters can use roguelike mechanics—the third person shooter *Returnal* (2021) has its astronaut protagonist trapped in a time-loop, so that every time they die, they are thrown back into the world, which changes every time the player has to traverse it. Procedural generation is also very common in games where the platform has limited memory, so giving the computer a set of instructions on how to create the level is a way of saving space and memory. Games such as the space trading game *Elite* (1984) or the side-scrolling racing game *Tiny Wings* (2011) use procedural generation to keep players engaged without using a lot of storage space. Procedural generation can also be used to generate content and create large worlds—the role-playing game *The Elder Scrolls: Skyrim* (2012) uses procedurally generated quests in order to match the expansive space and population of the game world.[41]

Procedural generation is often associated with random generation, but the relationship is only partially true. The system may take a random starting point to generate the content, but the generation uses artificial intelligence (AI) to produce something that makes sense and is playable. If we generate a labyrinth or a dungeon completely at random, we may end up with a result that is not playable. There should be an entrance and an exit; if there is a locked door, there should be a key for it that is accessible. Procedural generation is very complex, but it also has the potential to create games that are constantly changing, where it is not possible to use rote memory to traverse them.

As we have seen, the use of artificial intelligence to generate game content already has a long tradition in games. The popularity and accessibility of Large Language Models (LLMs), which can understand human language and generate it, as well as their combinations with image generation based on text prompts, have given way to a flurry of articles and discussions about how computers can replace humans in creation. Although LLMs are a promising and fascinating resource, the decades-long history of games is evidence that artificial intelligence still needs human creators (game designers, programmers) in order to make games that are meaningful and resonate with players. Once the novelty dies down, we will probably see interesting uses of LLMs as tools to create games, perhaps new kinds or perhaps old kinds, with a fresh twist.

Questions to identify whether the content is hard-coded or procedurally generated:

- Does the content change whenever the player starts a new game?
- Can the player learn a sequence to play the game by heart and repeat it to master the game?
- Does the game create content (characters, animations, sounds, levels) that generates completely different behaviors in the game?

Further Reading

Crawford, Chris. *Chris Crawford on Game Design. New Riders Games.* Indianapolis, IN: New Riders, 2005, pp. 89–91.

Dormans, Joris. "Adventures in Level Design: Generating Missions and Spaces for Action-Adventure Games." In *Proceedings of the 2010 Workshop on Procedural Content Generation in Games*, PCGames '10. New York: ACM, 2010, pp. 1:1–1:8.

Short, Tanya, and Tarn Adams. *Procedural Generation in Game Design*. CRC Press, 2017.

Game Dynamics This concept is a bit complex to explain. The rules of the game establish the possible behaviors in the game, but then they have to be set in motion. The instruction manual of Monopoly (1935), for instance, sets up the rules, but it is just a box with boards, dice, and cards until the players start playing—then it becomes a game. The dynamics of the game consist of how the game plays out, the type of strategies that the game invites, and even the kind of exploits that can derive from the rules; these are all the result of the rules in action. For example, the dynamics of Monopoly include aiming at buying the most expensive properties first and building fast—it is not something that the manual describes, but a strategy that players figure out after repeated sessions.

The term *dynamics* is borrowed from the MDA framework,[42] which in turn is inspired by concepts from cybernetics and how computer programs work: one thing is the code, the set of instructions of the game, and the other is runtime, the program actually working.

The game plays out the moment the player (or players) sets it in motion. A simple set of rules can result in complex dynamics—the board game Go is a traditional example of this. The board has a grid, and players place black or white pieces on the intersections; the player placing the black pieces goes first. The goal is to capture as many spaces as possible by surrounding a group of the opponent's pieces by taking up all orthogonally adjacent points. Pieces remain in place, unless they are captured, in which case they are removed from the board. Players can skip their turn if they want; the game ends when neither player wants to continue moving or one of the players resigns. Although the basic rules of Go can be written in a paragraph, the different strategies have been the subject of stacks of treatises over many centuries, as well as mathematical and computer science research where the game becomes a challenge to understand combinatorics, or a tool to develop better decision-making algorithms in artificial intelligence.

The strategies that players deploy while playing the game can be part of the formal study of games; what is more interesting is to study the resulting player strategies that may not have been anticipated by the designers, and the novel ways in which players decide to play. Unexpected or unusual player behaviors and how players appropriate a game can be the foundation to argue for its special status. For example, David Sudnow wrote a book on how he tried to master *Breakout* (1978) by playing it as a musical score, as a sequence of actions that can be reproduced exactly in the same way, rather than reacting to the movements of the ball, moment to moment.[43] Sudnow understood the dynamics of the game differently from other players, showing how a relatively simple game can be played using very different approaches—Sudnow's being one that is not particularly conducive to mastering the game.

A complex game can foster different play styles, demonstrating its versatility, as well as the capacity of players to transform the game with their participation. Chess is a non-digital example of a rich game that gives way to different ways of playing; as a digital counterpart, the real-time strategy game *Starcraft* (1998) has generated competitions to the point where it is also considered a sport (actually, an *e-sport*). In both cases, players devise their own particular ways to play the game, selecting which pieces or units they deploy or are willing to sacrifice, for example. Another example of how games can be transformed by players is the *Grand Theft Auto* series after its third instalment (2001–2013). It is relatively easy to find videos online that show how players spend their time exploring the world, doing stunts, or playing the mini-games instead of taking up the missions of the game.

At times, one single factor may change the dynamics of the game, and how the player tackles it. Saving the game, as we saw, is one such case—depending on whether there is the possibility to return to a specific game state can change how a player tackles the challenges of a game, as we discussed above with the vita-chambers of *Bioshock* (2007). Dynamic difficulty adjustment is a feature of some games, which detects how many times the player may be unsuccessfully trying a task, and evaluates whether the player needs help to advance. (The building block Difficulty Levels/Game Balance discusses this in more detail.) *Super Mario 3D Land* (2012) makes a special power-up appear at the beginning of the level if the player makes too many unsuccessful attempts at reaching the end; the power-up is a white *tanooki* suit that allows the player to float and destroys enemies by touching them. Players can avoid picking up the power-up to keep trying without the extra help, so the player character can still die if it falls down a chasm, keeping enough challenge to keep the game engaging.

This building block also requires the reader to be familiar with the game—if we cannot count on our reader having played, we have to do a really good job of explaining its rules. It is very easy to get lost in the discussion of very concrete strategies and cases once one knows the game well enough, and it is just as easy to write an expert explanation that is completely opaque and very difficult to follow. You just have to go to an online forum for fans of a game or genre you do not know to appreciate how inaccessible the discussion can be. When you tackle the dynamics of a game, remember that you may not be speaking to fellow players with the same knowledge as you, so you need to provide enough framing to make the information intelligible.

Studying the dynamics of a game can be hard, since there is not a single way of playing most games—this is when our subjectivity as players becomes most evident. There is a whole slew of books dealing with strategies to play games—manuals on how to play Chess, Bridge, and Poker are some of the driest examples of in-depth discussions of game dynamics. On the other hand, this is also where this experience can provide some of the most interesting insights—Sudnow's book is fascinating precisely because he approaches the game in a somewhat unusual manner, and takes it so personally.

Questions to identify the dynamics of the game:

- Does the player have the opportunity to develop different ways to tackle the challenges of the game?
- How do specific formal elements encourage or discourage certain ways to play the game?
- What are the dominant strategies that players have developed?
- What types of gameplay may seem to differ from what the game was supposedly designed for?

Further Reading

Hunicke, Robin, Marc LeBlanc, and Robert Zubek. "MDA: A Formal Approach to Game Design and Game Research." In *Proceedings of the AAAI Workshop on Challenges in Game AI*. San Jose, CA: AAAI Press, 2004, pp. 1–5.

The Gap between the Player and the Game: Point of View

A game uses specific formal devices to present its contents to the player, from the point of view in the world, to using specific types of cards or boards that the player manipulates. The discussion of this building block focuses on how digital games are mediated, although non-digital games such as board games, card games, and even playground games may have similar elements to discuss.

The term *mediation* refers to the formal elements that allow the player to interact with the game, such as the user interface (UI), the point of view, and the player character. These elements position the player within the game both as a software program and in relation to the fictional world. The building block Spaces of the Game in Chapter 4 talked about the *mediated space*, which refers to how the game uses the screen itself to present the game to the player. Below, there is another overview of the interface elements that are outside of the screen (pieces of hardware such as controllers, cameras, or motion sensors). This building block focuses specifically on the point of view as part of the mediation, while the next three blocks tackle how the player affects the entities and the world of the game.

How the point of view is presented to the player is the first, most visible aspect of the mediation. If the game has graphics, it usually provides a camera view of the fictional world. Depending on where it is, it implies different roles in the world. If the world is shown from a first-person point of view, the identity of the player is defined by a specific, physical point of view. The player sees what the camera sees. The camera can also track back and follow the character that works as the surrogate of the player in the world—characters such as Lara Croft in *Tomb Raider* (2013) or Chun-Li in *Street Fighter II* (1992) are the ones whom the player controls to affect the game world. This is usually referred to as *third-person point of view*, in which identification is visual—the player points at that character and says: "That's me." The camera can track back even further, providing a view of the world and not identifying with a particular entity in it. Simulation and strategy games such as *The Sims* (2000) or *Sid Meier's Civilization V* (2010) use this removed point of view to allow the player to get a picture of what is going on in the world. The player identifies with the point of view again but in a generic role, such as a god, of sorts, or a commander ruling the world.

In contrast, text adventure games/interactive fiction, as well as multi-user dungeons (MUDs), use textual representation. Although not exclusively, these games usually use the second-person point of view—the game is addressing the player, telling them where their character surrogate is in the world. This voice has been inherited from the *Choose Your Own Adventure* books, as well as the game *Adventure* (1977), which also used the second person inspired by tabletop role-playing games. However, it does not have to be the norm—some interactive fiction pieces play with the voice so that it is not necessarily second person. For example, *Lost Pig* (2007) is written from the point of view of the linguistically challenged orc Grunk, who describes the world and events talking about himself in a broken third-person. Text games play with literary point of view, rather than visual, allowing us to analyze them as a hybrid between literature and games.[44]

Questions to identify the point of view of a game:

- What is the point of view of the game based on where the camera is?
- If there is no camera, is there another way to position the player in the world (e.g., through narration)?
- How does the point of view provide a role for the player?

Further Reading

Bolter, J. David, and Richard Grusin. *Remediation: Understanding New Media*. Cambridge, MA: The MIT Press, 1999.

Wolf, Mark J.P. *The Medium of the Video Game*. 1st edn. Austin, TX: University of Texas Press, 2002, Chapter 3.

The Gap between the Player and the Game: Entity and Object Manipulation The mediation between the player and the game also involves how the player becomes part of the fictional world and affects the things and characters in it. The element that structures this interaction is the *user interface* (UI). A basic dichotomy that can help us understand how the player intervenes in the world is the difference between direct and indirect manipulation.[45] In games, direct manipulation means the objects that can be manipulated are visible, and the player can affect them immediately, in consecutive actions, and the player can see the effect of the manipulation right away. This is now the most common way to interact with graphical games: in platform games, such as *Rayman: Origins* (2011) or *Super Mario 64* (1996), the player uses a controller to move the player character around the world and jump. Each button maps to an action that is immediately visible on the screen: if there is a wall, the player can see it is not possible to advance unless one jumps over it. If Mario runs into an enemy, the character loses health points, whereas if it is a coin, Mario will pick it up. Direct manipulation means that the player carries out an action, and immediately sees whether it is possible or not, and what the consequences are.

This is different from a text adventure, where the player reads about the world in paragraphs, and has to type in the commands before knowing whether something is possible or not. Some graphic adventure games that use text menus, such as *King's Quest* (1987) or *Maniac Mansion* (1988), have the player select a command from the menu ("pick up key") and then will show the character trying to perform the action. If it is possible, the character will pick up the key, whereas if it is not, there will be a message or animation telling the player the character cannot do that. There is no immediate feedback, but rather a dialogue between the player and the game where the player has to figure out what may be feasible or not—the player operates in the game using indirect manipulation. It is like telling the game what to do and then waiting to see how it responds.

Indirect manipulation is also very common in strategy games, either turn-based (e.g., *Civilization* series, 1991–2016) or real-time (e.g., *Starcraft* series, 1998–2017), as well as the tower defense genre (e.g., *Kingdom Rush*, 2011). The player operates on the world of the game by clicking on units and locations as well as operating on them through a series of menus. Even when the player issues a direct command, such as "create a specific type of unit," the result of that action may take either a series of turns or real time until we see the result, so the feedback on our decisions is not immediate.

Another example of indirect manipulation is the turn-based combat system of computer role-playing games (RPGs), probably inherited from their tabletop origins. In *Star Wars: Knights of the Old Republic* (2003), when the player enters combat, time in the world seems to stop so the player can plan every step of the fight. The player selects the actions from a menu, such as attacking with a certain weapon, and once the actions have been lined up, the player can go back to the world and the actions play out. *Knights of the Old Republic* is an interesting example because the player can navigate the world using direct manipulation, but the combat uses a menu. This shows how games can use different types of user interface depending on the phase or stage of the game; this example also points back to a previous building block (Diegetic vs. Extradiegetic Rules), where the planning is extradiegetic while the fight is diegetic.

Devices that allow gestural interfaces are in an interesting middle ground between direct and indirect manipulation—this is the case of technology such as the Microsoft Kinect, the Wiimotes, or the PlayStation Eye. On the one hand, the player imitates the movements that they want to see in the game—in the bowling section of *Wii Sports* (2006), players imitate the movements of picking up a bowling ball and then throwing it down the alley, so the movements seem to map directly to the screen. Although the perfect imitation of the movements helps, players can also play bowling from a chair, and still get to throw the ball with a flick of the wrist, showing that the mapping may not be as direct as it seems. Studying how the gestural interfaces cue the player to carry out certain movements, or how these gestures may break down, is also part of exploring the mediated participation of the player in the game.

Current technological developments also create new types of mediation in digital games, as is the case with both virtual reality (VR) and augmented reality (AR). VR technologies use a helmet display that covers our whole field of vision, and supposedly separates its users from the real world. In truth, the VR user is still moving and looking around using physical movements outside of the virtual world; one of the challenges of *immersion* (see Box 5.1 Beware of Buzzwords) is to create the sense that the player's body is in the virtual space—what in virtual reality jargon we call *presence*.[46] The player is often a disembodied head, or a pair of floating hands, most times the character we control does not have feet, while our body is still anchored to the physical space. This makes it easy to feel the disconnect between the virtual world and ourselves. Analyzing how a game is trying to create a connection between the player's physical space and the virtual space, or to cover up the mismatch between both can be a good exercise to explore how the technology shapes the fiction of a game. The player character of the VR game *Dead Secret* (2015), for example, carries their arm in a sling, as a way to explain that the player can only use one arm to control the game, so the mediation of the game influences the fictional world of the game.

Augmented reality (AR) can take different shapes, from using locations to determine what kind of content the player can access using a mobile platform, such as a mobile phone, as a lens to see the physical space through.

The essence of AR is to add layers between the user and the real world, which is what mediation means. Therefore, analyzing how an AR game mediates the space may be very productive. For example, *Pokémon Go* (2016) has players navigating the real world to find creatures and catch them, utilizing Pokéstops as locations to acquire items, or Gyms to battle creatures from other teams. The mediation of the game makes players move through urban spaces differently, looking for landmarks in the real world where items or creatures from the fictional world could be. Some businesses took advantage of this overlap between the fictional and the real, establishing Pokéstops in order to encourage players to patronize their establishment, if they wanted to obtain items.[47]

Questions to identify how the game allows the player to manipulate and participate in the world of the game:

- What are the onscreen elements that give information to the player on how to play the game?
- How does the player intervene in the fictional world? What are the entities and objects that they can manipulate?
- Does the interface use direct or indirect manipulation?

Further Reading

Isbister, Katherine, and Noah Schaffer. *Game Usability: Advancing the Player Experience.* Boca Raton, FL: CRC Press, 2008.

Shneiderman, Ben. "Direct Manipulation: A Step Beyond Programming Languages." In *The New Media Reader*, edited by Noah Wardrip-Fruin and Nick Montfort. Cambridge, MA: The MIT Press, 2003, pp. 486–499.

Control Schemes Whereas the previous building block focused on the screen and how it mediates the world of the game for the player, this building block deals with how the hardware allows the player to participate in the game. These formal aspects belong to the player and the social space of the game, as defined by Nitsche in the Spaces of the Game building block.[48] Control schemes point to this space in the form of pieces of hardware, such as the game controller or the keyboard and mouse. The specific design of the hardware won't be discussed here, since that often uses pre-made standards, but rather how the game utilizes the hardware. The following building block tackles specialized controllers and their design.

This building block helps us discuss how the hardware allows the player to participate in the game. While different screen mediations situate the player in the game, hardware controls may involve different skills to use them. While most players will know how to point and click with a mouse, using the WASD keys to move around a three-dimensional world can be a challenge for those who are not used to it. In a similar way, while a touchscreen may make it easier for players to manipulate objects in the world (resorting to direct manipulation—see above), a game controller and its many buttons can be very cryptic for people new to digital games. Even if one knows how to hold it, learning the button combinations to perform complex movements can be challenging.

Controllers use conventions, and conventions change over time—for example, I am used to looking up or steering a ship in 3D by pulling the joystick down or moving the mouse back, a habit I picked up from playing flight simulation games in the 1990s. Now most games map the forward movement to looking up, which confuses me no end, until I find how to configure the controls back to the conventions I feel comfortable with, namely playing with an inverted Y-axis.

Controllers involve a certain literacy, that is, knowing how to use them in order to play. Beware of thinking that controls are "intuitive"—even gesture and movement-based controls require some time to learn how to use them. Using a lot of buttons for game input requires being familiar with a lot of conventions, from how they match to actions to different button combinations. On the other hand, gestures and movement may seem easier to pick up because there is a direct match between the gesture and the action on the screen.

Some games may let players configure the controls to their taste and abilities, accommodating a certain range of skills. For example, *Mario Kart Wii* (2008) has different control schemes—some mapping the controls to a traditional controller where the control stick directs the kart, some using the motion sensor to allow players to place the controller in wheel to steer the vehicle. As another example, the Nintendo Switch console allows players to choose from a variety of control configurations, from using one component of the controller as a standalone device, or attaching both components to the sides of the screen. These different options allow to play in different ways, which can range from using the console as a mobile platform, in a more intimate setting, or playing with others on a big screen as a multiplayer experience, thus, using different spatial configurations that the hardware takes advantage of differently.

As part of player space, the hardware also dictates how the physical space is used. For example, touchscreens and portable consoles tend to reduce the space to play to where the player is sitting or standing, just as reading a book would, thus making them a better fit to play during one's commute on a train or a bus. On the other hand, hardware that involves cameras, such as the PlayStation Eye or the Microsoft Kinect, or that detects motion, such as the WiiMote, requires more physical space and seems to be a better match for games involving social interaction (and players who have enough space to play).

Hardware can also help extend the fictional world to the player space, often dictating how to play the game. The *Rock Band* (2007) controllers (drums, guitars, and microphones) transform the player space into a stage of sorts, where players have to physically perform the actions of the game. A more extreme example is the game *Steel Battalion* (2002), which requires a specialized controller that resembles the control panels of a cockpit. The enormous controller sits on the knees of the player, turning the physical space into the cockpit of a giant robot.

How the hardware provides input to the game is going to continue changing—apart from new gestural interfaces, there are technologies such as biofeedback sensors and improved virtual reality headsets that may open up novel ways to play games.

Questions to identify the formal traits of the control schemes:

- Does the game use standard hardware (keyboard, mouse, game controllers) or does it need custom/specialized hardware?
- Do the actions of the player map to the controller following the conventions of a specific genre? Or does the game provide a new way to use the hardware?
- Can the player customize how to use the controls?
- What type of familiarity with game controls and games does the game require?
- How does the hardware extend the fictional world to the space of the player?

Further Reading

Blomberg, Johan. 2018. "The Semiotics of the Game Controller." *Game Studies 18*, no. 2. https://gamestudies.org/1802/articles/blomberg. Accessed November 4, 2023.

Juul, Jesper. *A Casual Revolution: Reinventing Video Games and Their Players*. Cambridge, MA: The MIT Press, 2009, Chapter 5.

BOX 5.6 EXERCISE: HOW "INTUITIVE" ARE THE CONTROLS?

Run a little experiment, either by playing yourself, or observing someone else play. The goal is to evaluate how intuitive a control scheme is supposed to be. Give someone who does not play games in three-dimensional spaces a first-person game. Games that do not require a lot of shooting may be prepared, such as the beginning of *Half-Life 2* (2004), *Portal* (2007), or a so-called *walking simulator* such as *Dear Esther* (2012) or *The Stanley Parable* (2013). Another genre that is interesting to explore is fighting games, which seem to use direct manipulation but use indirect manipulation for special moves and combos (see building block The Gap between the Player and the Game: Entity and Object Manipulation). A third possibility is to get someone to play a game they know with a different control scheme. How fast does the player figure out how to move (if at all)? What are the common issues that they run into? Ask the player what their expectations are, how would they want to use the controller, and why. How does their supposed intuition match the control scheme they have to use?

Alternative Controllers This building block applies to a type of games which do not use controllers that are commercially available, but rather are customized for a concrete game. There are game creators who craft special controllers for their games, to the point that the controller shapes the game itself—the result is often referred to as *alternative controller games*, also *alt control*. These works are different from commercial games that require a specialized controller, such a plastic guitar, a steering wheel, or a light gun, because they use custom-made, one-of-a-kind controllers, and bring together the physicality of a controller with the digital world.

Alternative controller games can take many shapes and forms,[49] although usually the first thing that comes to mind as an alternative controller game is made specifically for the game. For example, Enric Llagostera's *Cook Your Way* (2018)[50] uses a cooking station controller, with a small pot, stove dials, and chopping board, where players have to cook a dish from their country in order to obtain a visa. The physicality of cooking, and the arbitrariness of how to evaluate how well the player cooks, is part of the political message of the game. The game can be played without the controller, but that means that the design and interactions are also altered. Another example is Carol Mertz and Francesca Carletto-Leon's *Hellcouch* (2018),[51] where the controller is a living room couch. The couch is "possessed," and players have to sit on the right section in order to liberate the demon. This second case is significant because it is a digital game but there is no display—a string of lights and a speaker give the information players need to figure out how to defeat the demon trapped inside the couch. The couch *is* the game—there cannot be a non-digital version.

These games are usually showcased in special physical events, such as festivals or gallery exhibits; their physicality also turns them into an exclusive event—to play them as designed you really need to play them with the controller. As Boluk and Lemieux argue, games with custom-made controllers are a way to challenge standardized ways of playing games, "alternative interfaces do not simply make videogames accessible, but radically transform what videogames are and what they can do."[52] As we discussed in the previous building block, we often take for granted that the way to play a game will be with a console controller, or with a mouse or keyboard as the default input, but we can also challenge the platform and its assumptions. Although at times they may seem gimmicky, alternate control games bring to the forefront the importance of the controller, which often is assumed to be "invisible" or "intuitive," and force us to rethink how we participate in a game, and emphasize the physical movement of moving the controller and how the interface works. Analyzing these games is important because it means documenting their existence and their novel approach to games, as well as making us reflect about what we think is a digital game, since many of these examples do run with digital technology but do not have displays: instead, lights, sound, and haptics may tell us what the state of the game is.

Questions to identify and describe games with alternate controllers:

- Does the game use a modified version of a standard game controller or computer input?

- Does the game use a piece of hardware that is not used as a game device (e.g., a dial-up telephone, a musical instrument, a puppet)?
- How does the game extend the fictional world of the game to the social space of the game?
- Can the game be played with a different controller? If so, how is the game different?
- How does the game controller comment or question the assumptions we make about how players interface with a game?

Further Reading

Boluk, Stephanie. 2017. *Metagaming: Playing, Competing, Spectating, Cheating, Trading, Making, and Breaking Videogames*. Electronic Mediations; v. 53. Chapter One.

Truesdell, Erin J.K., and Brian Magerko. 2023. "Three Design Themes for Collaborative Alternative Controllers." In *Proceedings of the 18th International Conference on the Foundations of Digital Games*. FDG '23. New York, NY: Association for Computing Machinery. https://doi.org/10.1145/3582437.3582473. Accessed November 4, 2023.

Difficulty Levels/Game Balance Determining how easy or difficult a game may be is rather subjective, since it depends on the expertise of each player—what is easy for one person may be impossible for another. A first-person 3D game can be inordinately difficult to navigate for someone who is not familiar with how to navigate a three-dimensional virtual space, whereas a seasoned first-person shooter may breeze through the environment. In order to be aware of your own skills and subjectivity, look back to the exercise in Chapter 2 to help figure out what your player profile is, and think about how your skills and expertise may make some games easier or more difficult than others.

Looking into specific formal elements can help analyze the difficulty in somewhat more objective terms, such as whether there are difficulty settings or different game modes. How often the game allows the player to save is another indicator (see the building block Save Games). Other formal elements that we can look into are:

- *The number of obstacles and their frequency*: how many challenges and how often the player has to deal with them can make a game more or less difficult.
- *The length of a level*: The longest a player has to play in order to reach a milestone/save point, the harder it can be.
- *The skills needed to play the game*: A game that requires quick reflexes may need training; we can check if the game introduces players to the skills needed bit by bit or expects them to already have them. For puzzle-based games, which require more thinking than twitch reflexes, we can look into how the game helps the players acquire the knowledge to solve the puzzles.

It may be the case that the game has variable settings for difficulty, which let players determine how they want to play. In modern games, this may be an indicator that the game is trying to attract different types of audiences. For example, *Bioshock* (2007) has four levels of difficulty: easy, normal, hard, survivor. In the easiest mode, enemy attacks do not hurt the player much; enemies do not have a lot of health points, making them easier to get rid of; using special powers (called plasmids) does not cost a lot of points; and helpful items such as weapons or power-ups appear frequently and are relatively powerful. In the hardest mode (survivor), enemies are twice as strong and attack very accurately, and the helpful items are rather scarce. The easiest mode accommodates players who are interested in the story of the game, whereas the higher levels of difficulty are not only for more seasoned players of first-person shooters, but also for those who may want to focus on honing their skills rather than exploring the environment and the stories in it.

Some games may be easy to learn, but difficult to master, establishing two different aspects to difficulty, as well as different expectations for the player. Many of the games considered "addictive" share this trait, such as *Tetris* (1987) or *Angry Birds* (2009). Other games have a steep curve in order to learn them, requiring attention and work from players to even start playing them, such as *Microsoft Flight Simulator* (2020), *Starcraft* (1998), or *Dwarf Fortress* (2006). How difficult it is to learn how to play also sets different expectations for the player because just starting the game supposes a significant time investment.

Some games are extremely difficult, and that is what makes them fun. In some cases, the difficulty derives from early games where game balancing was not yet part of the vocabulary of design—games designed for home computers in the 1980s, such as *Manic Miner* (1983), had players try each screen over and over again until they got the perfect sequence to overcome the challenges. More recently, there is a type of game identified as *masocore*, which is precisely designed for players to develop the skills to perform precise and well-timed moves. Independent games such as, *Super Meat Boy* (2010), *Hydorah* (2010), or *Limbo* (2012) can be labeled *masocore*. In *Getting Over It with Bennett Foddy* (2017), the developer himself comments on how difficult the game is, as well as philosophizing about failure, as the player struggles to advance in this surrealist platformer. Some games require exacting moves in order to compete each challenge. In genres such as the so-called bullet-hell shooter, exemplified by games such as *Ikaruga* (2001), players have to dodge showers of bullets while trying to attack the incoming enemies, while beat-matching games such as *Beat-Mania* (1998), or *Dance Dance Revolution* (1999) require a good sense of rhythm as well as physical resilience. These games are designed so that players fail a lot and keep trying but they are also games that allow their best players to perform and show off, since seeing someone be good at them is rather impressive.

In other cases, games want to help players learn how to play the game and keep playing, rather than punishing players if they do not do well, or to encourage them to purchase power-ups if they want to make the game more accessible, as free-to-play games tend to do. Some games have systems that keep track of how well (or badly) a player is doing, and can change the difficulty of the game in order to help the player get better at the game—the goal of these games is to keep the player in the game, accommodating the design to the skills of the player. This is the case of the *Mario Kart series* (1992–2020). In the single-player mode, if a player who lags behind picks up a power-up, it will likely be something that helps them speed up and catch up with the main group, whereas if the player is in first place, it is very likely that the other racers will pick up one of the infamous blue shells, which are effectively missiles targeted at whoever is in the first place. This is called *rubberbanding*, and it is a way to both adjust the difficulty so players can be part of the game, and also helps keep the game interesting—if a player is too far behind or too far ahead, there is no drama in the race and the challenge disappears.[53]

The term *game balancing* refers to the process of adjusting the dynamics of the system (see Difficulty Levels/Game Balance building block above) to make the game appropriately difficult for the intended audience, and to create a rhythm and sense of progress, so that the game becomes more difficult as the player gets better at it. Hence, the balance between the skills of the player and the challenge presented. This balance is not an objective, mathematical result—the factors listed above can explain how the difficulty increases, creating a pace in the game. Online games, such as multiplayer online battle arenas (MOBAs) or battle royale games, have matchmaking systems that allow players with the same level of proficiency to play against each other. It is a way to keep things fair, as well as a means to introduce new players into the game—if a player starts a game and is swiftly defeated by an expert player, they may get discouraged pretty fast and quit after a few rounds.

Portal (2007) and its sequel *Portal 2* (2011) are examples of a game where each level is more difficult than the previous one, but only because of the addition of a new element, which the player needs to master in order to advance. *Portal* starts by introducing the player to the concept of portals, then players learn how to use the portal gun to open one side of the portal, then both sides, then how to use switches to open and close doors, and so on. Thus, *Portal* manages to keep players engaged because it provides the player with some scaffolding as it becomes more challenging.

The concept of *flow*, as defined by Mihaly Csikszentmihalyi (2008), is often invoked as an ideal of game design, where the challenge is enough to keep the player interested, but it is not so easy that it becomes boring. This balance is difficult to achieve, but it seems to be a goal of many designers, because it keeps players focused on the activity—players are "in the zone" while they play: they become one with the activity. This means that the skills required, and the difficulty of the challenge are kept in balance (see Figure 5.2). Games that need fast reflexes, such as racing games or music games at a high level of difficulty, are designed to achieve that feeling of control and being able to use one's skills to overcome the challenge. It is a state that is associated with other pleasurable activities, such as yoga, meditation, or dancing.[54]

The design aesthetic of some games, however, does not seem to seek to invite players to achieve a state of flow. For example, some games do not seem to have increased challenges as the game goes on, which may be the case of adventure games. In adventure games, the puzzles are part of advancing the

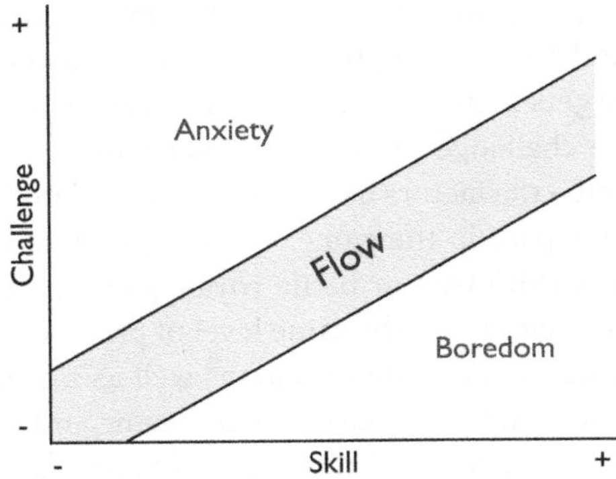

Figure 5.2 Illustration of how the zone of flow finds a balance between the skill required and the difficulty of the challenge

Source: adapted from Csikszentmihalyi (2008)

story, and the skill of the player is not as vital to advancing in the game as their capacity to solve puzzles and get to know the world of the game.

Remember that determining how difficult a game is should not be determined exclusively by how it "feels" to you—formal aspects are what will help you express the level of difficulty more precisely.

Questions to identify the formal elements that indicate the level of difficulty of a game:

- Does the game have specific settings to change the difficulty?
- How frequent are the challenges?
- How much leeway does the player have to recover from a mistake?
- What is the proportion between the powers/stats of the player and those of the opponents in the game?
- Does the game teach the player how to get better at the game? Or does it expect previous knowledge and skills to play it?
- Which elements of the game change as the player progresses to make it more difficult? How does the game become more difficult?

Further Reading

Asad, Mariam. "Making It Difficult: Modernist Poetry as Applied to Game Design Analysis." Thesis, Georgia Institute of Technology, 2011. Available at: https://smartech.gatech.edu/handle/1853/39617. Accessed November 4, 2023.

Juul, Jesper. *A Casual Revolution: Reinventing Video Games and Their Players*. Cambridge, MA: The MIT Press, 2009, Chapter 2.

Wilson, Douglas, and Miguel Sicart. "Now It's Personal: On Abusive Game Design." In *Proceedings of the International Academic Conference on the Future of Game Design and Technology*, Futureplay'10. New York: ACM, 2010, pp. 40–47.

BOX 5.7 EXERCISE: HARD GAMES ARE FUN TOO

Take one of the games listed as *masocore* above and try to get as far as you can without cheating, then find a video playthrough of the game by an expert player and examine how they play. The difficulty of those games is too much to enter a state of flow easily—and yet, they can still be fun, although maybe for a reduced number of players. It is also true that one way to beat these games may be actually entering that state of flow, as may be the case of bullet-hell shoot'em ups, or the hardest level of difficulty of music games such as *Rock Band* (2007). What makes them engaging? How can continual failure be pleasurable? Would these games be as successful if they were more forgiving?

Representation (Visual Design, Sound Design, and Music)

Examining the formal aspects of the audio-visual presentation of a game may be familiar to those coming from film, art, and music history. This is one of the building blocks that certainly benefits from the vocabulary of these fields, so, in order to write about this block, this section will refer to the methods of these other academic disciplines, while pointing out some of the medium-specific formal aspects that the discussion can focus on. This block focuses on the style and aesthetic presentation of the game, while the next one focuses on who and what is represented, and how that expresses certain understandings about the world.

The representation of the game helps in creating a mood, expressing themes, as well as contributing to the narrative of the game. Those coming from film or literature may be tempted to analyze a game in the same way as they write about their usual subjects of study. However, limiting oneself to methods borrowed from other media usually ignores the specifics of the participatory nature of games, as I have been pointing out throughout the book. An analysis that goes beyond merely reading a game like a film or a symphony should acknowledge what the player does in the game: for example, as already mentioned, the musical score of *Metal Gear Solid 2: Sons of Liberty* (2001) tells the player whether the guards are looking for the player character or not, and if they are, how long they have been searching for him. In this case, the music is both setting a mood and providing feedback to the player (as mentioned in the Diegetic vs. Extradiegetic building block). In *Puzzle Bobble* (1994), the music speeds up when time is running out or the player is close to losing, to deliver a sense of urgency, in both cases, indicating that the game may be over soon.

At times it can be difficult to divorce the audio-visual analysis from other building blocks, particularly the user interface (UI) design. Color-coding applied to objects, for example, can be both an expressive device and good interface design. For example, in the game *Ico* (2001), the save points are represented as an eerily white bench that stands out from the rest of the objects. The player character sits there to rest, which effectively pauses the game. The bench is a respite both for the character and the player, while the peculiar shade of white marks the location as a connection to the extradiegetic elements of the game: the saving menu in this case.

The audio-visual aesthetics of the game can evoke other media—*Comix Zone* (1995), for example, takes the panels from comics and transforms them into different screens of the game; as the player overcomes a challenge, the player character moves from panel to panel. Continuing with imitating print, *Gorogoa* (2017) evokes an illustrated book and panels, which the player re-arranges and reconnects in order to tell a story. The independent game *They Came from Verminest* (2012) evokes American sci-fi movies of the 1950s, including a mode that can be played with 3D glasses (one lens red, one blue), and the player can select a screen mode that imitates worn-out film stock. *Cuphead* (2017) is a 2D platformer that imitates the style of American cartoons of the 1930s, so the game looks like an interactive old-fashioned cartoon. The aesthetic choice, however, also inherits some of the problematic representations of that style. The characteristic visual style of *Cuphead* reproduces caricatured racial stereotypes wholesale, without acknowledging the history of the style and how it promoted negative stereotypes of black people.[55]

The history of videogames is long enough that they can make references to the aesthetics associated with previous game genres or technological platforms. Independent videogames often evoke the pixel visuals and music of games from the 1980s, such as *La-Mulana* (2005) which it is a straightforward homage to an obsolete platform, the MSX2, and a game that was released exclusively for it, *Knightmare II: The Maze of Gallious* (1987).

In short, the audio-visual representation is one aspect where the methods to analyze other audio-visual media can be directly applied; however, it is also important not to lose sight of the aspects of the representation that may relate to the medium itself, from technological constraints to the deliberate evocation of other technologies or media, to ideological connotations of certain styles.

Questions to start the discussion of the audio-visual aspects:

- How do the audio-visual aspects of the game indicate what the game is about?
- How does the audio-visual design provide cues for interaction or help understand what is going on in the game?
- How do the audio-visuals take advantage of the technology of the game?
- How does the game evoke the aesthetics of other media/other games/other platforms?

Further Reading

Camper, Brett. "Retro Reflexivity: La-Mulana, an 8-Bit Period Piece." In *The Video Game Theory Reader 2*, edited by Bernard Perron and Mark J.P Wolf. New York: Routledge, 2009, pp. 169–195.

Grant, Barry Keith. "Screams on Screens: Paradigms of Horror." *Loading ... 4*, no. 6 (2010). Available at: http://journals.sfu.ca/loading/index.php/loading/article/view/85. Accessed November 4, 2023.

Perron, Bernard. "From Gamers to Players and Gameplayers: The Example of Interactive Movies." In *The Video Game Theory Reader*, edited by Mark J.P. Wolf and Bernard Perron. New York: Routledge, 2003, pp. 259–280.

Summers, Tim. *Understanding Video Game Music*. Cambridge: Cambridge University Press, 2016.

Representation and Identity In relation to the building block Representation (Visual Design, Sound Design, and Music), as well as with mediation, there is another aspect that also deserves attention, which is how the representation of the game helps create an identity in the game, usually by controlling a character or characters. Who we are and what we look like can matter to many—some players enjoy becoming someone else, others like seeing themselves in the world of the game. We identify with the characters on the screen—you do not say "Mario needs to do a double jump to get there" but "I need to do a double jump." Therefore, players establish a connection with the characters they see on screen. Characters can be anthropomorphic, whether they are human, like Jill Valentine in *Resident Evil* (1996), or animals, like Sonic the Hedgehog. We also identify with vehicles as our character—be it a spaceship, as in the case of shoot'em ups like *Ikaruga* (2001), or racing cars, as in *Road Fighter* (1984) or the futuristic racing game *Wipeout* (1995). Board games also use tokens that are not anthropomorphic—see, for example, how Monopoly (1935) included an iron, a top hat, a shoe, a thimble, a cannon, and a battleship, as some of its early tokens.[56]

The characters that we control in games can be of two types. On the one hand, we have the *player character*, which is pre-designed and given to the player—Super Mario in the eponymous series (1985–2017), Nathan Drake in the *Uncharted* series (2007–2017) or Lara Croft in the *Tomb Raider* series (1996–2018). On the other, we have the avatar,[57] which is a configurable character, so the player can choose how their character will look in the game, or what their abilities are. Western role-playing games, such as *Mass Effect* (2007) typically let players configure their characters, inherited from the character sheets of *Dungeons and Dragons*, whereas Japanese RPGs such as the *Final Fantasy* series (1987–2023) provide player characters. Massively multiplayer online games (MMOs) let players configure their avatars, as a way to create their identity in the game.

Since players often establish a personal relationship with the character they control, it is important to examine the relationship between both. A 2009 survey examined 150 games from that year across platforms, looking for the characters that appeared in the first 30 minutes of the game, whether they could be controlled by the player or not. The survey found that white adult men were overrepresented and constituted the majority of player characters, whereas women, Hispanics, Native Americans, and the elderly were systematically underrepresented.[58] Although this is a relatively old survey, repeating the experiment now would likely yield similar results. Every few years, there is a different image collage of what MacDonald calls the "brooding white male videogame protagonists"[59]—white adult men with a five o'clock shadow and a permanently stern expression. Some key examples of this stereotype are Snake in the *Metal Gear* series (1987–2018) or Joel in *The Last of Us* (2013). Search for the term "video game protagonists" and you will see what they look like for yourself.

Why should it matter who gets represented in games? As Williams et al. discuss in their article:

> Media creates objects in what Price and Tewksbury term the 'knowledge store', which they describe as 'a network of constructs, including information about social objects and their attributes' … Imagery that is viewed or played repeatedly is more accessible when a person is attempting to recall information about that class of social objects.[60]

What this passage is pointing out is that representations that are more frequent are easier to recall or keep in mind, while other representations are erased. These representations also have values attached to them—if white adult men are recurrently represented as the hero, the perception is that only white men can lead the action, whereas if people of color are constantly presented as the sidekick or the enemy, or women are not controllable characters but a reward, players assume that they are less important, less active characters. Media representations help us understand our everyday life, they help create the *knowledge store* defined by Price and Tewksbury, and when media keeps repeating certain representations over and over, the values that those representations make keep getting reinforced, at the expense of those who are left out or represented in a less positive light. Understanding who the games has us to identify with, who is considered the protagonist, and what they look like has certain sets of values. When the game aligns with one's view of the world, these values may seem invisible, but for those who do not often see themselves in games, the discrimination can be painfully evident.

Questions to start the discussion of representation in relation to identity:

- Who does the player control? Is there a single character or many?
- Is the character pre-designed or is it configurable?

- What is the gender/age/ethnicity/sexuality of the characters (playable or not)? How is that meaningful in the world of the game?

Further Reading

Boudreau, Kelly. "Between Play and Design: The Emergence of Hybrid-Identity in Single-Player Videogames." PhD thesis, Université de Montréal, 2012.

Chess, Shira. *Ready Player Two*. Minneapolis, MN: University of Minnesota Press, 2017.

Everett, Anna, and S. Craig Watkins. "The Power of Play: The Portrayal and Performance of Race in Video Games." In *The Ecology of Games: Connecting Youth, Games, and Learning*, edited by Katie Salen, Cambridge, MA: The MIT Press, 2008, pp. 141–164.

Klevjer, Rune. "What Is the Avatar? Fiction and Embodiment in Avatar-Based Singleplayer Computer Games." Thesis, University of Bergen, 2006.

Shaw, Adrienne. *Gaming at the Edge: Sexuality and Gender at the Margins of Gamer Culture*. Minneapolis, MN: University of Minnesota Press, 2015, Chapter 2.

Rule-Driven vs. Goal-Driven Games Some definitions of games focus on their nature as rule systems[61]—there are other possible definitions, but this is the one that will be used in this particular building block. Here is a refresher from previous building blocks: rules indicate which actions and events are possible; the mechanics constrain the player to doing things in certain ways. For example, the rules of Monopoly (1935) tell us which parts of the board are valid spaces to place one's token, and how the tokens move (e.g., we cannot move them counter-clockwise, we have to throw the dice to know the number of spaces). The outcome of the system is going to be different each time—who gets which properties in Monopoly, how fast, and how the properties are traded will change in every session based on the roll of the dice, the chance or community chest cards, and the decisions each player makes.

Emergence is the term we use to define how the events and outcomes of the game are generated by the player interacting with the system, specifically referring to gameplay.[62] Although related, this concept is different from procedural content generation (see above), which refers to how the content is created by the computer. Emergence is the source of variability of the game because it is the reason why we often develop strategies rather than come up with a series of specific steps to complete a game.

Games can also have goals, which are the conditions that define how to advance or win. Scoring the highest points within a specific amount of time is the goal of sports games like basketball or handball, for example. There can also be sub-goals, which are milestones that mark player progress in the form of levels or stages that the player must complete to advance, for example. These progression markers are common in games with a strong story component, where advancing in the game is paired with advancing in the story. This is the case of computer role-playing games (e.g., the *Fallout* series, 1997–2018), where different quests provide a set of goals for the player, or mission-based games, such as action-adventure games like the *Uncharted* (2007–2017) or *Grand Theft Auto* (1997–2013) series. In a similar way, adventure games comprise a series of narrative puzzles that give way to the story of the game as the player solves them. *Progression* is the aspect of the game that regulates how the player advances in the game, and relates to its goal structure.

Thus, *emergence* refers to the aspects of the game that relate to the player making decisions, whereas *progression* refers to the goals and sub-goals of the game. Since most games have both rules and goals, most games also combine both progression and emergence, as Jesper Juul indicates;[63] some games lend prominence to either the rules or the goals. Non-digital games are usually clear examples of games of emergence because there is usually one goal (e.g., get a score higher than the opponent's, get the combination of cards that means the highest score). Strategy games, such as *Starcraft* (1998) or *Sid Meier's Civilization V* (2010), are also a good example of games of emergence, where the player interacts with a complex game system to achieve a specific goal (become the dominant race or civilization).

A game where consecutive goals dominate gameplay may be called a game of progression—Juul refers to the adventure game *The Hobbit* (1982) as a game of progression, because it requires solving one puzzle after another to complete it. The so-called walking simulator genre, where players explore a space in order to discover the story of a space, such as *Dear Esther* (2012), *Gone Home* (2013), or *What Remains of Edith Finch* (2017) have different areas and milestones which mark how much of the world has been traversed; once the player reaches the final space, the game is over. Music games such as *Beatmania* (1998) or *Rock Band* (2007), or rhythm games like *Dance Dance Revolution* (1999) or *Taiko no Tatsujin: Rhythm Festival* (2022), are also games of progression, since there is a clear set of actions (hit the note or move in time with the music) that must be completed in order to succeed in the game.

The distinction between emergence and progression is more useful than using the terms *linear/non-linear,* which do not reflect the nuance of the game design. Car-racing games may seem linear because they take place on a track, but they are really an example of a game of emergence: although there is usually a single path to get to the finish line, there is a single goal (get to the finish line first), whereas how we get to the end of the line depends on how we drive, speed up, slow down, and interact with other racers. In the case of computer racing games, the player's position may trigger different behaviors among the computer-controlled opponents—if the player is first, the other cars will speed up, whereas they will slow down if the player is last so that the player can catch up and still compete[64]—this is *rubberbanding,* as defined in the Difficulty Levels/Game Balance building block. In either case, the goal is to provide a challenge to the player, so that the game is not too easy in the first case, or too hard and will make the player give up. On the other hand, games that have branching paths, such as *Life is Strange* (2015), have very limited emergence—they provide the player with moment-to-moment goals, and depending on how they are achieved (based on the player's skill or choices), the story will take a different course, but in the end the branches are pre-set, even if the system is complex enough to make it hard to represent them.

The contrast between rule-driven vs. goal-driven games also helps us to account for some examples that defy the preconceptions that we have of games. *The Sims* (2000) was originally conceived as a digital dolls house,[65] where players come up with their own goals. The system is rich and complex enough that emergence is predominant. There may be other cases where the game is open for players to come up with their own way of achieving the goals—a game like Charades is a competition where players have to communicate a word or phrase without sound, but rather by acting it out. In this case, the emergence comes from the openness of the rules, which players can negotiate (e.g., no pointing to things or trying to spell the word), bend, or invent as they go.

Games of progression may seem to constrain the player to do a certain set of actions, but that is precisely why they are enjoyable—we synchronize to a set of actions, be it to a computer as in the case of *Rock Band,* or a song and movements, as in the case of the clapping game Pattycakes.

Progression and emergence are two complementary ways of structuring gameplay, so most games have a combination of both, and which one dominates will depend on the type of game, and it may change moment to moment.

Questions to help discuss emergence and progression:

- What is the balance between how the rules and the goals dictate gameplay?
- If you had to write how to complete the game, would it be a strategy guide, a walkthrough with a set of specific actions, or a combination of both?
- Does the gameplay change every time you play, even if the content is the same?

Further Reading

Egenfeldt-Nielsen, Simon, Jonas Heide Smith, and Susana Pajares Tosca. *Understanding Video Games: The Essential Introduction*. 4th edn. London: Routledge, 2020, pp. 213–217.

Juul, Jesper. *Half-Real: Video Games between Real Rules and Fictional Worlds*. Cambridge, MA: The MIT Press, 2005, pp. 71–92.

BOX 5.8 EXERCISE: GOAL STRUCTURE

We have broken down the game you are analyzing in terms of modes, episodes, and quests (see Context Inside the Game, Chapter 3) and verbs (see Game Mechanics, Chapter 4). Now let us create a structure in terms of its goals in order to determine whether it is a rule-driven or goal-driven game. List the goals of the game you are analyzing, dividing them into the overall/long-term goal(s) and the moment-to-moment/short-term goals.

Let us contrast two extreme examples—an adventure game, which is predominantly goal-driven, and a strategy game, which is predominantly rule-driven. In the adventure game *Loom* (1990), the player discovers the goals while exploring and interacting with the world. This would be a sample goal structure of the first act of the game:

- Discover the mystery of the player character's birth (long-term goal).
- Learn how to use the magic distaff (short-term goal).

(Continued)

(Continued)

- Learn all the notes (mid-term goal).
- Learn all the spells (mid-term goal).
    - Learn open spell (short-term goal).
    - Learn light-up spell (short-term goal).
    - Learn straw to gold spell (short-term goal).
    - Learn dye spell (short-term goal).
- Leave the weaver's village (mid-term goal).
    - Open the egg (short-term goal) → reveals information.
    - Open the shell (short-term goal) → gets a new note.
    - Open the skies (short-term goal) → lightning makes a branch fall on the dock.
- Use branch to leave village by sea.

The goals here are presented by the game itself; once they are fulfilled, they usually have immediate consequences—usually opening up a new goal or allowing the fulfilment of a longer-term goal.

In contrast, for Sid Meier's *Civilization V* (2010), the goal structure is much more vague:

- Long-term goal: become the dominant civilization in the world.
- Mid-term goal (the player chooses to follow one).
    - Use scientific dominance.
    - Use cultural influence.
    - Use diplomacy and political strategies.
    - Use military strategies.

In this case, it is much more difficult to write the goal structure, because the game does not quite have one beyond its long-term goal. How to achieve it is up to the player—the mid-term goals are different strategies to achieve them; the short-term goals are determined by the player, and discovered through practice and experimentation or by looking at strategy guides.

If listing the given goals of the game is easy, the game tends to be goal-driven. If you can only list one or two long-term goals, and you realize that the moment-to-moment goals are usually marked by the player, then you are probably dealing with a game that tends to be rule-driven.

Levels and Level Design Throughout this chapter, we have seen different ways to segment gameplay—from levels of difficulty to story chapters or quests. Many videogames are divided into levels, which are sections of gameplay marked by separate spaces. Levels divide what we called the rule-based space in the Spaces of the Game building block (see Chapter 4). Each level can be identified by having a goal, such as clearing all the pills from the screen (*Pac-Man*, 1980) to physically reaching the end of the level (*Super Mario Bros.*, 1985 and most platform games), or defeating a particularly difficult enemy (the dungeons in *The Legend of Zelda: A Link to the Past*, 1991).

Level design is its own specific discipline in game development because it refers to the specific moment-to-moment challenges, rather than general systems or overall goals. When analyzing the level design of a game, we refer to how the different challenges are distributed in the space and what the different goals of the game are. *Donkey Kong* (1981) is a clear example of how level design works. Each screen has the same goal—get to the top of the screen to rescue Lady Pauline from the giant ape—but there are different challenges to tackle.

- The first screen has the player character Jumpman going up the platforms while dodging the barrels that Donkey Kong is throwing at him.
- In the second screen, the platforms become conveyor belts that are continuously moving, and there are burning coals roaming the space. Thus, the challenge consists of coordinating one's jumps with the platforms moving sideways.
- In the third screen the climbing has to happen by jumping on elevators and dodging the springs that Donkey Kong again throws at Jumpman. The movement challenge is to time the jump to get on the right elevator without getting hit by a spring.
- In the last screen, rather than reaching the top, the goal is to remove eight rivets that hold the structure together while dodging the burning coals; once the rivets are removed, the platforms will collapse and Donkey Kong will fall with them. Whereas in other levels the player may be able to avoid certain areas, here the player needs to reach eight specific spots.

Each level of Donkey Kong shows how the core mechanics—moving and jumping—can find sufficient variation by providing different challenges, such as jumping on a moving platform or an elevator. The layout of the platforms, the frequency of the obstacles, as well as the distribution of items—the hammer that can destroy the barrels for a limited amount of time or items to increase the score—are defined by the level design.

Analyzing 2D platform games, such as *Super Mario Bros.* or *Rayman: Origins* (2011), is a good way to learn the basics of level design because the player is just supposed to go to the right and advance obstacles. These games usually coax the player to move following certain paths and time their movements well. When the virtual space becomes three-dimensional, discussing the level design becomes a bit more difficult because the critical path may not be as obvious. *Super Mario Bros.* allows players to skip levels if they find the hidden screens with the entrance to the shortcuts (called *warp zones* in the game), while *Rayman: Origins* has secret areas with small challenges to rescue the little creatures, Electoons, to get more points. Three-dimensional spaces, on the other hand, allow players to traverse them in different ways.

A quintessential example of this complexity is *Super Mario 64* (1996), the very first game in the *Super Mario* series that featured a three-dimensional space. Each level of the game is a separate space, which the player accesses through different portals. The final goal of each level is the same—pick up the golden star. After going through the portal, the player is presented with a title for the level, which gives a clue about how to obtain the star. For example, the very first level the player can play is called "Big Bob-Omb on the Summit," which is a hint for the player to climb to the top of the mountain in the level. What makes the game stand out, which later games in the series have not quite tackled, is that after finding the first star, the player can go back and find a different one. The space remains the same, whereas the layout is versatile enough to support a variety of ways to traverse it and fulfill the different goals of the level. For example, in practically every level there are five red coins; if the player picks up all of them, a golden star appears and becomes the goal of the level.

Other elements that define level design are the distribution of resources, such as power-ups, which provide the player with specific advantages that make it easier to play, often for a limited period of time. Ammunition or extra health work as power-ups, for example. As mentioned in the Difficulty Levels/Game Balance building block, how frequent or infrequent these resources are will determine how difficult the level is. In terms of spatial distribution, the closer these resources are to the critical path, the easier it will be. If there are hidden resources, it may be a sign of the game inviting players to explore and find alternate paths to traverse the space.

Alternate paths and secret zones are also part of the level design. When the goal of the level is to get from A to B, part of the challenge is to open up new areas that allow the player to advance. Closing off certain zones is a way to limit the player's movements and make sure they stick to the critical path.

This is very typical of the dungeons in the *Legend of Zelda: A Link to the Past*. While exploring the dungeon for the first time, the player may pass by a door that is locked, or see an area across a chasm that is inaccessible. These are indicators that there are areas the player needs to reach, and provides a sub-goal in the level. Now the player needs to find out how to get there, for example, by finding the fulcrum that will open a door. Using locked areas as part of the level design results in an interesting experiential paradox—while it is a tool for designers to dictate where players should go, it also makes players believe they are finding their own way, because they need to explore to find how to open up the new area.

Another level design element that uses the space to create a challenge is *choke points*. A choke point is a narrow space the player must go through in order to reach the goal, such as a corridor or a bridge. By forcing the player to go through a specific path, the level design fosters conflict for the player. Choke points are common in shooter games, especially maps for multi-player first-person shooters. By creating a choke point, the designer creates the opportunity for conflict. Players look for these points to ambush the other team because they know they have to go through it, and they will have limited space to maneuver. So, whichever team forces their opponents to the choke point will have the advantage.

Careful level design can also be an effective way of teaching the player the basic mechanics of a game, as an interactive instruction manual of sorts. Game designer Anna Anthropy explains how the first few seconds of *Super Mario Bros.* teach the player what to do.[66] The first thing the player sees is Mario on the left, looking to the right, where there is a flashing block with a question mark, so the prompt is to go right. As the player moves, the first enemy shows up: a goomba walking directly towards Mario. The player needs to dodge, and the only action possible is to jump. A timely jump can result in one of several things: the player can dodge, land on the goomba and destroy it, or can hit on the flashing block with a question mark, which makes a coin pop up. After this first discovery, the player sees that there are other blocks, so the level is inviting the player to keep hitting them. When the player hits the next block, a giant mushroom appears—if the player picks it up, Mario doubles his size and can jump higher. All this information is contained within a couple of screens. Granted, it may take novice players a few tries to figure all these features out, but it is a clear example of how level design can be used to let players figure out the game by playing, rather than by having it explained.

A game like *Portal* (2007) turns the incremental reveal of the mechanics into a feature, as we saw in the building block Difficulty Levels/Game Balance. The player character, Chell, is presented as an experimental subject that must go through a series of tests, and each test takes place in a different chamber. The player learns one game mechanic at a time. In the first chamber, the player learns that there are portals across space that allow non-topographical navigation, and that one can put cubes on switches to open doors. The second chamber shows that the portals can move, and there can only be two portals open at a time, and the next two chambers teach how to open one portal with a special gun. *Portal*'s core mechanics involve a type of spatial thinking that we cannot develop in the real world; these mechanics were innovative and uncommon; therefore, the progressive introduction of each mechanic is a way to present players with a new set of mechanics and problem-solving.

We have already discussed the field of narrative design in the Relationship Between Rules and the Fictional World building block—narrative design also counts with its own specialized type of level design. Narrative level design means designing the space of the game and how it should be navigated as a way to construct a story. This type of narrative design, for instance, is the core of walking simulators, where the interaction revolves around traversing the space, so players can figure out what has happened in it. Apart from setting up the challenges, a narrative level designer also sets up the objects and characters that tell the story, integrating narrative and game design. As the player traverses the space, the game invites the player to interpret the objects and characters in the environment. Games such as *Portal* or *Bioshock* (2007) are notable precisely because of their environmental storytelling. In *Portal*, the player can find traces left by other test subjects who have been in the facilities before. *Bioshock* makes environmental storytelling into its biggest boon by showing the story of the underwater city Rapture through its different areas, and how it went from utopia to civil war in a short period of time. The beginning of the game provides continuous examples of how the environment constructs a story. After seeing a brief film introducing the ideology that led to build Rapture, the player is thrown into a city ravaged by violence and conflict. The player reaches an area where there are placards littering the floor, with slogans such as "Rapture is dead" probably protesting the disintegration of the society and its values. The panel display listing the transports leaving the city reads "cancelled" whereas the floor is littered with abandoned suitcases. The objects tell the story of the collapse of ideals and how citizens were trying to leave the city but could not, all as the player navigates the first level.

Since level design defines moment-to-moment interaction, a breakdown of the elements of a level is a useful exercise for game designers, both novice and experienced, just as analyzing a poem word for word or a film scene shot for shot can reveal the complexity and care of the work. This practice, however, requires knowing the level well; as we saw in the examples, the analysis not only entails giving a detailed account of what happens, but also hypothesizes the rationale of the design, that is, why the level is laid out as it is.

Questions to analyze the level design of a game:

- How is the space segment defining the level?
- What is the goal of the level? Are there any sub-goals?
- What are the challenges in the level? How are they distributed in the space?
- Is there a critical path, i.e., is the player expected to traverse the level in a specific way?
- How does the level communicate to the player what to do?
- Does the level try to integrate gameplay and story? Or is the story separate from the players' actions (e.g., using cut-scenes)?
- How does the environment relate to the story of the game? How does the level construct a story for the player?

Further Reading

Anthropy, Anna, and Naomi Clark. *A Game Design Vocabulary: Exploring the Foundational Principles Behind Good Game Design*. Reading, MA: Addison-Wesley Professional, 2014.

Fernandez-Vara, Clara. "Game Spaces Speak Volumes: Indexical Storytelling". In *Proceedings of Think Design Play: Digital Games Research Association Conference 2011*. Utrecht, 2011.

Totten, Christopher W. *An Architectural Approach to Level Design: Second Edition*. 2nd edn. Boca Raton: A K Peters/CRC Press, 2019.

Treanor, Mike, and Michael Mateas. "BurgerTime: A Proceduralist Investigation". In *Conference of the Digital Games Research Association—DIGRA 2011*. Hilversum, The Netherlands, 2011.

Zagal, Jose P., Clara Fernández-Vara, and Michael Mateas. "Rounds, Levels and Waves: The Early Evolution of Gameplay Segmentation". *Games and Culture* 3, no. 2 (2008): 175–198.

BOX 5.9 EXERCISE: WORDLESS TUTORIALS

In the same way that we have provided a brief breakdown of the early moves in *Super Mario Bros.*, examine the first level of a game, focusing on how it introduces the players to the core mechanics. Does the game tell the player about the actions, or does it invite the player to perform them instead? Is it a mix of both? Is it optional to perform the core mechanics or not?

It may be the case that the game does not really introduce the player to the mechanics, and expects the player to read the manual or figure them out on their own, as is the case for example of the *Mario Kart* series (1992–2020). If this is the case, what does the level assume the player knows about the game already? What makes the level more accessible than others later in the game?

The tutorials of story-driven games often have a special status—the first level introduces the player to the fictional world of the game and to the mechanics. Justifying the process of learning the game is an interesting challenge, especially because it usually bridges the fictional space with the play space—the game needs to refer to the controller that the player is holding. Using another set of terms, the game needs to refer to extradiegetic elements in order to teach the player how to play. How does the tutorial deal with the gap between the player and the world of the game? How does it narrativize the process the player is following to learn about the fictional world and the rules of the game at the same time?

Choice Design Choice design relates to the previous building block Levels and Level Design; it refers to how the player may be presented with choices and their consequences. These choices can happen moment to moment, or can be a key part of the overall game design, where different choices may lead to different pre-set outcomes.

Salen and Zimmerman indicate that choices in games have five phases:[67]

1. The game in its current state.
2. The player is presented with a choice.
3. The player makes a choice.
4. The choice has consequences in the system.
5. The consequences are communicated to the player.

These five steps help us identify the choices of the game, evaluate their possible consequences, and how they are communicated to the player.

In rule-driven games, the player is constantly making decisions—see, for example, *Sid Meier's Civilization V* (2010), where the player has to choose what to do in each turn, such as develop an area, a technology, or more units; give commands to units; or attack other civilizations. In goal-driven games, choices are less frequent and also often very specific; the consequences tend to be pre-set from a limited number of options. The game will change in particular aspects as the player progresses, including different endings. This is more common in story-driven games, because if every choice changed the story, the content would have to contemplate every single permutation, which can make the development of the game unwieldy. There are different ways to structure narrative choices, and not all of them may be necessarily dependent on branching.[68] An example of this is *Overboard!* (2021), where the player controls a murderous actress, who is trying to get away with murder aboard a transatlantic ship, within a specific time. Players can choose to blame other people, plant evidence, or even murder additional witnesses. The game is meant to be replayed many times, not only to find different ways to escape jail, but also to learn the secrets of the rest of the passengers in the boat.

At times a choice may be apparent, but there are no consequences—it provides the illusion of choice. Japanese role-playing games do this all the time. *Dragon Warrior* (1986) is notorious for forcing the player to give a specific answer—the princess who invariably needs rescue asks the player character, "Dost thou love me, Kefka?" If the player chooses "No," the princess responds, "But thou must," presenting the dialogue choices again until the player chooses to reply affirmatively. *Dragon Warrior* is a blatant example of how games at times give players the illusion that they are making a choice. Whatever the player decides is irrelevant because the consequences will always be the same.

Comparing the differences between choices can provide insight on what the game is about. Some games reward certain choices and not others, or there may be a value system attached to the player's actions. Role-playing games such as *Star Wars: Knights of the Old Republic* (2003) or *Mass Effect* (2007) have systems that keep track of the players' actions, from how they talk to non-player characters, to whether they choose to help them or not. The more actions of a certain type that the player carries out, the more the player character tends to become a good or bad character (or, in the case of each game, *jedi* and *sith, paragon* and *renegade*). The issue with choosing to be good or bad seems to be that it reduces morality to an obvious spectrum, as a problem that has a single solution, and makes the decisions that push the player's counter one way or another relatively apparent.[69] The dialogue system positions the good, neutral, and bad options always in the same slot of the menu, for example, so it becomes clear what the moral consequences may be. The choice becomes a gimmick, rather than an interesting exploration of moral values, by making the choices too obvious.

The other extreme occurs when the choices are not obvious—the player is making a choice without realizing that specific actions will have consequences. One example of this is the game *Penguin Adventure* (1986), where the player controls Pentaro, a penguin who must find a golden apple and bring it to the royal palace to save the penguin princess. By default, the princess dies—the only way to get a good ending is to play the game from beginning to end, only pausing the game once (no more, no less). Supposedly, the final outcome is the result of the actions of the player, but there is no explicit mention of how these actions (which are extradiegetic) can have such dire consequences.[70]

Sid Meier, designer of the *Civilization* series, stated that games are a series of interesting choices.[71] How frequent these choices are, the extent of their consequences, and how obvious they are, also determine how interesting the game may become.

Questions to evaluate the choice design of a game:

- How often does the player have to make a choice?

- What types of choices are there (e.g., a binary choice vs. multiple actions from a menu)?
- Are the choices obvious?
- Is the relationship between the choice and its consequences clear? How far is the choice made from the resulting consequence, in space or in time?
- Does each choice have a value attached to it?

Further Reading

Salen, Katie, and Eric Zimmerman. *Rules of Play: Game Design Fundamentals.* Cambridge, MA: The MIT Press, 2004.

Sicart, Miguel. *Beyond Choices: The Design of Ethical Gameplay.* MIT Press, 2013.

BOX 5.10 EXERCISE: EXAMINING MORAL CHOICES

Choose a game where the choices are attached to a (presumed) moral system, or where choices are the core mechanic that determines how events evolve, such a *Planescape: Torment* (1999), *Mass Effect* (2007), *Undertale* (2015), or *Disco Elysium* (2019).

- How obvious are the choices?
- Can players track the consequences of their actions to what they chose? Examine what the function of the choices is: do the choices pat the player on the back to reinforce a worldview, or do they reflect on the consequences of our actions?

Cheats/Hacks/Mods/Bugs Chapter 2 discussed how it is good to specify the version of the game we are analyzing, including whether we use any alternative modes to enhance our gaming capital, that is, our knowledge and proficiency in the game.

These non-standard ways to play may change the supposed critical path/ideal experience, as already discussed. These alterations affect the formal properties of a game, often making more evident how some of those formal aspects affect gameplay. By being able to change the game, we can see how it is different when certain formal aspects are changed or completely omitted.

Cheats are devices that allow us to change the game and make it easier, such as getting infinite energy, hints, or skipping levels. Some of these cheats are codes that are already part of the game because they are a tool that developers use to facilitate testing during development. If they change something in a level late in the game, they want to have a shortcut to skip and play that level instead of having to play through the game from the beginning. Cheats can also be modifications done with external devices, such as a program that loads before the game, or a cartridge that allows the player to modify the game externally. Computer-savvy players may know how to modify the game by accessing the debug mode of the program (another development tool) or changing some of the settings in the configuration files. By changing these settings, we can see what makes a game difficult or engaging—is *Super Mario Bros.* (1985) still interesting to play if you get rid of all the enemies? What happens if Mario could jump higher than in the standard game?

Hacks and modifications (*mods*) are alterations that can also help us think about the game differently, to the extent of providing a critique on it. For example, expert programmers find ways to change the game to create new modes to play, or reveal content that is part of the code but is not accessible otherwise. The mod can be as basic as changing character sprites—a programmer changed *Donkey Kong* (1981) so that his daughter could play as the female character, Pauline.[72] By changing the images of the character, the hack critiques the assumptions made by many mainstream games where the protagonist is male and has to rescue the princess (see other Nintendo series *Legend of Zelda*, 1986–2017, or *Super Mario Bros.*, 1985–2013). The name of the character evokes a prototypical damsel in distress, Pauline from *The Perils of Pauline* film serial (1914), who kept taking deadly risks and had to be rescued in every episode. *Donkey Kong* does not let players identify with a strong, adventurous female player, but rather with stumpy, moustached Jumpman—the hacker found a way to let his daughter control a character that she felt comfortable playing and identifying with.

Modifications can also become an artwork on their own, which comments on and questions the original game(s) that it modifies. Cory Arcangel's *Super Mario Clouds* (2002) features only the background of the game *Super Mario Bros* (1985), with drifting clouds over a blue sky, projected on the walls of the exhibition room.[73] The mod, running on an original NES console, has been showcased in galleries all over the world. By erasing all the other elements from the game, the installation interpellates the viewer to interpret it—anyone familiar with the original game will recognize the clouds, appealing to their iconic status as well as nostalgia. The viewer can also ask questions the work itself—is it still a game if it is not interactive, but it is running on the original hardware? The clouds are also projected on the walls, as if they were a painting in motion—what does it say about *Super Mario Bros.* as an artwork?

Game modifications can also be encouraged by the game itself, which may come packaged with tools for players to make their own content. *Doom* (1993) was one of the first games to include a level editor, which contributed to its popularity, while role-playing games such as *Neverwinter Nights* (2002) or *The Elder Scrolls V: Skyrim* (2011) include a set of tools for players to create their own adventures. These modifications can become games in their own right—*Dear Esther* (2012) started as a mod using Source, the *Half-Life 2* (2004) toolset, which then garnered enough acclaim to be recognized as a game on its own. *DOTA* (2003), started as *Defense of the Ancients*, a mod for *Warcraft III: Reign of Chaos* (2002), and then went on to be one of the defining titles in the multiplayer online battle arena (MOBA) genre.

The inclusion of tools for players is often related to the intent of wanting to create a community who will create additional content for the game. Game series such as *The Sims* (2000) or *LittleBigPlanet* (2008) put a lot of weight on the tools, because user-generated content can help them both grow the game and the community of fans behind it. Other games depend on user-generated content, such as *Super Mario Maker 2* (2019), which is a tool that allows players to build their own platforming levels in 2D based on the Super Mario designs, share them online, and play other users' designs.

Going back to the tech-savvy players, hacks can unearth hidden content that is part of the code of the game, but is not accessible in a standard way. For example, a group of fans of the game *Star Wars: Knights of the Old Republic II: The Sith Lords* (2005) managed to restore a series of quests and parts of the story that are in the code but were incomplete, recovering deleted scenes that gave new insight into the story. Revealing hidden content can be the source of controversy and problems—fans of the game *Grand Theft Auto: San Andreas* (2004) found a discarded sex mini-game in the code, and made it available again in the modified PC version of the game that they nicknamed "Hot Coffee." This hack of the game created a controversy, since the inclusion of sexual content would change its age rating, at least in the USA.[74] After disastrously handling the situation by first saying that the content was not there and then admitting it was, Rockstar, the developer of the game, was forced to change the rating of the game in the USA to Adults Only, thus substantially reducing the audience of the game.[75] A discussion of whether discarded features left in the code but not available in a standard way are part of the game or not can help us explore the role of hacks in game studies.

Bugs can also open up non-standard ways of playing. A bug is a technical problem with a game, by which the program does not work as expected. At times, a bug can break the game in such a way that renders it unplayable; other times, it may make it too easy to play—that is called an exploit. In a third instance, the problems with the code create uncanny representations in the world of the game, even if the game is still playable.

An exploit (i.e., a bug that makes the game easy to play) usually means finding an easy way to get resources, skip difficult parts, or make some aspects of the game really easy. A clear example can be found in the game *The Elder Scrolls II: Daggerfall* (1996): if the player camps out in a store until it closes, the shopkeeper will leave, so the player can pick up all the items that may fit in the inventory. What is more, the player can come back to the store to sell the shopkeeper the items back, making this strategy an easy way to obtain a large number of resources. This makes it easy to acquire items and money, in a way that the developers probably did not plan for.

Bugs can transform our expectations about the game, often calling attention to the technology and its design convention. The original release of *Red Dead Redemption* (2010) has notorious bugs which are easy to come across and can be rather uncanny. Some of them have to do with the game assigning animal animations and sounds to a human shape, thus, we can find the so-called "cougar man," who moves around and attacks as a feline, or the "bird woman," who flies around flapping her arms.[76] The game seems to step over the line from Western to horror just because of these misallocated animations.

All these types of alternative content, whether they originate in the game itself, or whether they are player modifications, provide the opportunity for rich discussion, since they allow us to see the game in a new light. If we compare games with literature or film, the material can be similar to comparing different versions of the same text or film, or commenting on a homage or appropriation of a media text. The difference, particularly in the case of bugs, is that these alternative modes of playing may be an accident or derived from the technology itself, and probably were not intended by the developers.

Questions to discuss cheats, hacks, mods, and bugs:

- If discussing a cheat, does the modification of the standard way of playing derive from code from the developers or is it a modification by a third party?
- If it is another non-standard mode of playing, has it been developed using tools provided along with the game (modification) or has it been developed using external tools by expert programmers (hack)?
- Is the formal aspect being analyzed a programming issue that does not seem intended by the developers?
- What does this modification reveal about the game that is not observable in the supposedly standard mode?
- How does the modification allow us to critique the game? How does it change the values and assumptions of the original game?

Further Reading

Boluk, Stephanie. *Metagaming: Playing, Competing, Spectating, Cheating, Trading, Making, and Breaking Videogames*. Electronic Mediations; v. 53, 2017.

Champion, Erik. *Game Mods: Design, Theory and Criticism*. Pittsburgh, PA: ETC Press, 2013.

Lewis, Chris, Jim Whitehead, and Noah Wardrip-Fruin. "What Went Wrong: A Taxonomy of Video Game Bugs." In *Proceedings of the Fifth International Conference on the Foundations of Digital Games*. FDG'10. New York: ACM, 2010, pp. 108–115.

Postigo, Hector. "Video Game Appropriation through Modifications Attitudes Concerning Intellectual Property among Modders and Fans." *Convergence: The International Journal of Research into New Media Technologies 14*, no. *1* (2008): 59–74.

Taylor, T.L. "The Assemblage of Play." *Games and Culture 4*, no. *4* (October 1, 2009): 331–339.

BOX 5.11 EXERCISE: FAN REMAKES

In the same way that literature and film revisit the same stories and with different versions over time, game fans and developers also recreate their favorite games, or take the code of the original games and modify it as a way to provide commentary, as we have seen above. Find a mod or a hack that works as a critique on the original game. The *Donkey Kong* modification has been mentioned already; other examples would be *Kaizo Mario*, a hack of *Super Mario World* (1990) that turns it into an almost impossible platform game.[77] Alternatively, if you have the skills, you can create your own mod or hack of a game as a critical exercise. We have seen throughout the book different ways in which games can involve meaning, and in which players make sense of games; by appropriating the text and modifying it, fans and developers create new meanings as well.[78]

Discuss how the changes to the original game can be considered a comment on it. What elements does the modification take from the original game? What is changed—and why? Who is the audience of this modification?

▶ TO SUM UP

This area has provided the basic building blocks to discuss the formal elements of games. I have tried to be as comprehensive as possible, and although this is a lengthy collection of blocks, it is still a preliminary map of the different basic concepts. There are many different types of game genres, technologies, and play approaches—there are probably some games out there that already push the concepts described in these building blocks. The main takeaway of this chapter is to realize that, although some of the formal elements of games may overlap with those from other media, there are specific aspects that deal with their nature as regulated activities that players participate in that set them apart from film and literature, and situate them closer to activities such as theater or sports.

Remember that the goal of this area is not merely to provide a breakdown of the elements. This is not a laundry list; it is a discussion where you are finding out something new about the game and communicating it to others. It is not about what is in the game, but how and why it is distinctive.

So, now we have a whole box full of construction pieces. The possibilities are infinite—we can talk about a variety of aspects, and we have a repertoire of basic concepts and terms. At this point, I would imagine that the overview of the building blocks has already given you some ideas about what to discuss. I would hope that you already have some notes, and that some of the exercises in this chapter provide the foundation for your analysis. Now you need to organize them to express a coherent set of ideas, focusing on a specific topic and knowing who you are talking to.

Chapter 6 discusses how these building blocks can help construct a variety of analyses, depending on the goal and the area of study we come from. By putting things together, our analysis can help us, and our readers, understand better how games work, and how players participate in, appropriate, and transform them.

▶ NOTES

1 Rouse, Richard. *Game Design: Theory and Practice.* 2nd edn (Plano, TX: Wordware Publishing, 2001).

2 Smith, Lee, and Raymond Klein. "Evidence for Semantic Satiation: Repeating a Category Slows Subsequent Semantic Processing." *Journal of Experimental Psychology: Learning, Memory, and Cognition* 16, no. 5 (1990): 852–861.

3 Murray, Janet Horowitz. *Hamlet on the Holodeck: The Future of Narrative in Cyberspace* (Cambridge, MA: The MIT Press, 2001), pp. 97–125.

4 Ibid., p. 98.

5 McMahan, Alison. "Immersion, Engagement and Presence." In *The Video Game Theory Reader*, edited by Mark J.P. Wolf and Bernard Perron (New York: Routledge, 2003), pp. 67, 86.

6 Ryan, Marie-Laure. Narrative as Virtual Reality 2: Revisiting Immersion and Interactivity in Literature and Electronic Media (Baltimore, MD: Johns Hopkins University Press, 2015), Chapters 3 and 4.

7 See, for example, Linderoth's study of how players in *World of Warcraft* struggled to role-play and ignore happenings in the real world while playing: Linderoth, Jonas. "The Effort of Being in a Fictional World: Upkeyings and Laminated Frames in MMORPGs." *Symbolic Interaction* 35, no. 4 (2012): 474–492.

8 See a breakdown of the kind of spatial, cognitive, and participatory negotiation in Mäyrä, Frans, and Petri Lankoski. "Play in a Mixed Reality: Alternative Approaches into Game Design." In *Digital Cityscapes: Merging Digital and Urban Playspaces*, edited by Adriana de Souzo e Silva and Daniel M. Sutko (New York: Peter Lang, 2009), pp. 129–147.

9 Bogost defines the term in Bogost, Ian. "The Rhetoric of Video Games." In *The Ecology of Games: Connecting Youth, Games, and Learning*, edited by Katie Salen (Cambridge, MA: The MIT Press, 2008), pp. 117–140; Sicart provides a critique of the concept and how at times is used in a simplified way in Sicart, Miguel. "Against Procedurality." *Game Studies* 11, no. 3 (2011): 209.

10 Church, Doug. "Formal Abstract Design Tools." In *The Game Design Reader: A Rules of Play Anthology*, edited by Katie Salen and Eric Zimmerman (Cambridge, MA: The MIT Press, 2006).

11 Barwood, Hal. "The 400 Project." In *Hal Barwood: Writing and Design*. Available at: http://www.finitearts.com/Pages/400page.html (accessed November 4, 2023); Adams, Ernest, and Andrew Rollings. *Fundamentals of Game Design* (Berkeley, CA: Prentice Hall, 2006); Bates, Bob. *Game Design*. 2nd edn (Boston: Thompson Course Technology, 2004); Rouse, *Game Design: Theory and Practice.*

12 The Game Ontology's methodology is explained in Zagal, Jose P., Michael Mateas, Clara Fernández-Vara, Brian Hochhalter, and Nolan Lichti. "Towards an Ontological Language for Game Analysis." In *Changing Views: Worlds in Play* (Vancouver: University of Vancouver, 2005). Available at: http://www.digra.org/digital-library/publications/towards-an-ontological-language-for-game-analysis/ (accessed November 18, 2023). The Game Design Patterns are listed in a volume explaining their methodology and basic elements, Bjork, Staffan, and Jussi Holopainen. *Patterns in Game Design* (Game Development Series). 1st edn (Hingan, MA: Charles River Media, 2004). Operational Logics proposes a theoretical framework to explain how both games operate as well as how they communicate these operations to players; rationale and approach are explained in Osborn, Joseph C., Noah Wardrip-Fruin, and Michael Mateas. "Refining Operational Logics." In Proceedings of the 12th International Conference *on the Foundations of Digital Games* (New York: ACM, 2017), p. 27.

13 "Marc Laidlaw on Story and Narrative." Available at: www.gamasutra.com/view/feature/131227/marc_laidlaw_on_story_and_narrative.php (accessed November 4, 2023).

14 Eagleton, Terry. 1996. *Literary Theory: An Introduction Second Edition*. 2nd edn. Minneapolis, Minn: University of Minnesota Press, p. 3.

15 Gonzalo Frasca pointed out that the difference in approaches was really ludology and narrativism, i.e. interpreting games as a type of narrative, rather than narratology, which is the literary study of narrative and narrative theory (see Frasca, Gonzalo. "Simulation versus Narrative: Introduction to Ludology." In *The Video Game Theory Reader*, edited by Mark J. P. Wolf and Bernard Perron, 1st edn (Routledge, 2003).

16 See another Frasca paper for an early discussion of how ludological approaches were not necessarily antagonistic against narrative. Frasca, Gonzalo.

"Ludologists Love Stories Too: Notes from a Debate that Never Took Place." In *DiGRA '03 - Proceedings of the 2003 DiGRA International Conference: Level Up* (Utrecht: University of Utrecht, 2023). https://ludology.typepad.com/weblog/articles/frasca_levelUP2003.pdf (accessed November 4, 2023).

17 Jenkins, Henry. "Game Design as Narrative Architecture." In *First Person: New Media as Story, Performance, and Game*, edited by Noah Wardrip-Fruin and Pat Harrigan (Cambridge, Mass.: MIT Press, 2004), pp. 118–30.

18 Heussner, Tobias, Toiya Kristen Finley, Jennifer Brandes Hepler, and Ann Lemay. 2023. *The Game Narrative Toolbox*. 2nd edn (New York: Focal Place).

19 Propp, V., I. Fe, and A. Fe. *Morphology of the Folktale*. 2nd edn (Austin: University of Texas Press, 1968).

20 See for example Gervás, Pablo. "Propp's Morphology of the Folk Tale as a Grammar for Generation." In *2013 Workshop on Computational Models of Narrative*, edited by Mark A. Finlayson, Bernhard Fisseni, Benedikt Löwe, and Jan Christoph Meister. Open Access Series in Informatics (OASIcs) (Dagstuhl, Germany: Schloss Dagstuhl–Leibniz-Zentrum fuer Informatik, 2013), 32, pp. 106–22.

21 Flanagan, Mary, and Mikael Jakobsson. *Playing Oppression: The Legacy of Conquest and Empire in Colonialist Board Games* (The MIT Press, 2023).

22 In an early game studies article, Gonzalo Frasca proposes that games are simulations rather than narrative. Although this dichotomy is controversial and seems dated in light of later discussions, the description of how games as simulations allow us to experiment in the world is very insightful. Frasca, Gonzalo. "Simulation versus Narrative: Introduction to Ludology." In *The Video Game Theory Reader*, edited by Mark J.P. Wolf and Bernard Perron, 1st edn (New York: Routledge, 2003).

23 Seyalıoğlu, Hakan, and Kathryn Hymes. *Dialect: A Game about Language and How It Dies* (Thorny Games LLC, 2018).

24 Johnson, Soren. "GD Column 11: Theme Is Not Meaning (Part I)." *DESIGNER NOTES*. Available at: www.designer-notes.com/?p=237 (accessed November 4, 2023); "GD Column 12: Theme Is Not Meaning (Part II)." *DESIGNER NOTES*. Available at: www.designer-notes.com/?p=240 (accessed November 4, 2023).

25 For a definition of diegetic and extradiegetic sound in film, see Bordwell, David, and Kristin Thompson. *Film Art: An Introduction*. 9th edn (New York: McGraw-Hill, 2009), pp. 284–285.

26 This question is explored in Juul, Jesper. *Half-Real: Video Games between Real Rules and Fictional Worlds* (Cambridge, MA: The MIT Press, 2005), pp. 123–130.

27 Murray, *Hamlet on the Holodeck*, p. 79.

28 Weise, Matthew. "The Rules of Horror: Procedural Adaptation in Clock Tower, Resident Evil and Dead Rising." In *Horror Video Games: Essays on the Fusion of Fear and Play*, edited by Bernard Perron (Jefferson, NC: MacFarland, 2009), pp. 238–266.

29 Traitor mechanics are part of unilateral competition, one of the player configurations described in Chapter 4. In games with this configuration, players work towards a specific common goal, except for one player, who is the traitor and may be trying to sabotage the other players without revealing themselves. There may be more than one traitor; and the traitor is usually appointed through game mechanics, rather than players choosing to betray the others.

30 Hocking, Clint. "Ludonarrative Dissonance in Bioshock." *Click Nothing*, October 7, 2007. Available at: www.clicknothing.com/click_nothing/2007/10/ludonarrative-d.html (accessed November 4, 2023).

31 The game is playable online. Available at: http://unmanned.molleindustria.org (accessed November 4, 2023).

32 Juul, Jesper. "A Certain Level of Abstraction." In *Situated Play: DiGRA 2007 Conference Proceedings*, Tokyo, 2007. Available at: www.jesperjuul.net/text/acertain level/ (Accessed November 4, 2023).

33 Flanagan, Mary, Daniel C. Howe, and Helen Nissenbaum. "Values at Play: Design Tradeoffs in Socially-Oriented Game Design." In *Proceedings of the SIGCHI Conference on Human Factors in Computing Systems*, CHI'05 (New York: ACM, 2005), pp. 751–760.

34 Frasca, "Simulation versus Narrative," p. 231.

35 Karlsen, Faltin. "Analyzing Game Controversies: A Historical Approach to Moral Panics and Digital Games." In *The Dark Side of Game Play: Controversial Issues in Playful Environments*, edited by Torill Elvira Mortensen, Jonas Linderoth, and Ashley M.L. Brown (New York: Routledge, 2015), pp. 15–32. https://doi.org/10.4324/9781315738680.

36 Bogost, Ian. *Persuasive Games: The Expressive Power of Videogames* (Cambridge, MA: MIT Press, 2007), pp. 28–44.

37 Jayanth, Meghna. "Forget Protagonists: Writing NPCs with Agency for 80 Days and Beyond." *Medium* (blog), June 5, 2016. Available at: https://medium.com/@betterthemask/forget-protagonists-writing-npcs-with-agency-for-80-days-and-beyond-703201a2309 (accessed November 4, 2023).

38 Bogost, Ian. *Persuasive Games: The Expressive Power of Videogames* (Cambridge, MA: MIT Press, 2007), p. 50.

39 Mitgutsch, Konstantin, and Narda Alvarado. "Purposeful by Design?: A Serious Game Design Assessment Framework." In *Proceedings of the International Conference on the Foundations of Digital Games*, FDG'12 (New York: ACM, 2012), pp. 121–128.

40 Crawford, Chris. *Chris Crawford on Game Design*. New Riders Games (Indianapolis, IN: New Riders, 2005), pp. 89–92.

41 "Bethesda's Nesmith Reflects on the Difficult Birth of Skyrim's 'Radiant Story' System." *VentureBeat* (blog), January 27, 2012. Available at: https://venturebeat.com/2012/01/27/bethesdas-nesmith-reflects-on-the-difficult-birth-of-skyrims-radiant-story-system/ (accessed November 4, 2023).

42 Hunicke, Robin, Marc LeBlanc, and Robert Zubek. "MDA: A Formal Approach to Game Design and Game Research." In *Proceedings of the AAAI Workshop on Challenges in Game AI* (San Jose, CA. AAAI Press, 2004).

43 Sudnow, David. *Pilgrim in the Microworld* (New York: Warner Books, 1983).

44 For an in-depth exploration of the interactive fiction genre, see Montfort, Nick. *Twisty Little Passages: An Approach to Interactive Fiction* (Cambridge, MA: The MIT Press, 2003), pp. 50–51.

45 Schneiderman, Ben. "Direct Manipulation: A Step Beyond Programming Languages." In *The New Media Reader*, edited by Noah Wardrip-Fruin and Nick Montfort (Cambridge, MA: The MIT Press, 2003), pp. 486–499.

46 Ryan, Narrative as Virtual Reality 2, Chapter 3.

47 Humphreys, Lee. "Involvement Shield or Social Catalyst: Thoughts on Sociospatial Practice of Pokémon GO." *Mobile Media & Communication* 5, no. 1 (January 1, 2017): 15–19.

48 Nitsche, Michael. *Video Game Spaces: Image, Play, and Structure in 3D Worlds* (Cambridge, MA: The MIT Press), p. 16.

49 A good breakdown of different types of alternative controllers is "About Alternative Controllers—Shake that Button." n.d. https://shakethatbutton.com/about-alternative-controllers/ (accessed September 23, 2023).

50 More information about the project here https://enric.llagostera.com.br/cookyourway/ (accessed September 23, 2023).

51 You can see the game in action and further details here https://www.hellcouch.com/ (Accessed November 4, 2023).

52 Boluk, Stephanie, and Patrick LeMieux. *Metagaming: Playing, Competing, Spectating, Cheating, Trading, Making, and Breaking Videogames*. Vol. 53 (University of Minnesota Press, 2017), p. 36.

53 Nintendo has patented this system as part of a racing game. Ohyagi, Yasuyuki, and Katsuhisa Satou. Racing game program and video game device. United States US7278913B2, filed October 20, 2004, and issued October 9, 2007. Available at: https://patents.google.com/patent/US7278913/en. Accessed November 4, 2023.

54 Csikszentmihalyi, Mihaly. *Flow: The Psychology of Optimal Experience* (New York: Harper Perennial Modern Classics, 2008).

55 Two journalistic articles discuss the history of the visual style of *Cuphead* and how it is problematic. Blackmon, Samantha. "Pickaninnies and Pixels: On Race, Racism, and Cuphead at E3—NYMG." Available at: www.nymgamer.com/?p=9235 (accessed November 4, 2023) and Cole, Yussef. "Cuphead and the Racist Spectre of Fleischer Animation | Unwinnable." Available at: https://unwinnable.com/2017/11/10/cuphead-and-the-racist-spectre-of-fleischer-animation/ (accessed November 4, 2023).

56 Pilon, Mary. The Monopolists: Obsession, Fury, and the Scandal Behind the World's Favorite Board Game (New York: Bloomsbury Publishing USA, 2015).

57 Please note that the use of the term *avatar* can be considered problematic, since it has been appropriated by Western tech culture from the religion of the Indian subcontinent. See De Wildt, Lars, Thomas H. Apperley, Justin Clemens, Robbie Fordyce, and Souvik Mukherjee. "(Re-)Orienting the Video Game Avatar." *Games and Culture* 15, no. 8 (2020): 962–981.

58 Williams, Dmitri, Nicole Martins, Mia Consalvo, and James D. Ivory. "The Virtual Census: Representations of Gender, Race and Age in Video Games." *New Media & Society* 11, no. 5 (2009): 815–834. The survey has been recently updated, noting that the state of representation has not really changed much in over 10 years. Harrisson, Annie, Shawn Jones, Jessie Marchessault, Sâmia Pedraça, and Mia Consalvo. "The Virtual Census 2.0: A Continued Investigation on the Representations of Gender, Race and Age in Videogames." *AoIR Selected Papers of Internet Research* (2020).

59 MacDonald, Keza. "Brooding White Male Video Game Protagonists, Ranked." *Kotaku Australia*, March 7, 2016. Available at: www.kotaku.com.au/2016/03/brooding-white-male-video-game-protagonists-ranked/ (accessed November 4, 2023).

60 Ibid., p. 819. The article quoted in the paragraph is Price, Vincent, and David Tewksbury. "News Values and Public Opinion: A Theoretical Account of Media Priming and Framing." In *Progress in Communication Sciences* (New York: Ablex Publishing, 1997), pp. 173–212.

61 Juul, Jesper. *Half-Real: Video Games between Real Rules and Fictional Worlds* (Cambridge, MA: The MIT Press, 2005), pp. 23–45.

62 Ibid., pp. 76–82.

63 This building block revises Jesper Juul's dichotomy between games of progression and emergence (ibid., pp. 67–72). According to this definition, games of progression have a specific series of steps that the player needs to fulfill to achieve a specific outcome, and games of emergence are games where the outcome is unknown and is the result of interacting with the system. Since Juul indicates that most games usually combine emergence and progression, I decided to reformulate this dichotomy as a shift in the emphasis on pre-existing elements of the game, the rules and the goals.

64 Hunicke, et al. "MDA: A Formal Approach to Game Design and Game Research."

65 Pearce, Celia. "Sims, BattleBots, Cellular Automata God and Go: A Conversation with Will Wright." *Game Studies* 2, no. 1 (2002). Available at: www.gamestudies.org/0102/pearce/ (accessed November 4, 2023).

66 Anthropy, Anna, and Naomi Clark. *A Game Design Vocabulary: Exploring the Foundational Principles Behind Good Game Design* (Reading, MA: Addison-Wesley Professional, 2014), pp. 4, 54.

67 Salen, Katie, and Eric Zimmerman. *Rules of Play: Game Design Fundamentals* (Cambridge, MA: The MIT Press, 2004), pp. 62–66.

68 For an insightful breakdown on the structure of choice-based games, and how developers prevent content from expanding, see Ashwell, Sam Kabo. "Standard Patterns in Choice-Based Games." Blog. *These Heterogenous Tasks*, January 26, 2015. Available at: https://heterogenoustasks.wordpress.com/2015/01/26/standard-patterns-in-choice-based-games/ (accessed November 19, 2023).

69 A good critique of how games tend to model moral dilemmas as a solvable problem, rather than as philosophical ethical explorations is Sicart, Miguel. "Moral Dilemmas in Computer Games." *Design Issues* 29, no. 3 (2013): 28–37.

70 This is documented in "*Penguin Adventure's* Help and Trivia." Available at: www.angelfire.com/art2/unicorndreams/msx/PengnAdv.html (accessed November 4, 2023).

71 As quoted in Rollings, Andrew, and Dave Morris. *Game Architecture and Design* (Scottsdale, AZ: Coriolis, 2000), p. 38.

72 Kohler, Chris. "Why I Hacked Donkey Kong for My Daughter|Life | Wired.com." *Game\Life*, March 11, 2013. Available at: www.wired.com/gamelife/2013/03/donkey-kong-pauline-hack/ (accessed November 4, 2023).

73 Arcangel, Cory. "Super Mario Clouds." Cory Arcangel's Official Portfolio Website and Portal. Available at: https://coryarcangel.com/things-i-made/2002-001-super-mario-clouds.html (accessed November 19, 2023).

74 "*Hot Coffee* Mod." *Wikipedia*, last modified August 22, 2023. Available at: http://en.wikipedia.org/wiki/Hot_Coffee_mod.

75 "San Andreas Rated AO, Take-Two Suspends Production." *GameSpot*. Available at: www.gamespot.com/articles/san-andreas-rated-ao-take-two-suspends production/1100-6129500/ (accessed November 4, 2023).

76 "Glitches in Redemption." *Red Dead Wiki*. Available at: http://reddead.fandom.com/wiki/Glitches_in_Redemption (accessed November 4, 2023).

77 The Kaizo Mario mod, as well as documentation on how it came to be, are available at: http://kaizomario.techyoshi.com/index.html (accessed November 4, 2023).

78 For a detailed discussion of appropriation and participatory culture, see Jenkins, Henry. *Convergence Culture: Where Old and New Media Collide* (New York: New York University Press, 2006).

6

Writing the Analysis

▶ INTRODUCTION

At this point, we have done our research, and we are all ready to synthesize it as an assignment, a paper, an article or, if you are more ambitious, a thesis. In Chapter 5, we went through all the potential pieces of our analysis, which can also become the center of our discussion; the final stage is to select which pieces are the most relevant to what we want to get across. It is like playing with little plastic bricks—depending on what we want to build, we will choose different shapes and forms, so that a space rocket may not use the same pieces as a castle or an ambulance.

Your analysis is going to be informed by the assumptions that may be associated with your field.[1] In journalism, the assumption is that your writing should inform and enlighten readers by creating an accessible and clear narrative, and being faithful to your sources. Some humanities writing, on the other hand, values subjectivity and the exploration of ideas as a way to reach insight, although always supporting it with evidence. If your training is in computer science, or certain sections of social sciences, the scientific method and statistics may be what you most value as sources. These assumptions shape the strategies that we will use to understand our game better, as well as inform the specific methods with which we analyze it. The

DOI: 10.4324/9781003355779-6

field we are working within will share these assumptions, so we can appeal to them—or challenge them, if we feel ready—in our work.

If you are writing an academic analysis, this is the stage where you want to do a literature review, that is, read pre-existing academic works that provide the theoretical concepts to help you analyze your game, or find the adequate methodologies that will be relevant to your writing. For example, if you are writing about an online world, you probably want to read studies of virtual worlds. If you want to examine your game from a historical perspective, it may be useful to read historical analyses of different artifacts, from digital games to media texts, to technological artifacts (e.g., old cooking utensils,[2] or, more relevant to our study, early home computers[3]). In the field of game studies, we should feel free to take inspiration and poach from other disciplines that have a longer tradition in comparison. In order to innovate, the key may be to find unexpected but productive connections between our subject of study and pre-existing approaches, or to devise our own methods by transforming pre-existing ones.

As you read the notes you have been taking while playing the game and survey your secondary sources, remember not to be overambitious. This is the time to condense your ideas, to make a point. Making a contribution does not mean writing a whole treatise on your game, or demonstrating that you know everything about the game in question and then more. It should be possible to convey your insight in one or two sentences, as the core of what your analysis is about. This should ring a bell if you have done some essay writing already—it is the *thesis statement* of your analysis. Being able to express the main point of your analysis in a couple of sentences is not oversimplifying your ideas; it is making them clear. The thesis statement is the keystone that will hold your analysis together.

At times it can be challenging to figure out what the thesis statement may be at first, even after having prepared well. There is so much information that you do not know where to start. One good way to narrow down the focus of your writing is to ask a question of the information that you have as soon as you can. A game analysis is an inquiry about a game or games—so asking a question and devising the answer is a way to learn new things. Once you have your question, you can write the analysis to answer it, and the thesis statement becomes the summary of the answer to that question. The kinds of questions that are the most productive often start with "how?" or "why?," rather than a yes/no question (e.g., "Does this game engage players with their narrative?"). "How?" and "why?" help us understand process and/or hypothesize about the reasons, whereas a yes/no question often elicits a short answer as a thesis statement (yes or no).

For example, in my own work, I analyzed a collection of games based on the character of Sherlock Holmes,[4] in a comparative analysis of several titles through the years. Since I was comparing so many games, I needed a question to guide me through all of them. My question was "How do players become Sherlock Holmes in different games based on the character?" I already had a theoretical concept that was going to help me define this—players would recreate the behaviors of Sherlock Holmes' stories in an interactive manner, a process I called *restoration of behavior* based on previous works from performance studies.[5] I first came up with what those behaviors are by reading Arthur Conan Doyle's stories, then I played a selection of games. The answer to the question—which appeared in the introduction section of the paper—was that rather than trying to encourage the player to become Sherlock Holmes, by doing things like analyzing evidence, using disguises, carrying out chemical experiments, or actually deducing something, these games limited themselves to using design tropes from adventure games, such as lock-and-key puzzles or exploring dialogue trees.

Starting to write the analysis is also the stage when writer's block can appear. The concept for an essay can be great and you may be very excited to write it, but as every word goes down on the page, you may realize how hard it is to write. This stage can also be very difficult when you write about a game that you know very well. Your knowledge and passion, however, can also be a big hurdle, because you may feel like nothing you write does justice to the game, so it is easy to freeze and not write at all, or keep rewriting the same paragraph over and over. The key here is to know that this is a normal feeling, that yes, writing is hard, but there are also strategies to do a good job. In this case, the key is to keep writing and get to a first draft, which may not be good, but you can always rewrite it. Leaving time for revisions is the key to writing a good analysis—and any assignment, really. This is why spending too much time preparing your essay or starting to write the day before an assignment is due is a bad idea.

You are probably itching to write your analysis by now, so you can start by drafting the thesis statement, which should be one or two sentences at most, or come up with a question or two. Yes, coming up with a good question or a thesis statement is more difficult than starting to pour your thoughts on a paper and showing off how much you know. If you start doing that, the result may end up being a jumble of ideas, not an analysis. Your goal is not to overwhelm the reader, but to explain your ideas clearly and persuasively—the best analyses are not the ones that cram a lot of information into them, but the ones where we can remember what they were about. As a teacher, at times I have come across analyses from students who write about their favorite game, but they are more focused on showing off how well they know it rather than helping the reader learn something new and interesting about it. What is worse, the essays tend to be a mishmash of notions, which often get lost in jargon rather than make a point. Overwhelming your reader with information and presenting yourself as an expert player do not mean that you are writing a good essay; writing your ideas clearly is what will make the difference.

You may find yourself shifting your thesis statement as you write, and that is okay. It means that you are refining your arguments, which also includes refining and rewriting your thesis statement to make it stronger—remember, rewriting is a good thing. By the way, if you consider yourself a budding game designer, transmitting your ideas coherently and intelligently will also be your greatest asset. Being able to break down and explain other people's games is training for communicating your own design ideas to your collaborators.

A good thesis statement is going to take you a long way, because the rest of the analysis is providing arguments and evidence to support it. The thesis statement will provide the focus; it is a beacon to guide you through the mountains of knowledge that you have accrued during your research phase. You may not get to show off how much you know about the game, but you may demonstrate how you have found a compelling way to talk about it.

So, what makes a good thesis statement? Let us see an example from Kristine Jorgensen's article on the role of sound in digital games, which summarizes her topic in two sentences:

> Music with no source in the game world but still has the ability to inform about events in that world is an example of what I will call *transdiegetic* sounds in computer games. This is a new theoretical term that emphasises the specific functional aspects of sound in computer games while explaining how sound in computer games deviates from the common understanding in

film theory of diegetic sound (sound with an origin in the film world) and extradiegetic sound (sounds that stem from an external source).[6]

The goal of this paper is to explore a new concept related to sound, which the author needs to develop because the concepts borrowed from film studies of diegetic/extradiegetic do not quite explain it. This thesis statement does two things—on the one hand, it introduces the topic of the paper (sounds which have no source in the fictional world of the game, but are meaningful in the context of the game). It also defines *transdiegetic,* a new term that she is creating, and presenting in the context of terms from film studies. The thesis statement serves to contextualize the discussion and highlight the limitations of pre-existing theories when applying them to videogames.

Coming up with your thesis statement, however, is only half of the work. The other half involves framing your discussion, which means presenting it in a manner that is appropriate for your field and, therefore, your audience. We speak differently depending on who is listening—you would not retell the events at the party last night to your friends in the same way that you would tell them to your parents, for example. Knowing who we are talking to helps us select the building blocks and our words better, which again will contribute to the ultimate goal of writing a clear analysis. It is better to get across to selected people effectively, than to convey a muddled message to the masses.

An important prompt as you start writing is to think about who you are talking to. If you are writing a class assignment, it may be tempting to write it just with your teacher/professor in mind. That also means that you are learning to talk to one person. Is that what you really want? If you believe you really have something to say about games, you probably want to speak to a wider audience. Maybe your audience is not everyone, but a reduced group—from fellow game critics to people who are interested in games but may not be familiar with many of them. One of the challenges for those of us studying and making games is to create a discourse that evidences the socio-cultural relevance and artistic merit of games as a media form. We want to persuade those who still do not understand this with good academic, professional, or journalistic writing, creating an inclusive forum instead of just preaching to the converted.

Talking to everyone can be intimidating, though. Different people will have different pre-conceived ideas, concepts, and vocabulary. The analysis wants to appeal to the knowledge they already have first, in order to introduce new insights. That is the strategy that I am following in this book. I am writing the same way I talk to my students, because that is who my main audience is, and I want to make it accessible and useful to you. The teachers and researchers who may be reading this will notice that this book is not intended directly for them, since sections like these explain contents they may already know.

BOX 6.1 USING SPECIFIC EXAMPLES

Describing specific examples to illustrate your points is key to making your writing clear and accessible, as well as reinforcing the statements in your writing. Taking for granted that your reader is familiar with the game you are analyzing can lead to overstatements and vague affirmations that your reader may not agree with, even if they know the game. For example, if I were working on an analysis of *Dear Esther* (2012) and I wrote "The horror elements of *Dear Esther* are one of the main emotional draws of the game," I would need to specify what "horror elements" means. First of all, not many players of the game would agree with the game having anything to do with horror in the first place. So, I would have to give specific examples: there is a certain sense of uncertainty from the beginning of the game—who is the player character? Where does the action take place? Who is the Esther that the letters are addressed to? As the player explores, there are shadows that appear and disappear in different locations, which may be the ghosts of the previous inhabitants of the island, and appear at random. The uncertainty that pervades the game early on, the eerie space, as well as the ghosts would be elements of the game that relate to the horror genre—more of the uncanny type, as Freud defined it,[7] rather than jump scares.

The more specific your example is, the easier it will be to the reader to understand your point. Examples are both a way to provide context as well as help reinforce your statements—they are the evidence that your insights are not mere hunches but are grounded on specific moments, components, events of the game you are analyzing. You want your reader to see the game the way you do, rather than leaving gaps for players to fill with their own interpretations.

Your analysis then will probably be written within the conventions of the discipline that you are studying in. This is your opportunity to bring games to what you are studying, which should be pretty exciting. You can apply what you know about writing about film to games, for example, bringing it together with the strategies that we have been discussing in this book.

This is how you can show off how much you know, since you will be able to produce a piece of interdisciplinary writing.

If you are writing a journalistic piece, it should be briefer and to the point, and without in-text citations. Academic papers, on the other hand, invite the reader to examine the sources used, so including them is essential. In either case, both are types of writing that need research and documentation, and in both you need to use your sources accurately. In the case of academic papers, particularly in the social sciences, you also need to be explicit about your methods to demonstrate the scientific soundness of your paper.

There are a lot of limitations and guidelines that we need to take into account as we are writing, but do not let that stop you. You are not going to write the perfect analysis all at once—it takes writing, and rewriting and revising. If you try to follow all the advice in this book at once, you will probably freeze and never finish. So, write, then rewrite, and then rewrite some more.

▶ TYPES OF ANALYSES: OVERVIEW

The versatility of what we write also means that there are many ways in which to put it together. This book cannot overview every single one of them, but it can present a few sample ones that will serve as prototypes for some of the most common types of analysis that will constitute a class assignment. An analysis can focus on a specific area, which involves specific building blocks; therefore, the types of analysis that will be featured here will be organized according to the focus of the analysis. There are different types of analyses depending on their goal:

- *Journalistic review*: The goal is to provide a critical overview to future players of a game.
- *Historical analysis*: The goal is to understand the game as a historical artifact.
- *Game communities*: The goal is to use a game to understand the people who play it.
- *Illustration of a theory*: The goal is to provide evidence and support a theory through analyzing a game.

- *Interpretative analysis*: The goal is to communicate how the game may stand or mean something beyond the game itself.
- *Personal account*: The goal is to provide a subjective understanding of a game.

In the description of each type, we will include a discussion of what we can learn from that analysis, the fundamental building blocks it consists of, and examine some exemplary works. Each section points to the blocks that constitute the core of the analysis; you will still have to use other blocks to support your thesis and construct your arguments.

These are just a few models, but they are not the only possible ones. The type of analysis that you choose depends on who you are talking to, as we just discussed, as well as the point you want to make. That also means that you may want to find your own configuration of building blocks, or combine the different models. In the same way that the individual building blocks are at times difficult to tease apart and end up being discussed in conjunction, at times, the types of analyses merge and you may need to combine different types to make a point. Many of the sample analyses referred to here are combinations of different models. Game analysis is not an exact science, but a critical and subjective exercise. Which ones are relevant to your discussion will depend on your goals.

BOX 6.2 EXERCISE: ANALYZING THE ANALYSIS

Chapter 5 described the basic building blocks of how to analyze a game. Some of the building blocks are recurrent in every game analysis, of whatever type. Some others will only appear in certain types of analyses. A good way of seeing how they are assembled together is by breaking down the analyses into their corresponding building blocks.

Choose two game analyses from Appendix II, and identify the different building blocks. Which blocks are included? Which ones does the analysis focus on?

As an example, let us break down the building blocks of "Retro Reflexivity: *La-Mulana*, an 8-Bit Period Piece."[8]

1. Context: discusses the relationships between:
    - technological context
    - socio-historical context
    - economic context

(Continued)

(Continued)

2. Game overview:
    - production team
    - game genre
    - gameplay experience
    - story
3. Thesis statement: what sets the game apart:
    - representation and technological context
4. Supporting discussion:
    - technological context and representation
    - gameplay experience:
    - rules of the world
    - goal-driven game
    - relationship between the rules and the fictional world
    - production team: quotes
    - audience: reception
    - game modifications: fan translation
5. Application of theories to explain the game (remediation)
    - Application of the theory to the technological and economic context
6. Representation (discussion within the limits of the Technological Context)
7. Conclusion

▶ GAME SUMMARY: THE KEY SECTION

In order to get your reader situated in the discussion, independently of the type of analysis you choose to write, any analysis needs to include a summary to allow us to identify the game. This section will be common to all the analyses because it helps provide a basic context to our discussion. This summary condenses the following building blocks:

- Context: Production Team
- Context: Game Genre
- Game Overview: Number of Players
- Game Overview: Description of Gameplay
- Game Overview: Gameplay Experience

If the game is presented within a fictional world and has some sort of narrative, provide a brief synopsis based on these two building blocks:

- Game Overview: Story
- Game Overview: Fictional World

The following blocks are not always necessary, but can help us define the game in more detail:

- Formal Qualities: Difficulty Levels/Game Balance
- Formal Qualities: Control Schemes and Peripherals
- Formal Qualities: Representation (Visual Design, Sound Design, and Music)

This type of overview is not something that literary analyses usually do, since the writer often takes for granted that the reader is already familiar with the text and the analysis is a way to expand on it. The same may be said of cinema studies, although some analyses will include a brief synopsis if the film is not well known, and the purpose is precisely to call attention to its qualities.

In a game analysis, the overview helps us provide the context, so the reader understands the game even if they have not played it. We cannot count on our reader always being familiar with the game, so we have to provide a frame of reference. This is particularly necessary when our audience is not knowledgeable about videogames, or we are talking about an obscure, experimental game, for example, so we have to help them understand the basics of the game. The overview is a reminder that you are not writing this just for yourself or your friends, or even just your teacher—remember, your analysis should aim to speak to others.

We may be able to skip an overview in very limited instances, as would be the case if we are talking about an extremely popular or iconic game, such as the *Super Mario* series (1985–2023) or *Pac-Man* (1980). Even then, you may want to highlight the aspects of the game that the analysis is focusing on—you can always help your readers see the game in a new light. Imagine, for example, that our overview of *Pac-Man* becomes a bit interpretative:

Pac-Man could be understood as a game about a depressed man who has to take pills to forget about his problems, which are the ghosts that chase him. When he gets an extra dose of the medicine, he can fight the ghosts back. The rest of the analysis could use the rest of the building blocks, such as the relationship between the rules and the fictional world, to support it. Mind you, this is a somewhat facetious interpretation, proposing more of an exercise on style and provoking the reader, and it is probably hard to really sustain the interpretation with many building blocks. What I am trying to show with this extreme example is that our summary can encapsulate how we understand the game and how it differs from interpretations, for good or bad.

The summary should be a brief and succinct section to introduce the game. A good way to keep it short is to remember which are the game's distinctive features, what sets it apart, rather than what is common, and which aspects of the overview are going to help you set up the discussion that supports your thesis statement.

▶ JOURNALISTIC REVIEW

We are going to cover this type of analysis first, because it is likely that you have read game reviews before. (If you have not, it is not a problem—there are plenty of other writings that can serve us as a reference.) Perhaps your interest in talking about games comes from listening to podcasts, which can be a different journalistic format, or watching people review games on streaming, which do not tend to adhere to journalistic standards. As we advanced in Chapter 1, the journalistic review is also one of the most problematic modes of game analysis, which derives from being a type of writing that may not question its purpose as often as it should. It is hard to write a good game review, and as new formats arise and become popular, we need to be more critical about the discourse created by videogame reviews.

If you consider yourself someone who is knowledgeable about games, you probably have read your share of game reviews, and have these as the model of what game journalism is; it is also likely that streaming may be your main referent on how to talk about games. These kinds of discourses are probably what you associated with analyzing a game before reading this book; in this section we will focus on written reviews in a journalistic format. As you were going through the building blocks of the analysis, you likely recognized some of them from having seen them in these reviews. The building blocks that journalistic reviews feature are usually the ones already mentioned under the game overview section, because in a way the focus of the overview is to present the game to a new audience:

- Context: Production Team
- Context: Game Genre
- Game Overview: Number of Players
- Game Overview: Gameplay Experience
- Formal Qualities: Difficulty Levels/Game Balance
- Formal Qualities: Control Schemes and Peripherals
- Formal Qualities: Representation
- Formal Qualities: Representation and Identity

Because of how the review is written, listing the elements above may not be analyzing a game. This is all useful information to describe the game, but does not provide the reader with insight about it; what makes it interesting or engaging. If you write following this model of game review, you are basically writing a consumer report about specific generic features.

The goal of game reviews is usually to provide the reader with information about the game and its supposed qualities, in order to help the reader make the decision on whether they want to purchase the game or not. The key word here is *purchase*—a summary of the kinds of information the writer believes the reader needs to know before buying a game.

This is a specific trend in North American reviews—a sector of the game writers for mainstream outlets grew up reading magazines such as *Nintendo Power* (1988–2012) or *PlayStation Magazine* (1997–2012), and that became their writing model. Yet those publications were actually marketing vehicles for console makers, advertisements that consumers paid for, rather than a work of journalism. The line between writing a game review and a veiled advertisement can be quite blurred in some specialized websites and publications, although in the last 15 years there has been a growing journalistic trend to write independent reviews, as made explicit by the editorial guidelines and policies of some mainstream websites. Chapter 1 talked about how some game publications and specialized websites may depend on the income they get from game advertising; releasing a review before the time agreed with a publisher, or even negative reviews, may lose a website some important advertising revenue, or access to games before they are released, thus, not having access to the latest content.[9] However, this economic model seems to be shifting—some magazines and websites are based on subscriptions and donations, other websites make independence part of their mission statement.[10] Some game websites have started to diversify their content to include reviews of film and TV shows, while others have their advertising managed by external agencies, so, in either case, the revenue of the site is not exclusively tied to game-related advertising.

This takes me to another issue in game journalism: the need to review games well before they are released. Incidentally, this is not dissimilar to what film journalism does, with previews and interviews with filmmakers being featured in anticipation of new movies. The problem of writing at the service of selling game copies or tickets is that this type of writing falls into generating hype, and that often rubs out any critical approach that the writer may have initially intended.

The goal of your game review should not be creating hype, but reasoning with your readers about why a game may be worth their attention, and what they may get out of it. Game reviews should not be different from other game analyses: they should provide insight about the game. If you get a job as a game journalist, then you will probably have to face the economic constraints of the trade, which are also becoming insidious. But if you are not getting paid, or if they pay you no matter what you write, you should strive to deliver a worthy piece of writing.

The model that I have just described is currently in a state of flux—on the one hand, there is the work of game journalists who have improved the quality of game reviews to provide insightful comment and to create a more sophisticated discourse, often resorting to academic concepts in their reviews, but making them clear and accessible to the reader. In certain venues, game journalism has become more than a consumer report by providing critical reviews which make players intrigued about a game because of its concept or—more interestingly—invite players to read the review after playing to engage in the critical discourse about the game. On the other hand, the talent and brilliance of these journalists is not often supported by many publishing venues as it should be, often chasing them away from the journalistic discourse that they have helped improve.

The main shift in the videogame discourse has been to the subjective experience of the writer, rather than an evaluation, which started with the so-called New Games Journalism at the end of the 2000s. Kieron Gillen wrote a manifesto that pointed out the need to veer away from consumer reports and find a new way to write about games; in this article he advocates the personal point of view of the writer as a way to evoke the methods of the New Journalism in the 1960s.[11] Rather than appealing to the myth of journalistic objectivity, by which journalism only states facts and sidelines opinions, New Games Journalism (although not so new anymore) tackled the subjectivity of the writing full on, making these pieces personal and supposedly more relatable. The goal is to write about games as an experience, rather than as a system, or even a commercial product. Since reviews are not really objective anyway—they express the opinion of the writer—subjectivity becomes the main asset of this journalistic movement. Another milestone of New Games Journalism is the article "Bow, Nigger," where the writer/player always_black describes a session of playing online *Jedi Knight II: Jedi Outcast* (2002); the article is a blow-by-blow description of the abuse that the writer/player received in one of his encounters.[12]

The impetus behind New Games Journalism was met with resistance from certain critics[13]—some still advocated that game reviews should be a consumer report, while pushing back against the presumed academic aspirations of the manifesto, as well as what was perceived as a self-important attitude of the writer by putting their experience at the center of the review.

Gillen's manifesto and always_black's article gave way to a series of writers—some of them journalists—who aimed at writing about games in a more thoughtful way, looking for new insights. Some of these writers aim at producing articles with an academic tone, creating theories, and carrying out close readings of games. Others write breakdowns of games that are more relevant to the videogame industry, trying to speak their language. Initially, these writings took the form of blog posts, which appeared on the personal websites of journalists or aspiring game designers—this was their hobby, and yet, some produced criticism whose quality and insights were more interesting than writings found in commercial outlets. In later years, these writers have moved on to become professional journalists, game designers, and academics, thanks in part to these writings. Although blogging tends to use a more casual tone and does not follow rigorous academic standards, the drive for this type of analytical writing brought a blast of fresh air into the public discourse on game analysis.

Game reviews are now common in non-specialized outlets, such as *New York Times, The Guardian, Vanity Fair* or *Rolling Stone,* which now have their own game review sections, proving the relevance of games as socio-cultural artifacts, as well as the need to write for general audiences. These sections in newspapers and magazines also favor more independent game journalism since their economics are not tied exclusively to game advertising and reviews. The movement also seems limited to the English-speaking sphere, with some of the stronger examples of this type of writing coming from outside the USA. The main model of New Games Journalism writing will be expanded on below, in the personal account section.

By highlighting the subjectivity of the playing experience, New Games Journalism also opened the way to new voices in games, where many of the writers still tend to be predominantly white men.[14] Diverse writers have brought new and refreshing points of view to understanding games, even if their subjective voice is not as distinctive, they can highlight aspects of the games that may be overlooked by others. For example, it was two writers of color who brought up the problematic representations of *Cuphead* (2017), which evoked caricatures of blackness, as mentioned in the building block Representation and Identity in Chapter 5.[15] The edited volume, *The Offworld Collection*, compiles some of the best articles for the website Offworld,[16] showcasing a variety of points of view as well as games—from playing *Dungeons & Dragons* through a narrative lens, to how games vocabulary has become part of Chinese mainstream culture, to the queer undertones of stealth games, or how playing time-management games can be relaxing even for someone who has done the job in real life.[17] The articles in this volume also include a variety of games, from AAA to indie, from recent games to flashback reviews of games such as *Final Fantasy VII* (1997) or *Syberia* (2002). This collection shows how journalistic game analysis has so much to write about beyond reviews of the latest games, as well as how diverse writers can enrich the field. Some of the articles in the collection demonstrate how journalism and scholarship can go hand in hand in a game review—Katherine Cross' article on *80 Days* (2014)[18] follows a structure very similar to the one described here, and discusses the anti-colonial themes of the game, as well as providing a new alternate history of Native North America in its new version. The analysis cites an interview with the narrative designer of the game, Meghna Jayanth, as well as Cross' own in-depth play if the game. The article manages to intrigue the reader enough to play the game by highlighting meaningful examples, and inviting the reader to find their own. It is also an examination of the values of the game, as already covered in the Values and Procedural Rhetoric building block in Chapter 5.

Subjectivity seems to also be the predominant characteristic of streaming reviews, and to a certain extent of podcasts—part of their success seems to be tied to the personalities of the reviewers, as well as to the accessibility of these reviews. The casual language and off-the-cuff discourse seems to be easy to connect with, making their audience feel like it is a discourse that they can also participate in. Their accessibility, however, also derives from what can be, at times, a superficial approach to analyzing games—in the case of let's play videos, streamers may not have the chance of stopping to discuss a specific moment of a game, since they have to keep playing. The spontaneity of the conversation can be engaging but not lasting, and may not allow either the content creator nor their audience to achieve insights about the game at hand, learn something new, or leave a mark in the knowledge of the audience. Although these reviews are a good first approach to understanding a game, our goal with a review is to produce an organized, thoughtful, and clear piece of writing.

So, what makes a good game review? There are many ways to write one, in the same way that there are many ways to write a good film or book review. The core of the analysis will still be based on the building blocks listed above, and we can use any of the models below to make the case for why we should care about the game. You will have to work within journalistic constraints, such as length, tone, and style. A journalistic article tends to be shorter and more straightforward in its vocabulary than an academic paper, for example. Also, although journalistic writing often follows the structure of an essay, you want to have a concise, clear summary of your key insights early on; the important information goes first. This is not unlike other essay-like writing, except in journalistic writing you have to take into account that the reader is glancing through other articles, and may very well stop reading after the first paragraph. Part of the art of journalistic writing involves catching your readers' attention early on to keep them reading. If you're a journalism student, you probably are already used to it.

Writing constraints are not exclusive to journalistic reviews—every type of analysis has its own. Just make sure you are aware of what your constraints are. Journalists are still figuring out what a good journalistic review of games is. In order to compare two reviews that recommend a game, let us look at two articles that we already talked about: Chris Dahlen's review of *Cart Life* (2013) "Chasing the Dollar"[19] vs. Joel Goodwin's "Ahead...The Stars" reviewing the same title.[20]

The goal of both reviews is to call attention to Richard Hofmeier's *Cart Life*, an independent game where the player becomes a street-cart vendor. Although the game can be thought of as a "retail simulation," as the author calls it,[21] running the cart is only one of the challenges in the lives of the characters that the player can choose to become. The aim of both reviews is to persuade readers to play the game because they believe that its topic is unusual, and it demonstrates how videogames can be an expressive artistic medium as well as call attention to social issues. For both writers, the game is important, and they want more people to play it. *Cart Life* had not been widely publicized or made available through widespread channels of distribution—the creator at that point depended on word of mouth since he had no access to popular distribution channels and could not market it on a large scale. *Cart Life* went on to win awards and gain recognition in several festivals. It was available on Steam until its author decided to pull it from the service, and make it open source[22]; now a new commercial version of the game on Steam has been announced at the time of writing.[23]

Dahlen and Goodwin have different strategies to drive players to the game. "Chasing the Dollar" focuses on how the game helps players understand the value of money when you do not really have much, using money as a motif that holds together the critique of the game. Dahlen focuses on the mechanics of the game as a retail simulation rather than the story, which he avoids spoiling because he wants readers to go play and experience the emotional struggles of the game themselves. Throughout this article, Dahlen uses the second person "you" to explain what happens.

> *Cart Life* expects you to remember things. At the start of Melanie's story, your protagonist is talking to her sister about her plan to open a coffee

> stand. By way of a tutorial, the sister gives you a list of supplies to buy, the name of a woman who can sell you a cart and a location where you can set up shop.

By recurring constantly to the second person, the author is getting the readers involved in what happens in the game, emphasizing the personal experience.

In contrast, Joel Goodwin writes a journalistic blog post where he focuses on his own experience of the game, so that the review is closer to the personal accounts described a few sections later. Goodwin makes sure to acknowledge other reviews of the game to establish that he has something different to say about it. Rather than using a motif to hold the review together, Goodwin has an interpretation of the game, sustained by his own experience: "*Cart Life*'s message is not about the terrible lot of those people stuck at the bottom, but their determination and endurance in the face of that eternal wheel." "Ahead … The Stars" uses examples in the first person to explain the experience, then compares how the author understands the game with how the developer explained his artistic goals in the game forums, which are now unavailable. This review also sets itself aside from consumer reports by not caring about spoiling the game—part of *Cart Life*'s virtues are understood best by revealing some of the events that take place as one plays. This comparison shows two different ways to write about the same game, calling attention to its qualities using different formats—while Dahlen uses an essay-like format, Goodwin uses his personal experience as a central motif that is reinforced using comparisons with other reviews, other games, and the statements of the author himself.

That means that there is room for experimentation, as well as myriad models of reviews of other media, events, and artifacts that we could learn from. Film reviews are usually hailed as one standard that game reviews should be held up against, but there are many other types of reviews that we could learn from, such as theatre and music concerts (another performance activity), sports (another competitive activity where spectators take sides), restaurants (a space where food and how it is served create an experience). All these have established traditions—it is worth looking into how they are written in order to find what kinds of discussions and arguments we can make about videogames. Experimenting with new modes of writing is not only allowed but necessary at this point.

BOX 6.3 EXERCISE: WRITE A RETRO REVIEW

Choose a game that you have not played and that is more than ten years old. Write a review, but rather than holding it to the current standards, do some research to learn more about the types of games, technological platforms, and design aesthetics of the time. Try to examine the game with borrowed eyes, as if you were a contemporary player. Be brief—from 500 to 750 words—as you would be in a short review. After you have finished, find a review for the same game that is contemporary to it. What kinds of things does the review highlight? Is there anything that they appreciated that you skipped, or vice versa? What is the purpose of the contemporary review? What is the goal of your review?

BOX 6.4 IMITATING BAD WRITING

As you write, whether it is a journalistic review or not, it is easy to fall into adopting some of the traits that you have read in some of these reviews. So, think about whether you are imitating any of these things and, if you are, maybe you should do some revisions:

- Avoid hyping your game, resorting to overemotional vocabulary. You are not selling the game, and even when you are calling attention to how good it is, provide clear ideas, not only big words. "Best X ever" is probably a clear symptom that you are sliding into hype mode.
- Casual or overly chatty writing can indicate that you are writing for yourself and your friends, imitating casual blogs or popular game streamers. Although a more casual style can help get across to your audience, it also means that you will not be using the more precise, nuanced language that will help your analysis reach the level of sophistication we are aiming at in games discourse.
- Avoid listing the formal qualities or exclusively retelling the story premise of the game: although this may be a necessary part of the game overview, a laundry list is not the same as an analysis. Ask yourself: Why are these important? How do these make the game stand apart? How can the player engage with the game?
- Avoid repeating the terms and highlighting the aspects that are publicized on the box or the game ads: by parroting commercial mottos, you are just echoing marketing messages, not being a journalist.

Finding your voice as a writer is hard and requires a lot of practice. Until then, all you can do is find the kind of writing that you like, a voice that you feel comfortable imitating or following. The key to good writing about games is to be a good writer first. It does not have to be a games writer—there are plenty of good writers in literature and film criticism, journalism, philosophy, or media studies, to name but a few fields. So, find models that you want to sound like, read a lot, and write a lot.

▶ HISTORICAL ANALYSIS

Games are artifacts produced in specific socio-cultural circumstances, as seen in Chapter 5. As such, they can work as a snapshot of those circumstances, as well as provide insight on other contexts, such as different eras or across cultures. This is why, for example, Shakespeare is such a prominent figure in English-speaking cultures: we can learn a lot about Elizabethan culture and society by reading his plays and poems, but these works have also endured thanks to the ways that they have been replayed and understood later on, in the form of new productions, movies, translations, or appropriations by other cultures, apart from being upheld as part of the core of the Western literary canon. Using a media artifact as a lens, we can learn about the people and the material circumstances that surround them.

The history of games, although long, has not always been thoroughly documented. In the case of board and card games, their rules were transmitted orally most of the time, so that the only historical remnants may be boards, cards, or game bits. Games have been part of a folk tradition, like folk songs or stories, but they have not been recorded as often. One of the earliest books on games was a thirteenth-century volume commissioned by the Spanish king Alfonso X of Castile, *Juegos Diversos de Axedrez, Dados, y Tablas (Diverse Games of Chess, Dice, and Boards).* This book records the rules for different games, as well as certain Chess challenges, and includes illustrations for each game so the reader sees what the board looked like. Having a record like this is invaluable to learn about games, since we learn the rules and context for these games at a specific moment in time. In the same way that language changes through time, the way in which games are played also evolves, creating different strands and families of games, as mentioned earlier in the book.[24]

Digital games have a much shorter history; the earliest digital games that we have a record of were developed in the early 1950s.[25] As computers have become cheaper and smaller, we now have digital games in home computers, consoles, our phones and tablets, and even in the entertainment centers of planes. The proliferation of the technology also means that the number of games released grows exponentially every day. Digital game history is taking place right now; some of it is being recorded, but it is only partially being told in a critical and systematic manner.

Game analysis can help us record that history, by selecting games that help us gain insight on how we make and play games, as well as the time in which we play those games. It also helps us gain a very much needed historical perspective on games, particularly in the case of digital games. Digital technology is constantly evolving, forcing game makers to relearn how to make the best of the new technical possibilities. Having a knowledge of what has been done before will prevent the reinvention of the wheel, allowing us to move on from the design of games as a technical issue to focus on the human components of digital games. This perspective can also help us start relating digital and non-digital games, and understand games as an ecology that uses different material means (or none at all—think of "I Spy with My Little Eye") to create an experience.

As a teacher, I have seen my students talk about a very narrow set of games, which has usually been limited to the last ten years or less. It has always been my pleasure to show and discuss games that may have been pioneers in developing mechanics and themes, for example, with or without technology. At times, it is easy to become entranced by astounding digital graphics or sprawling virtual environments, without realizing that games can be engaging without the latest gizmos, or even sophisticated electronics. For example, while the game *L.A. Noire* (2011) may have been hailed as a novel and complex detective game, in the 1980s, several Infocom games already featured sophisticated mechanics that allowed players to become detectives, such as *Deadline* (1982), *The Witness* (1984), and *Suspect* (1984). These games were text-only, no graphics. This sense of history is not only important to be able to see the evolution of games, but also for up-and-coming designers to acquire a wide design vocabulary and learn from other people's designs, instead of redoing what has already been invented. By knowing our game past, we can discuss our current and future games in a more cultivated manner.

An historical analysis of a game is not only recording the rules of the game, as King Alfonso did, or discussing an older game. It is a discussion of a game *in context*; therefore, the main building blocks that we will use all belong to the context area. Although not exclusively, these will be the key building blocks:

- *Technological context*: Discussion of the platform for which the game was developed and how it determines and relates to the game. A discussion of related technologies (contemporary, antecedents, precedents) may also be relevant for the sake of contrast and to emphasize the relevance of the game in terms of technology.

- *Socio-historical context*: The time at which the game was developed, and the relationship between the game and social and cultural events, be it contemporary, or be it a revisitation or reinterpretation of past or future societies.

- *Economic context*: How the game was economically produced and marketed and distributed, including whether the game was commercial or not, and how it may have been monetized.

It is important to note that the analysis should give a diachronic sense, that is, reflecting changes through time. The reader has to understand how this game represents a change in certain aspects of a genre or series of games.

When writing a historical analysis, we explore the relationship between a game and its historical context. Thus, the kind of questions that we ask ourselves when writing a paper of this kind are:

- How does the game reflect the affordances of the technology it uses?

- How is the game an artifact that demonstrates the ideology and cultural concerns of the time?

- How does the game present a virtual recreation of a historical environment?

- How do marketing representations condition the way that the game is received?

A variation can be a comparative analysis of games based on the same aspect through time. In that case, the thesis statement focuses on one specific aspect (e.g., genre) and how it evolved through time. Juul's history of tile-matching games, which has already been discussed, is an example of this—tracing the origins of a genre by relating the formal aspects of different games.[26]

Focusing on the socio-historical context of a game to analyze it is a familiar practice for those who already have done some writing for the humanities. This kind of approach may be similar to certain types of writing in the history of art, where the properties of the work are observed through the lens of the society and culture of its time. A clear example of this is Kocurek's account of *Death Race* (1976), where the author focuses on the context of the game to provide a documented account of one of the earliest controversies about videogame violence in the United States.[27] The running argument of the analysis is that there were games that were just as violent released around the same time, but *Death Race*'s depiction of violence challenged the standards of what could be considered acceptable, which at the same time helped publicize the game and make it rather popular. The article hardly discusses any of the formal traits of the game—even the discussion of representation focuses on the cabinet of the game rather than on the gameplay. This is a fine approach too—it is a more traditional format to write about an artifact in its historical context.

An additional role of historical analyses can be to question contemporary perceptions of older games, which can be biased by nostalgia. Over time, our memory may change the way we remember a certain game and its impact at a personal as well as a general level. Other times, historical analysis can help challenge general perceptions of what the history of games was like. For example, Allison Gazzard's analysis of *Elite* (1984) sets out to reclaim the influence of British game development and the role of the BBC Micro home computer in the creation of a landmark title;[28] this claim also pushes against the commonplace perception that the "videogame crash" of 1983 was generalized, as at the same time the North American game industry was collapsing, European game developers and publishers were thriving, with popular titles like *Elite* in the UK. Gazzard also questions how *Elite* is often labeled as the first 3D space-trading game. Although there had been other games that created three-dimensional spaces, such as *Battlezone* (1980) or *3D Monster Maze* (1982), the real innovation of the game consisted of its clever technological use of the computer resources to create what we now call an open world, an expansive navigable space that was different with every new game. This analysis is an example of how telling the local histories of games all over the world can demonstrate that there is not a single narrative in the field, but rather many different ones.

The way a historical analysis of a game can be different from analyzing other media is that it usually refers to how the game is played and how participation can change through time, and how the technology shapes the work. Documenting how players' engagement with a game may have changed through time could illuminate the way attitudes and game strategies work, for example.

There are good examples of analyses that use technology as the lens to analyze a game or specific set of games. Focusing on the materiality of the medium is something that art historians may already be familiar with, while literary and film scholars tend to disregard the technical aspects of the medium they study. In the case of digital games, the technology is part of how the game is made and how players interact with it; it can be hard to obviate the technology as we analyze the game. It would be hard to talk about *Dance Central* (2010), for example, without discussing how the motion-tracking of the Kinect device allows players to dance rather than pressing buttons. In the same way that art historians talk about the materials of a sculpture, or literary scholars discuss concrete poetry, in which the arrangement of the words on the page is as important as the words, the technical aspects of a game add another layer of signification that we can break down and discuss.

Brett Camper's analysis of *La-Mulana* (2005), which has already been mentioned throughout the book, shows how the technical aspects of the game are part of its expressive devices.[29] The game utilizes contemporary computer and game technology to pay homage to a long-outdated home computing platform (the MSX2), not only through the game design, but also through the audio-visual representation that points to a technology of other times. Thus, Camper's analysis uses a historical perspective to understand the game, both in the context of the MSX platform, as well as contemporary games and how they evoke other platforms.

We have already seen how platform studies can help us understand games at the level beneath the code when discussing the Technological Context building block (Chapter 2). Through a nuanced discussion of how the technology works, we get to understand the design assumptions of the system, and how it affects the final result. A detailed example of a comprehensive historical analysis that is technology focused is Nick Montfort's analysis of the Atari VCS game *Combat* (1977).[30] The goal of the analysis is to understand the game in its historical context, not only economic and critical (the game overview includes quotes from contemporary reviews), but paying special attention to how the game uses technology, breaking it down in five layers, from the most material to the most external—the platform, the game code, the game form (how it plays), the interface, and the reception and operation. Each layer of the game relates to the next, so that the core of the article is to demonstrate how part of the importance of *Combat* is precisely how it makes the most of the technology it was developed for, and how it compares with other games.

As you may have realized, there are many ways in which we can write a historical analysis, all having to do with the context. In order to narrow down your approach, you may want to consider focusing on one of these aspects:

- *Production context*: The discussion centers on how the game was made; how it was distributed.
- *Reception*: Research and discussion of paratexts (magazines and interviews).
- *Platform Studies*: Focus on the hardware and how the game utilizes it.
- *Evolution*: A comparative analysis based on the formal features of the game, and how they transform over time.

The examples here cited show how, by discussing a game in its historical context, we can not only understand better its reach and relevance, but also can hypothesize about how certain design decisions were made, or where some ways of playing may come from. A historical perspective can also help us understand the ecology of games through time and across cultures—part of the value of the humanistic study of games derives from being able to connect one game and another, games and culture, and games and technology, among other relationships.

Historical analyses of games can be rich and complex; some titles can give us enough materials to write whole books. For example, *Doom* (1993) has a couple of monographs devoted to it[31]—Pinchbeck's (2013) is a detailed analysis of the game and its design, framed historically both by a history of its development as well as of the later games it influenced, whereas Kushner's book (2003) is a detailed account of the making of the game based on the personalities of his two main developers, John Romero and John Carmack. A game can tell many histories, depending on the questions we ask of it and the resources that we cite.

BOX 6.5 EXERCISE: KEY GAMES

Choose a game that can be considered influential on other games, a referent, or milestone in the history of games. The exercise for the building block Game Genre (Chapter 3) already invited you to trace the historical tree of a particular

(Continued)

(Continued)

genre; if you have already done that exercise, choose one of the games that appears as one of the origins of the tree. For example, the game *Alone in the Dark* (1992) was a key influence on the *Resident Evil* series (1996–2021), as well as later 3D survival horror games; the same year, *Wolfenstein 3D* heralded the advent of new 3D technology that would be used in first-person shooters.

The exercise can take two different forms:

- The game was influential at the time of its release; it stood out in its context and was innovative in some way. Focusing on the contextual and formal blocks, argue why its influence has endured.
- The game is influential because it created a new type of game, a new type of interaction, which has been picked up by other games. Focus on one specific aspect that makes it influential—e.g., a formal aspect of the design, or a way to engage players—and use a comparative analysis to make the argument. A comparative analysis is not resorting to the same building blocks twice, but drawing connections between both games to discuss them, including what they have in common, or not, and to present a hypothesis as to why this relationship can be traced.

GAME COMMUNITIES

An analysis of the communities that play a game tells us how the game is received and appropriated by its players, rather than the circumstances around its production or its materiality. In the case of game communities around an online virtual world, we will examine the social relationships of the players inside and outside the virtual world, how they make sense of it, and how they build an identity in the world. These communities can be formed in online forums, social media groups, fan websites, Discord servers, and online streaming, among other venues. The study of player communities brings about a shift in perspective from our discussions so far—an approach that will be familiar to those coming from communication studies, sociology, or anthropology. We can use a game as a lens to examine the community of people that participate in it. As in the case of the historical analysis, by studying game communities we place more emphasis on the context rather than the formal aspects of the game. This shift of emphasis also provides a very necessary perspective on games as a human activity—game studies at times seem to overemphasize their nature as systems and their materiality, overlooking that they are also a performance activity, by which there cannot be a game if nobody is playing it.

This type of analysis is probably one of the most complex and methodologically demanding, so a work of this kind is more likely to be an undergraduate thesis than a class paper. Whenever we start studying a game community, we have to plot a research plan carefully before we start—this is good practice in general, but it is essential here. You must ask yourself what it is that you want to learn from the community, as a general research question, and then consider what methods are going to help you answer it best. As Boellstroff et al. explain, however, one's methods must also be flexible to accommodate changes and allow us to explore the possibilities.[32] This type of study is not a scientific experiment where we are trying to prove a theory, but rather we are exploring the answers to general questions, and we should let our subjects surprise us—if the answers we start getting challenge our preconceptions, then we are on the way to a discovery!

Designing the study carefully is essential to the success of your research; if you are in a North American or European institution, it is also likely that you have to prepare a research protocol to study players, since they are considered research subjects. You may be required to have your experiment plan (called a protocol) approved by an IRB (Institutional Review Board) or an ethics review committee at your university before starting to gather data. If you are doing this type of research, be sure to consult your professor well in advance of the due date to check what the process at your institution is and whether you need a protocol or not.

Academics are not the only ones who perform this kind of study—developers and publishers also aim at understanding their audiences, so they will often carry out focus tests, send surveys, gather data with their games, or study game forums to appeal more to their consumers with each new game. The process of playtesting a game involves studying a group of people playing your game, so if your goal is to be a game developer, you should also be familiar with the approaches described in this section, as well as with the potential implications of your methods. For example, *The Last of Us* (2013) used focus groups as a way to gauge the interest of players in the game—a common practice from the marketing department, which uses some of the same methods that we use to study game communities. The issue, however, was that the research firm dealing with the focus groups started by only testing the game with male players—the developers of the game, Naughty Dog, had to request that the focus groups also included women.[33] Leaving them out of the experiment takes for granted that women do not play videogames, rather than asking the question of how interested they may be in the game directly. Inquiry is the soul of research.

The building blocks that will be the most relevant to this type of study are the following:

- *Context*: Audience: it points to the core of our study because it helps us understand who the game may be for. This block is somewhat abstract, based on marketing and economics, in contrast with the "Game Communities" block, which deals with specific players and their practices.

- *Game Overview*: Game Communities: the specific groups that are formed in and around a game. This is obviously the core of this type of analysis because we are examining a game through the players who engage with it. Each game community creates a culture of its own, from a series of behaviors, language, conventions, and expectations derived or inspired by the game; the community can also appropriate and transform the game from what was originally intended. That is, we analyze how a game brings people together, and how people make the game their own.

- *Formal Aspects*: Cheats/Mods/Hacks/Bugs: here we may want to focus on the *mods* (modifications) of the game, mostly because they are user-generated content. Game communities not only play together and generate information, but they can also create content for others to play, using tools provided along with the game, or creating their own. As the building block explains, including tools to generate content for a game already shows some intent to create a community around it.

We cannot dedicate this type of analysis the space it deserves, first, because it involves a complex research project, and also the methods and precepts of ethnographic research have been tackled in more detail elsewhere.[34] This section provides a brief overview of the issues that are specifically relevant to the study of games and their communities, which can be tackled from a variety of standpoints. The study of game communities, however, is more important now than ever, since they can reveal larger societal issues and dynamics in the microworlds in and around games. For example, Kishonna Gray's study of Black users in games is a monumental, interdisciplinary study of users and their everyday engagement with game technology, outlets and communities, and how they construct their identities in these environments, and is a prime example of the key contributions that the study of communities can bring to game studies.[35]

Quantitative vs. Qualitative One of the first things that you have to decide is what kind of data you will gather from your community, whether it is quantitative, qualitative, or a combination of both.

Quantitative Analysis

A quantitative approach is based on the assumption that the scientific method is the most reliable way of obtaining information. Using quantitative approaches requires setting up an experiment or designing a surveying order to obtain data that can be quantified and analyzed statistically.[36] Thus, this approach seems more adequate to deal with large amounts of subjects and variables, which can show us general trends and commonalities of a large group of players, and give us the chance to hypothesize where these come from, based on correlations in the data.

A quantitative analysis establishes a series of values that define the community and can be measured, and will be based on survey or data gathered from the games. A typical survey of this kind consists of a multiple-choice questionnaire or a scale to evaluate how much the subject agrees with a statement—which is called a Likert scale in social sciences research. For instance, Nick Yee created a forty-question survey to evaluate the variety of motivations of MMORPG players and his sample was 3,000 players.[37] He not only showed the nuances and interdependencies between motivations, from competition to role-playing or socializing, but also the differences in the motivations between male and female players.

Games can also have embedded systems to gather information on player activity, such as how long they play, their score, or where they get killed on a certain level. This information is rarely public, however, and in certain cases it is proprietary, so researchers depend on their own methods to gather this information, or work with developers to gain access to their data. These values give us data that is measurable and, therefore, easier to compare when we are dealing with large data samples. The industry and some branches of social sciences prefer quantitative studies because they follow the scientific method, and they believe that numbers provide objective results. The truth is, data still has to be interpreted by the researcher, who has to select which aspects are significant and hypothesize the reasons for certain correlations.

Qualitative Analysis

In contrast, qualitative approaches help us with smaller player samples where each participant is interviewed in depth. This can provide us with a more personal view of the community, where different voices can demonstrate both the heterogeneity of its members and the common traits in their behavior, as well as making it possible to understand the causes of those behaviors firsthand. The subjectivity of dealing with human subjects also makes qualitative analysis friendly to those in the humanities who want to borrow methods from the social sciences.

A qualitative study of a game community involves selecting a subset of players, interviewing them or playing with them; it may also involve wading through public forums to find what players may have posted about the game. Players provide their own experience and, by gathering a meaningful sample, their testimonies will display a variety of approaches to playing the game. Interviewing game players is a sobering exercise to realize one's own subjectivity when analyzing a game, which can also help to debunk myths about who plays games and how.[38] Because of the subjectivity of this approach, the privacy of the subjects can be a concern of the researcher, so you must consider how important it is to protect the identity of the people you are interviewing—this will be part of your protocol as well.

Another option is using what we call *mixed methods*, where we combine strategies in order to obtain the information we are looking for. For instance, Olson and Kutner's *Grand Theft Childhood* used a large-scale survey in order to learn which games children aged 12–14 years played, as well as their playing habits.[39] Then they set up group interviews with a much smaller sample to gain insight on the correlations that the data showed, as well as to learn in more detail about the specifics of how this population play together.

The Issue with Virtual Worlds Apart from the type of data that we can gather, there are also two basic types of game communities that we can study: communities around a game and communities within a virtual world:

- Communities around a game create a space to discuss it together, or play it together, either physically or online. For example, Mia Consalvo studied the reaction of fans of hidden-object games to the game *Return to Ravenhearst* (2008) by reading forum posts.[40] Other times we can observe players playing together in the physical space: for example, Nicholas Taylor studied boys and girls playing *Guitar Hero* (2005) together,[41] while Mikael Jakobsson studied a console game club playing *Super Smash Bros. Melee* (2001) and how they regulated the game.[42]

- Communities in a virtual world are formed in the virtual space of a game; in the case of massively-multiplayer online games (MMOGs), the world is so large that there will be many different types of communities that gather in it. Studying a virtual world usually involves becoming part of it as an inhabitant. Unlike a quantitative study, in which surveys and mined data give an abstract general idea of the workings of the world, this type of analysis requires us to become ethnographers to obtain information about specific people and situations that can provide insight on the general workings of the community. Studying the communities created around this virtual world, such as player-made tutorials, going to fan conventions, or interviews in real life, may be an additional resource to understand the community itself, but not the core of it as is the case above. These communities are also invaluable in the case of online games which periodically have large updates, such as *World of Warcraft* (2004–), or which have been disconnected and not available at all. The communities become secondary sources, as we saw in Chapter 2, that can help us understand what the game was like. The reconstruction through players' accounts is what Pearce did in her study of the community of players of *Myst Online: Uru* (2003–2004; 2007–2008; 2010–).[43] The dates of the game should already give you a sense that this virtual world has gone live and then disconnected repeatedly, so the interviews with its participants are key to understanding its different incarnations.

The second case requires us to become ethnographers and resort to potentially insightful methods we can apply to study game communities, namely, participant observation. The researcher becomes a member of the community, often self-identifying as such as part of the research methods. Participant observation is particularly common in the study of online games, mostly because we must also play the game to meet the people we study and understand how participants interact with each other through technology. This also may require identifying oneself to the participants as a researcher as part of the research protocol. If you do not disclose your identity to players, you need a good reason not to do it, and still be approved by the IRB or ethics committee. The identity of the researcher can even be broadcast—Professor Amy Bruckman had her students research *Second Life* (2003–), requesting that the avatars donned lab coats in the virtual world to indicate the purpose of their visit.[44] Being part of the community usually implies an expertise in the game and its workings, something very necessary in the case of complex, ever-changing virtual worlds such as *World of Warcraft* (2004–) or *Guild Wars 2* (2012–).

Being part of the virtual world that you are studying may also help you get a firsthand account of exceptional events in it. For example, Consalvo and Begy were studying the players of the casual MMO *Faunasphere* (2009–2011), when they got a notification that the game was going to close in the middle of their research. This gave them the rare opportunity of asking players how they felt about the disconnection of their game, and helped them understand how it was meaningful to them, as well as being there the moment that *Faunasphere* ended.[45]

Participant observation also invites subjective analysis, and revealing one's love—or hate—of a specific game can eclipse the careful methods that one must lay out before starting the study. Although the personal point of view may be one of the boons of participant observation, it should never be an excuse to justify one's gameplay—which may be excessive or compulsive—as research. Participant observation requires a lot of introspection, thinking about how our choices may affect the results of the research, why we are playing a certain way, and how our experience may be different from that of other players. How the researchers present themselves in the world has social and emotional consequences,[46] so this type of study is far from the mindless entertainment that videogames are often identified as, and more of an exhausting and meditative process that requires documenting yourself as well as your subjects.

Again, this is just a brief overview of the implications of studying game communities. Fortunately for us, the social sciences already provide us with a good repertoire of strategies and methods to analyze a game from the standpoint of the people who play it. That means that if this is the type of analysis you want to carry out, you should complement this book with manuals that describe those pre-existing strategies in more detail.

As Boellstroff et al. argue, ethnographic work relates to journalism in many ways, but it also differs in a few key specific aspects.[47] First, a journalist does not have to become part of the community that they are studying, or need consent from the people that they will talk about in the article; a journalistic article usually takes the form of a story and is prepared in a relatively short amount of time in most cases. However, it also depends on the type of journalistic article—as we have seen, certain types of game journalism resort to the personal account as a way to highlight the subjectivity of the experience in ways that may seem related to ethnographic research, although with some key differences, as we will see soon.

BOX 6.6 EXERCISE: EXPERT PLAYERS IN ONLINE GAMES

This is a brief qualitative exercise to study online communities, so you can get a sense of how this type of analysis works; in spite of its small scope, it can be an elaborate experiment. Choose an online game that has a competitive component, particularly of players against players. Your goal is to interview expert players (whom T.L. Taylor calls *power gamers*[48]) and understand how they play and what motivates them. Through interactions with the community, and looking at game forums and websites, identify two or three people whom you think may help you learn about how to acquire expertise and why. People who write strategy guides, for example, may be good people to interview.

The specific questions of the interview depend on the game of choice, but these are some of the general areas you may want to learn more about:

- How long have your subjects been playing?
- How many hours a week do they play?
- What kinds of strategies have they developed in order to become expert players?
- How do they relate to other players? Who do they compete with? Who do they collaborate with? Who do they ignore?
- What drives your subject to become a top player?

If it is not a game you already play, you will have to become familiar with the game itself in order to be able to understand how it works before finding your subjects. Remember to check if you need a protocol approved by the IRB or ethics committee before starting your research.

BOX 6.7 CLOSE READING

A method that will be common to some of the following analysis methods is using close reading, that is, selecting a specific aspect of a game and breaking it down into its basic elements. Close readings are in-depth, beat-by-beat analyses, and provide us with very specific examples to sustain our argument, be it explaining a high-level theory, an interpretation, or helping to deliver our personal account and approach to the game. The following three types of analyses (illustration of a theory, interpretation, and personal account) use close reading as their driving method, allowing for a study that resorts to detailed examples and discussion. The differences between them are defined by the goal of the analysis and who is going to read it, as explained in the introduction to this chapter.

Specific examples are key to any analysis—they support how you understand the game and help get it across. It may be easy to discuss games in abstract terms, but this also means that, while you are writing, you are too much in your own head. As you write, you are probably thinking of specific examples that you may think everyone knows. But not everyone is you, and the types of games and play are different enough that you want to ground your arguments with specific examples. That is why a close reading can help you ground and solidify your analysis.

Your examples need to be relevant to what you are analyzing—by carrying out a close reading, we make sure that the discussion is grounded. I have read more than one paper that supposedly discussed games where there was not a single game mentioned and all the examples were films. (I will avoid embarrassing the authors in print.) The authors were discussing games only in the abstract—the paper lacked the grounding that really made it a game studies paper. This whole book is advocating the use of game analysis to understand games and their culture better, so remember to not lose sight of your subject of study.

In doing a close reading, you still want to be selective. A close reading of an 80-hour game like *Demon's Souls* (2009) could be an encyclopedia and end up being difficult to follow. As with any other analysis, finding the core of the argument and providing supporting evidence are key to making your analysis readable, clear, and finished on time. For example, in the case of *Demon's Souls*, we could focus on how the main theme of the game is death as punishment. This theme is embodied in the mechanics (players can only save in specific points; players can see the ghosts of other players and see how they died; if the player kills any key non-player characters, then merchandise and wares will be unavailable and make it really hard to complete the game) as well as the fictional world (there has been a war and the world has been ravaged; the enemies are mostly living dead). Although it can be a fascinating exercise, not everyone has

(Continued)

(Continued)

the occasion to write an in-depth analysis of a whole game. *Killing Is Harmless*, a book-long close reading of *Spec Ops: The Line*, is a rare *tour de force*, and in spite of its length, it limits itself to a specific core argument (nothing is what it seems; the game challenges the player's perception), and limits its references to other media to songs and a couple of aspects of the film *Apocalypse Now* (1979).[49] One could write a different analysis of the game by drawing comparisons between the game and two of its source texts, the same movie and the book that inspired it, Joseph Conrad's *Heart of Darkness* (1899).

Close readings of specific sections of the game help in getting the point across. The basic building block that becomes your starting point is the Context Inside the Game building block (Chapter 3), which helps situate the moment you are discussing and what happens. This should be followed by the point you want to make—why is this example important? How does it contribute to the main argument you are making? The rest of the close reading can use any of the building blocks that relate to the game overview and the formal elements, either focusing on a single one across the game, or selecting a specific section and breaking it down. The key is to understand each section in the light of something else, such as pre-existing theories or metaphors, as the following sections explain.

▶ ILLUSTRATION OF A THEORY

Theories are abstractions that try to find commonalities and patterns in the world and ideas. They help us explain our world in almost any area—in biology, there is the theory of evolution, quantum theory in physics, while economists study macroeconomic and microeconomic theory. In the humanities, different schools of philosophy present us with different ways of making sense of the world, whereas the varieties of literary theory emphasize different aspects and approaches in the study of literature, from deconstructionism to studies of genre, or cultural studies.

We can resort to pre-existing theories to frame our understanding of games; we can also use games to illustrate our own theories. Since game studies is a relatively new field compared to other academic disciplines, we are still developing frameworks to help us understand our subject of study. However, developing new theories, although tempting, is also an advanced process more typical of Masters and PhD theses. So, unless you are an advanced student, you will get a better headstart by applying pre-existing theories to the study of games.

A reminder, again—always keep in mind what makes games different from other media. Their nature as performative, interactive, participatory media makes them different from a film or a novel, for example, and in the case of videogames, digital media also changes the nature of how we play.

Game studies as a field started with a controversy that put into question the application of literary theory to the study of games. Espen Aarseth vehemently criticized scholars who studied digital games as if they were novels, for example, arguing that literature and film critics would treat games like novels and films and lose sight of what sets them apart, without taking the time to figure out how the study of games may be different from other media.[50] Aarseth's critique was to the point—one of the most exciting things about being a games scholar is to realize that we need new frameworks and concepts to understand them. On the other hand, this should not preclude resorting to other fields to help us explore the vast field of games, both digital and non-digital.

Pre-existing theories can help us draw relationships between games and other fields, as well as put those theories to the test and show how they explain something novel about games—or not. If the theories do not quite apply to games, that usually means an invitation to come up with new theories and revisions to address the gaps or problems discovered as we tried to apply these theories to games.

Resorting to pre-existing theories to understand a text is probably familiar to most humanities students, since theory classes already use a variety of texts to exemplify it. Think of Genette's *Narrative Discourse*, which uses *À la Recherche du Temps Perdu* to illustrate the different ways in which narrative can organize a sequence of events, focusing on different aspects of temporality.[51] In film theory, Laura Mulvey uses Lacan's approach to psychoanalysis to find recurring patterns that reproduce the patriarchal discourse across different films; the basic pattern being that the woman becomes the passive object of the active male gaze as part of the story.[52] These concepts and theories have been applied to games too: Helen Kennedy used Mulvey's work when discussing Lara Croft,[53] while Diane Carr resorts to Seymour Chatman's and Genette's narrative theories to explain the narrative strategies of *Baldur's Gate*.[54] More recently, Bo Ruberg has bridged game studies and queer theory through the analysis of games such as

Pong (1972) or *Portal* (2007), inviting the reader to see these games through a new lens.[55] Theories help us understand the world better; we use examples from the world to illustrate and get them across, while theories in the abstract do not always go very far.

The key to this type of analysis is finding the theory that will be relevant and potentially insightful. You may start by applying a pre-existing theory that you have studied in class or that you may have read about already. Your teacher or university librarian can also help you find pre-existing literature that relates to specific approaches or topics. My first forays into studying videogames started in my doctoral courses of literature, when I read a late eighteenth-century short story that read like a videogame, "Sir Bertrand, A Fragment."[56] A knight fights a living armor, and when he defeats it, the armor transforms into a key; the knight uses the key to open the door to the next room. My professor at the time, Manuel Aguirre, was kind enough to listen as I wondered why videogames were still reproducing the events of an eighteenth-century story, so he directed me to the theories of Russian literary formalist Vladimir Propp and American anthropologist Joseph Campbell.[57] My first videogame paper used these theories to understand the event structures of games as recreating those of folk tales, including how they both appropriated and challenged the structures proposed by Propp and Campbell. For example, the trope of the princess who needs to be rescued comes from folk tales, and it is recurrent in videogames (e.g., *Prince of Persia*, 1989, *The Legend of Zelda* series, 1986–2017, *Super Mario* series, 1985–2023). These games tend to focus on the story elements that encourage action, rather than character development; that is why players can only control the hero after they have left their home to start the adventure until the princess is rescued. Some other story elements, such as defying a prohibition (e.g., "do not take the golden feather")[58] or initially refusing the call to adventure, result in a calamity that the hero needs to remedy.[59] Many of the story elements that both Propp and Campbell describe in folk tales are left out from the gameplay—they may be described or be part of the cut-scenes—which indicates that the types of narratives that we frequently find in videogames are not only the most essential human narratives, but also that they are included in a rather shallow way.

This type of analysis usually provides a summary of the theory, to make clear not only the theoretical concepts but also our own understanding of it.

In explaining the theory, we demonstrate a capacity to synthesize complex ideas in a few paragraphs, focusing on the core terms and ideas of the theory (see Box 6.8 Defining Your Terms).

BOX 6.8 DEFINING YOUR TERMS

In the same way that you need to determine who the audience of your paper is and what discipline you are writing within, you also have to consider the specific terms you are using to explain yourself. This is no small thing—a good part of the early days of game studies was spent trying to define *game* or whether one could consider games a type of narrative or not. The definition of academic terms invokes a tradition and situates your work as part of the pre-existing academic discourse; those terms will be the tools that you use to construct the argument of your analysis.

Defining your terms means explaining the theories and explaining the basic terminology that you are going to use through the paper. This is important because terms can mean different things depending on which discipline or area you come from.

Term definition should take place early in your writing, probably right after you present your thesis statement. These terms are the main concepts that will be your tools to construct your argument. By doing this, you demonstrate a familiarity with the pre-existing academic discourse, as well as preventing ambiguity or confusion about what you are talking about. In Chapter 5, the Box 5.1 Beware of Buzzwords listed reasons why using terms without thinking carefully what they mean will undermine the rigor of your writing, so taking some time to think about what your key terms mean will make sure that you are using your terms appropriately.

If your reader does not understand the terms the same way you do, by explaining how you understand them, you are preventing potential confusions or ambiguities. Even though you could get away with saying something like "*flow* as defined by Csikszentmihalyi"[63] or "*index* as defined by Peirce"[64] without including an explicit definition, it is always good to devote a few lines to explaining your terms.

Making your terms explicit is essential when discussing games for several reasons. To begin with, a good part of the early days of game studies was spent in defining the most basic terms. The recurring arguments about definitions can also be due to the interdisciplinarity of the study of games, where scholars come from a variety of backgrounds and provide a variety of perspectives. For example, the term *ontology* can be used by people coming from philosophy or computer science, so depending on who invokes it, the same word will mean different things. For philosophers, ontology is the study of existence, of how

(Continued)

(Continued)

things come into being, of reality, and how it can be classified, whereas, for computer scientists, ontology is a structural representation to organize knowledge and information. Even though conceptually related, if a researcher works on an ontology of game design components, it will sound confusing—and probably unfeasible—to a philosopher, so it is better to clarify what it means even before starting to describe the research.[65]

How do we define our terms? By listing them and providing a brief definition. It is fine to stop your discussion for a second and introduce your little glossary of terms; many of the exemplary analyses referred to in this book do that. For instance, Lisbeth Klastrup, in her analysis of *Everquest* (2003), characterizes her work as a *poetics* of virtual worlds.[66] She spends a whole section defining *poetics*, by invoking how others have used the term (from Aristotle to narratologist Shlomith Rimmon-Kenan[67]), and then providing her own definition. In order to make clear that the definition is important to the paper, she devotes a single paragraph to it, in italics. Her definition is based on Rimmon-Kenan's concept applied to virtual worlds rather than literature, and this is what it looks like:

> My point here is not to argue that virtual worlds are literature (or art, yet), but rather that if we replace "literature" with "virtual worlds" and "poet" with "developer" in the above quote, the contents of a possible poetics of virtual worlds emerges. As a guideline, I have rephrased Rimmon-Kenan:
>
> A poetics of virtual worlds deals with: the systematic study of virtual worlds as virtual worlds. It deals with the question "What is a virtual world?" and with all possible questions derived from it, such as: How is a virtual world an aesthetic form of expression? What are the forms and kinds of virtual worlds? What is the nature of one world genre or trend? What is the system of a particular developer's "art" and "means of expression"? How is a story constructed? What are the specific aspects of instances of virtual worlds? How are they constituted? How do virtual worlds embody "non-fictional" phenomena?[68]

In this case, Klastrup has come up with her own definition based on pre-existing work; this is an advanced example of what you should do. It is more likely that you will have to give a more straightforward definition, where you can quote the source directly or provide your own summary of the concept. By providing your own summary, you demonstrate how you understand the concept. For example, Consalvo needs to define the concept of *cultural capital* in her book

(Continued)

(Continued)

on cheating, as a foundation to define her own novel concept *gaming capital* (which was discussed already in Chapter 2).[69]

> ["Gaming capital"] is a reworking of Pierre Bourdieu's "cultural capital," which described a system of preferences and dispositions that ultimately served to classify groups by class. Of course, such a system was not apolitical, but Bourdieu's intention was to investigate how certain interests, pastimes, or preferences were conveyed (and kept) among groups, while kept carefully distinguishable from other interests or pastimes.

In both cases, defining the terms helps in setting up the discussion, as well as establishing relationships with previous works by quoting them. It is good academic practice, and it also helps you stop and think about the vocabulary you are using, preventing the use (and abuse) of buzzwords, which I have already warned about in previous sections (see Box 5.1 Beware of Buzzwords in Chapter 5).

The part where using a game to illustrate a theory gets tricky is the selection of the building blocks. Depending on the type of theory, the building blocks will be different. If the analysis is in the style of literary or film analysis, the formal qualities building blocks will be the most useful. The social sciences will more likely focus on the building blocks that refer to audience and game communities. Let us provide an example to illustrate how this would work.

Paul Martin tackles *The Elder Scrolls IV: Oblivion* (2006) with theories of the sublime and definitions of the pastoral in order to explain the function of the landscape throughout the adventures of the player in the realms of Tamriel and Oblivion.[60] The core argument is that the landscape initially stirs a sense of the sublime, the delightful fear as defined by Edmund Burke and Immanuel Kant,[61] which, throughout the game, is defused and becomes picturesque, still delightful but now mundane, as the player takes action and becomes familiar with the space. Incidentally, the discussion of the sublime in digital games is not unusual; see, for example, Simon Niedenthal's analysis of *Silent Hill 2* (2001) and *Resident Evil 4* (2005).[62] It is an engaging concept precisely because it refers to the experience of facing something that cannot be immediately grasped by our logic. Martin defines his terms (*pastoral, sublime*, as well as the role of space as part of gameplay) in order to make his argument. In the same way that the reaction to the sublime disappears as the spectator takes action, the feeling of the sublime set up by the expanding landscapes of *Oblivion* diminishes through the interaction with the game. The analysis focuses on the audio-visual representation of the game, although it also references game reviews, specific story events, and the role of the player character within the story, all in reference to understanding the space of the game. For example, after describing the player character creation and comparing it to other games, Martin brings the discussion back to discussing the landscape and by extension the core topics of the article:

> There is little possibility in the dialogue trees to really inject the hero with a unique personality. While the possibility of the hero becoming a compelling character exists, particularly for the genre fan, the hero can equally stay at the level of a functional object. The avatar's main function is not to develop the character of the hero, but to discover the character of the landscape.

The biggest challenge of applying pre-existing theories to the study of games is to demonstrate their relevance. Martin focuses on the landscape and then resorts to philosophical ideas that were devised to explain the reaction to magnificent, imposing, overwhelming spaces and nature, thus, managing to connect nineteenth-century concepts to a digital game in the early twenty-first century. These concepts are not the only connection—the examples from the game as well as other citations help to strengthen that relationship and make the concept relevant.

Pre-existing theories can also be integrated within the discussion without being its core, as it is in this example. On p. 265 I show how an analysis of *Head Over Heels* (1987) defines immersion and interactivity based on the works of several authors to explain how the player makes sense of the challenges of the game and identifies with the two characters that the player controls in the game. Theoretical concepts, in this case, support the overall discussion to interpret the game. Theories can also provide tools that we resort to in specific sections to make a point; on the other hand, we should not use somebody else's work to avoid having to make an argument. Remember to ask yourself why the theory is helpful to make your point, and whether you would be able to make the point without it. In the end, writing a game analysis is an art—the good news is that it is no different from other humanistic writing.

▶ INTERPRETATIVE ANALYSIS

This is the type of analysis that we usually associate with literature, less often with film. The text is read as representing something else, as a symbol of the undercurrent of cultural and social concerns that surround the text. Beware: an interpretation is not just your opinion. Interpretative analyses are exercises in observing the world, learning something new, and transmitting it to others in a persuasive manner.

In a way, almost any analysis of a game is going to be an interpretation of what it is about; we provide new knowledge by examining one specific aspect of a game. When the focus is the interpretation, the emphasis is precisely in finding new relationships between the game and what it means, or at least how it may be significant. Interpretative analyses can be as much about the game as about our capacity to argue our way of understanding it as valid and enriching.

Interpreting a game as an allegory of something else can provide novel and relevant insights, pointing to what parts of a text may resonate with its audience. A game may connect with players because it reflects a psychological state that many connect with, or because it reflects attitudes and concerns of a cultural or a historical moment. For example, Janet Murray talks about *Tetris* (1987) as

> a perfect enactment of the overtasked lives of Americans in the 1990s—of the constant bombardment of tasks that demand our attention and that we must somehow fit into our overcrowded schedules and clear off our desks in order to make room for the next onslaught.[70]

This insightful interpretation can explain why the game may have resonated with American players in the 1990s: it evokes something that rings true. This type of interpretative writing is typical of the humanities, which aim at understanding human activities better.

Although Murray acknowledges that the game was created by Alexei Patjinov, a Soviet scientist in the 1980s, some have read her analysis as attributing intentionality to its creator,[71] who did not intend it to be a commercial product.[72] In reading it closely, Murray's interpretation of *Tetris* focuses on the player's experience and explains it as a metaphor, rather than falling into this intentional fallacy. This controversy, however, shows how important it is to frame our interpretations, since different contexts will yield different analyses. Metaphorical interpretations can be very insightful and enriching, but also the most prone to be contested by people who may read the game—or your writing—following a different agenda.

This type of analysis mostly resorts to the building blocks in the formal qualities area; it is predominantly a formal analysis in which we examine how the formal qualities may point to socio-cultural concepts and events, or may construe a message, contributing to a coherent concept that explains the game. In certain cases, it is always preferable to ground our interpretation with building blocks belonging to the context area to avoid unfounded interpretations. The relevance of context to justify and strengthen the interpretation is clear when we examine the *Tetris* case above—in the context of American culture, Murray's interpretation is insightful because the activity of the game matches a specific aspect of the lifestyle. However, in the context of how it was produced, from the developer to the economic context in which it was initially conceived and distributed, it does not seem as relevant.[73]

The issues derived from understanding games as messages or how they are texts, because they are a participatory, performative medium, have already been discussed. The building block of Values and Procedural Rhetoric in Chapter 5 dealt briefly with how a game can express ideas persuasively as a system; the representation of the game and how it positions the player can also be interpreted and read.

Jan Van Looy carries out a close reading of *Head Over Heels*, "a 3D isometric arcade/puzzle game" developed in the UK in 1987.[74] The author focuses on the relationship between interactivity and signification, emphasizing that it is an interpretative analysis, whose core argument is how the interaction and representation in the game resonated among (British) players at the time because of the references to contemporary events as well as other games. In order to make that point, the author gives a very detailed overview of the context of the game, including the technology and the engine of the game, quotes from interviews with the developer, reviews from the time it was released, as well as a good game overview—the game was relatively popular in Europe at the time, but chances are that current readers around the world have not heard about it. In order to clarify the argument, the article also includes copious screenshots to explain the game, as well as a brief definition of theoretical terms in order to understand the argument being made.

In this case, the context and set-up seem to take more space than the interpretation, mostly because the author needs to provide a solid overview since the reader is mostly unlikely to have played the game. By giving the reader a detailed picture of the context, we can understand why the game was popular at the time, why it was innovative, and how it commented on different aspects of popular culture that may be lost to players now.

This *Head Over Heels* analysis demonstrates how examples and context help in legitimizing our interpretation of a game. In this case, Van Looy is analyzing a game where the player controls two different characters with complementary skills: "[Head...] can jump twice his own height and control his slow descent using his vestigial wings. Heels...has legs like pistons and is a powerful runner capable of leaping his own height." The core of the article is discussing how controlling two characters is what makes the game remarkable, because it uses the interaction to create meaning, as exemplified by the moment where the two characters meet and can combine, as one character sits on top of the other to move around together:

> Now that Head and Heels are together they combine strengths and lose weaknesses; "Head Over Heels" can run as fast as Heels and jump as high as Head. This entails, however, that they can jump further because of the faster take-off run and more easily escape from monsters, because they can jump over obstacles Heels alone would not dream of jumping over. Furthermore, they can solve more complex puzzles; for example, when one of the two guides the other across an electrified platform or when Heels builds a tower of boxes so that with Head's high jump they can go to the next room...Once joined, the couple is stronger than ever, but finishing the quest together is not self-evident. One of the two may die in the attempt or one may get stuck and give up underway. Interestingly, on this second allegorical level the player is no longer one of the protagonists or both, but rather unification itself. She finds the two forced to separate and she has to bring them back together. On the first level, the aim of the game is to avoid monsters, solve riddles and liberate planets. On the second level, it is to lead a fulfilling life with a loving partner.

Van Looy goes on to discuss how this may have resonated with British players at the time with further evidence. There is a statue in the game (a "chess piece" according to the article) that looks like a caricature of Prince Charles, which the player can move to reach places. The metaphor explained above is extended through this representation—the Prince has become a token the player manipulates, just like Princess Diana allegedly manipulated him; his missing other half in comparison with *Head Over Heels* points to how their marriage may be dysfunctional, something that was starting to become evident to the public at the time. Although this last interpretation may be reading more into the game than is there, the example is set up in such a way that the relationship is evident to the reader.

An interpretative analysis is rather difficult to get right, as the examples here evidence. As with other types of analysis, what is key here is to define our terms very carefully, setting up our discussion by explaining how we are going to approach the game. Then, using a close reading, we select the sections that help us make our point as concretely as possible, and explain how they connect—in the example above, the parallels between the interaction of the two player characters and the appearance of Prince Charles in the game are set up as a point of comparison. It is hard to write a bulletproof interpretation of a game, but if the points of comparison are convincing and well supported, we can make a pertinent contribution to the discourse of the game and its relevance in the cultural context. We do not need a complex hyper-realistic game to encourage interpretation—we have seen how we can interpret arcade games and platform games and hypothesize on how they resonate with us, thus, emphasizing the evocative potential of games.

▶ PERSONAL ACCOUNT

Another form of analysis that can resonate with readers is the personal account. This mode of writing turns to criticism that takes the form of a discussion where the point of view of the writer/player is emphasized. This type of analysis, thus, addresses the experiential aspects of games; some scholars have also flirted with this format (see Gonzalo Frasca's review of *The Sims*[75]), as a way to emphasize and reveal the role of the writer/player. The popularity of let's play videos as well as live video streaming of gameplay also demonstrate the cultural relevance of using one's own experience as the focus of an analysis. Personal accounts were one of the features of New Games Journalism, as we saw above, and their aim was breaking off with the types of commercial consumer reviews discussed in the Journalistic Review section.

The building blocks used, as in the other models based on close reading, can vary. A personal account is a detailed description of the gameplay experience, discussed in the game overview, using other blocks as examples to support it, mostly taken from game overview and formal elements. The personal account is an overview of the game where the subjectivity of the writer/player is emphasized to enrich and humanize the analysis.

This may seem like the easiest analysis to write, since it appears to be one's own experience of the game. But do not be deceived—it is probably the most complicated of them all. The key is not just to pour your thoughts on the game on paper, or transcribe everything that goes through your head as you go. A personal account is not about just writing a stream-of-consciousness account of your gameplay. Why should we care about what you think? It is easy to ramble; the challenge is to actually say something that makes your own experience unique and appreciative of the game. This same advice also applies to streaming or recording a let's play video, where players comment on the games while they play. Recording and broadcasting oneself requires preparation, from choosing the game and having a good technological set-up for broadcasting, to figuring out what persona you are constructing through play. Even if you think that you are going to play along with the audience, taking them through your journey of playing the game, the odds are that you may end up playing for the audience, ultimately playing in ways that are entertaining for the audience, and very differently from how you would play on your own.[76] Are you critiquing the design of the game? Are you playing the game satirically? Are you showing off your playing skills? Are you playing a horror game and want to transmit the fear to your audience? Or are you discovering an old game alongside your audience?[77] All these involve different ways of playing and talking to your spectators. If your goal is using a let's play format in your writing, you have to be even more specific on what your approach to the game is, what you are bringing to the analysis of the game, and how you are communicating that clearly to your reader.

What makes this type of writing potentially insightful is its relationship with *participant observation*, which was dealt with in the Game Communities analysis section above. Using one's own experience and know-how can be the method to provide insight into how we understand and engage with videogames, with the possibility of providing the kind of nuanced breakdown a close reading allows. A subjective point of view helps in dealing with the less systematic human factors of games—we cannot really measure "fun" objectively; by providing a personal approach to game writing, we can tackle and show the variety of ways to play.

One of the first examples of this type is David Sudnow's *Pilgrim in the Microworld,* a book-long account of the author's obsession with the Atari VCS version of *Breakout.*[78] The text is fascinating, first because Sudnow was a pioneer, and also for the exhaustive detail in which he explains his understanding of the game. The value of the book, however, has only been proved many years after its initial publication. Compared to how we play games now, Sudnow is certainly a naïve player, who thinks that he can perform the perfect *Breakout* game by figuring out the sequence, rather than understanding the game as a dynamic system that includes a certain level of randomness to keep it unpredictable and engaging. Sudnow tackles *Breakout* as if it was a difficult melody to play on the piano—he was a piano teacher—which one masters and performs perfectly. In his obsession with the game, he even interviews one of the developers in the hopes he will help him find the solution to get rid of all the bricks on the first screen. The developer gives him a detailed description of how the program works; a lot of this information, Sudnow admits, goes over his head: which types of shots to avoid, how the paddle is segmented, and how each segment has a different effect if it touches the ball. The key piece of information, however, is that there is nothing random in the behavior of the ball, which makes Sudnow believe that he can truly figure out the optimum game of *Breakout.*[79]

Sudnow's book, in the end, is more about him than the game, since he was using it to cope with other issues in his life at the time. He describes his actions in detail, from how he drives to a place, to setting up the console, to giving a beat-by-beat narration of his thought processes while playing. It is more about the experience than the game, and that is why we appreciate the work. Sudnow uses *Breakout* as an artifact to think with, exposing more of himself than revealing much about the game.

Because of the personal nature of this type of analysis, it also requires a lot of discipline and mindfulness about what one is doing in the game, just as in ethnographic analysis. Again, this is not simply your opinion—everyone has one, and we can agree or disagree—and the goal is to support it with an argument, just as in a regular essay-form type of writing. Just because it is personal does not mean you can stop being systematic. The goal is to relate your experience in playing, how you played the game, and what factors shaped that experience, from how the game may set up specific responses to how your personal background conditioned your reaction and interpretation of the game.

As is often the case in writing for the humanities, there is not really a right way or wrong way, but it is something that you need to consider. How are you portraying your experience? What do you mean when using *you* instead of *I?* Are you assuming that you are the ideal player? Why would you want to emphasize your subjective point of view? Why would you like to moderate your own voice? This reflection is important, because we must acknowledge that, as writers/players, we tend to generalize our way of approaching the gameplay. It is not uncommon—I do this often in my own work when I talk about aspects of the game that may seem given, which the player cannot get away without doing. As an adventure games scholar, I have written about solving puzzles in a specific way, because most times there is only one way to overcome the challenge. Generalization can help us connect with the reader, but it can also be a way to assume that other people are going to play the game in the same way.

Writing a personal account does not mean that you take notes as you play and then you simply repack them as an essay. All throughout this book, we have been dealing with how rich and complex the analysis of games can be—playing a game is one (crucial) source out of many.

In *Killing Is Harmless*, a book-long analysis of *Spec Ops: The Line* (2012), Brendan Keogh constantly talks about having played it multiple times, and using videos of other players' play-throughs to double-check on what happens in the game, or how other people may make different choices and their results. He did not play alone—he worked with students who helped him explore the game and all the possible options in it. As part of his research, he also references the work of other game critics, whose take on the game is different from his own.[80]

So, how does one write a personal account? The notes that you take are essential, yes, but the process of converting them into a personal account is a bit more sophisticated than just presenting your experience as a narrative. This type of writing is yet another essay, where you have a core idea that you want to elaborate and support; your personal point of view, your perspective, serves as the foundation of your argument. So, before you start writing, try to articulate what it is about your experience that provides a special insight on the game, what makes it significant. What is more, what makes you different as a player that can bring a fresh perspective on the game? Figuring out your premise early on, as is the case with all the other models, helps to keep your writing focused. Then the key is supporting that idea with specific examples from your play experience, moments of the game as well as what you were thinking, in the hope that how you played and understood the game resonates with your readers' experiences.

In *Killing Is Harmless*, Keogh writes from the point of view of both a videogame critic and an academic. In a way, this analysis feels like an experiment in writing a personal close reading of the game, trying to figure out the process of what a full-length analysis requires. The book takes the reader from the beginning to the end of the game as an idealized walkthrough—if the reader has not played the game, they get a sense of what it is like; if they have, they can contrast their own experience with Keogh's interpretation. The analysis also takes the time to show what happens at specific points of the game if the player chooses to do something different, thus giving a sense of how the player may have different options to play the game, by using techniques of close reading (see Box 6.7 Close Reading on p. 256). There is a core that drives the lengthy study, which provides the coherence that helps the writer get across.

Killing Is Harmless is remarkable in its detail and exhaustiveness precisely because it takes advantage of its subjectivity. *Spec Ops: The Line* is a shooter game whose main trope is subverting the expectations of the player, foreshadowing events with information that may seem irrelevant, and commenting on the action through songs and references to popular culture. The relevance of the game comes from paying attention to how the game slowly creates an hallucination for the player. By providing a personal interpretation, Keogh is highlighting how much the game toys with player expectations, and how it tricks players who may not tackle the game critically. The book also provides recurring references to its methods, such as noting that it is the product of multiple replays, as well as viewing online videos of other players both for reference and contrast.

The value of the personal account depends on the purpose of using subjectivity. As we have seen, in spite of the method, the subjectivity of personal accounts is not explicitly acknowledged often, and yet it drives all their content. What is often missing, though, is supporting some of the affirmations with more scholarly or educated texts—some journalists often cite each other, and may refer to scholarly affirmations from a blog rather than its original scholarly source. The legitimacy of this type of analysis can be grounded with scholarly work, but that does not quite happen—this could be a good vehicle to introduce players to a more complex academic discourse. Remember: your analysis is as good as your sources, so self-awareness combined with solid, well-researched journalistic or academic references is the best way to ground your view and get it across.

BOX 6.9 EXERCISE: REWRITE THE ANALYSIS

This chapter started by identifying the different building blocks of a game analysis; it will finish with a challenge. Find a game analysis of a game you know, or that you can play, or the one that you may already be analyzing. Write an analysis of the game from a different perspective—from history to a personal account, from a community to demonstrating a theory. Which aspects of the original analysis can inform your own? What building blocks would you lose? Which ones do you need to add? How does your analysis provide a different perspective?

This exercise is also good training both for writing analyses and other work in general. Our writing is part of a larger discourse, so it is always worth spending a moment thinking about how our work extends or makes a contribution to the field.

PUTTING IT ALL TOGETHER

As we have seen in this chapter, there are many ways to write a game analysis. At times, it seems unavoidable to combine several types of analysis, even though our goal may be predominantly one. When this is the case, ask yourself why you need this multifaceted analysis, what the role of each section is, and how the different approaches will relate to each other.

If you find yourself thinking of writing a holistic analysis that includes several types and you have not done this before, step back. Combining different approaches is something you will do comfortably when you become familiar with writing about games and media in general. Also, being overambitious as a novice writer will probably result in a superficial analysis or a piece of writing that you will not be able to finish on time. So, focus.

The multifaceted approach seems better suited for long-form analysis, such as theses or books, which may use different types of analysis to highlight different aspects of the game in depth. Pearce's book-length analysis of the community of *Uru* players uses two chapters to introduce the theories, another one to provide the historical precedents of the game being studied, *Myst Online: Uru* (2003–2004; 2007–2008; 2010–), and another to explain the history of this short-lived MMOG, before talking about the community itself.[81] This is particularly necessary because the version of the game that is being analyzed is not available online anymore, even though there is a fan-run version live at the time of writing.[82] This is why the author needs to give readers a holistic perspective, so they can learn about the game and its community without having played. Pearce's approach also manages to combine ethnography with a personal account—she credits her avatar Artemesia as the co-author of the book—which now that we have examined the relationship between both does not sound far-fetched.

This chapter has provided an overview both of some of the key sections of an analysis, and of a selection of different models. Writing the analysis means zeroing-in to specific aspects of the game, so we know which building blocks are going to be relevant. We start by formulating what the goal of the analysis is (e.g., calling attention to a little-known game, writing a journalistic review, doing some videogame archeology to understand a game in its historical context, to understand a game better through its players) and being well aware of who we are writing for. Introspection and knowledge of who we are as players, as well as identifying our voice as writers, can be challenging, but it is only for the best—writing about games often involves resorting to our own experience, so we have to know how to make the best of it. Your best allies to convey your ideas to your reader and construct a solid work are clear definitions of your terms and specific examples—for this type of analytical writing, the particulars of a game or games can help us develop higher-level concepts and theories that will advance the field of game studies.

The best thing about game analysis is that we are creating the best practices through writing. This book is a compendium of what I have learned after researching and teaching game studies for more than 15 years, as well as reading the work of many others, which is growing every day—and I still feel I have barely scratched the surface. The more we write and experiment, the better we can all become at writing for games, reaching the level of sophistication that other disciplines have already achieved.

▶ NOTES

1 Creswell, John W. *Research Design: Qualitative, Quantitative, and Mixed Method Approaches* (Thousand Oaks, CA: Sage Publications, 2003), pp. 13–21.

2 Eveleigh, David J. *Old Cooking Utensils* (Princes Risborough: Shire, 1986).

3 Murrell, Kevin. *Early Home Computers* (Oxford: Shire Publications, 2013).

4 Fernández-Vara, Clara. "The Game's Afoot: Designing Sherlock Holmes." In *Proceedings of DiGRA 2013: Defragging Game Studies. Atlanta*, GA, 2013. http://www.digra.org/digital-library/publications/the-games-afoot-designing-sherlock-holmes/ (accessed November 19, 2023).

5 Schechner, Richard. *Between Theater and Anthropology* (Philadelphia, PA: University of Pennsylvania Press, 1985).

6 Jorgensen, Kristine. "On Transdiegetic Sounds in Computer Games." *Northern Lights* 5, no. 1 (September 2007): 105–117.

7 Freud, Sigmund. "The 'Uncanny.'" In *The Standard Edition of the Complete Psychological Works of Sigmund Freud*, edited by Angela Richards, Vol. XVII (London: Hogarth Press, 1964), pp. 217–256.

8 Camper, Brett. "Retro Reflexivity: La-Mulana, an 8-Bit Period Piece." *The Video Game Theory Reader* 2 (2009): 169–195.

9 See Chapter 1, notes 5 and 6.

10 See examples of editorial statements in Chapter 1, note 7.

11 Gillen, Kieron. "The New Games Journalism." *Kieron Gillen's Workblog*. Available at: https://web.archive.org/web/20181114121101/http://gillen.cream.org/wordpress_html/assorted-essays/the-new-games-journalism/ (accessed November 19, 2023).

12 With apologies, we see the need to use the expletive in order to be able to identify the article and search it online; the term is also an essential part of the story it tells. The full text can be found as always_black. "Bow Nigger." In *The Game Design Reader: A Rules of Play Anthology*, edited by Katie Salen and Eric Zimmerman (Cambridge, MA: The MIT Press, 2006), pp. 602–609.

13 "Off the Grid with Walker Spaight: A Bow to the New Games Journalism | The Alphaville Herald." Available at: http://alphavilleherald.com/2005/03/off_the_grid_wi_1.html (accessed November 4, 2023).

14 See "Why the Games Media Has a Diversity Problem—This Website Especially." *Eurogamer* (blog), April 11, 2018. Available at: www.eurogamer.net/articles/2018-04-11-why-the-games-media-has-a-diversity-problem-this-website-especially (accessed November 4, 2023).

15 Blackmon, Samantha. "Pickaninnies and Pixels: On Race, Racism, and Cuphead at E3—NYMG." Available at: http://www.nymgamer.com/?p=9235 (accessed November 4, 2023); Cole, Yussef. "Cuphead and the Racist Spectre of Fleischer Animation | Unwinnable." Available at https://unwinnable.com/2017/11/10/cuphead-and-the-racist-spectre-of-fleischer-animation/ (accessed November 19, 2023, 2018).

16 Hudson, Laura, and Leigh Alexander. *The Offworld Collection* (TopatoCo, 2016).

17 Ibid.; Starkey, Daniel. "Playing on 'Indian Time.'" pp. 31–34; Xu, Christina. "China Loves the Lingo of Games." pp. 124–126; MacLeod, Riley. "The Queer Masculinity of Stealth Games." pp. 108–111; Hudson, Laura. "Subversive Games about Waitresses and Hairdressers." pp. 108–111.

18 Apart from The Offworld Collection, the original version of the article can be read online. Cross, Katherine. "There's Never Been a Better Time to Take an Adventure 'Round the World/Offworld." *Boing Boing—Offworld*, October 5, 2015. Available at: https://boingboing.net/2015/10/05/theres-never-been-a-better-t.html (accessed November 19, 2023.).

19 Dahlen, Chris. "Chasing the Dollar," *Unwinnable: Life with Culture*, February 28, 2013. Available at: www.unwinnable.com/2013/02/28/chasing-the-dollar/ (accessed November 4, 2023).

20 Goodwin, Joel. "Ahead ... The Stars," *Electron Dance: Words on PC Gaming*, January 17, 2012. Available at: www.electrondance.com/ahead-the-stars/ (accessed November 4, 2023).

21 The *Cart Life* Official page (now unavailable) described the game as "a retail simulator ... which showcases the lives of street vendors in a small city which is located in the Western United States. Each of the playable characters has specific goals and special traits, but also unique addictions which the player must accommodate in order to succeed within the game. Permits are required but expensive".

22 The executable of the game is downloadable from The Internet Archive. Available at: https://archive.org/details/cart-life-v1.6 while its source code is also available on Github https://github.com/gondur/cartlife_src (both accessed November 4, 2023).

23 Farokhmanesh, Megan. "The Untold Tale of a Disappearing Video Game—And Its Resurrection." *Wired*. https://www.wired.com/story/mystery-of-cart-life-death-rebirth/ (accessed November 19, 2023).

24 Partlett, David. *The Oxford History of Board Games* (Oxford: Oxford University Press, 1999).

25 One of the earliest digital games that we have a record of is Noughts and Crosses, which Alexander Douglas wrote for his PhD thesis in 1952. See Donovan, Tristan. *Replay: The History of Video Games* (Lewes, East Sussex: Yellow Ant Media Ltd, 2010), p. 6.

26 Juul, Jesper. "Swap Adjacent Gems to Make Sets of Three: A History of Matching Tile Games." *Artifact* 1, no. 4 (2007): 205–216.

27 Kocurek, Carly A. "The Agony and the Exidy: A History of Video Game Violence and the Legacy of Death Race." *Game Studies: The International Journal of Computer Game Research* 12, no. 1 (September 2012). Available at: http://gamestudies.org/1201/articles/carly_kocurek (accessed November 4, 2023).

28 Gazzard, Alison. "The Platform and the Player: Exploring the (hi)Stories of Elite." *Game Studies* 13, no. 2 (December 2013). Available at: http://gamestudies.org/1302/articles/agazzard (accessed November 4, 2023).

29 Camper, Brett. "Retro Reflexivity: La-Mulana, an 8-Bit Period Piece." In *The Video Game Theory Reader 2*, edited by Bernard Perron and Mark J.P. Wolf (New York: Routledge, 2009), pp. 169–195.

30 Montfort, Nick. "Combat in Context." *Game Studies: The International Journal of Computer Game Research* 6, no. 1 (2006). Available at: http://gamestudies.org/0601/articles/montfort (accessed November 4, 2023).

31 Pinchbeck, Dan. *Doom: Scarydarkfast* (Ann Arbor, MI: University of Michigan Press, 2013); Kushner, David. *Masters of Doom: How Two Guys Created an Empire and Transformed Pop Culture* (New York: Random House Publishing Group, 2003).

32 Boellstorff, Tom, Bonnie Nardi, Celia Pearce, and T.L. Taylor. *Ethnography and Virtual Worlds: A Handbook of Method* (Princeton, NJ: Princeton University Press, 2012), pp. 3–4.

33 Wehner, Mike. "Devs Had to Demand Female Focus Testers for the Last of Us." *The Escapist*, April 8, 2013. Available at: https://www.escapistmagazine.com/devs-had-to-demand-female-focus-testers-for-the-last-of-us/ (accessed November 19, 2023).

34 Some long-form works that are worth looking into, if you are interested in studying game communities, are Boellstorff et al. *Ethnography and Virtual Worlds*; Taylor, T.L. *Play between Worlds: Exploring Online Game Culture* (Cambridge, MA: The MIT Press, 2006); Pearce, Celia, and Artemesia. *Communities of Play: Emergent Cultures in Multiplayer Games and Virtual Worlds* (Cambridge, MA:

The MIT Press, 2009). For a good overview on methods to interview subjects, see Seidman, Irving. *Interviewing as Qualitative Research: A Guide for Researchers in Education and the Social Sciences* (New York: Teachers College Press, 2006).

35 Gray, Kishonna L. *Intersectional Tech: Black Users in Digital Gaming* (LSU Press, 2020).

36 Creswell, John W. *Research Design: Qualitative, Quantitative, and Mixed Method Approaches* (Thousand Oaks, CA: Sage Publications, 2003), pp. 153–168.

37 Yee, Nick. "Motivations for Play in Online Games." *CyberPsychology & Behavior* 9, no. 6 (2006): 772–775.

38 For example, T.L. Taylor reveals how meeting power gamers of Everquest (1999–) and how they played, using more than one computer to play, and looking for all the best items and most difficult quests, made her realize that she did not play the game the same way, even though she considered herself a devoted player. Taylor. *Play Between Worlds*, pp. 67–69.

39 Kutner, Lawrence, and Cheryl Olson. *Grand Theft Childhood: The Surprising Truth about Violent Video Games and What Parents Can Do* (New York: Simon & Schuster, 2008).

40 Consalvo, Mia. "Hardcore Casual: Game Culture Return(s) to Ravenhearst." In *Proceedings of the 4th International Conference on Foundations of Digital Games*, FDG '09 (New York: ACM, 2009), pp. 50–54.

41 Taylor, Nicholas, Jennifer Jenson, and Suzanne de Castell. "Gender in Play: Mapping a Girls' Gaming Club." In *Situated Play: DiGRA 2007 Conference Proceedings* (Tokyo, Japan: Akira Baba, 2007), pp. 302–308.

42 Jakobsson, Michael. "Playing with the Rules: Social and Cultural Aspects of Game Rules in a Console Game Club." In *Situated Play: DiGRA 2007 Conference Proceedings* (Tokyo, Japan: Akira Baba, 2007), pp. 386–392.

43 Pearce and Artemesia. *Communities of Play.*

44 Bruckman, Amy. "Interviewing Members of Online Communities: A Practical Guide to Recruiting Participants." In *Research Methods for Studying Groups*, edited by Andrea Hollingshead and Marshall Scott Poole (London: Routledge, 2012), pp. 200–210.

45 Consalvo, Mia, and Jason Begy. *Players and Their Pets: Gaming Communities from Beta to Sunset* (Minneapolis, MN: University of Minnesota Press, 2015).

46 See, for example, Taylor. *Play Between Worlds*, p. 12.

47 Boellstorff, et al. *Ethnography and Virtual Worlds*, pp. 21–22.

48 Taylor. *Play between Worlds*, pp. 67–92.

49 Keogh, Brendan, Daniel Purvis, Rob Zacny, and Benjamin Abraham. *Killing Is Harmless: A Critical Reading of Spec Ops: The Line*. 1st edn (Stolen Projects, 2013).

50 Aarseth, Espen J. *Cybertext: Perspectives on Ergodic Literature* (Baltimore, MD: Johns Hopkins University Press, 1997), pp. 18–19.

51 Genette, Gérard. *Narrative Discourse: An Essay in Method* (Ithaca, NY: Cornell University Press, 1980).

52 Mulvey's article is a referent in feminist film studies. Mulvey, Laura. "Visual Pleasure and Narrative Cinema." *Screen* 16, no. 3 (1975): 6–18.

53 Kennedy, H.W. "Lara Croft: Feminist Icon or Cyberbimbo? On the Limits of Textual Analysis." *Game Studies: International Journal of Computer Games Research* 2, no. 2 (December 2002). Available at: www.gamestudies.org/0202/kennedy/ (accessed November 4, 2023).

54 Carr, Diane. "Play and Pleasure." In *Computer Games: Text, Narrative and Play* (Cambridge: Polity, 2006), pp. 45–58.

55 Ruberg, Bo. *Video Games Have Always Been Queer* (New York: New York University Press, 2019).

56 Aikin, Anna Letitia. "Sir Bertrand: A Fragment." In *Gothic Short Stories*, edited by David Blair (London: Wordsworth Editions, 2002).

57 Propp, Vladimir. *Morphology of the Folktale*. 2nd edn (Austin, TX: University of Texas Press, 1968); Campbell, Joseph. *The Hero with a Thousand Faces* (Princeton, NJ: Princeton University Press, 1972).

58 Propp. *Morphology of the Folktale*, p. 26.

59 Campbell. *The Hero with a Thousand Faces*, pp. 59–68.

60 Martin, Paul. "The Pastoral and the Sublime in Elder Scrolls IV: Oblivion." *Game Studies* 11, no. 3 (2011). Available at: http://gamestudies.org/1103/articles/martin (accessed November 4, 2023).

61 Kant, Immanuel, and Werner S. Pluhar. *Critique of Judgment* (Indianapolis, IN: Hackett Publishing, 1987); Burke, Edmund. *A Philosophical Enquiry into the Origin of Our Ideas of the Sublime and Beautiful* ... (London: F.C. and J. Rivington, Otridge and Son, 1812).

62 Niedenthal, Simon. "Patterns of Obscurity: Gothic Setting and Light in Resident Evil 4 and Silent Hill 2." In *Horror Video Games: Essays on the Fusion of Fear and Play*, edited by Bernard Perron (Jefferson, NC: McFarland, 2009), pp. 168–180.

63 Csikszentmihalyi, Mihaly. *Flow: The Psychology of Optimal Experience* (New York: HarperPerennial Modern Classics, 2008).

64 Peirce, Charles. *Essential Peirce: Selected Philosophical Writings*, Vol. 2 (Bloomington, IN: Indiana University Press, 1998).

65 I know this from experience—see one of the papers I collaborated in where we needed to distinguish between the humanities and the computer science definition. Jose P. Zagal, Michael Mateas, Clara Fernández-Vara, Brian Hochhalter, and Nolan Lichti. "Towards an Ontological Language for Game Analysis." In *Changing Views: Worlds in Play* (Vancouver: University of Vancouver, 2005). Available at: www.digra.org/wp-content/uploads/digital-library/06276.09313.pdf (accessed November 4, 2023).

66 Klastrup, Lisbeth. "A Poetics of Virtual Worlds." In *Proceedings of Digital Arts and Culture* (Melbourne, 2003).

67 Rimmon-Kenan, Shlomith. *Narrative Fiction: Contemporary Poetics* (London: Psychology Press, 2002).

68 Klastrup. "A Poetics of Virtual Worlds," p. 101.

69 Consalvo, Mia. *Cheating: Gaining Advantage in Videogames* (Cambridge, MA: The MIT Press, 2007), p. 4.

70 Murray, Janet. *Hamlet on the Holodeck: The Future of Narrative in Cyberspace* (Cambridge, MA: The MIT Press, 2001), p. 144.

71 See, for instance, Eskelinen, Markku. "The Gaming Situation." *Game Studies* 1, no. 1 (2001): 68.

72 Donovan. *Replay*, pp. 199–201.

73 For more discussion on metaphors and how they relate to experience, see Begy, Jason. "Experiential Metaphors in Abstract Games." *Transactions of the Digital Games Research Association* 1, no. 1 (2013); Rusch, Doris C. "Exploring the Meaning Potential of Image Schemata in Fictional Games." In *Proceedings of DiGRA 2013: Defragging Game Studies* (Atlanta, 2013).

74 Van Looy, Jan. "Uneasy Lies the Head that Wears a Crown: Interactivity and Signification in Head Over Heels." *Game Studies: The International Journal of Computer Game Research* 3, no. 2 (2003). Available at: www.gamestudies.org/0302/vanlooy/ (accessed November 4, 2023).

75 Frasca, Gonzalo. "The Sims: Grandmothers Are Cooler than Trolls." *Game Studies* 1, no. 1 (2001). Available at: www.gamestudies.org/0101/frasca/ (accessed November 4, 2023).

76 Scully-Blaker et al. discuss how tandem play (playing alongside someone else) may be possible during a livestream of a game, but it ends up becoming a performance for the audience, playing for them to keep them interested. See Scully-Blaker, Rainforest, Jason Begy, Mia Consalvo, and Sarah Ganzon. "Playing Along and Playing for on Twitch: Livestreaming from Tandem Play to Performance." In *Proceedings of the 50th Hawaii International Conference on System Sciences* (Kona, 2017).

77 See, for example, Leigh Alexander's video series Lo-Fi Let's Play, which tackles different obscure home computer games from the 1980s. Available at: www.youtube.com/user/leighalexander1/videos (accessed November 4, 2023). Jess Morrisette also runs his own channel on Twitch where he plays mainly adventure games from the 1980s and 1990s; his videos are also available as an archive at https://www.youtube.com/decafjedi (accessed November 19, 2023).

78 Sudnow, David. *Pilgrim in the Microworld* (New York: Warner Books, 1983). This work was already mentioned in the Game Dynamics building block in Chapter 5.

79 Ibid., pp. 91–95.

80 Keogh et al. *Killing Is Harmless.*

81 Pearce and Artemesia. *Communities of Play.*

82 The current incarnation of *Uru* is available at http://mystonline.com/ (accessed November 4, 2023).

7 Wrapping Things Up

▶ SO YOU HAVE WRITTEN YOUR ANALYSIS. WHAT NOW?

Well, you are not done yet. In order to check whether your research and writing process has gone well, try to explain what your assignment/paper/thesis is about in a couple of sentences. You have been thinking about your game for a while now; synthesizing your ideas is a sign that you are close to learning something new. One good way to check that your analysis is focused is to go back to your original question, and then try to answer it briefly in a sentence or two—that will be your thesis statement. If writing a couple of paragraphs is too difficult, it probably means your ideas are still too fuzzy. You should write what you believe your analysis is about anyway and see where your ideas take you—then revise and synthesize.

Start by checking for consistency and reread your essay. Is there a conclusion that summarizes what you have learned from this process? Does your conclusion match your thesis statement? The conclusion addresses the issues that you called attention to in your introductory paragraph and thesis; if your thesis was explicitly formulated as a question, the conclusion should summarize the answer. It may be the case that your thesis and conclusion may not match—do not panic. As you were writing, you were probably

DOI: 10.4324/9781003355779-7

thinking through your argument and your evidence, so when you reach the end, you have refined what you are discussing. That is perfectly okay; the mismatch means that your thesis statement is in the last paragraph, and you have to move it to the introduction section and rewrite both the beginning and end of your analysis.

▶ THE ART OF THE REWRITE

Chapter 2 has already mentioned the need to budget time for rewrites—now is the time for them. Preparing any type of writing includes spending some time taking care of its final presentation before it reaches the reader. If you are studying game design, this will ring a bell—in the same way that you iterate and revise your game after you get feedback from players, your writing also needs revisions in order to be in the best shape possible. This last phase, although it does not take as much time in proportion with the rest of the process, is what differentiates a committed writer from an amateur.

Apart from rereading and revising what you have written, another good writing practice—of any kind—is to get feedback from others to make your analysis as good as it can be. In school, the writing cycle is usually cut short because of time constraints—you write an essay, give it to your teacher, the teacher gives feedback and grade, and that is the end of it. Some teachers give students the opportunity to rewrite their essays based on feedback, but that is relatively rare. You do not have to wait for your teacher to give you a grade. Getting together with other students in your class and providing feedback to each other helps you learn how the paper gets across and you have the chance to make it better, as well as helping you develop a critical vocabulary by having to explain to others what you think about their work. All writing is rewriting, so if you can squeeze in a rewrite before handing it to your teacher, your work can only get better.

▶ ACADEMIC INTEGRITY: INCLUDE YOUR SOURCES

Some institutions have specific rules or codes that students have to abide by—look for the academic integrity rules, honor code, or policies on plagiarism of your place of study. The goal of these policies is to ensure that the work you produce is honest and the product of your own intellect and effort. Plagiarizing (i.e., presenting other people's work as your own) is not only frowned upon, it can also mean automatically failing a class, or even academic dismissal from an educational institution. This is why it is important to keep track of your sources and include them in your writing—throughout this book, you can see how I have referred to the ideas of different authors, including the full reference in the endnotes.

Copying other people's work without providing attribution, or paying someone to write a paper for you might be a way to pass a class, or so you think. Experienced teachers can spot plagiarism quite fast—we read so many papers that everyone develops a "plagiarist detector instinct" early on. There are also automated tools that will run your electronic assignment and compare it to pre-existing works. Since the field of game studies is relatively small, it is also likely that the tools will spot where you are copying from right away. With regard to digital tools, there are also websites and applications that use Large Language Models (LLMs) to generate papers and essays that may sound convincingly human, but which can only tackle topics superficially and at a level that is not considered good academic quality. As already explained in Box 1.2: Using AI Generation to Write Your Essays in Chapter 1, these tools also "hallucinate" and make up sources and facts in their writing. If you submit an essay written with these tools and obtain a passing grade, maybe you should consider changing academic programs. Cheating is also detrimental for the cheater, since they are missing the opportunity to learn and grow, even if the lesson is not the contents of the class but how to make the effort to succeed at one difficult task.

If you are reading this, however, it probably means that you are committed enough to do the work—good for you! You should still carefully account for your sources in your text, from including in-text citations, to listing your resources either as endnotes (as in this book) or as a final compiled bibliography. If you have a document where you have listed all your sources, or used a reference manager system or database, this is where you will realize how much these facilitate your work, as well as help you prevent committing plagiarism accidentally.

▶ THE CHALLENGE OF INCLUDING GAMES IN YOUR SOURCES

Including one's sources is essential for academic practice—it is not only a matter of professional integrity, but also allows our readers to identify and consult works related to the topic of discussion. That is the reason why every analysis building block includes a "further reading" section, so you can find those sources if you wish to understand and learn more about any of those building blocks for your own work. Your work is part of a conversation, and being explicit about your sources helps situate it as part of a larger discourse.

One of the hurdles of writing academically about games is figuring out how to include citations. What is worse, since game studies is an interdisciplinary field, there is a wide variety of citation formats that we may end up using. In my own papers I have had to use citation formats from the humanities (Modern Language Association (MLA)), social sciences (American Psychology Association (APA)), computer science (Association for Computer Machinery (ACM)), and engineering (Institute of Electrical and Electronics Engineers (IEEE)). The Digital Games Research Association (DiGRA), the main international organization dealing with game studies, has its own formatting style based on the Chicago Manual of Style—the same used in this book. *The MLA Handbook*, in its ninth edition, now proposes a media-inclusive way to refer to formats, and has a section that lists examples of how to cite a videogame, which is a welcome change.[1] Each citation style also includes guidelines on how to format the paper, including font type, size, and page layout. Writing a game studies paper requires being ready to learn all the formatting tricks of your text editor of choice. The changing citation formats in game studies are another good reason to use a reference management system, because they keep the information for each source and then the computer application can format it in whichever format you need.

The main problem is that the citation standards listed above do not include a citation format for games, digital or non-digital, or when they do, they still fall short on accounting for the sources properly. For example, while the MLA format now allows us to account for videogames, their examples include the "director" of the game as key contributor, a term that seems to equate games to films, and a title that is actually not standard practice in the industry, at least in Western countries. In contrast, the ACM format does not have any citation guidelines from anything media-related other than video recordings. The APA style, on the other hand, does have a way to cite computer software, which may be one of the reasons why it is frequently used in game studies.[2]

As a way to fill this gap, DiGRA suggests the following reference format for digital games for the papers submitted to its conferences:

> Developer/designer. Year. *Title*. Platform, Version. Release City, State, Country: Publisher.

What does this information indicate? Why do we need it as part of our work?

- **Developer**: The people who made the game. Would be the equivalent of the author of a work; in the case of games developed by a team, it is preferable to name the team who made it. In some cases, there may be more than one team developing the game in conjunction. Some people put the designer in this section, but that means making a value judgment about what the authorship of a game means (unless the game is a solo project).

- **Year**: This is when the game was released. In the case of virtual worlds, whose development is ongoing, or may have been available only for a limited period of time, the date indicates the year it started. If the virtual world is closed, it is useful to indicate the year it ended. Throughout this book, I have included an en dash after the year to indicate that the world is still open, for example, *World of Warcraft* (2004–).

- **Platform, version**: This is the equivalent to the edition of a book. A game may have different versions even for the same platform. For example, Sony used to re-release bestselling games as "Game of the Year Edition," which included all the downloadable content (DLCs) of the game on the disk, meaning that the game in the new release now had additional content that was not available in the original release disk.

- **Publisher**: This is who distributes the game in a specific area. The same game may have different publishers in different parts of the world, which may also mean that the game is a different version. Although online distribution has made markets more uniform, and many publishers operate at a global level, publishers may still have to respond to the content regulations of specific countries and adapt their games accordingly.

- **Release City/State and Country**: These references have been handed down from printed sources; in the realm of digital media geographical locations seem less meaningful, particularly if the release is through online distribution. For consistency's sake, here you should state the country where the game was acquired, which should be the country of the publisher.

When you have to provide a reference to a digital game, and the style that you have to use does not accommodate software programs or games, find how a book would be cited, and fill it out with the equivalent fields listed above. It may be good to have a separate section for all the games (a "ludography" like the one at the end of this book) if the format allows it. If not, at times the citation format allows including the type of medium that you are citing.

In a way, non-digital games are easier to cite. Role-playing books can obviously follow the citation format of books. Commercial table-top games usually have a designer (*inventor* in old-fashioned jargon) and a publisher/year, as well as indicating different editions. One invaluable resource to learn about the different versions of a card or board game is the website Board Game Geek, where users maintain a large database of board games, including photos of different editions of the same game.[3]

As you may have noticed, the in-text citations in this book are formatted differently depending on whether the game is digital or non-digital. Non-digital games are capitalized but not in italics, while digital games are both capitalized and in italics, and include the date of release. Once your sources have been accounted for properly in your paper, it is now ready to go.

▶ WHAT NEXT?

You may have noticed that this book is way longer than the assignment you have to write. This is because the goal of this book is not to help you write one essay, but to introduce you to how to write about games, whichever your discipline is. Writing about games, like any other skill, takes time and dedication. You will probably not get it right the first time around. I certainly did not, and this book is the result of almost two decades of figuring out how to write about games and working with students. This is the third edition of the book, because in the period between its initial release and of this writing, there have been new research, journalistic articles, technologies, games, and ways of playing that have changed the way we write an analysis. The advice here is meant for you to avoid some of the pitfalls that I have come across and that I have seen my students struggle with, so you can find your own way to express yourself in writing.

This is the end of the book, but I would hope this is the beginning of your own way to finding more persuasive, engaging, and innovative ways to write about games. It will be you who will be writing the analyses that will serve as examples in the future.

▶ NOTES

1 *MLA Handbook*. 9th edn (Modern Language Association of America, 2021).

2 For a more detailed discussion of the challenges and issues in when citing games, see Stefano, Gualeni, Fassone Riccardo, and Linderoth Jonas. "How to Reference a Digital Game." In *DiGRA '19 - Proceedings of the 2019 DiGRA International Conference: Game, Play and the Emerging Ludo-Mix*, 2019.

3 The portal to the community of Board Game Geek is http://boardgamegeek.com/ (accessed November 5, 2023).

Appendix I
Sample Analyses

This appendix includes a few examples of game analysis of the same game (*The Secret of Monkey Island* (1990)) from different standpoints: A review, a historical analysis, using the game as an example of specific theories, and a personal account. The first analysis focuses on the remake of the game for iPad, whereas the historical analysis and the example of theories deal with the DOS version; the personal account is based on the Spanish translation of the game, using my own experience as a guide to understand the impact of the game on my generation.[1] The thesis statement of each analysis is in bold, so you can easily identify it.

These are all short, focused examples, which are closer to the kind of assignments that one may do in an undergraduate class. Given its complexity, there is no sample of a game communities analysis here—you can refer to Appendix II to find some exemplary discussions of game communities, as well as in the references to other works throughout the book. These samples are all skewed toward design analyses, too, partly because it is one of the aspects that other fields may not discuss in as much depth.

▶ SAMPLE ANALYSIS 1: JOURNALISTIC REVIEW

Almost 20 years after its original release, the point-and-click adventure game *The Secret of Monkey Island* (1990) gets a facelift for current game platforms with new graphics and voice acting. This new version wants to attract new players to a classic game and allow fans of the genre to play it again on their new gadgets; the iPad in this case. **The game seems more geared towards players who have not played the game before, or are not familiar with the adventure game genre, leaving the elements to please nostalgic players almost as an Easter egg.**

The player is Guybrush Threepwood, a wannabe pirate who arrives on Mêlée Island in order to learn his trade. Pirating is on hold, however. The Ghost Pirate LeChuck is now attacking pirate ships and turning their crews into their ghost slaves, so everyone is marooned until he is off the map. Before Guybrush can face the ghost pirate, he has to pass the three trials that will qualify him as a pirate: master the sword, find treasure, and steal a valuable idol.

The exploits of Guybrush Threepwood are a referent in the history of video games. Many players still remember the lines, especially when learning how to swordfight turns into a battle of wits. The witty writing also trickles down to the puzzles, which are often amusing or surprising, and require the player to come up with off-the-wall solutions that still make sense in the context of the game. Although some of the puzzles and the interactions may feel old-fashioned, *The Secret of Monkey Island* still retains all the charisma that has turned it into a recurrent in-joke in more recent games.

The Secret of Monkey Island: Special Edition (2009) is a re-release of classic adventure games for tablet PCs, contemporary to other re-releases such as *Beneath a Steel Sky* (2009), or *Broken Sword: Shadow of the Templars—The Director's Cut* (2009). What sets *Monkey Island* apart is the complete overhaul of the pixilated graphics, which now sport a comic book style, as well as a new graphical user interface. The new cartoonish style is closer to Telltale's sequel *Tales of Monkey Island* (2009), rather than artist Steve Purcell's original covers. It feels as if some graffiti artists have redone the graphics—a painterly stylization that seems to cover up the old graphics but does not quite fit or provide depth; an awkwardness that will be more evident to those familiar with the early 1990s version.

The hilarious dialogue is now delivered by voice actors; most of the cast has already worked in several of the sequels, which lends a nice continuity to the series. Listening to the dialogue demonstrates how well the writing has withstood the passage of time, and although it is obvious that it was not originally written to be performed, it is still a delight to hear the actors.

The renovated aesthetics are not the only shiny thing for new players—a new user interface and hint system adapt the mouse clicks into a touch interface that is more accessible to new players. The game selects the default action in most cases, so that if the player touches a closed door, the automatic action will be to open it. Some puzzles require actions that are a bit more complex, such as giving an object to someone, or pushing/pulling objects, which require using an action from the menu and then the object one wants to interact with. This means that the interface is more complex than games that use a native touch interface. The game requires a precision in selecting that touch interfaces do not quite allow—for example, in the Scumm Bar, it can be tricky to find the spot that allows going back and forth between the front and back of the house. Overall, the user interface remake strikes a fine balance between the old and the new, although the touch interface can occasionally get in the way.

The major addition to the game is the hint system, which gives the player pointers about what to do next. In a way, this feature is in keeping with the design of *Tales of Monkey Island,* where players can choose whether to get hints or not, and the game would detect when the player clicks around without knowing what to do; the hint is Guybrush thinking aloud what to do next. *The Secret of Monkey Island: Special Edition* is not as subtle: hold three fingers and a banner provides a hint; hold it again, and a huge arrow will tell you where to go. Although the original *Monkey Island* features finely set up puzzles for the most part and the solutions are mostly logical, some of the original clues may not be evident to those who do not usually play adventure games, thus, the bold hints.

So what is left for the old-school fans? The new graphics can be a bit off-putting, and the new interface may feel a bit strange. The "classic version" of the game is available but it is more of an Easter egg. The menus provide no indication of how to play the game in its original form; after some experimenting I found out holding two fingers on the screen swaps between versions. Seeing the old, pixilated graphics on the iPad screen is endearing, but the charm is fleeting the moment one tries to play. The classic version keeps the cursor pointer, which the player needs to drag and then pat in order to imitate the click, making it practically unplayable on a touch screen. These unwieldy controls are probably the reason why there is no direct access to it, as if burying a feature that does not quite work.

In short, *The Secret of Monkey Island: Special Edition* is a worthy revisitation for the iPad, and a must play as one of the cornerstones in the history of adventure games. For those who want to revive the old days, the writing and the puzzles retain their allure, while the voice acting can enhance the charm. The new graphics can feel a bit alienating, but in the end, it is a matter of preference.

▶ SAMPLE ANALYSIS 2: HISTORICAL ANALYSIS

Adventure games have one of longest traditions in digital games. There are many milestones in this history: *Adventure* (1976) is the first game in the genre and gives it its name;[2] *Mystery House* (1980) is acknowledged with being the first adventure game with graphics.[3] **The milestone that marks the design aesthetics of many of the point-and-click adventure games that encourage exploration are the games *Loom* and *The Secret of Monkey Island,* both released in 1990. What started as a novel design philosophy became a referent for adventure game designers in later years that still endures.**

1990 was the heyday of graphic adventure games. There was a plethora of companies dedicated to adventure games on both sides of the Atlantic, such as Sierra On-Line, Legend Entertainment, and Coktel Vision. Other companies were including adventure games as part of their catalogue, such as Access Software, Westwood Studios, or Delphine Software International.[4] With so many developers devoted to the genre, the generalization of point-and-click interfaces, and the continuous improvement of graphic and sound capabilities, every adventure game usually brought some innovation or improvement (as well as some failed experiments). It was an exciting time to be an adventure game fan, with so many topics and developers to choose from.

The games division of Lucasfilm—later renamed LucasArts—had also made some previous incursions in the genre, with *Labyrinth* (1986), and *Maniac Mansion* (1988); the latter was the first game to create a landmark. *Maniac Mansion* featured the SCUMM system (Script Creation Utility for Maniac Mansion), a development tool that made it easier to develop adventure games in a team and for multiple platforms. *Maniac Mansion*'s point-and-click interface was another attempt at making the input of commands more accessible by allowing players to select them from a menu, and then clicking on the object or character they wanted to operate on.

SCUMMM is the engine that both *Loom* (released in January 1990) and *The Secret of Monkey Island* (October 1990) use. While *Monkey Island* uses a command menu similar to that of *Maniac Mansion, Loom* turns the input command into a musical instrument. The lower part of the screen features a musical distaff divided into segments; each segment plays a note when clicking on it. Rather than clicking on a command, players have to play a short melody as an incantation to perform the action, from opening or closing things, to dyeing things green or white, or turning straw to gold. The player has to learn the magical melodies through the game, a novel mechanic at the time that later appeared in games such as *The Legend of Zelda: Ocarina of Time* (1998).

Both games stand out for their unusual fictional worlds. *Loom* takes place in a fantasy world where different city-states are led by different guilds, such as weavers or blacksmiths. The player character is Bobbin Threadbare, a young weaver apprentice who is about to learn about his origins, while the world is on the brink of the apocalypse. *The Secret of Monkey Island*, on the other hand, takes place in the Caribbean. The player character is Guybrush Threepwood—both games have protagonists with peculiar names—a young pirate apprentice who is learning his trade while all pirating has come to a halt, since the fearsome ghost pirate, LeChuck, threatens to turn any pirate ship crew into his ghost slaves. The two games share a coming-of-age premise, in which players learn about the world and grow along with their player characters.

What sets both *Loom* and *The Secret of Monkey Island apart*, however, is not their interface—other developers were coming up with their own point-and-click solutions to make input more accessible. For example, Sierra On-Line had deployed its Sierra Creative Interpreter (SCI) in 1988 with *King's Quest IV: The Perils of Rosella*.[5] The novelty of the games by Lucasfilm games was the design philosophy, important enough to appear in the manual of both games:

> We believe that you buy games to be entertained, not to be whacked over the head every time you make a mistake. So, we don't bring the game to a screeching halt when you poke your nose into a place you haven't visited before. We make it clear, however, when you are in a dangerous situation.
>
> We think you'd prefer to solve the game's mysteries by exploring and discovering, not by dying a thousand deaths. We also think you like to spend your time involved in the STORY, not typing in synonyms until you stumble upon the computer's word for a certain object.
>
> Unlike conventional computer adventures, you won't find yourself accidentally stepping off a path, or dying because you've picked up a sharp object. There are a few dangerous situations where Guybrush

> can die, but to anticipate them takes a little common sense, not excessive paranoia. Save the game when you think you may be entering a dangerous area, but don't assume that every wrong step will result in death. Usually, you'll get another chance.[6]

This design philosophy was an overt jab at the adventure game designs of other companies, specifically Sierra On-Line, which had turned killing the player character into an art. In some of their series, such as *King's Quest* (1984–1998) or *Space Quest* (1984–1995), making the wrong move usually meant the player character died instantly. Whereas killing the player character is a clear way of telling the player that the action does not lead to advancing in the game, it can be frustrating if one has not saved the game recently. In these Sierra games, there are times where the death seems unwarranted because the player was just exploring, and it was not clear that the situation was dangerous. In some cases, the player character has to die in order to learn that something is not possible or is dangerous. For example, in *King's Quest V*, a game released the same year, there is a cave full of treasure. The player can only take a brass bottle and one gold coin—trying to pick up any other treasure will kill the player character instantly because it is cursed. If the player spends too much time in the cave, it will seal off and also, again, kill the player. Neither of these impending dangers are quite communicated to the player.

Both *Loom* and *The Secret of Monkey Island* allow players to explore and figure out how the world works, without having to save every five minutes. This also means that, at times, players can wander around without knowing what to do next, because there is no feedback pointing to what they are missing or doing wrong. In the long run, this design approach also means an emphasis on exploring of the world, and letting the players figure out the puzzles and reveal the story at their own pace.

The jab at Sierra On-Line was not only in the manual of these games—*The Secret of Monkey Island* took advantage of its comedic tone to include an irreverent joke about their competitor's games. In the last act of the game, the player can fall from a cliff, which makes a "death screen" appear in the fashion of Sierra's games. The card reads "Oh, no! You've really screwed up this time! Guess you'll have to start over! Hope you saved the game!" After a few seconds in which players may be in shock, the player character bounces back to the cliff and says, "Rubber tree." Years later, Sierra would return the poke in the manual of *Space Quest V: The Next Mutation* (1993) with a fictional job ad from "Scumsoft," although rather than making fun of the design, they critiqued how overworked the LucasArts game designers were, as well as their lack of profits.

In the end, the LucasArts school of design seems to have become the referent for modern adventure game design: most point-and-click adventure games now let the player explore and do not force players to save constantly. Games such as *Ben There, Dan That!* (2009), the *Blackwell* series (2006–2014), *Ceville* (2009) or *Botanicula* (2012) emphasize exploration and let the player get the puzzles right on their own. It has become an identifiable aesthetic of adventure games, which establishes certain expectations from players. Also, not having to save constantly seems to fit better with how other genres deal with save games, since the auto-save feature is the default in game consoles and mobile platforms. This also means that there are other types of design aesthetics rising up in adventure games: *Kentucky Route Zero* (2020) is an adventure game with no puzzles, focusing on exploration; and *The Walking Dead* (2012) features difficult choices and time limits. The LucasArts model has been very influential for many years, and has given way to games that emphasize exploration of worlds where players can reveal the story through smaller interactions, as may be the case of walking simulators. Contemporary story-driven games tend to focus on helping players traverse the story, rather than punishing them until they solve convoluted puzzles—and Lucasfilm games marked the way to that aesthetic.

▶ SAMPLE ANALYSIS 3: GAMES AS EXAMPLES TO ILLUSTRATE A THEORY

Puzzles hold a special status in game design—whereas game designers often talk about systems and balancing, puzzle design means providing the player with a challenge that has one solution, and requires thinking rather than skills. There are many different types of game genres that incorporate puzzle elements, such as *The Legend of Zelda: A Link to the Past* (1991), which requires a specific sequence of events to open doors or reach a switch. In platform games such as *Rayman: Origins* (2011), the player needs to get from the starting point of the level to the end by figuring out the path, so that the player not only needs to have the skills to move on time, but also to plan the path in advance.

Adventure games thrive on puzzles, but most of them are of a different type—the puzzles are part of the events of the story. The player has to give an object, fix a machine, open a door, which are all events in the story. Therefore, we can call this type of challenge *narrative puzzle*, which brings together literature and game design. The relationship between adventure game puzzles and literature or word play is not new: while Graham Nelson referred to interactive fiction (aka text adventures, the origins of the genre) as "a narrative at war with a crossword,"[7] Nick Montfort has also traced the relationship between interactive fiction and riddles.[8]

The hybrid nature of narrative puzzles also makes them a prime source to understand how we think when we solve puzzles. **Adventure games encourage *insight thinking*, that is, the thought process that leads to new knowledge. With this analysis, we will demonstrate that narrative puzzles can encourage all types of insight thinking, which is not as common in other genres.**

In order to illustrate how narrative puzzles exemplify all these different types, this analysis focuses on *The Secret of Monkey Island*. This game from 1990 is particularly apt to illustrate this theory because of the variety of its puzzles; it is also referent in the adventure game genre, with many of its puzzles having served as a template or inspiration to many other games afterwards.

In this game, the player is Guybrush Threepwood, a wannabe pirate who arrives on Mêlée Island in order to learn his trade. Pirating is on hold, because the Ghost Pirate LeChuck is now attacking pirate ships and turning their crews into his ghost slaves, so everyone is marooned and cowering in fear. LeChuck has also fallen in love with Governor Elaine Marley, although she seems to have been able to keep him in check. Before he can face the ghost pirate or find the words to talk to the Governor, Guybrush has to pass the three trials that will qualify him as a pirate: master the sword, find treasure, and steal a valuable idol.

Before analyzing the puzzles, let us understand what *insight thinking* is and how it plays a part in solving puzzles. Puzzles are a mystery, an open question that the player has to answer.[9] When a player faces a puzzle, the key to coming up with a solution is using one's knowledge in order to find that piece of missing information. The moment the player figures out the missing piece of information is what we call the moment of insight, also known as the "a-ha" moment, or "eureka moment" for those familiar with Archimedes' story.

The knowledge to solve the puzzle usually belongs to a specific domain, such as carpentry, driving, or fishing, to name but a few. In adventure games, the fictional genre of the game can appeal to specific domains. *The Secret of Monkey Island*, with its references to pirate stories and magic, relates to domain knowledge such as sailing, sword fighting, using magic, as well as other more mundane knowledge, such as cooking or economic transactions.

When the knowledge becomes very specific, it may be the case that the players may not be familiar with it. For example, the final puzzle of *Monkey Island* requires the player to find a root to create a magic potion that will defeat the Ghost Pirate LeChuck. Which potions are effective against ghost pirates is a domain that is not part of everyday knowledge, and it is limited to the fictional world of this particular game. Therefore, the game sets up this information so that the player knows that the root is the main ingredient the player needs to defeat the villain—in a cut-scene, the Ghost Pirate LeChuck, asks his henchman to lock up a root, indicating that it may be something valuable; later on, the cannibals on Monkey Island tell the player character, Guybrush, that LeChuck stole the root from them and that the root is rare and they use it to make an exorcism potion. Without the root, they cannot concoct the potion to drive the ghosts away. This information provides the player with a goal (get the root) as well as with a solution to the problem of getting rid of a fearsome ghost pirate (make a potion with the root).

Setting up specific domain information like this is what sets *The Secret of Monkey Island* apart from other adventure games, where the information necessary to solve some puzzles was either really hidden or completely absent, requiring the player to guess what the designer was thinking, and to solve the problem with random actions in the hope one thing would work. Bob Bates calls this a "designer's puzzle," which is a notorious game design element that many players associate with their frustrations with adventure games.[10] In *The Secret of Monkey Island*, we can find the information needed to solve every puzzle somewhere in the world, as part of the dialogue or in the descriptions of objects; the information placement at times may be too subtle, particularly to players who believe that dialogue and descriptions are "flavor text" rather than potentially useful information.

Once the domain has been identified, coming up with the solution is much easier. It is a matter of identifying what specific information will help solve the puzzle—that is when insight happens. According to Sternberg, there are three different ways in which insight thinking uses reflective memory, which is the type of mental process that leads to finding the solution to a problem:

1. Selective encoding: making apparently irrelevant information relevant.
2. Selective comparison: using analogies and metaphors, in order to draw a non-obvious relationship between two pieces of information.
3. Selective combination: combining two items in order to form a novel one.[11]

Selective encoding means that the information is hidden, often in plain sight, and the player has to decode the information to achieve insight. The example above where we described how the game tells the player the key ingredient of the potion to defeat LeChuck is an example of selective encoding.

Disguising important information is what most adventure games do, since players need to have that information, but if it is too evident, it would not be a challenge, nor would players experience a moment of insight—they are told what to do and they just do it.

Selective comparison means finding similarities between two pieces of information, so that the insight derives from finding a new relationship between them. This type of insight thinking is one of the most obvious links between narrative puzzles and literature since literary metaphors are an example of selective comparison. A metaphor represents an object or concept (the *tenor*) in terms of another object or concept (the *vehicle*) that has some proximity or relation of similarity to it. For example, in the metaphor "three mouths to feed," "three mouths" is a vehicle for the tenor "three people." Specifically, this type of metaphor is a synecdoche, where one part represents the whole. Riddles are often metaphors, where the riddlee needs to identify the tenor based on the vehicle. For example, in *The Hobbit*, Gollum poses this riddle to Bilbo:

> This thing all things devours:
> Birds, beasts, trees, flowers;

Gnaws iron, bites steel;
Grinds hard stones to meal;
Slays king, ruins town,
And beats mountain down.[12]

Given their relationship with literature, adventure games can also use metaphors that the player needs to read correctly. In a way, it is another way of hiding information; the difference lies in that the insight comes from realizing what the relationship between the information and the solution is. There are multiple examples of selective comparison in the design of *The Secret of Monkey Island*; one of the most obvious happens early in the game. A circus needs a test subject to see if their cannon works—and Guybrush needs the money. The owners of the circus, however, will not let him take the job unless he provides his own helmet. The problem is that there are no helmets on the island; however, a cooking pot where "someone has cooked a headcheese," according to the description, is good enough. The circus runners agree that the pot is close enough, and give Guybrush the human bullet job. Here the similarity in shape and consistency between a pot and a helmet is the relationship that the player needs to draw in order to solve the puzzle.

Selective combination means incorporating two separate pieces of information to obtain a new one. This type of puzzle is probably the most common in adventure games. For example, lock-and-key puzzles are a typical example—the player needs to find the information that will provide access to a new location, such as a key, a password, or a disguise. In *The Secret of Monkey Island*, recipes are a clear example of selective combination. For example, the Governor's House is guarded by a pack of fierce poodles who chase away intruders. In order to get rid of them, the player must prepare a stew with meat and a special type of flower—by combining these two items, the player obtains the way to put the poodles to sleep and get into the house. Incidentally, the game uses selective encoding to indicate that the flowers are part of the recipe—the name of the flowers is "caniche endormi," which means "sleeping poodle" in French.

Sternberg's types of insight thinking help us understand different types of puzzles and how we reach the solution. They also show how we resort to different kinds of thinking in order to solve puzzles, and how at times different types of thinking can be combined every step of the way, each puzzle being a step closer to finishing the game. What is more, by understanding how the different types of thinking work, designers can also understand better how to create their puzzles, by making sure that the design sets up the knowledge the player needs to solve the puzzle, and by understanding how players may try to make sense of the puzzle.

These types of insight also reveal the particularity of narrative puzzles, since they can require all three types of insight thinking. Selective combination can be fostered through other types of puzzles, such as jigsaws, but the other two are more common and particularly apt for narrative puzzles. In particular, selective comparison puzzles are relatively rare in games outside of adventure games—they not only have strong ties to riddles as a narrative form, they are also puzzles that require players to interpret the information, in the same way that poetry can require readers to decode its metaphors.

Puzzles in other video games may be based on trial and error as well, as is the case, for example, of platform games, where the player may figure out the most efficient path after several attempts, each attempt providing incremental information about how to reach the goal. This gradual way of figuring out the path eventually leads to insight, but is not quite as revelatory as figuring out an adventure game puzzle, where the whole point is to make the connection between two pieces of information.

The Secret of Monkey Island also exemplifies how the moment of insight can be pleasurable, because, at times, on top of being able to connect two pieces of information, the relationship is original and amusing. We saw this with the pot-as-helmet example—the image of using a pot as a security helmet is ridiculous, and yet selective comparison tells us it makes sense. Apart from the "a-ha" moment, the player also gets to see Guybrush being shot out of the cannon and crashing into one of the circus tent poles, extending the pleasure of figuring out the puzzle with a funny short scene.

Adventure games encourage a variety of insight thinking, as *The Secret of Monkey Island* demonstrates, whereas other genres may stick to one single type. On the one hand, this is probably due to the puzzle-driven nature of adventure games, where solving puzzles is the core mechanic. On the other, the fact that they are a story-driven genre links them to a tradition of other literary games, such as riddles or mystery stories. This richness of adventure games that is often overlooked—it is games like *Monkey Island* that exemplify the range and nuance needed in the design of narrative puzzles.

▶ SAMPLE ANALYSIS 4: PERSONAL ACCOUNT

One of my favorite classes to teach is how writing dialogue can also be game design. I show two examples in that session—a repartee between Beatrice and Benedict from the film version of Shakespeare's *Much Ado About Nothing* (1993), and the sword fighting from *The Secret of Monkey Island* (1990). In this session, I get to demonstrate how my background in theatre and film is relevant to studying and making games, and how much I love both. Both works have a dear space in my heart, and have marked my professional career through the years. *The Secret of Monkey Island* is far from holding the canonical space in Western culture that Shakespeare does, but the way in which the game resonated with me when I first played it can explain its influence on other players and game developers, as well as its enduring appeal.

In *The Secret of Monkey Island,* I played as Guybrush Threepwood, a young boy who wants to become a pirate. The action starts on Mêlée Island, where soon it becomes obvious there is something wrong. Pirating is on hold, and all the pirates are taking refuge at the Scumm Bar. Early in the game, we learn about how the Ghost Pirate LeChuck, is now attacking pirate ships and turning their crews into his ghost slaves, so all the pirates are too scared to go sailing while he is around. Apparently, LeChuck has also fallen in love with Governor Elaine Marley, although she seems to have been able to keep him in check. Before he can face the ghost pirate or find the words to talk to the Governor, Guybrush has to pass the three trials that will qualify him as a pirate: master the sword, find treasure, and steal a valuable idol.

I belong to a generation of Spanish videogame players who grew up playing point-and-click adventure games, and who still remember the insults and their corresponding ripostes in the sword fighting section of *The Secret of Monkey Island.* The game somehow made an impression on the collective minds of young Spanish players in the early 1990s, as well as in other countries. **Why this game is such an important reference for me and for other people of my generation has to do with its accessibility, the world, and the writing.**

The Lucasfilm adventure games have had a stronger influence on Spanish players because they were translated into Spanish, while the Sierra On-Line games, which are a stronger referent in the USA, were translated into Italian, German, and French. The Castilian Spanish translations did not appear until a few years later—*King's Quest V* was the first one in 1990—and some of them were never translated, such as *Gabriel Knight: Sins of the Fathers* (1990). In a country where dubbed films are the still norm and understanding English was a specialized skill at the time, translating a game into the local language could take it rather far. At the time of playing the game, my English would not have been good enough to understand what to do.

Apart from the socio-economic circumstances, *The Secret of Monkey Island* also managed to engage me as a young player in ways that I now realize are marks of the quality of the game. First of all, a game about pirates was rather unusual, even if it was not unique—I had played a graphical text adventure based on Stevenson's *Treasure Island* (1985) a couple of years before. Although the home computer games I played before that featured more varied themes than most current games (from being a naughty child in *Jack the Nipper*, 1986, to a magical fairy in *Elidon*, 1985), wanting to be a pirate sounded exotic enough.

The writing is what really got me, though. The game is funny from the very first scene, when the player character Guybrush Threepwood appears on the scene.

> *Guybrush:* Hi! My name's Guybrush Threepwood, and I want to be a pirate!
>
> *Lookout:* Yikes! Don't sneak up on me like that!
>
> *Guybrush:* Er ...I'm over this way.
> [Turns out the lookout of the island is *blind.*]

There is something about the absurd humor of the game that also translates well, from the blind lookout to the gruff pirate with two hooks for hands who is terrified of his own parrot. It may have to do with the tradition of Spanish absurdist humor, where the jokes are based on off-the-wall references or changes of tone. The lack of reverence and casual tone of the game, where the characters speak more like one's neighbor instead of having semi-literary aspirations, also fit with how Spanish parody treats the myths from other cultures. This is particularly evident in comics: the Spanish response to James Bond is *Mortadelo y Filemón* (*Mort & Phil* in English), two clueless spies who can never get anything right; while the Spanish counterpart to Superman is *Superlópez,* a clumsy superhero who looks like a sour civil servant.[13] The irreverence of *Monkey Island* and Spanish parody seem to be attuned to each other, in spite of coming from different countries.

Perhaps the reason that the game has endured in the common memory of players, especially in Spain, is that many of us played it with other people. I played most of the game and its sequel with my brother, side by side. Part of the fun is reading the dialogues aloud, which is even more enjoyable because they have a healthy range between being witty and silly. Since adventure games are puzzle-driven, and depend on mental challenges rather than skills, we sat down and played together, giving suggestions and trying to solve the puzzles together. When we got stuck, we would ask other friends or family who had played for help. The game lends itself to communal play, so that the interpersonal experience reinforces the memories of the experience.

Some of the friends and family that I exchanged tips on the *Monkey Island* games are now jealous that I have a career that allows me to analyze and replay it and write about it for books. My view of the game is certainly biased, based on happy memories and personal enjoyment, so I have to remind myself to retain some critical distance. I have been lucky that the game is rich enough to allow me to make the best of it and learn from it—something that, unfortunately, I cannot say of other games that I have played before and after *Monkey Island*.

▶ NOTES

1 I analyzed *The Secret of Monkey Island* for another article, with an analysis that combined the personal account with using the game to illustrate a theory. Fernández-Vara, Clara. "The Secret of Monkey Island: Playing Between Cultures." In *Well Played 1.0: Video Games, Value and Meaning* (Pittsburgh, PA: ETC Press, 2009), pp. 147–156.

2 Jerz, Dennis G. "Somewhere Nearby Is Colossal Cave: Examining Will Crowther's Original 'Adventure' in Code and in Kentucky." *Digital Humanities Quarterly* 1, no. 2 (2007).

3 Montfort, Nick. *Twisty Little Passages: An Approach to Interactive Fiction* (Cambridge, MA: MIT Press, 2003), p. 169.

4 Kalata, Kurt. *The Guide to Classic Graphic Adventures.* [S.l.]: Hardcoregaming101.net, 2011.

5 "Sierra Creative Interpreter - SCI Wiki." http://sciwiki.sierrahelp.com//index.php/Sierra_Creative_Interpreter (accessed November 21, 2023).

6 *The Secret of Monkey Island*, Instruction Manual, p. 7.

7 Nelson, Graham. "The Craft of Adventure: Five Articles on the Design of Adventure Games." *IF Archive*, 1995. Available at: www.ifarchive.org/if-archive/info/Craft.Of.Adventure.txt (accessed November 4, 2023).

8 Montfort. *Twisty Little Passages*, pp. 50–51.

9 For a more detailed definition of puzzle games, see Danesi, Marcel. *The Puzzle Instinct* (Bloomington, IN: Indiana University Press, 2002).

10 Bates, Bob. *Game Design: The Art and Business of Creating Games*. 2nd edn (Thompson Course Technology, 2004), p. 128.

11 Sternberg, Robert J. *Beyond IQ: A Triarchic Theory of Human Intelligence* (Cambridge: Cambridge University Press, 1985).

12 Tolkien, J. R. R. *The Hobbit, or, There and Back Again* (Boston: Houghton Mifflin Co., 1996), p. 72. The solution to the puzzle is *time*.

13 The Wikipedia page on the characters can serve as an introduction to *Mortadelo y Filemón and Superlópez*. "Mort & Phil." *Wikipedia*, last modified September 6, 2023, http://en.wikipedia.org/wiki/Mort_%26_Phil; "Superlópez," Wikipedia, last modified July 6, 2023.

Appendix II
List of Other Published Analyses

This is a list of different game analyses which have been published in other sources, from books to journals. These examples are more complex than what you are probably expected to do, and they use a wider array of building blocks. These are the kinds of analyses that you can aspire to write once you feel more comfortable writing.

▶ ANALYSES OF INDIVIDUAL GAMES: ARTICLES

Austin, Jodie. "'The Hardest Battles Are Fought in the Mind': Representations of Mental Illness in Ninja Theory's Hellblade: Senua's Sacrifice." *Game Studies 21*, no. 4 (2021). Available at: https://gamestudies.org/2104/articles/austin. Accessed November 20, 2023.

Backe, Hans-Joachim. ""Deathloop": The Meta (Modern) Immersive Simulation Game." *Game Studies 22*, no. *2* (2022). Available at: https://gamestudies.org/2202/articles/gap_backe. Accessed November 20, 2023.

Bjørkelo, Kristian A. "'Elves Are Jews with Pointy Ears and Gay Magic': White Nationalist Readings of The Elder Scrolls V: Skyrim." (2020). Available at: https://gamestudies.org/2003/articles/bjorkelo. Accessed November 20, 2023.

Blackmon, Samantha. "Pickaninnies and Pixels: On Race, Racism, and Cuphead at E3 – NYMG." *NYMG Feminist Game Studies* (blog), June 17, 2015. Available at: www.nymgamer.com/?p=9235. Accessed November 4, 2023.

Camper, Brett. "Retro Reflexivity: La-Mulana, an 8-Bit Period Piece." In *The Video Game Theory Reader 2*, edited by Bernard Perron and Mark J. P. Wolf. London: Routledge, 2009, pp. 169–195.

Cole, Yussef. "Cuphead and the Racist Spectre of Fleischer Animation." *Unwinnable* (blog), November 10, 2017. Available at: https://unwinnable.com/2017/11/10/cuphead-and-the-racist-spectre-of-fleischer-animation/. Accessed November 4, 2023.

Cremin, Colin. "The Formal Qualities of the Video Game: An Exploration of Super Mario Galaxy with Gilles Deleuze." *Games and Culture 7*, no. *1* (January 1, 2012): 72–86.

Consalvo, Mia. "Persistence Meets Performance: Phoenix Wright, Ace Attorney." In *Well Played 1.0: Video Games, Value and Meaning*. Pittsburgh, PA: ETC Press, 2009, pp. 69–75.

Dennin, Kimberly, and Adrianna Burton. "Experiential Play as an Analytical Framework: Empathetic and Grating Queerness in The Last of Us Part II." *Game Studies 23*, no. *2* (2023). Available at: https://gamestudies.org/2302/articles/denninburton. Accessed November 20, 2023.

Dwyer, Lyne. "Sex and the City: A Sonic Analysis of Sex Work and Socioeconomic Class in Watch_Dogs 2." *Game Studies 22*, no. *2* (2022). Available at: https://gamestudies.org/2202/articles/gap_dwyer. Accessed November 20, 2023.

Frasca, Gonzalo. "The Sims: Grandmothers Are Cooler than Trolls." *Game Studies: The International Journal of Computer Game Research 1*, no. *1* (2001). Available at: www.gamestudies.org/0101/frasca/. Accessed November 4, 2023.

Gazzard, Alison. "The Platform and the Player: Exploring the (hi)Stories of Elite." *Game Studies: The International Journal of Computer Game Research 13*, no. *2* (2013). Available at: http://gamestudies.org/1302/articles/agazzard/. Accessed November 4, 2023.

Geyser, Hanli, and Pippa Tshabalala. "Return to Darkness: Representations of Africa in Resident Evil 5." In *Proceedings of the 2011 DiGRA International Conference: Think Design Play*, Vol. 6. Utrecht, 2011. http://www.digra.org/digital-library/publications/return-to-darkness-representations-of-africa-in-resident-evil-5/. Accessed November 20, 2023.

Harper, Todd. "Rules, Rhetoric, and Genre: Procedural Rhetoric in Persona 3." *Games and Culture* 6, no. 5 (September 1, 2011): 395–413.

Hutchinson, Rachael. "Observant Play: Colonial Ideology in The Legend of Zelda: Breath of the Wild." *Game Studies 21*, no. *3* (2021). Available at: https://gamestudies.org/2103/articles/hutchinson. Accessed November 20, 2023.

Iversen, Sara Mosberg. "In the Double Grip of the Game: Challenge and Fallout 3." *Game Studies 12*, no. *2* (December 2012). Available at: http://gamestudies.org/1202/articles/in_the_double_grip_of_the_game/. Accessed November 4, 2023.

Kocurek, Carly A. "The Agony and the Exidy: A History of Video Game Violence and the Legacy of Death Race." *Game Studies: The International Journal of Computer Game Research 12*, no. 1 (September 2012). Available at: http://gamestudies.org/1201/articles/carly_kocurek/. Accessed November 4, 2023.

Kohn, Martin Gibbs, Joji Mori, Michael Arnold, and Tamara. "Tombstones, Uncanny Monuments and EpicQuests: Memorials in World of Warcraft."

Game Studies 12, no. 1 (September 2012). Available at: http://gamestudies.org/1201/articles/gibbs_martin/. Accessed November 4, 2023.

Hammar, Emil Lundedal. "Playing Virtual Jim Crow in Mafia III-Prosthetic Memory via Historical Digital Games and the Limits of Mass Culture." *Game Studies 20,* no. *1* (2020). Available at: https://gamestudies.org/2001/articles/hammar. Accessed November 20, 2023.

Martin, Paul. "The Pastoral and the Sublime in Elder Scrolls IV: Oblivion." *Game Studies 11,* no. *3* (December 2011). Available at: http://gamestudies.org/1103/articles/martin/. Accessed November 4, 2023.

Montfort, Nick. "Combat in Context." *Game Studies 6,* no. 1 (December 2006). Available at: http://gamestudies.org/0601/articles/montfort/. Accessed November 4, 2023.

Montfort, Nick, and Stuart Moulthrop. "Face It, Tiger, You Just Hit the Jackpot: Reading and Playing Cadre's Varicella." *Fineart Forum 17,* no. *8* (August 2003). Available at: http://nickm.com/if/Varicella.pdf/. Accessed November 4, 2023.

Nijdam, E. B. "Playing against Real Time: Queer (ing) Temporalities in Bury Me, My Love." *Game Studies 22,* no. *1* (2022). https://gamestudies.org/2201/articles/nijdam. Accessed November 20, 2023.

Pötzsch, Holger, and Agata Waszkiewicz. "Life is Bleak (in Particular for Women Who Exert Power and Try to Change the World): The Poetics and Politics of Life Is Strange." (2019). Available at: https://gamestudies.org/2201/articles/nijdam. Accessed November 20, 2023.

Pruett, Chris. "The Anthropology of Fear: Learning about Japan through Horror Games." *Loading ... 4,* no. 6 (2010). Available at: http://journals.sfu.ca/loading/index.php/loading/article/view/90/. Accessed November 4, 2023.

▶ ANALYSES OF INDIVIDUAL GAMES: BOOKS

Anthropy, Anna. *ZZT.* Boss Fight Books, 2014.

Bowman, James and James McLean, eds. "Kingdom Hearts Special." *Loading...The Journal of the Canadian Game Studies Association 15,* no. *25* (August 31, 2022). https://journals.sfu.ca/loading/index.php/loading/issue/view/31. Accessed November 20, 2023.

Hall, L.E. *Katamari Damacy.* Boss Fight Books, 2018.

Kazemi, Darius, and Rob Zacny. *Jagged Alliance 2.* Boss Fight Books, 2014.

Keogh, Brendan, Daniel Purvis, Rob Zacny, and Benjamin Abraham. *Killing Is Harmless: A Critical Reading of Spec Ops: The Line*. 1st edn. Stolen Projects, 2013.

Perron, Bernard. *Silent Hill: The Terror Engine*. Ann Arbor, MI: University of Michigan Press, 2012.

Pinchbeck, Dan. *Doom: Scarydarkfast*. Ann Arbor, MI: University of Michigan Press, 2013.

Pilon, Mary. *The Monopolists: Obsession, Fury, and the Scandal Behind the World's Favorite Board Game*. New York: Bloomsbury Publishing USA, 2015.

Ruggill, Judd E., and Ken S. McAllister. *Tempest: Geometries of Play*. Ann Arbor, MI: University of Michigan Press, 2015.

Scully-Blaker, Rainforest, and Emily Flynn-Jones, eds. "Animal Crossing Special." *Loading...The Journal of the Canadian Game Studies Association 13*, no. *22* (August 31, 2022). https://journals.sfu.ca/loading/index.php/loading/issue/view/31. Accessed November 20, 2023.

Sudnow, David. *Pilgrim in the Microworld*. New York: Warner Books, 1983.

Wolf, Mark J. P. *Myst and Riven*. Landmark Videogames. Ann Arbor, MI: University of Michigan Press, 2011.

▶ COLLECTIONS OF GAME ANALYSES

Carr, Diane. *Computer Games: Text, Narrative and Play*. Cambridge: Polity, 2006.

Fernández-Vara, Clara, and Bennett Foddy, eds. "Well Played: Special Issue on European Videogames of the 1980s." *Well Played Journal* 6, no. *2* (2017).

Harrigan, Pat, and Noah Wardrip-Fruin. *Second Person: Role-Playing and Story in Games and Playable Media*. Cambridge, MA: The MIT Press, 2007.

Hudson, Laura, and Leigh Alexander. *The Offworld Collection*. TopatoCo, 2016.

Maher, Jimmy. *The Future Was Here: The Commodore Amiga*. Cambridge, MA: MIT Press, 2012.

Montfort, Nick, and Ian Bogost. *Racing the Beam: The Atari Video Computer System*. Cambridge, MA: The MIT Press, 2009.

Perron, Bernard. *Horror Video Games: Essays on the Fusion of Fear and Play*. Jefferson, NC: McFarland, 2009.

Rouse, Richard. *Game Design: Theory and Practice*. 2nd edn. Plano, TX: Wordware Publishing, 2001.

Ruberg, Bo. *Video Games Have Always Been Queer*. New York: New York University Press, 2019.

▶ ANALYSES OF GAME COMMUNITIES

Consalvo, Mia. "Hardcore Casual: Game Culture Return(s) to Ravenhearst." In *Proceedings of the 4th International Conference on Foundations of Digital Games, FDG'09*. New York: ACM, 2009, pp. 50–54. doi: 10.1145/1536513.1536531

Consalvo, Mia, and Jason Begy. *Players and Their Pets: Gaming Communities from Beta to Sunset*. Minneapolis, MN: University of Minnesota Press, 2015.

Gray, Kishonna L. *Intersectional Tech: Black Users in Digital Gaming*. LSU Press, 2020.

Harper, Todd. *The Culture of Digital Fighting Games: Performance and Practice*. New York, NY: Routledge, 2013.

Nardi, Bonnie. *My Life as a Night Elf Priest: An Anthropological Account of World of Warcraft*. Ann Arbor, MI: University of Michigan Press, 2010.

Pearce, Celia, and Artemesia. *Communities of Play: Emergent Cultures in Multiplayer Games and Virtual Worlds*. Cambridge. MA: The MIT Press, 2009.

Taylor, T.L. *Play between Worlds: Exploring Online Game Culture*. Cambridge, MA: The MIT Press, 2009.

Glossary

AAA games Commercial digital games with a very large budget, developed by large teams that are usually supported by large publishers. They are distributed using mainstream channels and often are supported by sizable marketing campaigns. The term is usually used in opposition to **independent games**.

adventure games Story-driven games, where the player controls a player character and the challenges are mostly puzzle-based, which are usually part of the story. The player needs to explore the fictional world of the game and experiment to gather information on how to solve the puzzle.

affordance A term borrowed from psychology, it is the property of an item or artifact that allows us to carry out a specific action. For example, a padlock can be locked and unlocked, or a music volume slider allows us to turn the volume up or down.

alternate reality games A cross-media game that blurs the boundaries between the game and everyday life. Alternate reality games use a variety of media technologies to create fictional worlds, from websites and email to phone calls and physical artifacts. Games such as *The Beast,* tied to the film *A.I.: Artificial Intelligence* (2001), and *I Love Bees,* tied to the release of the game *Halo 2* (2004), are two well-known examples of this type of game.

ARG The acronym can refer to **alternate reality games** or **augmented reality games**.

artificial intelligence The science and engineering of computing systems that imitate the thinking and actions of humans. It is a wide field of research and development, and has a multiplicity of fields, including robotics, and machine learning. Digital games use artificial intelligence in the creation of behaviors of **non-player characters** (NPCs) and **procedural generation**.

augmented reality games Games that use digital technology to copy and augment reality, usually by capturing an image of the real world and providing a layer of information and interaction. For example, the Nintendo 3DS gaming console comes packaged with a set of games that allow players to see mini-games on top of flat surfaces in the real world.

avatar The configurable anthropomorphic representation that the player controls within the fictional world of a game. The player can change its properties, such as its appearance or statistics. Often used in opposition to **player character**.

battle royale Online videogame genre in which players have to survive in a hostile environment, as well as being the last player standing during a play session. These games are often shooter games, such as *Fortnite Battle Royale*, but not exclusively, as is the case of *Tetris 99*.

bracketing A term borrowed from phenomenology, it is the process of suppressing the observer's beliefs in order to study the essential qualities of the real world. In practical terms, this means being able to identify and separate our world view from the subject we are studying.

casual games A type of game whose core mechanics are easy to pick up, that features accessible interfaces (such as a touchscreen interface), and that can be played in short, interruptible sessions. Casual games are also associated with having a lower level of difficulty at the beginning, making them more friendly to new players; they often do not require specialized hardware to play them. The term is often used in opposition to **hardcore games**.

checkpoint A specific point in a game level where the player saves the game state when reaching it. The game is usually saved automatically.

choke point A narrow, limited space in a game level that players are forced to go through in order to reach a goal. A choke point usually propitiates conflict that players have to deal with, since it physically narrows navigation and coaxes the player to stick to the critical path.

core mechanic One of the basic actions that a player has to perform repeatedly while playing a game. Every game usually has a set of core mechanics that make up a repertoire of actions. For example, the core mechanics of *Super Mario Bros.* (1985) are *walk, run, jump,* and *pick up.*

Throwing fireballs and swimming, although they are both part of the mechanics, are not core mechanics because they are possible only in certain parts of the game. See also **mechanics**.

critical distance Refers to the process by which the writer/researcher carrying out a study separates themself from the object of study. The distance can be achieved through different processes, such as not being personally invested in that object, or by tackling an event after a certain time has passed. See also **bracketing**.

critical path In certain videogames, the optimal way of traversing a game from beginning to end, which game designers have anticipated and designed for. The term also refers to the gameplay events that players have to participate in by necessity.

DiGRA Digital Games Research Association, an academic and professional organization that encourages the research of digital games and related phenomena and promotes the spread of that knowledge. The study is interdisciplinary, although the social sciences and the humanities are dominant in the types of research that the association promotes.

direct manipulation A term introduced by Ben Shneiderman to define the type of human-computer interaction that involves continuous representation of the objects that the user interacts with, and rapid, reversible, and incremental actions and feedback. In this type of interaction, the user can visualize the actions, and see immediately whether the action will be successful or not, as opposed to a command line interface, where the player has to type the action and wait to see the result.

DLC Short for *downloadable content*. It refers to the additional missions, outfits, weapons, or new storylines that players can download once they own a game. Since all these materials are expansions, they need the original game to run, as opposed to sequels to a title. See also **free-to-play**.

dynamics A term from the MDA framework, it refers to the behaviors that take place in the game as it is being played; the system of the game in action, including the relationship between players and the system.

e-sport Short for *electronic sport*; refers to competitive professional play of videogames. The genres that most commonly foster this type of play are first-person shooters, fighting games, real-time strategy games, and multiplayer online battle arena (MOBA) games. E-sports favor games where players start at an equal level and can gain an advantage through their own prowess.

emulator A virtual machine, that is, a type of program that duplicates or imitates the behavior of one computer system inside another computer system. In the study of games, emulators can allow access to certain games when the original hardware is not readily available.

F2P See **free-to-play**.

fictional world An imaginary world: in games, the world in which the actions and events of the game take place. The fictional world includes a space, the characters who inhabit it, and the actions and events that take place in it.

first-person shooter A game genre where the core mechanic is shooting, and the world is seen from the point of view of the player character. The space is usually represented in a three-dimensional space.

FPS See **first-person shooter**.

free-to-play Downloadable games, either on a computer or a mobile device, which the player does not have to pay for initially, but which include additional content that can be purchased later. This additional content can include levels, characters, gear, power-ups, and other new abilities.

gameplay The process of playing a game, that is, players interacting with the system or with each other.

gamer Said of an individual who plays videogames, especially someone who plays them assiduously and for whom videogames are a way to define themselves.

hardcore games A type of game that requires significant investment to play it, be it developing skills, investing time voluntarily, or purchasing specialized video gaming hardware. They are often defined in opposition to **casual games**.

independent games Games—often digital—with a limited budget, developed by an individual or a small team, which do not count with a publisher or large publisher while they are being developed. They tend to have limited distribution and/or marketing to promote them. The term is often used in opposition to **AAA games**.

indie games See **independent games**.

interactive fiction A type of adventure game where the input to the game is exclusively textual; the representation of the fictional world is also done through text. Also known as **text adventure**.

interface (Usually *user interface*.) The material objects or visual representation that serve as the point of communication between the player and a computer program. A mouse or game controller are different types of hardware interface between the player and the computer; a drop-down menu or a text prompt are software interfaces for the player.

kill screen The final level in a game before the software stops working. Specifically, they are the last possible playable stage that could be played in vintage arcade games from the 1980s before a software glitch made the program stop, since the game developers had not included any further stages after that.

LARP See **live action role-playing**.

level A spatial segment of a videogame, separate from the rest of the game, which has at least one goal.

level design The discipline in game development that consists of configuring the layout and item distribution within a level. The term also refers to the final result of creating a level.

live action role-playing (Usually abbreviated as *LARP*.) A type of non-digital role-playing game where the players enact the actions of their characters in the fictional world. It brings together games with improvisational theater.

masocore A type of game that is very, or excessively, difficult, and forces players to fail repeatedly in order to learn how to play; the gameplay consists of continuing trial and error. The term is a portmanteau word that combines "masochist" and "hardcore."

meaningful play Actions that the player is allowed to carry out and that have a consequence, either because they change the game state or because they provide a reward to the player. Dusting off a Chess piece is not meaningful, whereas moving a rook along a file where there are no other pieces in the way to get to a checkmate position is a meaningful movement.

mechanics (1) The rules of the game that refer to what the player can do, as opposed to the parts of the game system that act independently of player input. See also **core mechanic**. (2) According to the MDA framework, the data representation of the game, its rules.

MMOG Short for *massively multiplayer online game*.

MMORPG Short for *massively multiplayer online role-playing game*. This game genre allows for large numbers of players to play and interact with each other in a virtual world, usually by controlling an **avatar**.

MOBA Acronym for *multiplayer online battle arena*. Refers to a specific type of competitive, real-time, strategy games.

narrative design The game development discipline that combines game design with storytelling, so that the game elements and progress are framed and can be understood as a story.

non-player character A character in the fictional world that is not controlled by the player, but rather by the computer or the game master (in the case of a table-top role-playing game).

platform In videogames, the system that runs the game. Although it is often identified with the hardware in which the game is played, platform can also refer to the operating system (e.g., Windows 98) or a specific standard software (e.g., an Internet browser).

platformer See **platform game**.

platform game (Also known as *platformer*.) A game genre where the player controls a **player character**, and the challenge consists of traversing a **level** from beginning to end by jumping between elevated platforms and avoiding obstacles. The **core mechanics** of this genre are running and jumping.

player character The non-configurable anthropomorphic representation that the player controls within the fictional world of a game. The player cannot change its properties since they are usually determined by the design. Often used in opposition to **avatar**.

port The version of a game for a platform that is different from the one it was originally developed for. It usually requires translating and adapting the game for the new target platform.

power-up A game item that provides the player with an advantage or additional ability to tackle the challenges of the game, often for a limited period of time. For example, in *Super Mario Bros.* (1985), a mushroom grows the player character to twice its size, allowing it to jump higher and destroy bricks. In *Doom* (1993), first-aid kits help to restore health.

primary source A source of information that is original and has not been modified or distorted. In game studies, playing a copy of the original game is considered a primary source.

procedural generation In programming, the use of algorithmic processes to create content during the runtime of the program, rather than as pre-generated content in the form of data.

procedural rhetoric According to Ian Bogost in *Persuasive Games: The Expressive Power of Videogames*, the use of computer processes in order to create persuasive arguments, where the system embodies a set of values that the player interacts with.

role-playing game A game genre, both digital and non-digital, where the players take on the roles of characters in a **fictional world**; the challenges of the game and the way that the players tackle them become a narrative.

RPG See **role-playing game**.

save game A videogame feature that allows players to keep the state of their progress to be able to revisit the game at a later time.

secondary source A source of information that provides an interpretation or modification of the original material we need for research. In game studies, a walkthrough of a game is a secondary source, in lieu of actually playing the game.

serious games A type of game whose goal is to have an effect on everyday life, be it to educate or persuade players to change their behavior.

social deduction games A game genre, both digital and non-digital, where players have secret roles that the rest of the players are trying to uncover. Players can try to use deductions and observe each other's behaviors, while those who do not want to be discovered can lie or distract the others.

space of possibility The potential actions and events in a game; what the player could do and the potential results of those actions, as opposed to actual specific actions that have already been carried out.

survival horror A game genre that uses the horror genre as an inspiration for its fictional world and its events, in which the resources to fight enemies back are scarce. It is the one videogame genre where the fictional world is part of what defines it.

text adventure See **interactive fiction**.

walking simulator A first-person, story-driven, 3D game, where the player traverses a space in order to uncover a story told predominantly through environmental design, documents, and recordings. The origins of the terms are pejorative, but creators have appropriated it as a way to define the genre.

Ludography

(Titles are organized in alphabetical order by title.)

Evans, Malcolm. (1982). *3D Monster Maze*. Spectrum, J.K. Greye Software. United Kingdom.

Square. (1987). *3D World Runner*. Nintendo Entertainment System, Nintendo Entertainment System, Acclaim Entertainment Inc., U.S.A.

Inkle. (2014). *80 Days*. iOS, Inkle, United Kingdom.

Menéndez, Paco and Juan Delcán. (1987). *La Abadía del Crimen*. MSX, Opera Soft, Spain.

Pazos, Manuel and Daniel Celemín. (2016). *The Abbey of Crime Extensum*. OSX, Manuel Pazos and Daniel Celemín. Spain.

Infogrames. (1992). *Alone in the Dark*. DOS, Infogrames, France.

Frictional Games. (2010). *Amnesia: The Dark Descent*. OSX, Frictional Games, Sweden.

Innersloth. (2018). *Among Us*. iOS, Innersloth, U.S.A.

Christine Love. (2012). *Analogue: A Hate Story*. OSX, Christine Love, U.S.A.

Rovio Mobile. (2009). *Angry Birds*. iOS, Clickgamer Technologies Ltd., U.S.A.

Nintendo and Monolith Soft. (2015). *Animal Crossing: Happy Home Designer*. Nintendo 3DS, Nintendo of America, U.S.A.

Nintendo and Monolith Soft. (2020). *Animal Crossing: New Horizons*. Nintendo Switch, Nintendo of America, U.S.A.

Nintendo and Monolith Soft. (2013). *Animal Crossing: New Leaf*. Nintendo 3DS, Nintendo of America, U.S.A.

Ubisoft Montreal. (2007). *Assassin's Creed*. PlayStation 3, Ubisoft, France.

Atari Inc. (1979). *Asteroids*. Arcade, Atari Inc., U.S.A.

Konieczka, Corey. (2008). *Battlestar Galactica: The Board Game*. Fantasy Flight Games, U.S.A.

Atari. (1980). *Battlezone*. Arcade, Atari, U.S.A.

Konami. (1997). *Beatmania*. Arcade, Konami, Japan.

Everything Unlimited Ltd. (2015). *The Beginner's Guide*. OSX, Everything Unlimited Ltd, U.S.A.

PopCap Games. (2004). *Bejeweled 2*. OSX, PopCap Games, U.S.A.

Zombie Cow Limited. (2008). *Ben There, Dan That!*. Windows, Zombie Cow Limited, United Kingdom.

Revolution Software. (2009). *Beneath a Steel Sky*. iOS, Revolution Software, United Kingdom.

Cosmo D. (2022). *Betrayal at Club Low*. OSX, Cosmo D, United States.

2K Boston and 2K Australia. (2007). *Bioshock*. Xbox 360, 2K Games, U.S.A.

Wadjet Eye Games. (2006). *The Blackwell Legacy*. Windows, Wadjet Eye Games, U.S.A.

FromSoftware. (2015). *Bloodborne*. PlayStation 4, Sony Computer Entertainment, U.S.A.

Amanita Design. (2012). *Botanicula*. Windows, Amanita Design, Czech Republic.

Number None Games. (2009). *Braid*. Xbox 360, Microsoft Game Studios, U.S.A.

Atari. (1978). *Breakout*. Atari 2600, Sears, Roebuck and Co., U.S.A.

Revolution Sofware. (2009). *Broken Sword: Shadow of the Templars – Director's Cut*. iOS, Ubisoft Entertainment, United Kingdom.

Infocom. (1987). *Bureaucracy*. DOS, Infocom, U.S.A.

Bally Midway. (1982). *BurgerTime*. Arcade, Bally Midway, U.S.A.

Saltsman, Adam. (2009). *Cannabalt*. Flash/Web. Semi-Secret Software, U.S.A.

ERE Infomatique. (1988). *Captain Blood*. Amstrad CPC, Emulator, Exxos, France.

Stainless Software. (1997). *Carmageddon.* [DOS/Windows], Interplay Entertainment, U.S.A.

Richard Hofmeier. (2011). *Cart Life.* Windows, Richard Hofmeier, U.S.A.

Atari. (1980). *Centipede.* Arcade, Atari, U.S.A.

Realmforge. (2009). *Ceville.* Windows, Kalypso Media, Germany.

Square. (1995). *Chrono Trigger.* Super Nintendo Entertainment System, Square, Japan.

Firaxis Games. (2010). *Civilization V.* OSX, 2K Games, U.S.A.

Sega Technical Institute. (1995). *Comix Zone.* Sega Genesis, Sega of America, U.S.A.

Nutting Associates. (1971). *Computer Space.* Arcade, Nutting Associates, U.S.A.

Llagostera, Enric. (2018). *Cook Your Way.* Windows/Custom Controller.

Office Create. (2006). *Cooking Mama.* Nintendo DS, Majesco Entertainment Company, U.S.A.

LucasArts Entertainment Company. (1998). *The Curse of Monkey Island.* Windows, LucasArts Entertainment Company, U.S.A.

Takagi, Toshimitsu. (2004). *Crimson Room.* Flash/Web.

Harmonix Music Systems. (2010). *Dance Central.* Xbox 360, MTV Games, U.S.A.

Konami. (1999). *Dance Dance Revolution.* Arcade, Konami, Japan.

Sigman, Tyler. (2016). *Darkest Dungeon.* Windows, Red Hook Studios, U.S.A.

Capcom. (2006). *Dead Rising.* Xbox 360, Capcom, U.S.A.

Robot Invader (2015). *Dead Secret.* OSX andVR], Robot Invader, U.S.A.

Infocom. (1982). *Deadline.* Apple II, Infocom, U.S.A.

The Chinese Room. (2012). *Dear Esther.* OSX, The Chinese Room, United Kingdom.

Exity. (1976). *Death Race.* Arcade, Exity, U.S.A.

Williams Electronics. (1981). *Defender.* Arcade, Williams Electronics, U.S.A.

FromSoftware. (2009). *Demon's Souls.* PlayStation 3, Atlus, U.S.A.

Imagineering. (n.d. Unreleased). *Desert Bus (Penn and Teller's Smoke and Mirrors).* Sega CD, Absolute Entertainment, U.S.A.

Ion Storm. (2000). *Deus Ex.* Windows, Eidos Interactive, U.S.A.

Blizzard North. (1996). *Diablo.* Windows, Blizzard Entertainment, U.S.A.

Seyalıoğlu, Hakan and Kathryn Hymes. *Dialect: A Game about Language and How It Dies.* Thorny Games LLC, 2018.

Anthropy, Anna. (2012). *Dis4ia.* Flash, Newgrounds, U.S.A.

ZA/UM. (2019). *Disco Elysium.* Windows, ZA/UM, Estonia and United Kingdom.

Arkane Studios. (2012). *Dishonored.* PlayStation3, Bethesda Softworks, U.S.A.

Nintendo. (1981). *Donkey Kong.* Arcade, Nintendo, Japan.

Valve. (2003–). *DOTA.* Windows, Valve, U.S.A.

id Software. (1993). *Doom.* DOS, id Software, U.S.A.

BioWare Corporation. (2009). *Dragon Age: Origins.* Windows, Electronic Arts, U.S.A.

Chunsoft. (1986). *Dragon Warrior.* Nintendo Entertainment System, Enix Corporation, U.S.A.

Nintendo. (1984). *Duck Hunt.* Nintendo Entertainment System, Nintendo, Japan.

Gygax, Gary and Dave Arneson. *Dungeons and Dragons.* Tactical Studies Rules (TSR), 1974.

Bay 12 Games. (2006). *Dwarf Fortress.* OSX, Bay 12 Games, U.S.A.

Bethesda Softworks. (1996). *The Elder Scrolls II – Daggerfall.* DOS, Bethesda Softworks, U.S.A.

Bethesda Game Studios. (2006). *The Elder Scrolls IV – Oblivion.* Xbox 360, 2K Games/Bethesda Softworks, U.S.A.

Bethesda Game Studios. (2011). *The Elder Scrolls V: Skyrim.* Xbox 360, Bethesda Softworks, U.S.A.

Orpheus. (1985). *Elidon.* MSX, Aacksoft, The Netherlands.

Braven, David and Ian Bell. (1984). *Elite.* BBC Micro, Acornsoft, United Kingdom.

iNiS Corporation. (2006). *Elite Beat Agents.* Nintendo DS, Nintendo of America, U.S.A.

LucasArts Entertainment Company. (2000). *Escape from Monkey Island.* Windows, LucasArts Entertainment Company, U.S.A.

CCP Games. (2003). *Eve Online.* Windows, CCP Games, Iceland.

Sony Online Entertainment. (1999). *EverQuest.* Windows, Sony Online Entertainment, U.S.A.

JSH. (2011). *Factory Panic.* Game Gear, Sega Enterprises, U.S.A. (see also *Ganbare Gorby*).

Quantic Dream. (2005). *Fahrenheit.* Windows, Atari Europe, United Kingdom (see also *Indigo Prophecy*).

Interplay Entertainment. (1997). *Fallout.* Windows, Interplay Entertainment, U.S.A.

Bethesda Game Studios. (2008). *Fallout 3.* Xbox 360, Bethesda Softworks, U.S.A.

Obsidian Entertainment. (2010). *Fallout: New Vegas.* Xbox 360, Bethesda Softworks, U.S.A.

Big Fish Games. (2009–2011). *Faunasphere.* Flash/Web, Big Fish Games, U.S.A.

Ma, Justin and Matthew Davis. (2012). *FTL: Faster Than Light.* OSX, Subset Games, U.S.A.

EA Vancouver/EA Romania. (2022). *FIFA 23.* PlayStation 4, EA Sports, U.S.A.

Square. (1997). *Final Fantasy VII.* PlayStation, Sony Computer Entertainment America. U.S.A.

Square Enix. (2010–2012, 2013–). *Final Fantasy XIV.* Windows, Square Enix, Japan.

Epic Games. (2017–). *Fortnite: Battle Royale.* Windows/Android, Epic Games, U.S.A.

Activision. (1983). *Frostbite.* Atari 2600, Activision, U.S.A.

Sierra On-Line. (1993). *Gabriel Knight: Sins of the Fathers.* DOS, Sierra On-Line, U.S.A.

Namco. (1979). *Galaxian.* Arcade, Midway, U.S.A.

JHT. (1991). *Ganbare Gorby !*. Game Gear, Sega, Japan.

miHoYo. (2020–). *Genshin Impact*. iOS, HoYoverse, U.S.A.

Foddy, Bennett. (2017). *Getting Over It with Bennett Foddy*. OSX, Humble Bundle, U.S.A.

Ismail, Rami et al. (2011). *Glitchhiker*. Windows, Global Game Jam, The Netherlands.

Buried Signal. (2017). *Gorogoa*. iOS, Annapurna Interactive, U.S.A.

DMA Design. (2001). *Grand Theft Auto III*. PlayStation 2, Rockstar Games, U.S.A.

Rockstar North. (2008). *Grand Theft Auto IV*. PlayStation 3, Rockstar Games, U.S.A.

Rockstar North. (2004). *Grand Theft Auto: San Andreas*. PlayStation 2, Rockstar Games, U.S.A.

Rockstar North. (2002). *Grand Theft Auto: Vice City*. PlayStation 3, Rockstar Games, U.S.A.

ArenaNet. (2012–). *Guild Wars 2*. OSX, NCsoft, U.S.A.

Harmonix Music Systems. (2005). *Guitar Hero*. PlayStation 2, RedOctane, U.S.A.

Valve. (1998). *Half-Life*. Windows, Sierra On-Line, U.S.A.

Valve Corporation. (2004). *Half-Life 2*. Windows, Sierra Entertainment, U.S.A.

Bungie Studios. (2001). *Halo: Combat Evolved*. Xbox, Microsoft Corporation, U.S.A.

Bungie Studios. (2004). *Halo 2*. Xbox, Microsoft Game Studios, U.S.A.

Ocean Software. (1988). *Head Over Heels*. MSX, ERBE Software, Spain.

Quantic Dream. (2010). *Heavy Rain*. PlayStation 3, Sony Computer Entertainment America, U.S.A.

Mertz, Carol and Francesca Carletto-Leon. (2019). *Hellcouch*. Arduino/Custom controller.

Infocom. (1984). *The Hitchhiker's Guide to the Galaxy*. DOS, Infocom, U.S.A.

Beam Software. (1982). *The Hobbit*. ZX Spectrum, Melbourne House, United Kingdom.

Locomalito. (2010). *Hydorah*. Windows, Locomalito, Spain.

Team Ico. (2001). *Ico*. PlayStation 2, Sony Computer Entertainment America, U.S.A.

Treasure. (2001). *Ikaruga*. Dreamcast, SEGA, Japan.

42 Entertainment. (2004). *I Love Bees*. Alternate Reality Game, U.S.A.

Gremlin Graphics Software. (2010). *Jack the Nipper*. MSX, Gremlin Graphics Software, United Kingdom.

Smith, Matthew. (1984). *Jet Set Willy*. ZX Spectrum, Software Projects, United Kingdom.

Telltale Games. (2011). *Jurassic Park: The Game*. [Mac OSX], Telltale Games, United States.

Activision. (1981). *Kaboom*. Atari 2600, Activision, U.S.A.

Takemoto, T. (2007). *Kaizo Mario*. Super Nintendo Entertainment System and Emulator, Japan.

Mechner, Jordan. (2012). *Karateka*. iOS, Karateka LLC, U.S.A.

Cardboard Computer. (2020). *Kentucky Route Zero*. OSX, Annapurna Interactive, U.S.A.

DeBonis, Josh and Nikita Mikros. (2013). *Killer Queen*. Arcade, Bumblebear Games, U.S.A.

Ironhide. (2011). *Kingdom Rush*. iOS, Armor Games, U.S.A.

Sierra On-Line. (n.d.). *King's Quest: Quest for the Crown*. DOS, Sierra On-Line, U.S.A.

Team Bondi. (2011). *L.A. Noire*. PlayStation 3, Rockstar Games, U.S.A.

Lucasfilm Games. (1986). *Labyrinth*. MSX, Activision, U.S.A.

GR3 Project. (2005). *La-Mulana*. Windows, GR3 Project, Japan.

Naughty Dog. (2013). *The Last of Us*. PlayStation 3, Sony Computer Entertainment, U.S.A.

Nintendo. (1986). *The Legend of Zelda*. Nintendo Entertainment System, Nintendo of America, U.S.A.

Nintendo. (1991). *The Legend of Zelda: A Link of The Past.* Super Nintendo Entertainment System, Nintendo of America, U.S.A.

Nintendo. (1998). *The Legend of Zelda: Ocarina of Time.* Nintendo 64, Nintendo of America, U.S.A.

Dontnod Entertainment. (2015). *Life is Strange.* PlayStation 3, Square Enix, France.

Playdead. (2010). *Limbo.* OSX, Playdead, Denmark.

Baumgarten, Robin. (2015). *Line Wobbler.* Custom hardware, United Kingdom.

Media Molecule. (2008). *LittleBigPlanet.* PlayStation 3, Sony Computer Entertainment of America, U.S.A.

Lucasfilm Games. (1988). *Maniac Mansion.* DOS, Lucasfilm Games, U.S.A.

Smith, Matthew. (1983). *Manic Miner.* ZX Spectrum, Software Projects, United Kingdom.

Nintendo. (2008). *Mario Kart Wii.* Wii, Nintendo of America, U.S.A.

Failbetter Games. (2023). *Mask of the Rose.* Nintendo Switch, Failbetter Games, United Kingdom.

Bioware. (2007). *Mass Effect.* Xbox 360, Microsoft Game Studios, U.S.A.

Konami. (1987). *Metal Gear.* MSX2, Konami, Japan.

Konami. (1988). *Metal Gear.* Nintendo Entertainment System, Konami, U.S.A.

Konami. (1998). *Metal Gear Solid.* PlayStation, Konami of America, U.S.A.

Konami. (2001). *Metal Gear Solid 2: Sons of Liberty.* PlayStation 2, Konami of America, U.S.A.

Asobo Studio. (2020). *Microsoft Flight Simulator.* Windows, Xbox Game Studios, U.S.A.

Synapse Software Corporation. (1984). *Mindwheel.* DOS, Brøderbund Software, U.S.A.

Mojang. (2011). *Minecraft.* OSX, Mojang, Sweden.

EA DICE. (2008). *Mirror's Edge.* PlayStation 3, EA, Sweden.

Charles, Darrow. (1935). *Monopoly.* Parker Brothers, U.S.A.

Trubshaw, Roy and Richard Bartle. (1978). *MUD1*. PDP-10, United Kingdom.

Ozark Softscape. (1983). *M.U.L.E.* Commodore 64, U.S.A.

Alcachofa Soft. (2008). *Murder in the Abbey*. Windows, The Adventure Company, U.S.A.

Cyan. (1995). *Myst*. Windows, Brøderbund Software, U.S.A.

Cyan Worlds. (2003). *Myst Online: Uru Live*. Windows, Ubisoft, U.S.A.

On-Line Systems. (1980). *Mystery House*. Apple II, On-Line Systems, U.S.A.

Frogwares Development Studio. (2003). *The Mystery of the Mummy*. Windows, Th e Adventure Company, U.S.A.

Bungie Studios. (1997). *Myth: The Fallen Lords*. Windows, Eidos, U.S.A.

Visual Concepts. (2016). *NBA 2K17*. PlayStation 4, 2K Sports, U.S.A.

Nickleodeon Kids & Family Virtual Worlds Group. (1999–). *Neopets*. Browser, Nickleodeon Kids & Family Virtual Worlds Group, U.S.A.

Nintendo. (2006). *New Super Mario Bros*. Nintendo DS, Nintendo of America, U.S.A.

Nintendo. (2012). *Nintendo Land*. WiiU, Nintendo of America, U.S.A.

Taito. (1988). *Operation Wolf*. MSX, Erbe Software, Spain.

iNiS. (2005). *Osu! Tatakae! Ouendan*. Nintendo DS, Nintendo, U.S.A.

LucasArts Entertainment Company. (1997). *Outlaws*. Windows, LucasArts Entertainment Company, U.S.A.

Inkle. (2021). *Overboard!*. OSX, Inkle, United Kingdom.

Ghost Town Games. (2016). *Overcooked*. PlayStation 4, Team 17, United Kingdom.

Namco. (1980). *Pac-Man*. Arcade, Midway, U.S.A.

Nintendo. (2003). *Pac-Man Vs*. GameCube, Namco, U.S.A.

Matt, Leacock. (2008). *Pandemic*. Z-Man Games.

3909 LLC. (2013). *Papers, Please*. OSX, 3909 LLC.

Rohrer, Jason. (2007). *Passage*. Windows, U.S.A.

Konami. (1986). *Penguin Adventure*. MSX, Konami, Japan.

Cook, David "Zeb", Robh Ruppel, Dana Knutson, Tony DiTerlizzi and Rob Lazza-Retti. (1994). *Planescape Campaign Setting (Advanced Dungeons and Dragons)*. Wizards of the Coast, U.S.A.

Black Isle Studios. (1999). *Planescape: Torment*. Windows, Interplay Entertainment, U.S.A.

Niantic. (2016). *Pokémon Go*. iOS, Niantic, U.S.A.

Atari. (1972). *Pong*. Arcade, Atari, U.S.A.

Valve Corporation. (2007). *Portal*. OSX, Valve Corporation, U.S.A.

Valve Corporation. (2012). *Portal 2*. OSX, Valve Corporation, U.S.A.

Brøderbund. (1989). *Prince of Persia*. [DOS], Brøderbund, U.S.A.

7780s Studio. (2014). *P.T.* PlayStation 4, Konami, Japan.

Taito. (1994). *Puzzle Bobble*. Arcade, Taito, Japan.

Three Rings Design. (2003–). *Puzzle Pirates*. Java, Three Rings Design/Ubisoft, U.S.A.

Square Co. (1987). *Rad Racer*. Nintendo Entertainment System, Nintendo of America, U.S.A.

Gravity. (2002–). *Ragnarok Online*. Windows, Gravity, Korea.

Ubisoft Montpellier, Ubisoft Paris Studios SARL, Ubisoft SARL. (2011). *Rayman Origins*. PlayStation 3, Ubisoft, U.S.A.

Rockstar San Diego. (2010). *Red Dead Redemption*. Xbox 360, Rockstar Games, U.S.A.

Capcom. (1996). *Resident Evil*. PlayStation, Capcom Entertainment, U.S.A.

Capcom Production Studio 4. (2005). *Resident Evil 4*. GameCube, Capcom Entertainment, U.S.A.

Insomniac Games. (2006). *Resistance: Fall of Man*. PlayStation 3, Sony Computer Entertainment America, U.S.A.

3909 LLC. (2018). *Return of the Obra Dinn*. OSX, 3909 LLC, U.S.A.

Big Fish Games. (2008). *Return to Ravenhearst.* Windows, Big Fish Games, U.S.A.

Housemarque. (2021). *Returnal.* PlayStation 5, Sony Interactive Entertainment, U.S.A.

United Game Artists. (2001). *Rez.* Dreamcast, SEGA, U.S.A.

Konami. (1984). *Road Fighter.* MSX, Konami, Japan.

Harmonix Music Systems. (2007). *Rock Band.* Xbox 360, MTV Games, U.S.A.

Harmonix Music Systems. (2008). *Rock Band 2.* Xbox 360, MTV Games, U.S.A.

Davis, Corey. (2015). *Rocket League.* PlayStation 4, Psyonix, U.S.A.

Toy, Michael, Glenn Wichman, Ken Arnold and Jon Lane. (1980), *Rogue.* Linux, U.S.A.

Linden Research. (2003–). *Second Life.* OSX, Linden Labs, U.S.A.

Lucasfilm Games. (1990). *The Secret of Monkey Island.* DOS, Lucasfilm Games, U.S.A.

LucasArts Entertainment Company. (2009). *The Secret of Monkey Island: Special Edition.* iOS, LucasArts Entertainment Company, U.S.A.

Teuber, Klaus. *Settlers of Catan.* Mayfair Games, 1995.

Wadjet Eye Games. (2006). *The Shivah.* Windows, Wadjet Eye Games, U.S.A.

Konami Computer Entertainment Tokyo. (2001). *Silent Hill 2.* PlayStation, Konami, Japan.

Maxis Software. (1992). *SimCity.* Windows, Maxis Software, U.S.A.

Maxis Software. (1996). *SimCopter.* Windows, Electronic Arts, U.S.A.

Maxis Software. (2000). *The Sims.* Windows, Electronic Arts, U.S.A.

Sonic Team. (1991). *Sonic the Hedgehog.* Sega Genesis, Sega of America, U.S.A.

Project Soul. (2004). *Soul Calibur II.* GameCube, Namco Hometek, U.S.A.

Sierra On-Line. (1986). *Space Quest: The Sarien Encounter.* DOS, Sierra On-Line, U.S.A.

Sierra On-Line. (1993). *Space Quest V: The Next Mutation.* DOS, Sierra On-Line, U.S.A.

Russell, Steve, Martin Graetz and Wayne Wiitanen. (1961). *Spacewar!*. PDP1, U.S.A.

Darkside Game Studios and YAGER Development. (2012). *Spec Ops: The Line*. Windows, 2K Games, U.S.A.

Yu, Derek et al. (2009). *Spelunky*. Windows, Mossmouth, U.S.A.

Maxis Software. (2008). *Spore*. OSX, Electronic Arts, U.S.A.

Galactic Cafe. (2013). *The Stanley Parable*. OSX, Galactic Cafe, U.S.A.

Blizzard Entertainment. (1998). *Starcraft*. Windows, Blizzard Entertainment, U.S.A.

Raven Software. (2002). *Star Wars: Jedi Knight II – Jedi Outcast*. Windows, Activision, U.S.A.

Bioware. (2003). *Star Wars: Knights of the Old Republic*. Windows, LucasArts Entertainment Company, U.S.A.

Obsidian Entertainment. (2005). *Star Wars: Knights of the Old Republic II: The Sith Lords*. Windows, LucasArts Entertainment Company, U.S.A.

Capcom and Nude Maker. (2002). *Steel Battalion*. Xbox, Capcom, U.S.A.

Capcom. (1992). *Street Fighter II*. Super Nintendo Entertainment System, Capcom, U.S.A.

Capcom and Dimps Corporation. (2009). *Street Fighter IV*. PlayStation 3, Capcom, U.S.A.

Atari. (1979). *Super Breakout*. Atari 2600, Atari, U.S.A.

Uncredited. (2010). *Super Chick Sisters*. Browser, PETA, U.S.A.

Locomalito. (2017). *Super Hydorah*. Windows, Abylight Studios, Spain.

Nintendo. (1996). *Super Mario 64*. Nintendo 64, Nintendo, U.S.A.

Nintendo. (1985). *Super Mario Bros*. Nintendo Entertainment System, Nintendo of America, U.S.A.

Nintendo. (2019). *Super Mario Maker 2*. Switch, Nintendo of America, U.S.A.

Nintendo. (1991). *Super Mario World*. Nintendo Entertainment System, Nintendo of America, U.S.A.

Team Meat. (2010). *Super Meat Boy*. Windows, Team Meat, U.S.A.

HAL Laboratory. (2001). *Super Smash Bros. Melee.* GameCube, Nintendo, U.S.A.

Infocom. (1984). *Suspect.* DOS, Infocom, U.S.A.

Microïds. (2002). *Syberia.* Windows, Microïds, France.

Bandai Namco. (2022). *Taiko no Tatsujin: Rhythm Festival.* Switch, Bandai Namco Entertainment America.

Telltale Games. (2009). *Tales of Monkey Island.* OSX, Telltale Games, U.S.A.

Patjinov, Alexey. (1987). *Tetris.* DOS, Spectrum Holobyte, U.S.A.

Arika. (2019). *Tetris 99.* Nintendo Switch, Nintendo, Japan.

Makena Technologies. (2003–2010, 2012–). *There.* OSX, Makena Technologies, U.S.A.

Locomalito. (2012). *They Came from Verminest.* Windows, Locomalito, Spain.

Other Tales Interactive. (2019). *Tick Tock: A Tale for Two.* OSX, Other Tales Interactive, Denmark.

Crystal Dynamics. (2013). *Tomb Raider.* PlayStation 3, Square Enix, U.S.A.

Romero, Brenda. (2009). Train.

Windham Classics and Idealogic. (1985). *Treasure Island.* MSX2, Philips Spain, Spain.

Origin Systems. (1992). *Ultima VII: The Black Gate.* DOS, Origin Systems, U.S.A.

Naughty Dog. (2007). *Uncharted: Drake's Fortune.* PlayStation 3, Sony Computer Entertainment America, U.S.A.

Fox, Toby. (2015). *Undertale.* OSX, tobyfox, U.S.A.

ICOM Simulations. (1988). *Uninvited.* DOS, Mindscape, U.S.A.

Molleindustria. (2012). *Unmanned.* [Browser], Molleindustria, Italy.

Digital Extremes and Epic Games. (1999). *Unreal Tournament.* Windows, GT Interactive Software Corp, U.S.A.

OSX, VRChat Inc. (2014–). *VRChat.* Occulus Rift. VRChat Inc., U.S.A.

Telltale Games. (2012). *The Walking Dead.* iOS, Telltale Games, U.S.A.

Crowther, Anthony. (1984). *Wanted: Monty Mole*. Commodore 64, Gremlin Graphics, United Kingdom.

Blizzard Entertainment. (2002). *Warcraft III: Reign of Chaos*. Windows, Blizzard Entertainment, U.S.A.

Ostrich Banditos. (2015). *Westerado: Double Barreled*. OSX, Adult Swim, U.S.A.

Giant Sparrow. (2017). *What Remains of Edith Finch*. PlayStation 4, Annapurna Interactive, U.S.A.

Nintendo. (2006). *Wii Sports*. Wii, Nintendo of America, U.S.A.

Psygnosis. (1995). *Wipeout*. PlayStation, Psygnosis, United Kingdom.

Infocom. (1983). *The Witness*. DOS, Infocom, U.S.A.

Id Software. (1992). *Wolfestein 3D*. DOS, Apogee Software, U.S.A.

Blizzard Entertainment. (2004–). *World of Warcraft*. OSX, Blizzard Entertainment, U.S.A.

Nintendo R&D2. (2002). *Yoshi's Island: Super Mario Advanced 3*. GameBoy Advance, Nintendo of America, U.S.A.

Ubisoft Montpellier. (2012). *ZombiU*. WiiU, Ubisoft, France.

Index

Pages in *italics* refer to figures and pages followed by "n" refer to notes.

For Product Safety Concerns and Information please contact our EU representative GPSR@taylorandfrancis.com Taylor & Francis Verlag GmbH, Kaufingerstraße 24, 80331 München, Germany

Printed and bound by CPI Group (UK) Ltd, Croydon, CR0 4YY
08/06/2025
01897008-0005